Flawed Criminal Justice Policies

Flawed Criminal Justice Policies

At the Intersection of the Media,
Public Fear and Legislative Response

SECOND EDITION

Edited by

Frances P. Reddington

and

Gene Bonham, Jr.

Carolina Academic Press
Durham, North Carolina

Library of Congress Cataloging-in-Publication Data

Names: Reddington, Frances P., editor. | Bonham, Gene, editor.
Title: Flawed criminal justice policies : at the intersection of the media,
   public fear and legislative response / edited by Frances P. Reddington,
   Gene Bonham, Jr.
Description: Second edition. | Durham, North Carolina : Carolina Academic
   Press, [2019] | Includes bibliographical references and index.
Identifiers: LCCN 2018050640 | ISBN 9781611637335 (alk. paper)
Subjects: LCSH: Criminal justice, Administration of--United States. |
   Juvenile justice, Administration of--United States. | Law
   enforcement--United States. | United States--Politics and government--21st
   century.
Classification: LCC HV9950 .F56 2019 | DDC 364.973--dc23
LC record available at https://lccn.loc.gov/2018050640
e-ISBN 978-1-5310-1137-6

CAROLINA ACADEMIC PRESS, LLC
700 Kent Street
Durham, North Carolina 27701
Telephone (919) 489-7486
Fax (919) 493-5668
www.cap-press.com

Printed in the United States of America
2024 Printing

To my family.

FPR

To my wife, Marty, who has been my friend for life.

GB

Contents

Online Chapter · Policy Watch Special Issue: Treatment of Pregnant Incarcerated Women
Stephanie Shipwash

Introduction
Shackling
Prenatal Care
Bonding
Cost
Recommendations
Action
Conclusion
References

Preface

This book examines various aspects of the American criminal justice system and how policies that govern criminal justice procedures can sometimes be flawed. Basically a flawed criminal justice policy would not produce the desired effect intended by the policy, or may, in fact, produce unintended and negative consequences. While this book focuses somewhat on policies that may have produced negative and unintended consequences associated with our criminal justice system, it is not meant to imply that the criminal justice system is ineffective or unsuccessful. In fact, there currently exists a growing trend in our criminal justice system to improve policy creation and evaluation.

We asked the contributors to this book to write a chapter for this reader because of their expertise in certain critical areas of the criminal justice system, and because they also have some knowledge and insight into the role of public policy in their area of expertise. In addition, when we asked the contributors to write their chapters, we asked that they include both some recommendations for positive change as well as an overview of any positive progress that had or is occurring in their area of discussion. We believe that it would not be enough to simply point out flaws in how our system works, but that this reader also should offer recommendations on how to fix or improve the situation. Each chapter provides some discussion as to how flawed policy in a specific area can be addressed and remedied.

Chapter One opens the book with a discussion about criminal justice policy and how it evolves. It sets the stage for the rest of the chapters which follow. The basic framework provided in Chapter One will help the reader to examine each remaining chapter within the broader context of what is known about the policy making process and what is thought to work.

The remaining chapters focus on specific policy issues found in a certain segment of the criminal justice system today. Detailed analysis of a criminal justice policy and its consequences is provided by the contributors who then also provide suggestions for the creation of good, sound, evidence-based policy. Specific topics include the use of force, the War on Drugs, the enforcement of immigration laws, the sentencing revolution, solitary confinement, the death penalty, sex offender policies, adultifying juvenile justice, mental illness and the criminal justice system, and conceal and carry on college campuses.

In addition, we are including an online component to this second edition. The online component consists of shorter essays on important topics that we will post periodically. We call this Special Issues Policy Watch. The essays address the major issues and current status of policy and/ or procedure in criminal justice. Go to the book's webpage on the publisher's website (cap-press.com) to access these free supplements.

Frances P. Reddington
Gene Bonham, Jr.
May 29, 2018

Acknowledgments

Many people did a lot of work to make this book happen. First and foremost, no reader would happen without the collection of contributors who are at the heart of the work. The contributors to this reader are, in a word, exceptional.

We would like to acknowledge Carolina Academic Press for their support, and specifically Beth Hall, our editor, who kept us on task and offered us her support. From day one, she believed this was a work that needed to be done.

We would like to thank The University of Central Missouri for the support we receive. Putting together a reader of this nature takes a great deal of work, much of it very detail oriented and time consuming. We would like to thank two former Graduate Assistants from the Criminal Justice Department at the University of Central Missouri. Erica Lehmuth and Hillary McNeel both put in numerous hours checking references, creating indexes and helping to format the first edition. We thank them so much for their assistance—it really was invaluable to us and helped make this project possible.

And finally, we would like to acknowledge the people who work in the criminal justice field, those who make laws regarding criminal justice policy, those who cover criminal justice in the media, and the public who indicate that crime and the system designed to deal with this social issue remains a major American concern. We hope this work serves to raise awareness, foster discussion, and provides a little information as we move forward in finding what works best.

About the Contributors

Alissa R. Ackerman, **Ph.D.**, is a criminal justice professor at California State University, Fullerton. She has published extensively on sex crimes policy and practice, with her work appearing in *Criminal Justice & Behavior, Contemporary Justice Review, Sexual Abuse,* and the *Journal of Offender Rehabilitation.* Her most recent book *The New Campus Anti-Rape Movement* will be published in 2018.

Barbara Belbot, **J.D., Ph.D.**, is a Professor of Criminal Justice at the University of Houston-Downtown. She holds a J.D. from the University of Law Center and a Ph.D. from Same Houston State University. Dr. Belbot has published articles and books on criminal-justice-related topics. Her primary research interests are institutional corrections, corrections law, and civil liability issues for criminal justice professionals.

Gene Bonham, Jr., Ph.D., is currently a Professor in the Department of Criminal Justice at the University of Central Missouri where he teaches both undergraduate and graduate criminal justice classes. He holds a Master's degree in Administration of Justice from Wichita State University and a Ph.D. in Criminal Justice from Sam Houston State University. His work experience includes ten years as a state parole officer and almost ten years as Director of Community Corrections in Kansas, where he was responsible for operations of a multi-county adult and juvenile Community Corrections Act program. Currently Dr. Bonham's research interests include program evaluation, civil liability in corrections, restorative models, as well as systems and policy analysis. He has co-authored two books and published numerous articles in his areas of interest.

Jacqueline Buffington, Ph.D., is a forensic clinical psychologist and an associate professor at the University of Minnesota Duluth Criminology Department, where her focus of teaching and research is offenders with mental illness. She completed her masters and doctorate at Sam Houston State University in Texas, a postdoctoral fellowship at the University of Virginia Medical School's Institute of Law, Psychiatry, and Public Policy, and worked at several state forensic psychiatric hospitals. In addition to being a professor, she has been performing forensic evaluations (e.g., competency to stand trial, sanity at the time of the offense) for the past 12 years. She has trained hundreds of law enforcement officers, jail officers, and community members on mental illness and de-escalation. She consults on a variety of projects for the 6th Judicial District Courts in Minnesota, including the area's treatment courts.

Benecia Carmack, J.D., M.B.A. is an Assistant Professor with the Criminal Justice Department of the University of Central Missouri. She teaches Criminal Law and Criminal Procedure, White Collar Crime, Legal Aspects, Innocence Case Review Course, Introduction to Criminal Justice, Evidence and Courtroom Procedure, and serves as Undergraduate and Internship Coordinator. She previously served as municipal judge for the city of Clinton, Missouri in Henry County for over sixteen years. While serving as a municipal judge she was a board member of the Missouri Municipal and Associate Circuit Judges Association for four years. She graduated from University of Missouri at Kansas City Law School and also holds a Master in Business Administration from the University of Central Missouri.

Scott Chenault, Ph.D., is an Associate Professor of Criminal Justice at the University of Central Missouri. His primary research is in the area of correctional staff and programming. He has published research in the *Journal of Qualitative Criminal Justice and Criminology*, the *Journal of Criminal Justice Education*, and in the Sociology journal *Symbolic Interaction*.

Patricia Dahl, Ph.D., is an associate professor in the Criminal Justice and Legal Studies Department at Washburn University. Dr. Dahl received her master's degree in criminal justice and her Ph.D. in Public Administration/Criminal Justice from the University of Colorado in Denver. Prior to teaching at the college level, Dr. Dahl worked in the criminal justice field for 20 years at the county, state and federal level in Colorado. Her research interests include the juvenile justice system, institutional corrections, and crime victims.

Anthony Gassaway, M.S. has served as an Assistant Professor of Criminal Justice at the University of Central Missouri since July of 2014. Prior to that appointment, he was employed in various capacities with the U.S. Marshals Service, Department of Justice for approximately 31 years. During his tenure in the U.S. Marshals, he was assigned to numerous projects which required the creation, review, and revision of agency policies, to include those regarding the use of force and intermediate weapons. He additionally created several of the agency's intermediate weapon programs (expandable baton, OC spray, Taser) and also served as the agency's subject matter expert in federal court proceedings regarding the use of intermediate weapons and restraint devices. His final agency assignment was as the Chief Deputy U.S. Marshal for the Western District of Missouri. He received a Master's Degree in Criminal Justice from the University of Central Missouri in 2008 and a Bachelor's Degree in Criminology from Indiana State University in 1983.

Michael Gomila, Ph.D. is a project monitor for the State of Louisiana's Office of Behavioral Health. In his role with the agency, he is the state representative for substance abuse services and oversees forensic behavioral health programming. Dr. Gomila has a vast amount of experience in the administration of substance abuse and psychiatric facilities having managed both inpatient and outpatient behavioral health units in North Carolina and Louisiana. Dr. Gomila teaches as an adjunct professor within the Criminal Justice Department at the University of Louisiana at Monroe. As a matter of coincidence, Dr. Gomila has ties to the issue of drug policy through his family history. His distant relative (Frank R. Gomila, M.D. from New Orleans, LA) lent expert testimony to the hearings surrounding the Marijuana Tax Act of 1937, which lea to the criminalization of marijuana.

Robert Hanser, Ph.D., is the Coordinator of the Department of Criminal Justice at the University of Louisiana at Monroe. Rob is a past administrator of a regional police training academy and has been the director of Offender Programming for LaSalle Corrections for nearly 7 years. Rob has written several textbooks and numerous other publications related to his various fields of interest.

Amy Memmer, J.D., is an assistant professor in the Criminal Justice and Legal Studies Department at Washburn University and the director of the Washburn University Legal Studies Program. Ms. Memmer received a law degree and a master's degree in criminal justice from Washburn University. She is licensed to practice law and is a State approved mediator for the State of Kansas. Previously, she worked for the Kansas Supreme Court, the U.S. Department of Justice Civil Rights Division, the Kansas Court of Appeals, and the Shawnee County District Attorney's Office.

Natalie Perron, MSW, LGSW, has her Bachelor's degree in Criminology from the University of Minnesota Duluth and her Master's degree in Social Work from The College of Saint Scholastica. She has worked with both inmates in a prison re-entry program and with victims as a sexual assault advocate. Most recently, she has been assisting offenders with mental illness in a jail diversion program. She is currently employed as a research assistant on the Duluth Sexual Assault Kit Initiative, a joint project between the Duluth Police Department and the Program for Aid to Victims of Sexual Assault that is committed to testing old sexual assault evidentiary kits from unsolved cases.

Frances P. Reddington, Ph.D., is a professor of Criminal Justice at the University of Central Missouri. She earned her Ph.D. in Criminal Justice from Sam Houston State University. Her main areas of research interest include all aspects of juvenile justice. She has published in the areas of: juvenile law, juvenile law in Texas, juveniles in adult jails, transfer of juveniles to the adult court, juveniles and the age of criminal responsibility, training of juvenile probation officers, the use of charter schools, and the role of Guardians ad Litem in abuse and neglect cases in juvenile court. She has served as a consultant for the National Institute of Corrections and the Office of Juvenile Justice and Delinquency Prevention in the area of juvenile justice staff training. Dr. Reddington is a past chair of the Academy of Criminal Justice Sciences Juvenile Justice Section and past chair of the Student Affairs Committee of the American Correctional Association. She is a past editor for Youth Violence and Juvenile Justice: An Interdisciplinary Journal. She has been on the Board of Directors for both the Missouri Juvenile Justice Association and the Missouri State CASA (Court Appointed Special Advocate) Association and is on the board of the Missouri Corrections Association. She is currently researching in the area of juvenile justice policy.

Stephanie Shipwash, M.S., finished her Master's Degree in Criminal Justice in 2017 from the University of Central Missouri. Prior to graduate school, she was in the United States Air Force and worked in logistics and was also a victim advocate for sexual assault survivors. She received her Bachelor's Degree in Criminal Justice from Appalachian State University in 2009.

Karen Terry, Ph.D., is a Professor at John Jay College of Criminal Justice in New York City. She holds a doctorate in Criminology from Cambridge University. Her primary research interest is sexual offending and victimization and sex offender policy. Her current research focus is on abuse of children in an institutional setting, and she was the principal investigator for two studies on sexual abuse of minors by Catholic priests in the United States.

Scott Vollum, Ph.D., is Department Head and Associate Professor in The Department of Anthropology, Sociology & Criminology at the University of Minnesota Duluth. At this time, his primary areas of academic interest and research are violence, the death penalty, restorative justice, media and crime, and moral disengagement. He is currently working on a variety of research projects including an evaluation of a restorative justice program for domestic violence offenders, an examination of death penalty attitudes and the impact of wrongful convictions in capital cases, and a qualitative study of people who kill. He is author of the book *Last Words and The Death Penalty: Voices of the Condemned and Their Co-Victims* and co-author of the book *The Death Penalty: Constitutional Issues, Commentaries and Case Briefs.* His previous research has been published in a variety of scholarly journals, his most recent ("Gender Politics and *The Walking Dead*: Gendered Violence and the Reestablishment of Patriarchy") in the journal *Feminist Criminology*. He lives in Duluth, MN with his son Kai and their dogs Milo & Cooper.

Flawed Criminal Justice Policies

Chapter 1

Flawed Policy

Concepts and Issues in Criminal Justice Policy Making: General Propositions

Gene Bonham, Jr.

Introduction

This book is about the criminal justice system in the United States and how public policy, even though well intentioned and advocated in good faith, can sometimes be flawed. A flawed policy, in a general sense, is one that does not produce the desired effect intended by the policy or produces unintended consequences that work against the intended goals of the policy. While this book focuses somewhat on negatives associated with our criminal justice system, it is not meant to imply that our system is all bad. To the contrary, there is a growing trend in our criminal justice system to improve the manner in which policies are made as well as establishing means of evaluating policies, once implemented. Contributing authors for this book were selected based on their having some expertise in certain critical areas of our system and some knowledge and insight into the role of public policy in these areas. It is not enough to simply point out flaws in how our system works; one must also be prepared to offer recommendations on how to fix or improve the problems. Each chapter will provide some discussion as to how perceived flaws in the system can be improved.

General criticisms of our criminal justice system are plentiful and seem to be grounded in whether one is most concerned about victims, with a crime control emphasis, or on offenders, with a more due process emphasis (Ebbesen & Konecni, 1985). Those concerned primarily about victims, for example, point to the following concerns:

- rising crime rates in the United States in general,

- law enforcement being too constrained by limitations and rules related to probable cause and search and seizure,
- courts releasing dangerous offenders on bail who subsequently commit additional crimes,
- perceptions that too many guilty criminals end up released because of the insanity defense or legal defenses related to diminished capacity,
- soft approaches on offenders who are alcohol or drug users who end up being released, and
- the notion that prosecutors may not fully prosecute certain cases because they are not certain they will win (Ebbesen & Konecni, 1985).

On the other hand, those who are more focused on and concerned about offenders offer their own criticisms of the criminal justice system. Some of their concerns include the following:

- basic human rights of offenders are frequently violated;
- offenders going to prison are not rehabilitated and, in fact, are worse when they are ultimately released;
- too many times, important decisions made in the criminal justice system are based on extralegal factors rather than legal ones;
- innocent people are convicted in our system, in spite of the protections in place, due to faulty evidence;
- disparity in sentencing by the courts;
- the long history of emphasizing punishment, rather than rehabilitation, in our system of justice; and
- the selective prosecution of the weak and powerless in our society (Ebbesen & Konecni, 1985).

Increasingly, it is becoming recognized that there is more to the study of public policy in the arena of criminal justice than just the policies themselves. "The policy-making process continues to be neglected in studies of crime policy" (Ismali, 2006, p. 256). A full understanding of policies cannot be achieved unless one examines both the policies themselves and the processes in which they are formulated and shaped (Jones & Newburn, 2005). Furthermore, special attention must also be made to the actors involved in the process, the role of the public, professionals in criminal justice, politicians, and how these players interact in the policy decisions that are made (Ismali, 2006, p. 260).

A wide variety of policy making processes have been identified in the literature. Early models focused on a more technocratic orientation, that is, a series of clearly defined steps followed in a very rational manner (Ismali, 2006). This rational problem-solving approach included the following steps:

1. Identify the objectives to be achieved by the policy.
2. Identify alternative courses of action.
3. Predict and evaluate all the potential consequences of each course of action.
4. Select those alternatives that maximize the chances of attaining the stated objectives (Ismali, 2006).

While the technocratic approach is rational and works to a degree, it does not really fully take into account the larger issues involved in the policy making process or the players who participate or have some impact on the end product. Public policy does not occur in a vacuum and is not somehow "preordained, but are human creations of the public policy making process" (Stolz, 2002, p. 1; Banks, 2009). Public policies can generally be identified by one of three different primary motivators:

1. ideologically based,
2. empirically based, and
3. ethically based (Banks, 2009).

Ideologically based grounds include policies that are desirable simply because they fit into the assumptions and preconceived notions of ideologically motivated actors (Banks, 2009). For example, one may oppose policies related to the death penalty based on personal religious beliefs that prohibit the killing of another human being. Or, politicians frequently favor one policy over another based upon ideological reference points that are either conservative or liberal in nature. "Public policy in the United States in recent years has increasingly been conceived, debated, and evaluated through the lenses of politics and ideology—policies are Democratic or Republican, liberal or conservative, free market or government controlled" (Dunworth, Hannaway, Holahan, & Turner, 2003, p. 1). Politicians, also, of course, are influenced to one degree or another by the media, their constituents, and professional lobby groups (Banks, 2009). In general, politicians are very concerned about being reelected and may not be that open to technical evidence (Cook & Russo, 1999). In fact, it has been said that "there is nothing a politician likes so little as to be well informed; it makes decision-making so complex and difficult" (Davies, Nutley, & Smith, 1999, p. 3).

Empirical-based grounds include policies that somehow are founded upon science and research and what that research shows about any potential outcomes related to a particular policy (Banks, 2009). Bringing research into the policy making arena, in general, has always been a difficult challenge. Historically, practitioners especially have been somewhat suspect of academics and researchers. Bridging the gap between the two has shown promise in recent years, as many criminal justice agencies are recognizing the benefits of collaborating with academics in implementing programs and policies that are based upon research findings. Evidence-based practices has grown exponentially in the last decade or two. More on these specific approaches will be provided later. Suffice it to say here that empirically grounded policy making shows much promise for future decision-making in criminal justice policy fields.

Finally, ethically grounded policies "rely on conclusions drawn from an analysis of what is 'right' and 'wrong' or 'good or bad' in a moral sense" (Banks, 2009, p. 220). Such policies may be made more on the basis of reacting to events or issues in our society that take on an intense moral nature, that is, exaggerated to a point of creating a "moral panic" of sorts (Banks, 2009). Cohen (1973) referred to moral panic as having certain key features:

- defining a specific condition, event, or group as a threat to the values and interests of society; and
- this condition, event, or group is portrayed in a stereotypical manner by the media and those identified as being experts and who take on moral positions, make judgments, and suggest how the threat should be ameliorated.

These moral panics may be fed by the high visibility afforded by media portrayal of the events or issues in an inaccurate or exaggerated fashion. When such events are in the public spotlight, politicians are very sensitive to the public concerns and pay less attention to policy professionals (Ismali, 2006). They react almost in a visceral and instinctive manner rather than in a rational, reasoned, and informed manner (Banks, 2009). The role of the media in socially constructing issues and events in criminal justice has been widely researched, so only a cursory reference to this phenomena will be provided here as it relates to policy making. It is widely reported that the public reports, in overwhelming numbers, that "the media represents the principle source of information about crime (Beckett, 1997, p. 62). However, unethical policy making would include the making of policy in an "ad hoc, capricious, and arbitrary" manner, as opposed to a more reasoned and rational approach (Banks, 2009, p. 221). Such policies, referred to as morality polices, are "viewed and constructed by media, politicians, and sections of the public as involving moral and ethical issues" (Banks, 2009, p. 224). An example of morality policy making would include a state legislator or governor who, in order to get elected, might bring about policy changes they know will not achieve the goals or objectives of the policy but would rather likely create new injustices (Banks, 2009). Such behavior would be firmly based in ethically grounded policy making.

Graphically depicted, we see two divergent areas of foci with regard to criminal justice policy making, as shown below in Figure 1.

Figure 1. Contrast between Morality Policy Making Based on Moral Panics and Ideological Stances Compared to Rational, Reasoned, and Ethical Approaches

Morality Policy Making   Rational

Moral Panics   Reasoned

Ideological Stances   Ethical

Policy Communities

Public policies develop within the broader context of policy communities. "A policy community is that part of a political system that—by virtue of its functional responsibilities, its vested interests, and its specialized knowledge—acquires a dominant voice in determining government decisions in a specific field of public activity, and is generally permitted by society at large and the public authorities in particular to determine public policy in that field" (Pross, 1986, p. 68). Such policy communities can include elected stakeholders at the federal, state, and local levels of governments. Examples of these would include the president of the United States, state governors, city mayors, Congress, state legislators, as well as city councils.

Other nonelected stakeholders are "directly responsible for translating the political priorities of elected officials into public policy" (Ismali, 2006, p. 264). These can include a host of appointed government bureaucrats, including agency heads who monitor policies and advise elected officials (Solomon, 1981). These groups are many times considered experts and are called upon frequently by elected officials to advise them on policy issues.

Even more powerful, at times, are various interest groups who represent various components of the criminal justice system and outsiders who have a major influence of focusing the attention of elected officials on issues of importance to them. These groups include, among others, police associations, bar associations, judicial organizations, and correctional associations (Fairchild, 1981). Other examples, outside of criminal justice agencies, include various pressure groups, media groups, academics, consultants, and other "experts" (Pross, 1986; Coleman & Skogstad, 1990).

Elitist and Populist Models of Policy Making

Another essential feature of the policy making process has to do with who actually makes public policy and the extent to which the public or citizenry participate in that process. In this regard, there are two models: the elitist model and the populist model. The elitist model of penal policy making was prominent in the two decades prior to 1945. Here, policy was determined and "dominated by small, male, metropolitan elite" (Ryan, 1999, p. 3–4). This model is a top down approach in which public policy is set by a small minority who are believed to be in a position of superior knowledge, thus the source of their authority. The citizenry, or general public, do not have the requisite knowledge or information with which to make appropriate decisions and therefore are essentially locked out of the process.

However, "an elitist model is giving way to a more populist model, in which governments consult ordinary people, especially those living in areas undermined by crime and disorder, before formulating and implementing policies to tackle crime" (Johnstone, 2000, p. 161). Part of the reason for a hesitancy to bring the public into the policy making process is the general belief by some that the public is by nature very punitive in attitudes. This could result in harsh policies that may be inappropriate. Indeed, "polls have consistently painted a picture of a punitive public" (Hough, 1996, p. 192). This has resulted in the idea that, in general, the public reacts to events in an exaggerated manner that is disproportionate to any particular event. Some have even suggested that there are deep-seated psychological impulses that lie behind a drive to punish (Johnstone, 2000). An alternative explanation, which on the surface garners more credibility, is the influence of the media in shaping public opinion and attitudes. "An important cause of punitive attitudes are the systematically distorted images of crime and criminal justice which people receive from the media" (Johnstone, 2000, p. 408). There is also the issue of a systematic ignorance and lack of understanding by the public as to how the criminal justice system really works, crime and criminals, and sentencing policies. Much of the workings of the criminal justice system occur outside the view of the general public, leaving them to a perspective based largely on distorted media representations of the system and its players.

Research on public attitudes toward criminal justice issues, however, reflect that public opinion is actually more diverse than was thought, and there is more of a willingness to consider other than punitive approaches to specific problems approaches to specific problems that are not punitive (Hough, 1996). Also, there is considerable evidence that a lot of survey research regarding opinions is dependent upon what questions are asked and how they are asked. When the public is asked multiple questions instead of just one question and is given more than one option, they tend to express less punitive attitudes (Banks, 2009). To further complicate the matter of public opinion, there is good reason to believe that opinions expressed in polls may very well not be a good guide as to what people might do if they were actually provided an opportunity to have some real role in the decision-making process (Johnstone, 2000).

Banks (2009) described Cullen and others' seven main conclusions regarding public attitudes in the criminal justice sphere as follows:

1. Generally, the public is punitive toward crime.
2. This punitiveness is not rock solid, however, as even when the public describes a punitive opinion, they are also flexible enough to consider a range of sentencing options when given adequate information.
3. In order to moderate their punitive views, the public must be provided a good reason not to be punitive.
4. The public has no hesitancy to put dangerous offenders in prison. However, nondangerous or violent offenders are given a more wide range of sentencing options.
5. The general public continues to believe in a more rehabilitative approach in spite of the many attacks on treatment and rehabilitation by many.
6. The public is very interested in child saving, that is, the rehabilitation and treatment of young offenders. Also, there is general public support for diverting children away from criminality through alternative programming.
7. The public generally favors approaches that are balanced and focused on achieving the stated objectives of criminal justice, that is, justice, public safety, and reforming offenders (p. 227).

So, the trend in recent years has been a move from the more elitist model of policy making to one that includes the input of the public at large. A number of suggestions have been proffered as ways of improving the public's sentiment away from an overreliance on punitive approaches. Some of these suggestions include the following:

- Make the public more knowledgeable about criminal justice and punishment.
- Make people more better educated.
- Try to better deal with the wider social issues that tend to engender more punitive and harsh attitudes.
- Deal with the economic and structural problems in our society.
- Provide more support for victims.
- Make greater use of restorative justice programs.

- Work to strengthen social control capacities of families and communities, i.e., reintegrative shaming (Banks, 2009, p. 166).

With such improvements, it is thought that citizens can certainly play a much greater role in the policy making process, resulting in more informed policies that are more widely accepted by the public. The idea is that citizens could play a meaningful role in public policy decision-making, much like the "upper rungs" of the participatory ladder as described by Arnstein (1969). In this ladder, you have lower rungs in which the public is essentially manipulated and only involved in decision-making processes to persuade them to accept the decisions desired by the elite policy makers. Then, there are the middle rungs, where citizens are relegated to being informed, consulted with, and placated. The citizens are heard but not given any power to really be heeded. And, finally, on the upper rungs, this is where citizens truly participate and have a good amount of control of the policies that are developed and implemented (Arnstein, 1969, p. 169).

Evidence-Based Policy Making: The Interplay Between Theory, Research, and Policy

In this section, the role of theory and research will be examined as they inform evidence-based policy making. There has been a growing trend in both criminal justice agencies and public policy arenas to at least consider the important role of criminological theory and empirical research in the process. There is an increasing recognition that for governments to be effective, its actions and policies must be informed by reason and some form of evidence (Sanderson, 2002). Evidence is obtained by careful theory formulation and a continuous examination and reexamination of hypotheses that can be either confirmed or falsified. Theory, research, and evidence are all closely tied together and in combination add to our understanding (Bardach, 2003).

Duke (2001) identified seven models of the research–policy relationship, as first developed by Weiss in 1986:

1. Knowledge-driven model: basic research leads to opportunities, and applied research is then conducted to better define and test the findings. Then, technologies are developed and application of the new technologies are implemented.
2. Problem-solving model: this model utilizes evidence that may help to solve or better elucidate the policy issue and, in turn, this then influences policy choices and decisions.
3. Interactive model: information is sought from many types of actors, including politicians, government workers, journalists, special interest

groups, practitioners, planners, and even clients. This model is more fluid and does not follow a strictly linear process but may result in very useful information that leads to better policy making.

4. Political model: various interests and ideologies come together to determine the stances of policy makers on particular issues and problems. Here, research is unlikely to have a major impact on the policy makers. Many times, it serves as a way of legitimizing or justifying particular policy decisions.

5. Tactical model: where specific research findings are considered unimportant. Instead, what is critical is just the fact that there is research out there that is being done. Then, when governments are pressed for action, they can attempt to delay action by playing the research card.

6. Enlightenment model: focuses on the cumulative effects of research and information over time rather than single pieces of research, or even a body of related studies. Such focus helps to sensitize policy makers to new issues and helps to shape the way problems are handled by them.

7. Part of the intellectual enterprise of society: whereby research is viewed as a dependent variable rather than an independent variable. That is, policy influences and sets the parameters of research rather than the other way around. It helps to determine which social issues or problems are studied. The relationship is considered "reflexive," meaning that policy and research constantly interacts and influences each other (p. 279).

So, given that evidence-based policy appears to be a growing trend in criminal justice, exactly what does the term mean? According to the Dunworth et al. (2003), "evidence-based policy is a rigorous approach that draws on careful data collection, experimentation, and both quantitative and qualitative analysis to answer three questions: What exactly is the problem? What are the possible ways to address the problem? And what are the possible impacts of each?" (Dunworth et al., 2003, p. 1). These approaches, then, harken back to the early days when a rational, problem-solving approach was used, only whereas here, we add the notion of policies "based on systematic, objective evidence from empirical research. It has scientific findings as its base" (Hall & Jennings, 2006, p. 11). Policy makers and practitioners alike have come to recognize the importance of science in this process. In a sense, all policy is underpinned by theory, which is developed through empirical research and use of the scientific methods, designs, and analyses. Theories are either tentatively confirmed or falsified. This is a continuous, iterative process in which the growing body of knowledge that results can then be utilized in the formulation of evidence-based policy in criminal justice.

Such evidence may be used to inform the development and implementation of policy in at least a couple of ways. First, there may be evidence that the policy is effective and therefore helps to determine what policy actions to take. And, secondly, evidence as to how implemented policy options may be adjusted to improve or continue, which in turn provides impetus for future policy options (Plewis, 2000).

The move toward evidence-based policy "attempts to insure that practitioners use methods which have been found to be effective rather than the ones they prefer" (Duke, 2001, p. 292). Effectiveness, in this instance, has come to mean "what works." Whether or not a policy actually works is often given little consideration or totally ignored (Dunworth et al., 2003). Policies borne out of issues of morality or driven largely by media portrayal, which is often exaggerated or inaccurate, are many times developed and implemented with little regard to whether or not it is supported by evidence or has some chance of actually working. Such policies, unfortunately, are many times doomed to fail in the sense that they do not achieve the goals or objectives of the policy. That is, the problem(s) motivating the policy do not really get better and in some instances actually become worse. For many, the real task is to "understand what works, for whom, in what circumstances, and why as a basis for piecemeal social reform; indeed, the phrase 'what matters is what works' has become something of a mantra in evidence-based policy circles" (Sanderson, 2002, p. 8). So, with the advent of empirical-based policy making, "research and evidence have become increasingly important dimensions within the policy process" (Duke, 2001, p. 277).

According to Sanderson (2002), there are at least two forms of evidence that are helpful in the policy making process:

1. evidence to promote accountability in terms of results—evidence that government is working effectively, and
2. evidence to promote improvement through more effective policies and programs—the increasing use of performance indicators and targets, for example, in government departments (p. 3).

Benefits and Criticisms of
Evidence-Based Policy Making

In addition to effectiveness, evidence-based policies help to provide an acceptable rate of return on the enormous investment paid by taxpayers for the criminal justice expenditures on courts, law enforcement, prisons, and community-based programs (Dunworth et al., 2003). This is no insignificant benefit. With dwindling resources and a justice system that is bursting at the seams with too many offenders, it is critical that public policies be both effective and provide a reasonable return on investment for dollars spent. In this environment, policy makers can no longer do what is just politically popular without regard to effectiveness. "Politically acceptable doesn't necessarily mean effective, affordable, or otherwise viable" (Dunworth et al., 2003). Additionally, grounding policy making in the realm of "what works" helps to preserve the relevance and integrity of the entire process (Sanderson, 2002).

However, evidence-based policy making is not without some criticism, nor is it fully embraced into the policy making process. Despite the increased demand for evidence-based practices, there is not the total integration of research and evidence production into the making of public policy (Maynard, 2006). There are some limitations to evidence-based approaches:

1. The evidence can be ambiguous or contradictory at times.
2. The evidence can be very complex and difficult to interpret.
3. There is always the issue of human bias. Research methods strive to control for researcher bias, but it may not completely eliminate this issue (Dunworth et al., 2003, p. 2).

There is also the very real possibility that results from research may be misused by politicians and others for their own devices. Politicians may, for example, attempt to bring some legitimacy to the notion of evidence-based policies by only using research evidence when it supports the political or ideologically driven priorities (Kogan, 1999). This is not so much a limitation of evidence-based policy making itself as it is the misapplication of these approaches for political or ideological motivations.

Evidence based policy making cannot be a panacea for all policy issues or problems. However, "it can illuminate the path to more effective public policy" over the long haul (Dunworth et al., 2003). It is effectively the best we have.

Researchers themselves, as producers of evidence, can have a major impact on policy making in criminal justice. Duke (2001) argued that researchers should actually become more active agents at every step in the policy making process, especially at the beginning. "It is clear that many researchers have been successful in exploiting the opportunities presented by such research to embed themselves within policy networks, interpret and present their data critically and influence decision making" (Duke, 2001, p. 292). Furthermore, researchers can actually shape the policy making agenda by getting more involved at the beginning of the process, rather than just through their efforts in the evaluative process at the end (Duke, 2001).

Best Practices in Criminal Justice Policy Making

Now, let us discuss some of the reforms and what is emerging as policy communities develop what they call *best practices* for their particular criminal justice domains of expertise. "The use of best practices and evidence-based practice to inform and influence public policy is on the rise" (Hall & Jennings, 2006, p. 2). Sometimes, these best practices are collected and placed into a catalog, compendium, or database of best practices dealing with some specific policy area (Bardach, 2003).

Best practices have been defined as "results oriented decision making based upon scientific evidence" (Cannon & Kilburn, 2003, p. 2). The use of best practices attempts to rationalize government (Hall & Jennings, 2006) and is motivated by

- improving organizational performance,
- meeting national standards,
- providing effective interventions,
- improving accountability,
- ensuring professionalism,
- providing policy direction, and
- providing legislative requirements (p. 16).

Policy Making Reform and Guidelines

Reformers of policy making certainly agree that best practices based on evidence produced by scientific, rational processes is a move in the right direction. For example, we should be more rational about how we allocate our limited resources in our "War on Crime." We should strive to be effective, that is, achieve our stated policy goals. We should be sure to make good investments in the manner in which we formulate and implement our public policies in the justice system. We should reduce recidivism, or reoffending by offenders, when that is our aim. And, finally, we should help ex-offenders become productive citizens who do not return to crime (Steen & Bandy, 2007).

Foster (2009, slides 6–14) outlined what he considers to be seven essential criteria of good policy as follows:

1. Effectiveness. What is the bottom line? What is the policy intended to do? Is the policy working? Are goals being met, as opposed to just activity taking place? Too many times we may mistake frenetic activity for actually getting something done. This is especially true when horrendous events are highly publicized and policy makers feel a desperate

need to do something because they feel pressure from the public. Legislation and policy made in this knee-jerk fashion is rarely good or effective.

2.   Externalities. What might be the side effects of the policy? What are the intended consequences? Can we identify any potential unintended consequences, positive or negative? An example of this might be where residence requirements and restrictions are placed on where sex offenders can live, only to inadvertently create small geographical areas that are left for them to reside, all in close proximity to each other, with negative consequences.

3.   Theory. What are the underlying assumptions of our proposed policy? Nearly all justice policy is founded in theory. What is that theory or theories? How does our policy match up in terms of consistency with that theory or theories?

4.   Efficiency. Are we doing things right with our policy? Are we using the least amount of resources to produce the desired results?

5.   Compliance. Does our policy comply with the fundamentals of our system of law? Is it constitutional? Is it consistent with American systems of justice?

6.   Equity. Are the outputs and burdens of our policy equitably distributed?

7.   Intervention effect. Can the effects of our policy be accurately measured?

These criteria can, and should, be applied to all of our current policies in criminal justice retrospectively as well as new ones being contemplated. Foster (2009) also discussed other things to consider when contemplating policy options. He referred to these as the six Cs of policy options. There is *concentration*, which refers to the issue of whether or not we have the resources to implement a particular policy, i.e., personnel, time, equipment, and money. There have been times when policies were implemented without much thought about how it will be possible to pay for it, otherwise referred to as an unfunded mandate. *Clarity* refers to whether or not the goals of the policy are clearly outlined. Are the stakeholders identified, and do the identified stakeholders implementing the policy understand what their role is? Do stakeholders who are actually affected by the policy understand it? *Challenge* refers to whether or not the policy is doable? Is it a realistic policy so far as availability of resources, stakeholder support, and outcomes? Then, there is *changeability*. How flexible is the policy to change? If conditions change, can the policy easily change? If not, then there are those who argue that many times in criminal justice we just keep doing the same thing, even though we know it doesn't work. Are stakeholders who are responsible for and affected by the policy able to adapt to the change in policy, if that happens? *Coordination* asks whether or not there is effective coordination and communication between all stakeholders. Is there a feedback mechanism for course corrections? And, finally, there is *consistency*. Are the actions required by the policy consistent with the objectives of the policy? Are the objectives consistent with the goal? Is the policy consistent with other policies? Is the policy action delivered consistently?

Dunworth et al. (2003) summarized some of the key elements of sound policy analysis as

- identifying the most important issues and putting them first,
- gathering as much data as time and money allow,
- turning to informed and unbiased experts for analysis,
- applying the most appropriate methodologies for the problem and data,
- pursuing evidence without preconceived conclusions in mind,
- subjecting findings to independent review, and
- sharing results—whether positive or negative—with the public (p. 7).

The remaining chapters in this book will focus on specific policy issues found in the criminal justice system today. Detailed analysis is provided by the authors who have developed expertise in each area and who provide suggestions for the creation of good, sound evidence-based policy. Specific topics highlighted include the War on Drugs, immigration laws, the bail process, the Patriot Act and terrorist laws, sentencing guidelines, three-strikes laws, capital punishment, sex offender laws, "get tough" juvenile policies, zero-tolerance policies in schools, policies for mental health offenders, and policies affecting pregnant offenders.

The basic framework provided in Chapter 1 will help the reader to examine each remaining chapter within the broader context of what is known about the policy making process and what is thought to work.

References

Arnstein, S. (1969). Ladder of participation. *American Institute of Planners Journal, 35,* 216–224.

Banks, C. (2009). The ethics of criminal justice policy making. In *Criminal justice ethics: Theory and practice* (2nd ed.). Thousand Oaks, CA: Sage.

Bardach, E. (2003). Creating compendia of "best practices." *Journal of Policy Analysis and Management, 22*(4), 661–665.

Beckett, K. (1977). *Making crime pay: Law and order in contemporary American politics.* New York, NY: Oxford University Press.

Cannon, J. S., & Kilburn, M. R. (2003). Meeting decision makers' needs for evidence-based information on child and family policy. *Journal of Policy Analysis and Management, 22*(4), 665–668.

Cohen, S. (1973). *Folk devils and moral panics.* St. Albans, England: Paladin.

Coleman, W. D., & Skogstad, G. (1990). *Policy communities and public policy in Canada.* Mississauga, ON: Copp Clark Pitman.

Cook, D. T., & Russo, M. J. (1999). Lessons learned in evaluation over the past 25 years. In E. Chelimsky & W. R. Shadish (Eds.), *Evaluation for the 21st century: A handbook.* Thousand Oaks, CA: Sage.

Davies, H. T. O., Nutley, S. M., & Smith, P. C. (1999). Editorial: What works? The role of evidence in public sector policy and practice. *Public Money and Management, 19*(1), 3–5.

Duke, K. (2001). Evidence-based policy making? The interplay between research and the development of prison drugs policy. *Criminology and Criminal Justice, 1*, 277–300.

Dunworth, T., Hannaway, J., Holahan, J., & Turner, M. A. (2003). *The case for evidence-based policy: Beyond ideology, politics, and guess work.* Washington, DC: Urban Institute.

Ebbesen, E., & Konecni, V. (1985). Criticisms of the criminal justice system: A decision-making analysis. *Behavioral Science and the Law, 3*(2), 177–194.

Fairchild, E. S. (1981). Interest groups in the criminal justice process. *Journal of Criminal Justice, 9*, 181–194.

Foster, R. (2009). *Public policy and practice in criminal justice: Decision-making part II* [PowerPoint presentation]. Retrieved from https://www.slideshare.net/PoliceConsultant/public-policy-and-practice-decision-making-part-two.

Hall, J., & Jennings, Jr., E. (2006, August). *Using best practices to inform public policy decision making.* Paper delivered at the annual meeting of the American Political Science Association, Philadelphia, PA.

Hough, M. (1996). People talking about punishment. *Howard Journal of Criminal Justice, 35*(3), 191–214.

Ismali, K. (2006). Contextualizing the criminal justice policy-making process. *Criminal Justice Policy Review, 17*(3), 255–269.

Johnstone, G. (2000). Penal policy making: Elitist, populist or participatory? *Punishment & Society, 2*(2), 161–180.

Jones, T., & Newburn, T. (2005). Comparative criminal justice policy-making in the United States and the United Kingdom. *British Journal of Criminology, 45*(1), 58–80.

Kogan, M. (1999). The impact of research on policy. In F. Coffield (Ed.), *Research and policy in lifelong learning.* Bristol, England: Policy Press.

Maynard, R. A. (2006). Presidential address: Evidence-based decision making: What will it take for decision makers to decide? *Journal of Policy Analysis and Management, 25*(1), 249–266.

Plewis, I. (2000). Educational inequalities and education action zones. In C. Pantazis & D. Gordon (Eds.), *Tackling inequalities: Where are we now and what can be done?* Bristol, England: Policy Press.

Pross, A. P. (1986). *Group politics and public policy.* Toronto, Canada: Oxford University Press.

Ryan, M. (1999). Penal policy making towards the millennium: Elites and populists; New labour and the new criminology. *International Journal of the Sociology of Law, 27*(1), 1–22.

Sanderson, I. (2002). Evaluation, policy learning and evidence-based policy making. *Public Administration, 80*(1), 1–22.

Solomon, P. (1981). The policy process in Canadian criminal justice: A perspective and research agenda. *Canadian Journal of Criminology, 23,* 5–25.

Steen, S., & Bandy, R. (2007).When the policy becomes the problem: Criminal justice in the new millennium. *Punishment & Society, 9,* 5–26.

Stolz, B. A. (2002). *Criminal justice policy making: Federal roles and processes.* Westport, CT: Praeger Publishers.

Weiss, C. H. (1986). Introduction. In C. H. Weis (Ed.), *Using social research in public policy-making.* Farnborough, England: Saxon House.

Chapter 2

Police and the Use of Force
Dilemmas in Policy Making

Anthony Gassaway

"The discretion whether to employ deadly force is, because of its irreversible consequences, the gravest power that a society can delegate to one of its agencies. Accordingly, the development of strict guidelines to govern its use should receive the highest community priority."
—Honorable Wade H. McCree, Jr., Solicitor General
(U.S. Department of Justice, 1979, p. v.)

Introduction

The use of force, and in particular, coercive force, is considered by many to be the defining feature of policing in the United States. Some scholars contend that the ability to rightfully use coercive force separates policing and its officers from all other professions and citizens. Egon Bittner, in his work, *The Functions of the Police in Modern Society, A Review of Background Factors, Current Practices, and Possible Role Models* (1970), described police use of force in this manner: "the role of police is to address all sorts of human problems when and insofar as their solutions do and may require the use of force at the point of their occurrence" (Bittner, 1970, p. 44). Unique to this public institution we call policing, our designated governmental agents, in order to do their jobs efficiently and effectively, have been granted the authority to use force (on occasion) against the citizens they serve. Pate, Fridell, and Hamilton (1993) stated, "Indeed, the legitimate use of force is the defining characteristic of the institution of policing" (Pate et al., 1993, p. 5).

Yet consistently, among the most publicly scrutinized and controversial actions that occur in policing, both in a historical context and even yet today, are those occasions when police do use force. The use of force by police is arguably one of the predominant topics continuously discussed throughout the entire criminal justice community, academia, the media, politicians, and society in general.

Of specific concern, debate, and consideration are often those incidents where deadly force is used. Fyfe (1981) stated, "the subject of police use of deadly force has generated considerable controversy in recent years. Questions related to deadly force have been raised and analyzed by presidential commissions, police practitioners, researchers contracted by police practitioners, radical criminologists, more traditional academics, social activists, law reviews, and popular writers" (Fyfe, 1981, p. 376).

Invariably, similar questions often arise when police use of force incidents are analyzed and discussed. Was the force used necessary and appropriate to the circumstance? Did the officer possess other measures that would have been prudent? What training did the officer receive in this area? And for the purposes of our discussion, what was the department's use of force policy, and more importantly, was it followed? The recent headlines noted below are reflective of the extreme scrutiny that is occurring across the country regarding police use of force and the policy making associated with those actions.

"Chicago Police Finalize Tighter Rules on When to Shoot, Other Uses of Force" (Hinkle, 2017)
"Las Vegas Police Revise Use-of-Force Policies" (Shoro & Apgar, 2017)
"Fewer Shootings by Police—That's the Goal of New Rules Adopted by the L.A. Police Commission" (Mather & Chang, 2017)
"Baltimore Police Department Overhauls Decade-Old Use of Force Policy" (DelValle, 2016)
"Minneapolis Police Reveal Changes to Use-of-Force Policy" (Jany, 2016)

Analysis and Definitions

To analyze any police usage of force, it is critical to understand that at the core of every police officer–citizen interaction is an intervention. Most often, this is an authorized intervention on behalf of the government into the life of a citizen of that government. Statistically, this intervention is usually benign in nature; it is basically just a brief conversation and the encounter is concluded. No force by the officer is generally needed or utilized. During some of these interventions, however, the governmental agent may be required to use some level of force to gain compliance from the citizen. This often very difficult and dangerous task falls to the men and women who do policing in the United

States. It is also undisputed that rarely some of these interventions by our police officers are not conducted in an acceptable or legal manner.

As citizens, we fully expect that our police will have to, on occasion, use various levels of coercive force during their duties, including deadly force. Yet, we also rightly demand that those using force follow the laws, policies, and procedures created to regulate that police conduct. If they do not, then the offending officer(s) must simply be held accountable for their improper behavior. Ultimately, it is a normally held expectation that police must possess the ability to use justifiable force to perform their duties. Fridell (2005) aptly described this use of police force as "that force ... used to the extent necessary so that the officers are able to conduct law enforcement functions. Force is not used when it could be avoided, and force is used only in the amounts necessary to achieve legitimate objectives" (Fridell, 2005, p. 21).

What legitimately raises questions, as well as concerns, in our society, and is the topic of our discussion on policy making, are those incidents when police are perceived to or have actually used "excessive" force in their duties. Excessive force has been defined as "the amount of physical force that is more than reasonably necessary to effect a legal function" (Pate et al., 1993, p. 19). Kania and Mackey (1977) have defined excessive force as "violence of a degree that is more than necessary or justified to effect a legitimate police function" (p. 29). Lastly, it has simply been described as "the abuse of force" (Morgan & Allen, 2009, p. 95). Whatever the definition applied, there is no lack of consensus that this type of inappropriate conduct by our police is not acceptable within a democratic society. Certainly, one primary component to achieving a measure of force accountability in a police agency is through the use of appropriate policy making by that department. A primary mechanism to achieve this goal is the implementation and enforcement of detailed, written policies that formally guide and constrain officers in their use of force. Multiple research studies conducted since the 1960s have consistently shown that when a police agency possesses a comprehensive use of force policy, those policies do influence the nature and frequency of force used by their police officers (Fridell, 2005, p. 22). Yet, even with a thoroughly researched and meticulously constructed force policy, the hazardous nature of the policing function may still ultimately lead to the injury or death of the citizen to whom force is applied. The following incident is an example of the extraordinary discretion that a police officer possesses to use force, the life changing consequences that follow that force, and the implications to all parties based on that force.

On October 20, 2014, a 17-year-old African American man, Laquan McDonald, was in the midst of a formal governmental intervention conducted by members of the Chicago Police Department. According to official reports, the police had been dispatched to investigate citizen complaints that McDonald was observed carrying a knife and possibly breaking into motor vehicles. There is no question that McDonald's erratic behavior required the police to intervene in this matter. Ample video recordings of that encounter currently exist that explicitly detail the results of that intervention and unequivocally demonstrate the often-tragic results of a violent police–citizen encounter.

When officers initially confronted McDonald, he reportedly used a small bladed knife to slice the tire on a patrol vehicle and also damaged its windshield. The officers repeatedly ordered McDonald to drop the knife, which he refused to do. Hoping to end the encounter using a less than lethal option, the officers on scene requested a conducted energy device (Taser) be brought to the site. While awaiting the arrival of that device, Chicago Police Officer Jason Van Dyke also arrived on scene to assist the initial responding officers. Within 6 seconds of exiting his vehicle, Van Dyke subsequently shot Laquan McDonald 16 times in the span of 14 to 15 seconds. He was later pronounced dead upon being transported to an area hospital (Austen, 2016).

Within the larger societal scheme, just one more police use of force on a citizen had occurred. In this case, a young man of color, whose behavior had certainly required a governmental intervention, was tragically killed in the process. The designated governmental official who responded to McDonald's actions, Officer Van Dyke, determined on that evening that his firearm was the most appropriate level of force to control this situation.

The aftermath of that encounter is still being discussed to date. After a preliminary investigation was conducted in this incident, Officer Van Dyke was charged in November 2015 with first-degree murder and was initially held without bail at the Cook County Jail located in Chicago, Illinois. Van Dyke was subsequently released from custody and is currently awaiting trial as of the date of this writing (March, 2018). Additionally, the city of Chicago has reached an undisclosed settlement with McDonald's family. Numerous protests denouncing McDonald's death have occurred at both at the local and national level. Angry citizens have demanded changes be immediately made in Chicago Police Department procedures, particularly in their use of force. There have been numerous calls for the dismissal or resignation of city and county officials over this incident, including Mayor Rahm Emanuel.

This tremendous cascade of negative results from a single police use of force incident has created not only a major public trust issue for the Chicago Police Department but also has prompted extensive internal change within that department. The outcry from the McDonald incident ultimately led to a comprehensive review of the Chicago Police's use of force policies, whereby additional guidelines were added to their force policy that purportedly will provide additional protections to the citizens of Chicago from excessive force by their police. Presumably, these same additions will also not impede the safety of the officers who would be mandated to follow them. Among the new rules, one now requires Chicago police officers to intervene verbally if they observe their colleagues using unnecessary force. In the McDonald case, it has been contended that the accounts given by other officers at the scene supported the initial story of the officer who fired the shots, but their statements were eventually contradicted by video evidence.

Per the updated policy, Chicago officers also face new restrictions on using deadly force against fleeing suspects, only allowing it's use when the person poses an "immediate threat." The previous policy allowed an officer to fire on anyone who has committed or attempted a felony using force. Experts in the policing field have stated the new rules go beyond U.S. Supreme Court case law that guides this behavior. According to the *New York Post*, some national supporters of police reform have praised Chicago's new force guidelines, stating they went beyond the policies of many other departments around the nation. "This represents the next generation of use-of-force policy," said David A. Harris, a professor at the University of Pittsburgh School of Law who has written extensively about police accountability (Hinkle, 2017).

Since the beginnings of policing in the United States, perhaps even during the colonial period of our country, incidents of police force of varying degrees have certainly been commonplace. The ability to force a citizen to comply to a lawful order is integral to the task of effectively policing our population. The goal of that authority is that a designated governmental agent would be able to intervene, to take control when necessary, in the safest and most efficient manner possible. Without that rightful authority, our police, and the citizenry they protect, would definitively be put at great physical risk. The decisions police must make as to whether to use force, at whatever the level, are among the most difficult ones that an officer will be required to do in their careers.

Bittner (1970) noted:

> Police intervention means above all making use of the capacity and authority to overpower resistance to an attempted solution in the native habitat of the problem. There can be no doubt that this feature of police work is uppermost in the minds of people who solicit police aid or direct the attention of the police to problems, that person against whom the police proceed have this feature in mind and conduct themselves accordingly, and that every conceivable police intervention projects the message that force maybe, and may have to be, used to achieve a desired objective. (p. 43)

Despite what current public misconceptions may exist regarding the use of deadly force by police, the large majority of officers are never required to discharge their firearms at a citizen during the midst of making these official interventions. Perhaps over thousands of contacts with citizens over an entire career, the overwhelming majority of police officers in the United States are never once required to use of the highest authorized level of police force (deadly force). Regarding the use of lesser levels of force by police, statistics demonstrate that any use of force by a police officer against a citizen is an infrequent incident when compared to the overall contacts that occur each day in the United States. For the sake of our discussion, why are these infrequent events so closely scrutinized and critiqued by the general population?

At the heart of this contentious issue is the inherent difficulty that police officers must frequently make these force decisions under very difficult and dangerous conditions. It is a unique conundrum unlike those faced in any other profession, one that officers may face in each and every direct encounter with the citizens they serve. Should they underestimate the level of force necessary to gain compliance, they or another person could potentially be injured or killed. On the other hand, should they overreact and then utilize an excessive level of force, a citizen may be unnecessarily killed or injured. To compound this entire decision-making process, officers must often make this very precise force decision under extreme stress and in a time frame of split seconds. Certainly, it is an unenviable task for any public servant. In the case of Laquan McDonald, some segments of society have contended the officer involved used an inappropriate and unnecessary level of force when he intervened in McDonald's life. That matter has yet to be fully resolved. What is readily apparent from the McDonald case is that the tremendous police discretion and authority, in this instance the use of deadly force, is the most serious act an officer must ever determine to utilize. As a 1979 Department of Justice (DOJ) report aptly noted, "A reverence for the value of human life should always guide officers in considering the use of force (deadly). It is in the public interest that law enforcement officers be guided by a policy which the people believe to be fair and appropriate" (p. v.). Of continued discussion is what exactly would be considered "fair and appropriate" policy by the citizenry of the United States?

Media Impact on Public Perceptions

A potential issue that arises from the public's conceptions regarding "proper" police conduct, such as in the McDonald case, is the general lack of technical expertise in law enforcement matters by those who criticize and make external judgments on that conduct. In some instances, the use of excessive force by an officer is so egregious that it is readily apparent to all that the actions were improper. Unfortunately, what is often found to be true here is that public perceptions of police use of force, and particularly excessive force, are heavily influenced by the power of the media and, consequently, are sometimes not based in fact. It is well known that all of us readily, and in an immediate fashion, receive all types of information, from news to popular culture. This instant information is disseminated through numerous venues such as television, the Internet, Facebook, Twitter, and the like. Thompson (2011) stated, "Studies have demonstrated the strong correlation between the amount of media coverage on a particular topic with public knowledge and interest on that topic. When it comes to crime coverage, television programming not only tends to suggest that crime happens at greater frequency than it does, but it also exaggerates the amount of violent crime in the world relative to property crime" (Thompson, 2011, p. 776).

Unfortunately, some of the media depictions of incidents similar to Laquan McDonald, and of police work in general, are not presenting an accurate overall picture as to what the data tells us regarding police use of force. In fact, the public's perception of these incidents regarding the frequency and appropriateness of police force are sometimes framed in large part by media descriptions (International Association of Chiefs of Police/Office of Community Oriented Policing Services, 2012, p.11). These misconceptions can unfortunately skew the public's overall attitude and support toward the police in general, and, particularly, in their use of force. Regarding this media distortion and the policy making aspects of use of force, Thompson (2011) went on to state, "Informed public policy demands at a minimum rigorous debate and ideas driven by evidence rather than heat. Criminal justice policy without a grounded evidentiary basis holds serious implications for both the public perception of effective public policy, and the administration of criminal justice policy" (Thompson, 2011, p. 778). Bernard Melekian, former director of the DOJ's Office of Community Oriented Policing Services, summarized this phenomenon: "This perception (public's use of force by police) is heavily influenced by a variety of factors, including depictions in the media, and is exacerbated by the increasing power of social media. In today's age, incidents of use of force can create a false narrative for the public concerning the appropriateness of police actions, albeit one that is not statistically representative or supported by data" (International Association of Chiefs of Police/Office of Community Oriented Policing Services, 2012, p.1).

Before a discussion of appropriate use of force policy making is undertaken, what do we accurately know regarding the use of force against citizens by police?

One fact that is sometimes not well understood by the general public is that force used by police against a citizen is statistically low in comparison to the overall contacts that occur between the two groups each and every day in the United States. The most recently published Bureau of Justice (BJS) report, "Census of State and Local Law Enforcement Agencies, 2008" stated that there are approximately 765,000 sworn police officers in the United States. A collateral 2008 BJS report on contacts between the police and the public reports that those 765,000 police officers had approximately 40 million contacts with U.S. citizens in 2008. Of those contacts, only an estimated 770,000 contacts out of the 40 million overall resulted in the threatened use or application of force during that encounter. This equates to any level of force being used by police against a civilian in only 1.9% of the overall contacts (International Association of Chiefs of Police/Office of Community Oriented Policing Services, 2012, p. 11).

It has been additionally reported in similar studies that only 15%–20% of the overall arrests that occur in the United States result in a low-level use of force to control a resistant suspect. Most importantly, the majority of these incidents are believed to just have involved a very minor level of force, simply the use of an officer's hands, arms, and/or body to push or pull a suspect to gain control. No higher levels of force, specifically a firearm or intermediate control device (such as a baton) were typically utilized (Smith et al., 2010, p. 1–1). An earlier 2002 study on contacts between police and the public demonstrated about the same frequency; 1.5% of the citizens who had police contact had force threatened or used against them. Only 14% of the respondents in this study reported any injury because of that use of force (Smith et al., 2011, p. 2–3).

In a 2001 Police Use of Force in America report conducted by the International Association of Chiefs of Police (IACP), it was noted that the IACP's National Police Use of Force Database was the first known attempt at a substantial aggregation of local, county, and state law enforcement use of force data. Information for this database was compiled from the years 1991–2000 and represented, among other items, 45,913,161 calls for service to police; 177,215 use of force incidents reported in those calls; and 8,082 complaints based on those use of force incidents. The analysis of this data demonstrated that U.S. police used force at a rate of 3.61 times per 10,000 calls for service, which translated to a rate of use of force of 0.0361%. As noted in the report, "Expressed another way, police_did not use force 99.9639% of the time" (IACP, 2001, p. i).

What can be construed from all this available research is that the use of force by police against citizens is an infrequent event, and in those cases where it does occur, only a very small percentage of those citizens actually report any injury from the contact. It can also be construed that the improper use of force by a police officer is statistically a very rare event. Unfortunately, these statistically small, yet improper, force interventions can have devastating and long-lasting effects on the image of the police department involved, as well as the resultant loss of public trust by the community served. Kenneth Adams (1999) described this situation:

> In characterizing police use of force as infrequent or rare, the intention is neither to minimize the problem nor to suggest that the issue can be dismissed as unworthy of serious attention. Society's ends are best achieved peaceably, and we should strive to minimize the use of force by police as much as possible. However, it is important to put police use of force in context in order to understand the potential magnitude of use-of-force problems. Although estimates may not completely reassure everyone that police are doing everything they can to minimize the use of force, the data do not support the notion that we have a national epidemic of police violence. (Adams et al., 1999, p. 12)

Conversely, one also cannot ignore the danger that our police face when they must intervene in the lives of our population. The Federal Bureau of Investigation's (FBI) 2016 Law Enforcement Killed and Assaulted (LEOKA) report demonstrated that a total of 118 U.S. law enforcement officers were killed in the line of duty in 2016. Of those deaths, 52 were accidental and 66 were felonious. Additionally, in that same year, 57,180 officers were assaulted in the line of duty, with nearly 30% of those officers being physically injured in the incidents (FBI, 2017).

Hall (1993) stated:

> The number of officers slain or seriously injured while performing their duties graphically illustrates the inherent risks associated with law enforcement. For example, during the period 1981–1990, 762 State and local law enforcement officers were slain as the result of adversarial action; an additional 617,969 officers were assaulted, of whom 210,109 (34%) suffered significant injury.... Society recognizes these risks and grants law enforcement officers the authority to protect themselves as they perform their duties. Obviously, the exercise of that authority must be constantly and carefully monitored to discourage abuse, and officers know that any use of force, particularly deadly force, will certainly be subjected to administrative, and probably judicial, review. (p. 27)

What is evident from these statistics is that the inherent dangers posed in the policing profession require officers to possess the authority to use reasonable and necessary force. It is also vitally critical that every police officer possesses the ability, training, and tools to forcefully execute their duties under the proper circumstances and in accordance with the law and their agency's policies and procedures. And as the 2016 LEOKA statistics demonstrate, even while possessing the tremendous authority and discretion to use force if necessary, a large number of police officers every year in the United States are still assaulted, injured, or killed.

To summarize our discussion thus far, for centuries, mankind, from practitioners to scholars from various disciplines and fields of study, have attempted to analyze and truly understand the use of force by our designated governmental agents. Compounding that difficulty is the inability to generate a common definition. What exactly is "use of force"? It can certainly be an ambiguous and difficult concept to specifically define, and consequently, administer by a policy. The IACP (2001) provided the following definition: " 'Use of force' refers to the 'amount of effort required by police to compel compliance by an unwilling subject' " (p.1). Martin, Gwynne, and Gruber (2009) defined it as "Force (police) is a broad term and its use can be defined as deadly force, less than deadly force, and the depravation of liberty through arrest" (p. 21). Champion (2009) defined police use of force as:

> Most broadly defined, police use of force involves any type of physical control or restraint imposed upon a member of the public. Use of force may occur during arrests, in the course of interventions in ongoing assaults, or in crowd control situations. Officers use various levels of force to protect themselves or others, to sustain an apprehension or to maintain control of a situation. Most broadly defined, police use of force involves any type of physical control or restraint imposed upon a member of the public. Use of force may occur during arrests, in the course of interventions in ongoing assaults, or in crowd control situations. Officers use various levels of force to protect themselves or others, to sustain an apprehension or to maintain control of a situation. (p. 632)

In whatever manner police force is defined, agreement is generally universal that police must not exercise it in an unrestrained fashion. The implications of the use of unnecessary and improper force to the communities that are being served by police are far-reaching. The subsequent loss of public support and trust for their police forces due to perceived or actual police misconduct can have a long-lasting impact on a community. Geller and Karales (1981) stated, "Even a single, well-publicized shooting can foster a hostility between police and community which can take years to undo. As a result, much of the scholarly, legislative, and administrative attention to deadly force questions is prompted by both a moral and utilitarian concern over the social turmoil which police shootings can produce. The social costs clearly can go beyond the individual and family suffering which follow the shooting of a police officer" (p. 1814). The remainder of this chapter will attempt to provide some clarity on the police use of force, specifically related to the policy making efforts of various entities to regulate this ability. Ultimately, it is those policies and procedures adopted by police that will frame what we accept as the appropriate usage of this ability.

Role of Use of Force Policy and Procedures

The appropriateness of Chicago Officer Jason Van Dyke's actions in the Laquan McDonald case certainly, and rightly so, is a matter that will be determined through designated and thorough review processes. Ultimately, the true tragedy of this situation was that a young man's life was extinguished. What must be a critical component of that review was the question of whether or not Van Dyke operated within the bounds of the Chicago Police Department's use of force policy. Under the specific circumstances he was facing at the time with McDonald, did the officer utilize his firearm in conjunction with the parameters outlined in the department's policy?

This key question is often at the core issue regarding the many police–citizen interactions that occur daily in the United States. It goes to the appropriateness of the use of force, if any, measured against the resistance the officer faced in the situation. The policies and procedures created by our police departments, legislatures, and courts regulate and guide this use of force and are paramount in regulating police conduct in this area. Compounding this issue is the conundrum that a policy regulating this area must be written in a manner as to provide broad parameters that still allow for tremendous officer discretion to make those critical decisions. Should the policy be too restrictive, an officer or another person might be injured or killed. Too little guidance and the officer may utilize excessive force, potentially killing a subject.

The many issues and perspectives surrounding use of force policies by police has certainly been extensively analyzed and discussed at all levels, including by academics, practitioners, courts, politicians, attorneys, and the citizens that police serve. Unfortunately, this is a difficult and perplexing scenario that is not easily defined. There is no clear and easily definable answer to what exactly a use of force policy must and should contain. The members of the public being served by a police department generally agree that their designated governmental officials (the police) must be granted the authority to "intervene" in situations that tend to threaten public safety and order. However, they would also agree that authority must be carefully measured and executed.

Historical Background

From where do our police receive their "permission" to use force? Pate et al. (1993) noted that concern over the power of law enforcement officers goes as far back to the year 1215 as reflected in the articles of the Magna Carta. Fearful of misuse of the authority by the "police" of that timeframe, the articles reflected numerous safeguards to protect citizens from abuse. In another early instance of control over police use of force, in approximately 1830, the London Metropolitan Police Department issued strict policy to its officers on the proper use of the police truncheon. This direction reportedly coming after a rash of citizen complaints regarding the excessive use of the baton (Pate et al., 1993, p. 6).

Regarding policing in the United States, Hicks (2009) noted, "the social contract theory provides a firm foundation to rest an understanding and evaluation of police practices" (p. 5). This "social contract" philosophy extends back to the framers of the Declaration of Independence and the U.S. Constitution, such as Thomas Jefferson. In essence, these early leaders believed that citizens of a society grant their government the authority to make and enforce laws in order to provide security, safety, and peace to each of the citizens as a whole. As a part of that contract, each citizen consequently gives up a small portion of their individual freedom to the government to live in this peaceful collective. The police in the United States were created as the formal governmental mechanism to provide for that protection of all its members under laws drafted by their elected officials. The power to properly enforce those laws, including using force against citizens, is thus vested in our police forces (Hicks, 2009).

The continuing question is what exactly is the "right and proper" use of that force? Compounding the issue of fully analyzing this use of force by police and attempting to apply a singular policy standard to it nationwide is the practice in U.S. policing known as *fragmentation*. Rather than subject our citizens to a singular entity to provide police services across the United States, our country undertook the process of creating police protection at all the various levels of governmental entities: city, county, state, and federal. Walker and Katz (2018) stated, "The independence of local governments is deeply rooted in American history. The principle of local control, not just of police but of schools and other governmental services" (p. 77). To maintain local control over police services, in many cases, each city, county, and state in the United States created their "own" law enforcement entity to provide policing. This fragmented system of policing services today equals approximately 18,000 law enforcement agencies in the United States. Overall, that number equates to approximately 12,500 local police departments, 3,000 sheriff's departments, 50 state police entities, 1,700 special police agencies, and 73 federal agencies. For the purposes of this discussion, each with their own policy of designating the appropriate use of force by its officers.

Based on this direction, the United States undertook of police agency fragmentation. Consequently, there exists no singular entity in the United States that provides direct oversight to those 18,000 agencies, including in the area of policy making. Unfortunately, our tradition of local police control has led to inconsistent standards across all our law enforcement entities and, potentially, in no more a divisive area than in the use of force. Interestingly, multiple police agencies located even within a close geographic range can possess vastly different approaches to the same mission, including different uniforms, weapons, procedures, and specifically, in the construction of their use of force policies.

Walker and Katz (2018) compare the U.S. approach with that of Japan. Japan possesses a singular law enforcement agency that exerts central coordination over their entire police function yet still allows for local control in their designated jurisdictions. This entity, the National Police Agency, is responsible for coordinating the operations of the 47 Japanese prefectural police. While each prefecture is considered independent, the national office can recommend operational standards, in this case, the use of force by police officers (Walker and Katz, 2018, p. 73).

Unlike Japan, the resultant issue for the United States, which is also the topic of our discussion, is the inability to apply a singular policy or standard to all our 18,000 police agencies across the country so that each of them individually exercises one direct set of standards that will guide them in the rightful and appropriate use of force. The earlier discussed issue of fragmentation compounds that issue even further.

A rightful question in regulating police use of force would be how about court decisions providing that singular guidance? Potentially the U.S. Supreme Court? Unfortunately, even recent Supreme Court decisions have not specified universal force standards and instead have allowed police agencies substantial discretion in use of force policy making. The IACP's (2017) "National Consensus Policy and Discussion Paper on the Use of Force" stated, "The United States Supreme Court has provided clear parameters regarding the use of force. However, how this guidance is operationalized in the policies of individual law enforcement agencies varies greatly. This creates a landscape where each agency, even neighboring jurisdictions, are potentially operating under differing, inconsistent, or varied policies when it comes to the most critical of topics" (p. 5). The result is approximately 18,000 differing police entities in the United States possessing potentially 18,000 differing approaches to the use of force, both in practice and policy making.

In their research on use of force policies currently in use by police agencies, Terrill, Paoline, and Ingram (2011) stated, "Moreover, it was difficult to identify a standard of practice that is used by police departments across the country. While some departments are quite restrictive in terms of allowing officers to use more severe forms of force only on actively aggressive suspects, other agencies are quite liberal and place a large amount of discretion in officers hands by allowing them to use nearly all types of force against nearly all types of resistance faced short of extreme imbalance" (p. iii).

Since it is apparent that a great diversity in approach currently exists regarding use of force policies, what is the current status of the revision of use of force policies among U.S. police agencies, and more importantly, what direction is necessary for today's police entity? First, why is a written policy in this area so vital? According to Walker and Katz (2018), the use of administrative rulemaking, the creation of written policies to limit police discretion, is the dominant approach in policing today to confine police behavior. Specifically, these policies generally specific three areas: "1. What the officer must do in certain situations, 2. What he or she may not do in these situations, and 3. What factors an officer should take into consideration in deciding on a course of action" (Walker & Katz, 2018, p. 388). Terrill and Paoline (2017) noted, "There is perhaps no greater example of the influence that organizational policy can have on police behavior than that of lethal force" (p. 193).

A policy is defined as "a statement of intent, of general goals, of what an organization is trying to achieve" (Bard and Shellow, 1976, p. 31). Within the policing profession, policies, procedures, and regulations are the mechanisms created by administrators to properly guide and constrain an officer's behavior. This direction occurs in all the various areas of police operation, from the appearance of a uniform to the use of force. Without that written guidance, each individual officer would be left to their own discretion to determine what is right and proper behavior. When forming and implementing these policies, and particularly on the use of force, governments must develop them within the applicable law created by their legislatures as well as the decisions rendered by the courts. The administrators of the police agencies must also intertwine the goals and missions of their individual agency within that policy so their "boots on the ground" representatives have sufficient direction to properly interact with the citizen during their daily duties. Once that policy has been issued, the various layers of police management now possess a living document to evaluate whether an individual officer acted properly according to their agency's direction.

Wilson's seminal 1950 textbook on police administration is among the first known efforts to direct police departments to utilize a written directive system to guide their operations. Wilson and McLaren (1972) stated that written directives "defined policy, established procedures, and set forth the rules and regulations that guide the efforts of the department" (pp. 128–129). In a 2000 FBI bulletin, Carpenter (2000) stated, "A well written policy and procedures manual serves as the foundation of a professional law enforcement agency. He describes it as a "powerful communication tool" that not only outlines the acceptable procedures to follow but also ensures consistency among all personnel and informs them of their personal responsibilities" (pp.1–2).

Interestingly, even with the definable benefits of rulemaking, written policies and procedures on the use of force by police are still considered a fairly recent phenomenon in the overall history of U.S. policing. According to Hicks (2009), what was evidenced during the early years of policing in the United States was a general ambivalence by our citizenry on directly constraining the use of force by police. This ambivalence was reflected in the lack of clear guidance in policy or procedure, as demonstrated in our early police departments (Hicks, 2009, p. 6). As previously stated, without a policy in place, the decisions being made on the necessary level and extent of force to control a person was often left solely up to the officer's discretion. It is believed that prior to the 1950s, the police profession in the United States paid little attention to use of force issues. Additionally, police agencies generally offered little guidance to their officers through policy or training on the proper use of force and, unfortunately, retained very minimal, if any, records on instances when officers used force (Terrill & Mastrofski, 2002).

In 1967, the Presidential Commission openly expressed concern that many police departments lacked a formal use of force policy (Fridell, 2005). Police reform across the United States began occurring in earnest during the 1950s and 1960s, simultaneously with African Americans' effort to gain civil rights. Greater public and governmental scrutiny was occurring on police and their conduct and, in particular, how force was being used by police against the citizenry. In response to this increased review, police across the United States generally implemented numerous improvements in these areas, including a greater prevalence of detailed force policies and regular and enhanced officer training on the proper use of force, and measures were adopted that improved accountability to the public on force usage (Luna, 2005). Today, it is believed that all U.S. police agencies have created policies that outline the use of deadly and nonlethal force.

Within the last quarter century, however, specific direction by the courts, a renewed interest by outside entities, the creation of laws by legislatures, and the formulation of use of force policies by the police themselves have all had a major impact in this area. Particularly, the U.S. Supreme Court has intervened and had major impact on directing police use of force nationwide. To some that direction has not gone far enough in regulating the behavior. According to Gross (2016), "The United States Supreme Court seldom addresses the issue of police officer use of force; when the issue is addressed, legal justification for the use of force, and the limitations on when the use of force is appropriate are not analyzed or discussed in any great detail" (p. 157).

Regardless, prior court decisions have consistently demonstrated that police may lawfully use force in various circumstances, including in defense of themselves or others, to accomplish a lawful objective, to prevent a suspect from injuring themselves, and to overcome unlawful resistance. Generally, the primary issue still at question is what is the amount of force necessary to reasonably accomplish those goals? What exactly is reasonable, and how do police define that in a policy statement? It was not until 1989 that the Supreme Court of the United States outlined what is reasonable when a police officer uses force in the landmark decision of *Graham v. Connor* (1989). Prior to Graham, the Court also addressed police use of force, specifically using deadly force to stop fleeing felons, in the landmark case of *Tennessee v. Garner* (1985).

In *Garner*, a 15-year-old burglary suspect (Edward Garner) was shot in the back while fleeing officers of the Memphis (TN) Police Department. The officers at the time of the shooting did not believe that Edward Garner was armed, yet they still shot him in the back while he was fleeing. The officers used that level of force following the guidance of a Tennessee statute that allowed officers to use any necessary means to stop a fleeing felon, regardless of their potential dangerousness.

Flanders and Welling (2015) explained the implications of the Supreme Court ruling in *Garner*:

> The Tennessee rule, the Court concluded, was "pure" common law, but that common law rule when literally applied made no sense in our changed "legal and technological context." Proof that the rule was no longer good could be found in the evolving practices of states but even more "impressive[ly]" in polices "adopted by police departments themselves." "Overwhelmingly" police departments had chosen policies that were more restrictive than the common law rule. They allowed force when there was a risk of serious harm, or death, and not merely when there was a fleeing felon. According to the Court, over 85% of departments had rejected the common law rule. The Court found the trend of departments to be especially persuasive, because it demonstrated that sound policing did not require the common law rule in order to protect citizens and prevent crime. (p. 116)

The new force standard issued by the *Garner* ruling was to replace the prevailing "common law" rule. Prior to this decision, many jurisdictions utilized their state laws and subsequent police force policies, an approach that emanated from English common law. Under this early approach, since all felonies were essentially punishable by death, then it was acceptable for a peace officer to be allowed to kill a resisting or fleeing subject. When English law was eventually incorporated into American law, this common law standard was adopted into U.S. policing. Many states did, however, adopt stricter statutes on deadly force in the 1970s, and numerous police agencies followed suit with more restrictive use of force policies (Fridell, 2005).

Now, under the 1985 *Garner* ruling, the use of deadly force by the police was "not to be used unless it is necessary to prevent the escape and the officer has probable cause to believe that the suspect poses a significant threat of death or serious physical injury to the officer or others." The next line brings an even more specific statement of the Court's new standard: "Thus, if the suspect threatens the officer with a weapon or there is probable cause to believe that he has committed a crime involving the infliction or threatened infliction of serious physical harm, deadly force may be used if necessary to prevent escape, and if, where feasible, some warning has been given" (Flanders & Welling, 2015, p. 116).

Four years later in 1989, the U.S. Supreme Court was to again address police use of force, this time in *Graham v. Connor* (1989). The Court would now finally address the ambiguous concept of what specifically was a reasonable amount of force a police officer could utilize. In this case, Dethorne Graham was being driven to a convenience store by an associate to purportedly purchase orange juice. Graham, a diabetic, was experiencing the onset of an insulin reaction and wanted the juice to counteract the reaction. Unable to rapidly purchase the juice, Graham hurriedly left the store and requested his associate to instead drive him to a friend's home. Officer Connor of the Charlotte, North Carolina Police Department observed Graham leaving the store, and considering his actions suspicious, Connor conducted an investigatory stop on the vehicle in which Graham was a passenger. After some confusion at the scene by the officers present to fully understand that Graham was experiencing a medical condition, they briefly arrested him. After further investigation, he was eventually released at the scene and driven home. It was also reported that Graham experienced several minor injuries during the arrest.

In a subsequent legal action taken against Officer Connor and others by Graham during the pursuit of a federal civil action under 42 U.S.C. § 1983, both the U.S. District Court and the Fourth District Court of Appeals agreed that the force used against Graham did not rise to a constitutional action under 1983 and instead held for Officer Connor. The U.S. Supreme Court ultimately disagreed and overturned the decisions of both lower courts.

In their decision, the Supreme Court basically outlined what a police officer may legally do in a potential use of force situation but still did not provide specific standards on what officers should do. They, instead, left that specific guidance up to the individual police agencies to decide how to incorporate the Court's decision into their policies and training (Wexler, 2016, p.15).

However, the Court did address the idea of reasonableness as it applies to the use of force, and specifically, if that use of force can be deemed excessive, creating what is now known as the "objective reasonableness" standard (Champion, 2009, p. 634). Under the Graham ruling, a police officer's use of force is now judged against that reasonableness standard that reflects the Fourth Amendment to the U.S. Constitution's ban on unreasonable searches and seizures (Wexler, 2016). Specifically, the Supreme Court stated:

> Determining whether the force used to effect a particular seizure is "reasonable" under the Fourth Amendment requires a careful balancing of "the nature and quality of the intrusion on the individual's Fourth Amendment interests" against the countervailing governmental interests at stake.... Because "[t]he test of reasonableness under the Fourth Amendment is not capable of precise definition or mechanical application" ... its proper application requires careful attention to the facts and circumstances of each particular case, including the severity of the crime at issue, whether the suspect poses an immediate threat to the safety of the officers or others, and whether he is actively resisting arrest or attempting to evade arrest by flight.... The "reasonableness" of a particular use of force must be judged from the perspective of a reasonable officer on the scene, rather than with the 20/20 vision of hindsight.... The calculus of reasonableness must embody allowance for the fact that police officers are often forced to make split-second judgments—in circumstances that are tense, uncertain, and rapidly evolving—about the amount of force that is necessary in a particular situation. (Wexler, 2016, pp. 15–16)

With this brief, 10-page Supreme Court decision, police agencies across the United States now possessed a "common" standard by which to formulate their use of force policies. Unfortunately, in regard to forming a universal policy for all police agencies, Graham's ambiguity does not specify on exactly how police should formulate their force policies, in what manner training should be provided to their officers on the topic, and in many ways, how to apply *Graham* to a street level perspective. As Wexler (2016) noted, "*Graham v. Connor* allows for significant variations in police agencies' individual policies and practices" (p. 16). Regardless, the ruling has been called by some as the "common denominator" that now exists among all police agencies. All agencies must possess use of force policies which at a minimum least meet that standard (*Graham*), even though significant variations still exist among the 18,000 police agencies' policies.

If *Graham* has provided U.S. police with a standard to follow in use of force, then why do we often see the current and consistent push in some jurisdictions to modify use of force policies to a "higher standard?" One can speculate on the many factors in the currently observed "frenzied pace" across many of the U.S. police departments to modify their force policies. Media depictions? Legislative over reach? In addition, several recently published reports from various workgroups and commissions have made extensive recommendations to law enforcement in how they should construct their use of force polices.

In January 2016, a Police Executive Research Forum (PERF) document titled "Use of Force: Taking Policing to a Higher Standard (30 Guiding Principles)" outlined several principles that they believe are integral in modifying the use of force by police. Policy revision is at the forefront of some of those principles. Specifically, principle number two is paramount for our discussion on policy making. It is partially as follows: "Agencies should continue to develop best policies, practices, and training on use-of-force issues that go beyond the minimum requirements of *Graham v. Connor*" (Police Executive Research Forum, 2016, p. 35). The recommended practice goes on to suggest that police agency use of force policies should go beyond the legal standard of "objective reasonableness" outlined in the 1989 U.S. Supreme Court decision *Graham v. Connor*, and that the Court's guidance should be seen as "necessary but not sufficient," because it does not provide police with sufficient guidance on use of force." On the positive side, guiding principle number two goes on to state that "many police departments already have policies that exceed legal standards." These modifications include placing restrictions on force actions such as shooting at a moving vehicle, firing warning shots, restricting or prohibiting vehicle pursuits, and the like (PERF, 2016, pp. 35–36).

With similar guidance to the 2016 PERF report, in the "May 2015 Final Report of the President's Task Force on 21st Century Policing," the second pillar encompasses policy and oversight suggestions for police agencies. It stated, "Paramount among the policies of law enforcement organizations are those controlling use of force. Not only should there be policies for deadly and nondeadly uses of force but a clearly stated 'sanctity of life' philosophy must also be in the forefront of every officer's mind" (President's Task Force on 21st Century Policing, 2015, p.19). The task force goes on to recommend specific items to achieve that philosophy. One example was "2.2 Recommendation: Law enforcement agencies should have comprehensive policies on the use of force that include training, investigations, prosecutions, data collection, and information sharing. These policies must be clear, concise, and openly available for public inspection" (President's Task Force on 21st Century Policing, 2015, p. 20).

A rightly posed question at this juncture is can a police agency make productive use of force policy changes despite whatever factors, external or internal, are driving the change? As we have observed, pressure to do so is currently being applied to multiple police departments from the various "clients" that they serve. Paramount to any revision process is that proposed changes made to a use of force policy are not only reasonable and realistic but also allow officers the necessary discretion to properly perform their tasks. A prime example of a potentially "successful" effort to modify a large U.S. police department's use of force policies and practices is the Las Vegas Metropolitan Police Department (LVMPD). After several highly publicized instances of police force by the LVMPD, pressure was mounted by various external forces for the department to make changes to their use of force policy, as well as other components of their operations.

Las Vegas Metropolitan Police Department

In 2012, the American Civil Liberties Union (ACLU) of Nevada issued a blistering critique of the LVMPD's use of force policy in a document titled "Proposed Revisions to the Las Vegas Metropolitan Police Department's Use of Force Policy." Among the statements contained in the report was the following:

> After careful review of the LVMPD Policy and the other policies from around the nation, the ACLU of Nevada (2012) concluded the following:
> - *In contrast to many police departments and law enforcement agencies around the nation, the LVMPD Policy fails to emphasize the importance of human life above the use of force.*
> - *The LVMPD Policy does not provide officers with specific and adequate directives on the proper use of force.*
> - LVMPD's failure to provide its officers with adequate directives may lead officers to use force inappropriately and excessively. (pp. 2–3)

In January of 2012, the LVMPD agreed to take part in an initiative sponsored by the U.S. DOJ known as the Collaborative Reform Model. This initiative was spurred partly due to the reported growing community concern of LVMPD's use of force practices. Upon the conclusion of DOJ's eight-month in-depth review of their use of force policies and practices, a report was issued documenting a total of 75 reforms and recommendations. It was reported that some of the report's key recommendations had already been initiated prior to the assessment process being conducted. A 2014 DOJ follow-up report noted that LVMPD had completed 72 of the 75 previous recommendations (90%) to include "two key policy reforms, regarding its use of force policy. The policy is now divided into smaller sub-components that can stand alone, making them easier to teach and learn for LVMPD officers. LVMPD has also begun an annual review of its policy to ensure that it is up to date with recent court rulings and other major events that can influence the direction in which the department wants to take the policy" (Fachner & Carter, 2014, p. 7).

The results from LVMPD's proactive leadership in not only agreeing to have their operations scrutinized by DOJ but also making substantial policy and procedural changes based on that feedback has been heralded by all aspects of the community. According to Sheriff Joseph Lombardo, head of the LVMPD, "Today, the Las Vegas Metropolitan Police Department is recognized as a model agency on use-of-force practices. Our success is the result of learning from mistakes, changing our business practices and involving our community in the process. Police leaders from Chicago, Baltimore and several other cities have visited Las Vegas seeking methods to reduce the number of police shootings and rebuild community relations back home" (Lombardo, 2017).

Recent news headlines also reflect the general consensus that LVMPD has continued to modify and improve their use of force polices in a successful manner:

> Feds Praise Metro (LVMPD) on Use-of-Force Reforms as Police Shootings Plummet. Metro Police's leadership, tactics of de-escalation, community engagement and transparency, as well as a notable decrease in officer-involved shootings, were lauded in a report released Wednesday by the U.S. Justice Department. (Torres-Cortez, 2017)
> Las Vegas Police Revise Use-of-Force policies. Las Vegas police announced changes to the department's use-of-force policy on Thursday, including classifying the neck restraint highlighted in the May police custody death of Tashii Brown as a technique to be used only in serious or life-threatening situations. (Shoro & Apgar, 2017)

The LVMPD example demonstrates that the living document that a police use of force policy represents can be accomplished as a positive factor for change, to enhance transparency, and to develop closer relationships with the community the police serve. As observed in this example, careful planning and thoughtful consideration must be undertaken by a jurisdiction prior to making those changes. They certainly should not be considered lightly, nor conducted without due cause. Not only must the protection of the public they serve be considered in any policy making but also the safety and security of the police tasked with their difficult and hazardous functions. Although no singular standard can, or potentially should, be applied to each any every police department in the United States, each agency can learn valuable lessons from the examples provided by fellow departments who thoughtfully and carefully modify their force policies. In the LVMPS case, positive results were purportedly experienced.

Caution must also be exercised by policy makers when determining if a police force policy currently in use truly needs to be revised, and more importantly, to what extent. Not everyone in the policing field concurs that the currently used policies that meet the *Graham* standard are not pertinent and responsive to the needs of the community and their police officers. In response to the slew of police departments in the midst of revising force policies, some of those previously noted in this chapter, the IACP issued this email to their members:

> [T]he IACP is extremely concerned about calls to require law enforcement agencies to unilaterally, and haphazardly, establish use-of-force guidelines that exceed the "objectively reasonable" standard set forth by the U.S. Supreme Court nearly 30 years ago (*Graham v. Connor*). The creation of a multitude of differing policies and use-of-force standards throughout the United States would, undoubtedly, lead to both confusion and hesitation on behalf of law enforcement officers, which in turn would threaten both their safety and that of the citizens they are sworn to protect.... As we move forward in examining law enforcement's policies and training procedures regarding use of force it is imperative that any reforms be carefully researched and evidence-based. (Meyer, 2016)

A September 22, 2017, *Chicago Tribune* article titled "Chicago Police Union Files Labor Dispute over New Use-of-Force Changes" stated "Chicago's largest police union is fighting the implementation of a new policy governing police officers' use of force on the job. The Fraternal Order of Police Lodge 7, which represents thousands of rank-and-file police officers, filed a labor complaint against the city on Sept. 21 through the Illinois Labor Relations Board, arguing the new policy violates the union's labor contract and was not jointly agreed upon" (Gorner & Byrne, 2017).

An August 14, 2017, *Denver Post* article noted "Denver police officers are no longer helping revise the department's use-of-force policy." According to the article, based on disagreements on the approach taken to create a revised use of force police, a police union representative stopped attending meetings of, and eventually resigned from, a community group assembled to draft a revised use of policy. The assigned police officer stated in his resignation letter "that he had attempted to forge bonds with fellow committee members and keep an open mind to their opinions and ideas, but the early proposal from his work group does not reflect the type of policy all Denver citizens expect from police. Furthermore, it puts officers at risk in the performance of their duties." He went on to state, "Therefore, I cannot continue to participate nor does the draft reflect any of the input I have provided. I cannot endorse it." It was also reported that additional Denver police officers who were initially assigned as part of this policy committee had previously left the group over similar objections (Phillips, 2017).

Conclusion

It is apparent in our discussion that not all participants in this policy making process, including the police themselves, are in concurrence that extensive change must be applied to each and every police use of force policy across the United States. What has been also evidenced is that this is certainly a sensitive issue for some segments of our society, and most importantly, their voices must also be heard. Ultimately, this issue of policy making comes down to the question of what exactly do we as a people expect from our police and their ability to use force as necessary and proper in the performance of their duties? As observed, it is a difficult dilemma for all parties involved, one that is not clearly defined, is constantly evolving, and often not easily designated and managed by police in a policy format. In 1973, the National Advisory Commission on Criminal Justice Standards very aptly noted, "The degree to which society achieves public order through police action depends on the price that its members are willing to pay ... a balance must be struck that permits enough freedom to enjoy what is secured by sacrificing unlimited freedom. That balance must be determined by their people if a productive relationship with their police is to be achieved" (p. 15).

Approximately 45 years later, we are still wrestling with what is the acceptable balance that our society is willing to accept and still maintain a "productive relationship" with their police. In Klockars' 1985 book *The Idea of Police*, he asked this very pertinent question that we can still apply today to the issue of police use of force: "Why should it be that in a modern democratic society that a state should create an institution with a general right to use coercive force?" The author answered his own question by noting that even in the most democratic and free of societies there must be an institution with the ability to resolve situations with the use of force (Klockars, 1985, p. 14). In our case, these are the men and women in the United States who perform the critical function of policing.

It is also apparent that the conduct of police is under a public microscope, perhaps now more than ever, particularly in how they use force to perform their duties. As public servants, they should rightly be held to the highest standards of ethical conduct by the public the serve, the courts, the legislatures, and their own leadership. When an officer fails to live up to those high expectations, the ramifications can be extremely negative and extensive across the board. Public distrust of police, governmental scrutiny of their operations, civil lawsuits, and even criminal actions against the offending officer are all potential results. A well written and balanced use of force policy not only provides a sound foundation for proper conduct by our police but also designates an appropriate measure of accountability in all force actions. As a simultaneous benefit, a comprehensive use of force policy also gives a police officer the appropriate discretion to safely and effectively perform their duties, which is an admirable goal that each of the estimated 18,000 U.S. state and local law enforcement agencies should strive to attain.

References

Adams, K., Alpert, G. P., Dunham, R. G., Garner, J. H., Greenfield, L. A., Henriquez, M. A., Langan, P. A., & Smith, S. K. (1999). *Use of force by police: Overview of national and local data.* Report prepared for the National Institute of Justice.

American Civil Liberties Union of Nevada. (2012). *Proposed revisions to the Las Vegas Metropolitan Police Department's use of force policy.* Retrieved from https://cops.usdoj.gov/pdf/ACLU-changes.pdf.

Austen, B. (2016, April 24). Chicago after Laquan McDonald. *The New York Times Magazine.* Retrieved from https://www.nytimes.com/2016/04/24/magazine.

Bard, M., & Shellow, R. (1976). Professionalism in policing. In *Issues in law enforcement: Essays and case studies* (pp. 19–38). Reston, VA: Reston Publishing Company.

Bittner, E. (1970). *The functions of the police in modern society: A review of background factors, current practices, and possible role models.* Chevy Chase, MD: National Institute of Mental Health. Retrieved from https://www.ncjrs.gov/pdffiles1/Digitization/147822NCJRS.pdf.

Carpenter, M. (2000). Put it in writing: The police policy manual. *FBI Law Enforcement Bulletin, 69*(10), 1–5. Retrieved from https://search-proquest-com.cyrano.ucmo.edu/docview/204144659?pq-origsite=summon.

Champion, D. (2009) Police use of force. In H. Greene & S. Gabbidon (Eds.), *Encyclopedia of race and crime* (pp. 632–636). Thousand Oaks, CA: Sage Publications.

DelValle, L. (2016, June 30). Baltimore Police Department overhauls decade-old use of force policy. Retrieved from https://www.cnn.com/2016/06/30/us/baltimore-police-use-of-force-policy-freddie-gray/index.html.

Fachner, G., & Carter, S. (2014). *Collaborative reform model: Final assessment report of the Las Vegas Metropolitan Police Department.* Retrieved from https://ric-zai-inc.com/Publications/cops-p287-pub.pdf.

Federal Bureau of Investigation. (2017, October 16). *FBI releases 2016 statistics for law enforcement officers killed and assaulted in the line of duty* [Press release]. Retrieved from https://ucr.fbi.gov/leoka/2016/other-leoka-resources/press-relelase-for-oct-2017-_leoka-2016.

Flanders, C., & Welling, J. (2015) Police use of deadly force: State statutes 30 years after Garner. *Saint Louis University Public Law Review*, *35*, 109–156. Retrieved from http://law.slu.edu/sites/default/files/Journals/chad_flanders_and_joseph_welling_article.pdf.

Fridell, L. A. (2005). Improving use-of-force policy, policy enforcement, and training. In J. Ederheimer & L. Fridell (Eds.), *Chief concerns: Exploring the challenges of police use of force* (pp. 21–55). Washington, DC: Police Executive Research Forum.

Fyfe, J. J. (1981). Observations on police deadly force. *Crime and Delinquency*, *27*, 376–389.

Geller, W., & Karales, K. (1981) Shootings of and by Chicago police: Uncommon crises—part I: Shootings by Chicago police. *Journal of Criminal Law and Criminology*, *72*(4), 1813–1866.

Gorner, J., & Byrne, J. (2017, September 22). Chicago police union files labor complaint over new use of force changes. *Chicago Tribune.* Retrieved from http://www.chicagotribune.com/news/local/breaking/ct-fop-labor-board-complaint-met-20170922-story.html

Gross, J. P. (2016). Judge, jury, and executioner: The excessive use of deadly force by police officers. *Texas Journal on Civil Liberties & Civil Rights*, *21*(2), 155–181.

Hall, J. C. (1993, August). Deadly force in defense of life. *FBI Law Enforcement Bulletin*, *62*(8), 27–32. Retrieved from http://link.galegroup.com.cyrano.ucmo.edu:2048/apps/doc/A14507511/AONE?u=cent1000&sid=AONE&xid=04838b4f.

Hicks, W. L. (2009). A modern understanding of police use of force through consideration of the antiquated: The just war tradition in contemporary criminal justice. In T. Jurkanin & V. Sergevnin (Eds.), *Critical issues of use of force by law enforcement* (pp. 95–105). Macomb, IL: Western Illinois University.

Hinkle, D. (2017, May 17). Chicago police finalize tighter rules on when to shoot, other uses of force. *Chicago Tribune*. Retrieved from http://www.chicagotribune.com/news/local/breaking/ct-chicago-police-use-of-force-met-20170517-story.html.

International Association of Chiefs of Police (2001). *Police use of force in America*. Retrieved from http://www.theiacp.org/Portals/0/pdfs/Publications/2001useofforce.pdf.

International Association of Chiefs of Police (2017). *National consensus policy and discussion paper on the use of force*. Retrieved from http://www.theiacp.org/Portals/0/documents/pdfs/National_Consensus_Policy_On_Use_Of_Force.pdfchk.

International Association of Chiefs of Police/Office of Community Oriented Policing Services (2012). *Emerging use of force issues: Balancing public and officer safety*. Retrieved from http://www.theiacp.org/portals/0/pdfs/emerginguseofforceissues041612.pdf.

Jany, L. (2016, August 9). Minneapolis police reveal changes to use-of-force policy. *StarTribune*. Retrieved from http://www.startribune.com/minneapolis-police-reveal-changes-to-use-of-force-policy/389509371/.

Kania, R. R. E., & Mackey, W. C. (1977). Police violence as a function of community characteristics. *Criminology, 15*, 27–48.

Klockars, C. B. (1985). *The idea of police*. Beverly Hills, CA: Sage Publications.

Lombardo, J. (2016, August 14). Metro police a model on use-of-force practices. *Las Vegas Sun*. Retrieved from https://lasvegassun.com/news/2016/aug/14/metro-police-a-model-on-use-of-force-practices/.

Luna, A. M. (2005). Introduction. In J. Ederheimer & L. Fridell (Eds.), *Chief concerns: Exploring the challenges of police use of force* (pp. 1–20). Washington, DC: Police Executive Research Forum.

Martin, R. H., Gwynne, J. L., & Gruber, C. A. (2009). Investigating use of force before and after complaints: An operational template to avoid civil liability. In T. Jurkanin & V. Sergevnin (Eds.), *Critical issues of use of force by law enforcement* (pp. 95–105). Macomb, IL: Western Illinois University.

Mather, K., & Chang, C. (2017, April 18). Fewer shootings by police—that's the goal of new rules adopted by the L.A. Police Commission. *Los Angeles Times*. Retrieved from http://www.latimes.com/local/lanow/la-me-ln-lapd-commission-force-20170418-story.html.

Meyer, G. (2016, March 7). A revolution in use-of-force policy and training? *Police Magazine*. Retrieved from http://www.policemag.com/channel/patrol/articles/2016/03/a-revolution-in-use-of-force-policy-and-training.aspx.

Morgan, J., & Allen, J. (2009). Use of force and excited delirium syndrome. In T. Jurkanin & V. Sergevnin (Eds.), *Critical issues of use of force by law enforcement* (pp. 95–105). Macomb, IL: Western Illinois University.

National Advisory Commission on Criminal Justice Standards and Goals. (1973). *Police—report of the National Advisory Commission on Criminal Justice Standards and Goals*. Washington, DC: Author.

Pate, A. M., Fridell, L. A., & Hamilton, E. E. (1993). *Police use of force: Official reports, citizen complaints, and legal consequences, volumes I and II*. Police Foundation. Retrieved from https://www.ncjrs.gov/App/Publications/abstract.aspx?ID=146825.

Phillips, N. (2017, August 14). Denver police officers are no longer helping revise the department's use-of-force policy. *The Denver Post*. Retrieved from https://www.denverpost.com/2017/08/14/denver-police-officers-no-longer-helping-revise-use-of-force-policy/.

Police Executive Research Forum (2016). *Critical issues in policing series: Guiding principles on use of force*. Washington, D. C.

President's Task Force on 21st Century Policing. (2015). *Final Report of the President's Task Force on 21st Century Policing*. Retrieved from https://ric-zai-inc.com/Publications/cops-p311-pub.pdf.

Shoro, M., & Apgar, B. (2017, September 21). Las Vegas police revise use-of-force policies. *Las Vegas Review-Journal*. Retrieved from https://www.reviewjournal.com/crime/las-vegas-police-revise-use-of-force-policies/.

Smith, M. R., Kaminski, R. J., Alpert, G. P., Fridell, L. A., MacDonald, J., & Kubu, B. (2010). *A multi-method evaluation of police use of force outcomes: Final report to the National Institute of Justice*. Retrieved from https://www.ncjrs.gov/pdffiles1/nij/grants/231176.pdf.

Terrill, W., & Mastrofski, S. D. (2002). Situational and officer based determinants of police coercion. *Justice Quarterly*, *19*(2), 215–248.

Terrill, W., & Paoline, E. A. (2017). Police use of less lethal force: Does administrative policy matter? *Justice Quarterly*, *34*(2), 193–216.

Terrill, W., Paoline, E. A., & Ingram, J. (2011). *Final technical report draft: Assessing police use of force policy and outcomes*. Retrieved from https://www.ncjrs.gov/pdffiles1/nij/grants/237794.pdf.

Thompson, A. (2011). From sounds bites to sound policy: Reclaiming the high ground in criminal justice policy-making. *Fordham Urban Law Journal*, *38*, 775–820.

Torres-Cortez, R. (2017, January 19). Feds praise Metro on use-of-force reforms as police shootings plummet. *Las Vegas Sun*. Retrieved from https://lasvegassun.com/news/2017/jan/19/feds-praise-metro-police-transparency-use-of-force/.

U.S. Department of Justice. (1979). *A community concern: Police use of deadly force*. Washington, DC: Author.

Walker, S., & Katz, C. M. (2018). *The police in America: An introduction* (9th ed.). New York, NY: McGraw-Hill Education.

Wexler, C. (2016). Why we need to challenge conventional thinking on police use of force. In *Critical issues in policing series: Guiding principles on use of force*. Police Executive Research Forum. Retrieved from http://www.policeforum.org/assets/30%20guiding%20principles.pdf.

Wilson, O. W., & McLaren, R. C. (1972). *Police administration* (3rd ed.). New York, NY: McGraw Hill.

Cases Cited

Graham v. Connor, U. S. (1989)

Tennessee v. Garner, U. S. (1985).

Chapter 3

The War on Drugs
A Review of U.S. Drug Policy

Michael N. Gomila and Robert D. Hanser

Introduction

The debate over the regulation of mood altering substances is as old as the formation of the country itself. The historical mood altering drug of choice (not including tobacco and caffeine) by Americans is, and always has been, alcohol. Interestingly, although not having any chemical properties that make it distinctive (as far as the potential for abuse) from other abused drugs, alcohol emerged as somehow "different" and "unique" from other drugs. The vernacular by which we refer to alcohol remains distinct from other illicit drugs, yet its effects are no less harmful. Because of this, and given the attitudes and values that permeate American culture, much of our current thoughts about policy, enforcement, prevention, addiction, and treatment have developed out of our relationship with this drug. Any discussion about the War on Drugs is vastly incomplete without understanding regulation efforts involving alcohol. Suffice to say that the War on Drugs once included alcohol, but because of the dismal failures of Prohibition policy, alcohol was removed from the fight.

Another point to consider is the many political influences that have weighed in and ultimately created our public consciousness about drugs. Many of these policy decisions were crafted out of racial politics, and therefore racial politics, whether intentional or unintentional, are still represented in current policy decisions. To understand this statement, one need only to consider that, despite the fact that African Americans use drugs at about the same rate as white Americans, African Americans are incarcerated at a level six times greater than that of whites for drug crimes. There are a number of reasons why these disparities exist, but it is safe to say that either directly or indirectly, policy has helped create a culture where African Americans are overrepresented in the penal system. To understand how this has occurred, one might view the political process as one in which those in power attempt to retain power while those on the periphery are kept out. As such, minority classes have always received harsher treatments because of drug policies.

It will be helpful for the reader to keep in mind that all drugs are not equal in potential for abuse (addictive properties), thought distortion, mood alterations, or societal harm, and that public opinion has been formed around distinct properties for many of these chemicals. For instance, tobacco is arguably one of the most addictive substances on the planet. It has strong mood alteration properties as well as produces a greater societal harm in the form of death and disability than all other drugs combined. Yet, because it does not have strong thought inhibiting properties, it is regarded by laypersons as being less harmful than illicit drugs.

Public opinion has also been shaped by the legality of certain drugs. Alcohol is regarded by many in the public as being less harmful than marijuana. Juxtaposed to this view, alcohol has been linked to aggressive behavior, violent crime, domestic violence, etc., and it is responsible for more deaths annually than all illicit drugs combined. Marijuana, to the contrary, is known to make individuals less aggressive, has not been tied to violent crime, and produces very low amounts of societal harm related to disability and death. This is not to suggest that either substance should be made legal or illegal but that policy decisions are sometimes based on political considerations rather than scientific evidence.

There is little debate that substance abuse can and does thwart human potential. There are few families that have not been touched by the harmful effects of these substances. However, it is our contention that, although these substances may pose risks, rational policy decisions should be enacted that produce the least amount of harm for people and their communities.

As a final note, it is our hope that the reader can acknowledge that there are costs associated with the regulation of human behavior, particularly when the behaviors are mutually agreed upon. Crimes that do not have known victims (e.g., prostitution, drug use, gambling, etc.) are difficult to enforce, limit individual freedoms, as well as create alternate economies that are managed by a criminal underworld.

A Historical Overview

America's Romance

"Give strong drink unto him that is ready to perish, and wine to those that be of heavy heart. Let him drink and forget about his poverty, and remember his misery no more"

—Proverbs 31:6

The debate over the prohibition of mood altering substances is steeped in the historical, moral, and political establishment of the United States itself. Mimicking the values of English society, settlers of the colonial era regarded alcohol as "God's gift to mankind and a panacea for almost every ailment" (Behr, 1996, p. 8). Alcohol was seen as the social lubricant of society and therefore was incorporated to every aspect of early colonial life. Colicky babies were given rum in a bottle to sooth their nerves (Behr, 1996). Workers rarely went a few hours without requiring a break for another drink. Alcohol was so valued by early settlers that it became a form of currency often used to trade for slaves or other provisions needed in the plantation system. Slaves and indentured servants, the lowest order in the colonial system, were given daily allotments of alcohol (Behr, 1996). Saloons were often built next to churches, denoting that religion and the functions of the church were closely tied to the use of alcohol. Between services and at special functions (e.g., weddings, funerals) congregations would meet at the saloon for prolonged bouts of drinking (Behr, 1996). Consequentially, because the saloon was the center of social activity of the colonial era, it also became the political center. The tavern owner often was a political figure who would exchange drinks for votes.

As with much of the colonial period, life was marked by the changing values of Protestant Reformers in contrast to the English establishment. Upon the arrival of the United States as a nation, social reformations were taking hold that would form the identity of the nation. Temperance, a term coined to refer to the reduction of use of alcoholic beverages, slowly emerged as a moral/political issue of the early 1800s. Temperance groups preached that alcohol was responsible for the moral and social decline of society and therefore should be limited. The 1830s marked drastic change in the tone of this rhetoric, noting that temperance advocates prior to 1830 preached for moderation, whereas those that emerged after the 1830s took a much harder line on alcohol use, claiming that use of any amount was a sign that the user had turned away from God (Behr, 1996). Alcohol use, in this vein of thinking, was equivalent to being eternally damned to hell. The role of government and church, as seen by the temperance advocates, was to prevent persons from becoming ensnared by this evil and ultimately losing their souls (Behr, 1996).

In 1851, the Temperance Movement and the prohibitionists scored their first victory when Maine became the first state to make the sale of alcohol illegal. The Temperance Movement persisted, becoming "the political issue" over the next half century. Groups such as the Prohibition Party, the Women's Christian Temperance Union (WCTU), and the Anti-Saloon League (ASL) played an influential role in American politics regarding the use of alcohol, so much so that alcohol was made, in 1920, illegal through the adoption of the Eighteenth Amendment and the enabling language that was contained in the accompanying Volstead Act. In part, the political momentum to achieve passage of the Eighteenth Amendment was directly related to anti-German sentiment that existed as a result of the United States' involvement in World War I. Germans, who were the primary beer brewers in the United States, were seen as the enemy, and thus their profession of brewing beer was regarded as equally damaging to society (Behr, 1996).

Somewhat simultaneously, public opinion about drug use was being formed. Throughout the 1800s and early 1900s, narcotic drugs could be purchased without a prescription. In fact, in the 1890s, Sears and Roebuck's mail order catalogs offered a needle, syringe, and a small amount of cocaine for $1.50. Around the turn of the century, fueled by anti-immigrant and anti-African American sentiment, both opium and cocaine became linked in the public's mind to crime. The *Journal of American Medical Association*, in a 1900 article, stated that "Negroes in some parts of the South are reported as being addicted to a new form of vice—that of cocaine sniffing." Almost immediately, Southern newspapers seize on this article printing that "Negros were prone to raping white women while under the influence of cocaine" (Gray, 1998). Hysteria over the dangers of the drug swept through the South, conjuring images for the citizenry of black men that were "drug crazed zombies that were impervious to bullets" (Gray, 1998). Likewise in the West, Chinese immigrants had been characterized as corruptors of civilized society, "threatening to run off with white men's wives." Related to these fears, legislation was crafted to keep these immigrant groups in line (Gray, 1998). An example of this can be found in an 1875 San Francisco opium ordinance that targeted Chinese Americans. Chinese immigrants had come to America to build railroads and consequently glutted the labor market. A distinguishing feature of Chinese immigrants was their common use of opium. The San Francisco ordinance ensured that Chinese immigrants could be arrested and harshly dealt with because of their drug habits.

Dr. Hamilton Wright:
The Father of Modern Drug Enforcement

In 1909, seizing on the opportunity to make opium a wedge issue in U.S. diplomacy with China, Theodore Roosevelt appointed Dr. Hamilton Wright as the first opium drug commissioner of the United States (Gray, 1998). Perhaps more influential than any single individual in U.S. drug policies, Dr. Wright left a legacy that remains today. Dr. Wright, upon appointment to his post, began researching the U.S. opium problem. Through his research (which was mostly pseudoscientific), Wright convinced himself that the opium problem was a global scourge. Wright believed that narcotic drugs (including cocaine) were some of the greatest evils presented to civilized society. His view formed against the backdrop of prohibitionist's attitudes that were becoming the political issue of the day. The prohibitionists viewed addiction as a moral disease that could be cured. The individual that suffered from addiction was morally defective and needed to be restored by whatever means necessary. This meant that the addict should be restricted from engaging in addictive behaviors, as well as sufficiently punished, until repentance was obtained. Consequently, Wright settled into a similar belief that enforcement would "cure" the perceived scourge (Gray, 1998).

In retrospect, most of the opium addiction that Dr. Wright had observed was based on the fact that many cough elixirs and popular medicines were laced with opiate drugs. Unwitting consumers used these products and became physically addicted to their contents. In 1906, the Pure Food and Drug Act forced the labeling of the ingredients of these products. When consumers realized that what they were using had addictive potential, many discontinued their use. Ironically, what Wright noted as a global scourge was actually a period of decline for the use of narcotic drugs in the United States. Despite these facts, Wright would lobby for the passage of a national narcotics legislation that would regulate the distribution of narcotics by druggists, doctors, and manufacturers.

To have his enforcement policies adopted, Wright used a number of crafty maneuvers to ensure his end goal of federally regulating narcotics was achieved. One such method employed was crafting his legislation in the form of a tax law (Gray, 1998). Wright knew that for any enforcement of narcotics distribution to be taken into effect, there must be some form of enforcement agency. Under the Tenth Amendment, the federal government could not exceed its constitutional mandates by regulating narcotics. Wright knew that this power was not expressly given to the federal government but more appropriately fell under a state control. To sidestep this issue, Wright cleverly disguised his narcotics regulation as tax law, an area that was under the prevue of the federal government. Of this, Wright was quoted as saying that crafting this legislation had "been difficult business—the Constitution keeps getting in my way" (Gray, 1998). Secondly, Wright was all too eager to exploit racial fears that existed over African Americans in the South and Chinese immigrants in the West. It has been suggested that Wright went as far as to agree with the sentiment that "cocaine promoted rape of white women by African Americans," and that "white women were leaving their husbands and cohabitating with Chinese men because of opium use" (Gray, 1998). This strong racial rhetoric was enough to sway congressional opinion in favor of adopting a national narcotics policy. In the winter of 1914, Congress adopted the Harrison Narcotics Act, the first federal policy regulating this distribution of narcotic drugs.

The Harrison Narcotics Act

The Harrison Narcotics Act of 1914 appeared to be legislation that simply required anyone participating in narcotics distributions to purchase a license and precisely record the allocations of narcotics medication. Hidden in the language of the act were a few choice words that made dispensing narcotics to individuals who had addiction problems a crime (Gray, 1998). The specific wording that would hold physicians criminally liable for improperly dispensing medication noted that "a physician could only prescribe narcotic medications in the course of professional practice." At first glimpse, most physicians were supportive of this language, believing that the language actually protected their professional interests. Little did these physicians know, the Treasury Department would inherit almost limitless enforcement power. The Treasury Department was given the sole authority to determine whether or not a physician was operating within the scope of professional practice; if the agency determined that a physician was not operating within this scope, then he or she could be charged with a crime. Wright had added the language to thwart prescribing medications to persons that suffered from addictions. In his belief system, the addict could be morally and physically "cured" only if the drugs were removed. Once more, he alone would be responsible for ridding the country of drug addiction.

The Prohibition Unit:
The Beginning of Enforcement

In 1920, a year after the passage of the Volstead Act, the Prohibition Unit was formed. The Prohibition Unit was the agency responsible for the enforcement of the Prohibition Act of 1919 (commonly known as the Volstead Act), which made illegal the manufacture, sale, and transportation of alcoholic beverages. A separate division of the Prohibition Unit, known as the Narcotics Division, was the primary enforcement agency for the Harrison Act. The Prohibition Unit was initially established in the Bureau of Internal Revenue. Because of this, enforcement agents of the unit were commonly known as "revenuers" (Behr, 1996). In 1927, the Prohibition Unit became its own separate entity within the Department of Treasury, and as a consequence, the unit's name was changed to the Bureau of Prohibition. This unit would eventually be transferred into the Federal Bureau of Investigations for a brief time and then later emerged full circle back into the Internal Revenue Service (IRS), having been renamed to the modern Bureau of Alcohol, Tobacco, and Firearms (ATF).

The Narcotics Division of the Prohibition Unit split off from the Prohibition Unit in 1930 (through the Porter Act), creating the Federal Bureau of Narcotics (FBN). The first ever commissioner of the FBN was Harry Anslinger. Anslinger had been an agent for the Prohibition Units and transferred into the FBN right before Prohibition came to a close.

Harry Anslinger and the Marijuana Tax Act of 1937

As FBN commissioner, Harry Anslinger was credited with overseeing the criminalization of marijuana in the United States (Gray, 1998). Anslinger initially opposed the idea, noting that the stuff "grows like dandelions" and therefore did not believe that enforcement was possible. In 1935, in an about face move, Anslinger took up marijuana as being the "new cause," upgrading its societal ramifications from a low priority to an "evil as hellish as heroine" (Gray, 1998).

There is some speculation that Anslinger was approached by the DuPont Petrochemicals and William Randolph Hearst in their bid to eliminate hemp as an industrial competitor (Gray, 1998). This would, in part, explain Anslinger's sudden inexplicable change of heart about the dangers of marijuana. This suspicion is fueled by the fact that Hearst contributed substantial amounts of money to antimarijuana campaigns. Critics note that both DuPont Petrochemicals and Hearst had vested interests in industrial markets that were threatened by the emergence of hemp as an industrial crop. Processes involved in cultivating and processing hemp had recently been invented (in the form of the decorticator machine), making the potential uses for hemp limitless (Gray, 1998). Almost certainly, hemp production would have had severe negative impacts on both the forestry and nylon/rayon markets that Hearst and DuPont were invested in.

The primary offensive from Anslinger and the newly formed FBN would be in the form of mass media campaigns. Anslinger would compile a "Gore File" that he would use at public speaking events, hearings, etc., which would hyperbolically demonstrate the dangers of marijuana. Most of these stories came from Hearst's *New York American Journal,* which had made a routine habit of demonstrating the horrors of marijuana (Gray, 1998). The Gore File was composed of horrifying stories of brutal murders and rape that were supposedly a direct result of marijuana intoxication. Once more, a significant amount of the Gore File consisted of racist material (Gray, 1998).

In 1937, congressional hearings began regarding the taxation of marijuana. There was no input from the medical community, and from all accounts, few congressmen even knew what marijuana was. For the most part, Anslinger's account of the problems of marijuana was the only testimony considered. Excerpts of this material included the following:

> With an ax he had killed his father, mother, two brothers and a sister. He seemed to be in a daze. He had no recollection of committing the multiple crimes. The officers knew him ordinarily as a sane, rather quiet man; now he was pitifully crazed. They sought the reason. The boy said that he had been in the habit of smoking something which friends called "muggles," a childish name for marijuana.
>
> Colored students at the University of Minnesota partying with (white) female students, smoking [marijuana] and getting their sympathy with stories of racial persecution. Result: pregnancy.

With a lack of fanfare, the Marijuana Tax Act of 1937 would be passed in Congress.

The Modern War on Drugs

The 1960s set the stage for reform measures that would be implemented in the subsequent decade as well as form our current conceptions about the War on Drugs. The 1960s were defined by a dramatic cultural shift that involved civil rights issues, the Vietnam War, and the recreational use of drugs by teens. Once more, there was a perceived heroine epidemic that had been brought back from the war in Vietnam. The 1960s represented a cultural upheaval that threatened the more conservative views of previous generations. Capitalizing on conservative backlash, Richard Nixon, in his 1969 presidential campaign, highlighted the country's illicit drug use problem and promised to alleviate crime related to drug use. In keeping with his campaign promises, once elected, President Nixon declared a "War on Drugs" in which illicit drugs were "public enemy No. 1." Implicit to this concept of the War on Drugs was that it was to be fought with subsequent policy changes and governmental interventions that had not previously existed. To carry out this so-called war, the administration needed a legal framework as well as a governmental policy enforcing agency. These came in the form of the Comprehensive Drug Abuse Prevention Act of 1970 and through the creation of the Drug Enforcement Agency (DEA).

The Comprehensive Drug Abuse Prevention Act (CSA) of 1970 was federal legislation that required, among other things, pharmaceutical companies to maintain physical security and strict recordkeeping of certain types of drugs. The CSA mandated that controlled substance be divided into five schedules on the basis of potential for abuse, accepted medical use, and the accepted safety of the drug given through proper medical supervision. As it still exists today, Schedule I drugs have the highest potential for abuse, while Schedule II—VI drugs have a decreasing potential for abuse.

In addition to the CSA legislation, President Nixon sought to have a responsive agency of the executive branch in order to carry out the mandates of the CSA. In 1973, Nixon merged the Bureau of Narcotic and Dangerous Drugs and the Office of Drug Abuse Law Enforcement to form the DEA. The DEA was tasked with being the primary enforcement arm of the federal government for the War on Drugs. These tasks included domestic enforcement tasks as well as combating drug smuggling operations that emanated from abroad.

The trend toward a tough stance on drug related crime has persisted until the present time. The only changes in the efforts have mostly centered on the kinds of drugs being targeted. Roughly, there have been three drug epidemics for which presidential administrations have responded: the heroine epidemic of the late 1960s and early 1970s, the powder cocaine epidemic of the late 1970s and early 1980s, and the crack cocaine epidemic of the early 1980s until the late 1990s. Perhaps the most significant change since the War on Drugs began was the reinstatement of mandatory minimum sentencing guidelines that were part of the Anti Drug Abuse Acts of 1986 and 1988. Until the Anti-Drug Abuse Acts, mandatory minimum sentencing guidelines had been discarded by the Comprehensive Drug Abuse Prevention Act. In 1986, following the death of Boston Celtics star Len Bias in a cocaine-related death, a renewed public interest spawned the eventual adoption of the Anti-Drug Abuse Act. One of the key provisions of this act, mandatory minimum sentencing, ultimately led to an explosion of the penal population as well as well as wide racial disparities.

The specific provision that has been shown to target minorities is mandatory sentencing guidelines for crack cocaine. Under these sentencing guidelines, possession of crack cocaine brings a mandatory 5-year sentence. In contrast, 100 times the amount of powder cocaine is required to garner a 5-year sentence. According to Boyum and Reuter (2005), this sentencing guideline has resulted in a racially disparate outcome noting that African Americans are much more commonly charged with crack cocaine distribution, while whites are more commonly charged with powder cocaine distribution.

The Lessons of Prohibition

National prohibition transferred $2 billion a year from the hands of brewers, distillers, and shareholders to the hands of murderers, crooks, and illiterates

—Andrew Sinclair

To understand the current problems faced in waging the War on Drugs, it is important to reflect on past deterrence policies regarding the use of alcohol. From all accounts, what can be said of the policy of Prohibition was that it was an abject failure. Prohibition, as a stated goal, did reduce the annual consumption of alcohol; however, the reduction was only slight, and the problems created by deterrence strategies far outweighed the benefits.

Crime

The most significant result of Prohibition was the dramatic rise in crime that occurred between 1920 and 1933 (the Prohibition era). Before Prohibition, America had been on a steady and gradual decrease in criminal activities (Thornton, 1991). After Prohibition, general crime rates increased in most major cities along with murder, burglary rates, and assault rates. More crimes were said to have been committed because Prohibition destroyed legitimate jobs, created a violent black market, diverted resources from enforcement of other laws, as well as increased the cost of prohibited items (making individuals more likely to result to criminal activity to get prohibited items) (Thornton, 1991).

Introduction of Young Drinkers to More Potent Alcohol

Prohibition also encouraged drinking by a more youthful crowd as well as encouraged more potent forms of alcohol to be produced. The youth of the Prohibition period saw drinking as a "forbidden fruit" laced with intrigue and excitement (Thornton, 1991). Because of this, more youth were drawn to drinking than were in the period before Prohibition. The strength of the alcohol produced during the Prohibition period was also of a higher alcohol percentage. Before Prohibition, Americans consumed beer and spirits at approximately the same rate. After Prohibition, drinking was almost exclusively limited to spirits and high alcohol content drinks. This was a result of the need to have a potent drink that could be easily smuggled (e.g., white lightning, moonshine, etc.) (Thornton, 1991).

Unnecessary Death Related to a Lack of Regulation

The health problems related to Prohibition seemed to outweigh the health benefits. Although it is true that cirrhosis of the liver cases decreased during the Prohibition period, it is widely held that cirrhosis-related deaths were in decline before the Prohibition era, and that cirrhosis of the liver is rare in alcohol drinkers (less than 4%) (Thornton, 1991). To the contrary, Prohibition did cause many alcohol-related deaths due to adulterated product. There were thousands of poisonings related to the drinking of contaminated products. This was largely due to the fact that there were no standards for the production of alcohol (Thornton, 1991). Amateurs would make products in basements and hidden locations using inferior production means. Once more, the U.S. government had ordered the contamination of industrial alcohol with poison to prevent their consumption. The result of both poison-laced industrial alcohol and inferior production techniques produced a quadrupling of the death rate as a result of poisonings (Thornton, 1991).

Increased Incarceration Rates

Incarcerations rates were dramatically impacted by the prohibition of alcohol. Over the course of the 13 years of Prohibition, the prison population increased by 561% (Thornton, 1991). Of this increase, violations of the Volstead Act and other Prohibition laws represented the majority of the increase. By 1930, two thirds of all prisoners would be serving time for a drug- or alcohol-related crime (Thornton, 1991).

Corruption

In the years following the passage of the Volstead Act, the Prohibition Unit would be tasked with assuring that federal law was enforced. The peak number of agents reached 2,500, and their salaries were a modest $1,200 to $2,000 annually (Behr, 1996). Because of the low wages, corruption became commonplace, noting that many agents allied with bootleggers to make supplemental income (Behr, 1996). Agents were notorious for selling permits so that when bootleggers removed their stock from warehouses, the agents could simply look the other way when coming across illegal operations. It is estimated that in 1921 alone, 96% of the agents hired by the Prohibition Unit were fired or else resigned from their posts (Behr, 1996). Ten percent of those discharged were terminated for known crimes involving falsification of records, perjury, bribery extortion, theft, and other lesser crimes (Behr, 1996).

The Lessons of the Current War on Drugs

There are three predominate ways to intervene with drug use policy. The first method is through the use of prevention interventions. Prevention interventions are geared at the potential end consumer. The goal of prevention is to educate and/or remove stressors that might make an individual more prone to drug use. This kind of intervention is known as a demand side intervention because it attempts to reduce the demand for drugs and alcohol. The second policy strategy is known as treatment. Like prevention, treatment tries to limit the demand for alcohol and drugs by engaging the client in recovery-oriented programs that provide a social framework that encourages abstinence from drugs or alcohol or through harm reduction measures that moderate the kind and amount of substances used. The third form of intervention is enforcement interventions. Enforcement attempts to limit the supply of drugs reaching the end consumer as well as increase the street value of the drug. Increasing the value of the product is thought to keep end consumers from being able to afford the product, thus reducing use. This is typically done by using law enforcement to intercept drug supply lines that enter the United States; however, a substantial amount of funding is dedicated to foreign aid to assist countries addressing internal drug production problems.

Of all three of the aforementioned drug policy methods, enforcement is the predominant method used as the drug deterrence policy in the United States. Sixty-five percent of the federal drug policy budget is spent on enforcement strategies. Despite the fact that over $10 billion is spent on enforcement annually, no increase in the street value of drugs or reduction of supply has been noticed. This has convinced many policy makers that there is a need to rethink current budget allocations and focus more on treatment and prevention.

Much like Prohibition enforcement strategies, the current focus on drug enforcement has had unintended societal costs. Once more, there are several constitutional issues and racial questions that have developed out of the War on Drugs policy. The following paragraphs will outline these problems.

Constitutionality Questions

The early framers of the Constitution never envisioned that drug/alcohol enforcement would become a responsibility of the federal government. In fact, the framers resisted ceding too much power to a central government, fearing that the power instilled would cause a gradual erosion of liberties. The Tenth Amendment notes that powers not expressly given to the federal government are states' rights. Prohibitionists understood this concept and therefore opted for the adoption of the Eighteenth Amendment. However, current drug policy operates under broad discretion assumed by the Commerce Clause. Article I, Section 8, Clause 3 of the Constitution grants the federal government the ability to "regulate commerce with foreign nations, and among the several states, and with the Indian Tribes." Operating under the Commerce Clause, the federal government has drawn the position that it has a right to engage in the War on Drugs because drugs are sold through interstate commerce. In *Gonzales v. Raich*, the Supreme Court went as far as to conclude that the federal government's application of the Commerce Clause was extended to regulate medical marijuana grown for personal use. Many view the creation of the DEA and the massive enforcement structure of the United States government as being an overstepping of constitutional authority as was designed. Proponents of this view conclude that Congress should vote for the adoption of a constitutional amendment in order to legitimize drug enforcement on the part of the federal government.

States' Rights and Legalization of Marijuana

In 2012, voters in Colorado opted to legalize the recreational use of marijuana, making Colorado one of the first two states in the nation to legalize its use (Police Foundation & Colorado Association of Chiefs of Police, 2015). Washington is the other state that legalized recreational marijuana use in 2012. Other states would eventually follow suit as well, such as California (Zezima, 2018). This naturally presents challenges to law enforcement officials who are not tasked with regulating the use of marijuana rather than enforcing the legality of its use.

Indeed, the regulatory processes involved can be quite cumbersome for the legal growers of marijuana (Zezima, 2018). Much of this is because despite the fact that Colorado, Washington, and California have made marijuana use legal, it is still illegal according to federal law. Naturally, this showcases, once again, issues of constitutionality regarding state drug laws. What is important is that these changes in state laws reflect a cultural shift that has occurred in those states as well as others throughout the nation. Indeed, support for the use of marijuana throughout the nation is the highest that it has been during the past 50 years (McCarthy, 2017). This has been equated to an indication (along with other measures of social mores) of more liberal views on social issues. However, there has been resistance to this trend that has emerged during the past 10 years or so. For instance, states adjacent to Colorado, such as Nebraska and Oklahoma, have filed federal suits against Colorado in an effort to rescind the constitutional amendment that legalizes recreational marijuana in that state (Police Foundation & Colorado Association of Chiefs of Police, 2015). This is because state governments in Nebraska and Oklahoma claim that marijuana is bought legally in Colorado but is then brought into their borders on a constant basis. Child welfare advocates are concerned that marijuana use among youth will skyrocket as a result of this more permissive societal view of the drug. But to further demonstrate the difficulty in separating the hype from reality, it has recently been found that more recent data from the National Survey on Drug Use and Health shows that drug use for youth ages 12 through 17 has actually gone down (Substance Abuse and Mental Health Services Administration, 2017). Thus, the nation is still conflicted, it would seem, on the issue of marijuana legalization, but it is uncertain as to whether this conflict is steeped in myth or grounded in factual arguments one way or the other.

Crime and Incarceration

Ironically, in a country that purports to be one of the freest in human history, more persons are behind bars (2.29 million) than in any other place in the world (Walmsley, 2008). Closely tied to the actual number of persons locked up is a staggering percentage of the population that is incarcerated (as compared to the rest of the world), which is also the highest in the world (754 persons per 100,000 thousand) (Walmsley, 2008). In contrast, only China and Russia, two countries known for very punitive criminal justice systems, come close to incarcerating as many of its citizens as does the United States. Collectively, the United States (2.29 million), China (1.57 million), and Russia (0.89 million) house nearly half of all those behind bars in the world (Walmsley, 2008). As relative to population size, Russia is the only country that even remotely comes close to incarcerating as many of it citizenry as does the United States (629 persons per 100,000) (Walmsley, 2008). In contrast to other world nations, the incarceration rate in the United States is nearly five to eight times that of most developed countries. This reliance on incarceration as a primary form of societal deterrence and punishment has prompted many to term the practice as mass incarceration.

Since the early 1970s, the United States has experienced an expansive increase in the number of individuals incarcerated. It has been estimated that over the last 40 years, there has been a sixfold increase in the number of individuals confined in the United States. The reasons for this dramatic shift in incarceration rates are manifold. Perhaps the most simplistic reason for the increased reliance on incarceration is the prevalence of crime. The United States, when compared to other countries, has similar nonviolent crime rates; however, violent crime rates are exponentially higher. It is noteworthy that over 50% of all those incarcerated are for a violent crime offense (Boyum & Reuter, 2005). It has been estimated that, despite recent trends of decreases in homicides, the United States still maintains a rate that is four times higher than most countries in Europe. Largely, this difference in homicide rates is fueled by the prevalence of firearms in the United States. It is widely accepted that industrialized nations without strong gun control policy naturally have disparate murder rates (Boyum & Reuter, 2005).

Although an increase in the violent crime rate may explain some of the increase in the rise of incarceration rates, it, however, does not come close to being a driving force of this movement. Alfred Blumstein and Allen Beck (1999) concluded that of all the factors responsible for tripling the prison population between the years 1980–1996, none were as significant as sentencing policy changes. In this study, changes in crime rates were seen as contributing to a minor amount of the penal population growth (12%), whereas policy changes were seen as being responsible for the overwhelming amount of rise in this growth (88%). In a summary of their findings, Blumstein and Beck (1999) found that policy changes enacted since the 1970s had resulted in 1) persons arrested for felonies being far more likely to be sentenced to prison (51%), and 2) those that were sentenced to prison were given longer sentences (37%). Other studies have found similar results, noting population growth (7.7%), increased crime (19%), and increased arrests (5.3%) were all minor factors when compared to the 60.9% of cases that were a direct result of policy changes. These policies that coincide with the dramatic increase in incarceration rates take the form of mandatory sentencing requirements such as "truth in sentencing" and "three strikes and you're out" legislation. The implementation of these policy changes has resulted in casting an increasingly wider "incarceration net" that has ultimately been responsible for criminalizing, and subsequently incarcerating, an increasing number of drug related offenses. The greatest expansion of the prison population has been related to the incidence of drug-related crime. It has been estimated that in 60% of those in federal custody, drug involvement was a premeditating factor (Sabol, West, & Cooper, 2009).

Mass Commutation of Drug Offender Sentences

In 2016 all the way up to his last day in office in 2017, President Barack Obama commuted the sentences of hundreds of nonviolent drug offenders (Liptak, 2017). Many of these offenders had charges for distribution or production of drugs that were nonviolent in nature. The true goal of the Obama Administration was to reduce racial disparities in drug sentencing laws and outcomes. However, the gridlock of the nation's capital prevented progress at the level that was desired; thus, the commutation of sentences was the next-best strategy to attempt semblance of proportionality in sentencing (Liptak, 2017). What is important is the fact that the climate had substantially changed in regard to drug use and drug offenders, resulting in legalization of cannabis in some states, clemency of drug sentences, and better access to affordable drug treatment.

Loss of Tax Revenue

The War on Drugs, by criminalizing the sale and distribution of substances, has in effect delivered an industry that produces well over $40 billion annually into the hands of criminals. If drugs were a legal enterprise, the federal government could begin to appropriately tax the sale of these products. Tax revenues collected could be used to pay for prevention and treatment programs that have been shown to be more effective than enforcement measures.

Racial Bias and Minority Communities

Disadvantaged minority communities, particularly African American communities, are more likely to experience increased incidences of crime, drug sales, and poverty as well as a greater law enforcement presence than other communities. Other coalescing social ails may include a lack of meaningful employment opportunities, a lack of educational opportunities, and limited access to healthcare and treatment. In communities where there is a lack of opportunity for societal advancement, crime is regarded by many as if it were a legitimate enterprise. A criminal lifestyle is often regarded as an opportunity to escape the trappings of poverty. Many youth living in these communities lack education or employable skills, making them targets for drug sales involvement. Once ensnared, these youth often start using drugs themselves. In a spiral of behaviors, actions that once were used toward the promise of "getting ahead" are turned into a means of supporting addictive behaviors. This perpetuates a scene in these disadvantaged minority communities where hard drugs are sold in open view around an increased law enforcement presence. It is this climate of drug use and sales that led researchers Boyum and Reuter (2005) to conclude that heavy concentrations of drug sales in minority communities is perhaps the principle explanation for criminal justice disparities.

Emphasis on Treatment

In 2014, the Obama Administration not only supported treatment of drug abuse but also provided a financial stream where such help could be easily obtained through the Affordable Care Act. In 2014 alone, $1.4 billion more was requested for treatment than the previous year, which was the largest request for drug treatment money in decades (Sebelius, Holder, & Kerlikowske, 2014). Further, through this act, it became mandatory that U.S. citizens hold medical insurance. More importantly, insurance companies were required to cover treatment for addiction, with drug use being equated to a chronic medical disease. Through this act, millions of people, including offenders released from prison, have received expanded substance abuse assistance (Sebelius et al., 2014).

Portugal: Lessons for Policy Reform

In 2001, Portugal passed legislation that decriminalized the use of certain drugs of abuse (Greenwald, 2009). Decriminalization removes the legal penalties for possessing drugs for personal use. Portugal, in the enactment of decriminalization penalties, recognized three goals that it wanted to achieve through drug policy. These were to 1) redirect the focus to primary prevention, 2) extend and improve the quality and response capacity of the healthcare networks for drug addicts so as to ensure access to treatment for all drug addicts who seek treatment, and 3) guarantee the necessary mechanisms to allow competent bodies to enforce measures such as the enforcement such as voluntary treatment of drug addicts as an alternative to prison sentences (Greenwald, 2009). It is noteworthy that the Portuguese policy did not legalize the use of certain drugs of abuse but rather stripped criminal penalty from use that would be deemed personal only.

The fears associated with adopting the policy is that drug tourism would result because the new policy would cause crime and social problems to skyrocket. Contrary to this belief, after five years of having enacted the policy, drug use has decreased (or stayed very close to prepolicy levels), and healthcare concerns associated with drug use have made remarkable improvements (Greenwald, 2009). Persons involved in drug treatment doubled in the period between 1999 and 2003, suggesting that both funding levels and persons' willingness to participate in treatment improved as a result of policy changes (Greenwald,

2009). Criminalization of drug use is a known deterrent to persons with addiction seeking help; therefore, this increase was seen as a sign of success. HIV, Hepatitis C, and mortality all decreased in the same time period as a result of decriminalizing the use of drugs (Greenwald, 2009).

Conclusions: Possibilities for Policy Reform

The United States' War on Drugs, represented primarily as an enforcement strategy, was adopted based on political, racial, and moral philosophies of the past. As with Prohibition, there is an increasing awareness that enforcement as a primary means of dealing with drugs has failed. Criminalizing the use of drugs has resulted in the creation of a booming black market that has become a $40 billion industry. Those attracted to this industry are all too commonly minorities who have grown up around the black market and have few other opportunities for societal advancement. Enforcement agencies have also borne down on minority communities because more drugs are sold in these concentrated areas than other communities. This has resulted in casting an ever-widening net that continues to arrest more and more minorities for drug use and sales.

The fundamental questions that need to be asked are regarding alternative solutions to the U.S. drug problem. Decriminalization, legalization, and increasing treatment and prevention funding have begun to be implemented since the last revision of this chapter. There is little doubt that adopting any of these changes will reduce drug use and result in fewer people being incarcerated. In an era where state prison budgets are tightening, these new developments in drug laws, sentencing, incarceration, and treatment comport well with the current emphasis on offender reentry that is touted as a priority in modern-day correctional policy. Thus, the War on Drugs seems to have morphed into one that is better expressed as concern for the drug crisis. This is likely to be much more productive for the welfare of the nation.

References

Behr, E. (1996). *Prohibition: Thirteen years that changed America*. New York, NY: Arcade Publishing.

Blumstein, A., & Beck, A. J. (1999). Population growth in U.S. prisons, 1980–1996. In M. Tonry & J. Petersilia (Eds.), *Crime and justice: A review of the research, Vol. 26, Prisons* (pp. 17–61). Chicago, IL: University of Chicago Press.

Boyum, D., & Reuter, P. (2005). An analytic assessment of U.S. drug policy. Washington, DC: AEI Press.

Gray, M. (1998). *Drug crazy: How we got into this mess and how we can get out.* New York, NY: Random House.

Greenwald, G. (2009). *Drug decriminalization in Portugal: Lessons for creating fair and successful drug policies.* Washington, DC: Cato Institute.

Liptak, K. (2017). Obama cuts sentences of hundreds of drug offenders. *CNN Politics.* Retrieved from https://www.cnn.com/2017/01/17/politics/obama-cuts-sentences-of-hundreds-of-drug-offenders/index.html

McCarthy, J. (2017). *Record-high support for legalizing marijuana use in the United States.* New York, NY: Gallup. Retrieved from http://news.gallup.com/poll/221018/record-high-support-legalizing-marijuana.aspx

Police Foundation & Colorado Association of Chiefs of Police (2015). *Colorado's legalization of marijuana and the impact on public safety: A practical guide for law enforcement.* Washington, DC: Police Foundation.

Sabol, W. J., West, H. C., & Cooper, M. (2009). *Prisoners in 2008.* Bureau of Justice Statistics. Washington, DC: Office of Justice Programs.

Sebelius, K., Holder, E., & Kerlikowske, G. (2014). *A drug policy for the 21st Century.* Washington, DC: Office of the President.

Substance Abuse and Mental Health Services Administration (2019). *National Survey on Drug Use and Health: Comparison of 2014–2015 and 2015–2016 Population Percentages.* Retrieved from https://www.samhsa.gov/data/sites/default/files/NSDUHsaeShortTermCHG2016/NSDUHsaeShortTermCHG2016.htm

Thornton, M. (1991). *Alcohol prohibition was a failure.* Cato Institute. Retrieved from http://www.cato.org/pub_display.php?pub_id=1017

Walmsley, R. (2008). *World prison population list* (8th ed.). World Prison Brief. Retrieved from http://www.prisonstudies.org/sites/default/files/resources/downloads/world_prison_population_list_11th_edition_0.pdf

Zezima, K. (2017). Marijuana is legal in California January 1, but you won't be able to buy it everywhere. *Washington Post.* Retrieved from https://www.washingtonpost.com/national/marijuana-is-legal-in-california-jan-1-but-you-wont-be-able-to-buy-it-everywhere/2017/12/31/f76c26de-e031-11e7-89e8-edec16379010_story.html?utm_term=.f0284679acc7

Chapter 4

The Enforcement of Immigration Law by Police

Robert D. Hanser and Michael N. Gomilla

Introduction

During the past decade, growing concern over immigration issues has become a fixture within the news media, the public consciousness, and official policy makers alike. After 9/11, questions regarding entry into the United States were the source of serious scrutiny, and this led to numerous changes in the organizational structure of federal government enforcement agencies. Amidst, and well after, this catastrophic event, concerns about border security began to be a routine concern among policy makers and the lay public. Concern with border security eventually dovetailed with persistent concerns related to illegal immigration into the United States. These two issues—concern over potential Al Qaeda operatives getting through the porous borders of the United States and the influx of Mexican illegal immigrants seeking work and coming into the southwestern parts of the United States—provided the impetus behind numerous federal and state level developments that ultimately led to a renewed interest in having state and local law enforcement aid the federal government in enforcing immigration statutes.

While this may, in part, briefly explain how issues of internal security and immigration eventually became an area of enforcement for local and state police, the reason that this approach has been so controversial and the reason that this policy is flawed warrants considerable explanation. Before discussing these flaws in depth, it should be pointed out that immigration issues have not, in fact, been beyond the purview of local police enforcement; though immigration is a federal issue, many states have required that their officers turn over information to federal officials when they have detected persons who are within the nation's borders illegally. However, this is rooted in Section 287(g) of the Immigration and Nationality Act (INA), and according to Section 287(g), police possess an inherent authority to arrest illegal aliens who have violated criminal statutes. Once the person is arrested, local police officers are expected to contact federal immigration officials so that the illegal alien can be transferred to federal custody. As one may notice, this type of local police enforcement of immigration law is one that is incident to arrest but is not, unto itself, the basis for the initial arrest. While this tends to be generally true for all law enforcement, Section 287(g) also provides for more extensive broadening of police powers regarding immigration enforcement, provided that police agencies agree to adopt the parameters of Section 287(g).

The opportunity for broadened immigration enforcement powers and responsibility among police agencies followed the events of 9/11 and the creation of the Department of Homeland Security in 2002. Subsequently, it is estimated that there are about 275,000 arrests and deportations made annually by the Department of Homeland Security through its two primary immigration enforcement agencies—Customs and Border Protection (CBP) and Immigration and Customs Enforcement (ICE)—as well as the partnerships with state and local police that have signed formal agreements with ICE to grant them additional immigration authority as authorized by Section 287(g) of the INA. Because the events leading up to and including the implementation of Section 287(g) serve as a historical precedent to the current day media attention to police enforcement of immigration issues, we will provide a brief overview of this policy before commencing with the remainder of this chapter.

Section 287(g)

During the mid-1990s, there was significant social reaction to immigration issues in various areas of southwestern United States. In particular, the passage of Proposition 187 in California drew substantial attention because it denied illegal immigrants the ability to obtain a variety of social services. This proposition was passed in 1994 on the heels of other initiatives aimed at restricting illegal border crossings from Mexico to the United States. In 1996, Section 287(g) was established to aid the outdated Immigration and Naturalization Service (INS) in enforcing immigration issues within the nation's interior. However, it is important to note that resources were much more limited for the INS than they are today for the modern federal agencies—CBP and ICE—that are tasked with enforcing immigration issues. Importantly, the INA of 1996 broadened the types of crime for which immigrants could be deported, and it restricted their right to appeal after being arrested (Espenshade, Baraka, & Huber 1997). This act was the means by which the Section 287(g) program was established and also established many of the strategies that ICE currently uses in immigration enforcement. Despite this, the INA of 1996 did not create many sweeping changes to immigration enforcement effectiveness. In addition, the inclusion of Section 287(g) did not have immediate effects upon local police agencies.

Indeed, it was not until 2003 that the first agreement between the federal government and a police agency was established when the state of Florida and the state of Alabama signed an agreement in 2003. Later, there were a handful more agreements that were signed during the years of 2005 and 2006. But the year 2007 is considered the primary year when Section 287(g) became more commonly implemented, with over 50 police agencies signing agreements by the close of 2008. The signing of these agreements included a memorandum of agreement (MOA) between state or local police agencies and ICE to allow police officers to enforce immigration laws. Under these MOAs, police agencies designated officers for specialized training by ICE officials on immigration laws, identification of potential unauthorized immigrants, procedures for verifying documents, and the use of databases to validate identities. Once these officers were trained, the designated officers then would return to their home jurisdictions where they continued their original jobs as state or local police but were, in addition to their regular duties, supervised by ICE agents when conducting immigration enforcement operations (Capps, 2010). According to Capps (2010), there are two different MOAs for Section 287(g) agreements: jail enforcement and task force models. These agreements differ depending on the type of police agency that enters into these agreements. According to Capps (2010),

> Through Task Force agreements, designated officers (and only designated officers) may check the legal status of arrestees at the scene of arrest or participate with ICE agents in joint enforcement operations. The Task Force agreements generally designate officers to check immigration status as part of their regular policing duties and spell out which officers will become part of the Task Force. Jail Enforcement officers check the legal status of inmates as they are booked into jail, and Jail Enforcement agreements are mostly between ICE and county sheriffs' offices (p. 159).

As indicated above, the parameters of Section 287(g) officers who conduct immigration enforcement duties, whether as part of task force initiatives or as part of a custodial setting's operations, do so in addition to their regular duties. This means that police agencies, including their jail facilities, provide this additional service with no budgetary assistance from ICE or any other federal entity. While the reasons for doing this may, on occasion, benefit the agency, this generally would be a program designed to remedy a nuisance issue identified by the community. Typically, most police departments will not identify immigration enforcement as a priority objective within that agency's annual planning process. Further, agencies are not autonomous in fulfilling this mandate but are instead required to operate under the close supervision of ICE. Agencies willing to engage in immigration enforcement incur an additional cost in human resources, and they agree to close supervision from the federal government when doing so.

The limits of Section 287(g) begs the question of why do police agencies sign memorandums of agreement for immigration enforcement if there is extra cost and a relegation of supervision to a federal agency and when this does not fulfill their primary duty of crime fighting? The answer is provided by Capps (2010) who noted that agencies adopting this policy are in states where immigration issues are perceived as problematic by the public and/or where immigration has seen a sharp increase in occurrence. Political fervor against illegal immigration tended to weigh heavy on the agendas of elected officials such as governors who direct state police functions, city mayors who appoint police chiefs over their municipality, and sheriffs who are directly voted into office by the public. As a means of currying favor from the public, governors, police chiefs, and sheriffs have found it prudent to adopt this concern as part of their own agenda, with the public support being so great as to offset budgetary concerns within their agencies.

Going Beyond Section 287(g)

With this overview of previous laws and regulations regarding state and local police involvement in immigration enforcement, we are now in a position to discuss more recent events that have drawn attention during the past few years. In discussing these developments, we will provide attention to Arizona's controversial Senate Bill 1070 (SB 1070) on Immigration, Law Enforcement, and Safe Neighborhoods as well as California's Senate Bill 54. In addition, we will explain the legal distinctions in police involvement, explaining why the SB 1070's shift to the use of reasonable suspicion as grounds for police intervention is so important to understand. Then, we will expound on how relations between community members can be greatly impaired, and how this negatively impacts the police agency, local community, and even the broader U.S. society. Afterward, we will also discuss the lack of resources that have existed for federal Border Patrol personnel and how this same lack of resources places local police in a precarious position if they are to engage in immigration investigation. Issues with potential legal liabilities will be discussed, particularly in regard to concerns over potential racial profiling. Lastly, some recommendations for rectifying this problem will be provided in light of the issues presented throughout the chapter.

Recent State Developments with Immigration Enforcement

Currently, there is a backlog in processing potential work visas, which causes challenges for many businesses where documented immigrant workers are employed. Further, many undocumented immigrant workers are, in order to keep their jobs, willing to work in environments that are dangerous and/or not in compliance with many of the health and safety standards usually expected in work environments. Lastly, the emphasis on deportation tends to ignore the reality that most often, families in the southwestern region may consist of both legal and illegal immigrants; thereby, family members are separated in a manner that is detrimental to the social welfare of the family and the community around them. All of these and other issues are of importance when attempting to develop a practical approach to immigration control and enforcement, especially when involving local police as agents of migration enforcement.

Given this reality, several states have clashed with presidential administrations over the use of law enforcement resources in migration policy and procedures. These clashes are not limited to the current administration. Just a few years ago in Arizona, SB 1070 on Immigration, Law Enforcement, and Safe Neighborhoods was called into question by the federal government. This bill, which eventually did become law, expanded police arrest powers such that they can now make probable cause arrests solely on the grounds that the person has entered the United States illegally without the need for any other attendant charges or alleged crimes (Ward, 2008). In fact, Arizona's SB 1070 legislation required police to stop and question potential immigrants upon a reasonable suspicion that they may be illegally in the United States.

In response, the U.S. Department of Justice (DOJ) filed a lawsuit in 2010 against the state of Arizona in district court that declared SB 1070 invalid because it interfered with federal immigration regulations (Markon & Shear, 2010). Specifically, DOJ attorneys noted that federal preemption existed and that a development of patchwork policies among local and state agencies was likely to be ineffective, as it would likely confuse efforts in the future (Markon & Shear, 2010). At the heart of the matter, the DOJ contended that Congress and the various federal agencies constituted a careful, deliberate, and balanced approach that simultaneously included law enforcement public safety concerns, foreign relations concerns, and humanitarian concerns (Markon & Shear, 2010). These were concerns that were not likely as important to the state of Arizona but to the nation as a whole. As a result, the DOJ requested an injunction against Arizona to prevent enforcement of the law before it had a chance to go into effect (Markon & Shear, 2010).

Ultimately, in 2012, the U.S. Supreme Court handed down a ruling that upheld the practice of requiring immigration status checks during routine police stops in a 5–3 majority vote (Barnes, 2012). However, the Court cautioned against detaining individuals for prolonged periods of time if they do not have their immigration documents and expressed concern over the potential for racial profiling to occur. This resulted in limits to the use of racial factors in arrests so that police could not use race, color, or national origin beyond what was already established as permissible (Barnes, 2012).

As one can see, the contradictions between state and federal priorities leaves local police departments in a state of uncertainty on immigration enforcement. Amidst the legal wrangling, law enforcement is left to make decisions that are tenuous and fraught with peril. This also creates tension between state and federal agents in areas where migration is sensitive because many local agents have more investment in their locations than do the federal agents assigned to their regions. To add to the confusion, there has been a flip-flop from democratic to republican presidential administrations that has further exacerbated this uncertainty. Indeed, Arizona's SB 1070 entailed a democratic presidency and a conservative republican state. California's Senate Bill 54 is exactly the opposite, involving a conservative republican presidency and a state known for being liberal and progressive.

California and Senate Bill 54

California has had a longstanding back-and-forth tussle on the issue of involving local law enforcement in immigration policy. Recently, Senate Bill 54 (SB 54), known as the "California Values Act," restricts the type and amount of support that local law enforcement agencies may provide to federal ICE officials (Fry, 2017). One key feature of SB 54 in California is the prohibition against moving inmates in local jails to immigration detention facilities (Fry, 2017). While this does not prevent ICE agents from being present at the time that an offender is released from a jail facility, at which time ICE agents can take the offender into custody, it does limit the use of the jail facility as an additional conduit of migrants for ICE officials, especially if release dates and identities are not specifically sent to ICE in advance (Fry, 2017).

The reasons for SB 54 have more to do with the fact that persons in migrant communities still do not nearly contact the police as frequently as nonmigrant community members when a crime is afoot. Fear that ICE will become involved is a key reason for this lack of reporting. In many cases, because crime does tend to be intraracial, this means that both the offending party and the victim may both be illegally within U.S. borders. In fact, in most criminal incidents, the victim and the assailant know each other, at least remotely. Thus, crime in migrant communities often goes unreported.

In response, the current presidential administration has indicated that it will challenge the new law in court. Indeed, U.S. Attorney General Jeff Sessions recently filed a lawsuit against the state of California over three laws that were passed in the state (Fry, 2017). Collectively, these laws limit the ability of state and local agents and employers in aiding federal immigration agents (Fry, 2017). These laws also give the state of California authority to inspect and review the conditions of care that are provided by federal officials to migrant detainees in facilities where they are kept. The notion that state authorities could have oversight ability over federal services is one that is quite unorthodox and has seemingly struck the ire of the federal government (Fry, 2017).

Reasonable Suspicion Versus Probable Cause

For most persons familiar with police work, the distinction between reasonable suspicion and probable cause is readily understood. But because it cannot be presumed that citizens understand the important distinctions and because this application, as applied to the enforcement of immigration laws, is a bit unique, it is best that we explain the concept of reasonable suspicion. Reasonable suspicion is a term that was first coined by the U.S. Supreme Court in the landmark case of *Terry v. Ohio*. Reasonable suspicion is a standard of proof that is less than probable cause but is more than an "unparticularized suspicion or hunch" (*Terry v. Ohio*, 1968). This proof must be developed from "specific and articulable facts, taken together with rational inferences from those facts" (*Terry v. Ohio*, 1968). With reasonable suspicion, police officers may briefly detain an individual if they believe that the individual has been, is, or will be involved in criminal activity. This type of a stop is considered, technically speaking, a detention, since it is not an arrest.

Probable cause, on the other hand, is a burden of proof that exists when a crime has been committed and knowledge of facts and circumstances known to the officer would lead a prudent individual to conclude that a suspect has committed, is committing, or will commit a crime. Probable cause is the standard of proof necessary for police to arrest an individual; without this level of proof, the arrest is invalid. The reader should understand that typically when police make an arrest, it is due to a crime that the person was thought to have committed; their immigration status was an afterthought that, if found illegal, resulted in their contacting federal immigration authorities for transfer to federal (not state or local) custody. But while illegal immigration is illegal, it may not be a bona fide criminal offense. Rather, there are stipulations of federal immigration laws where illegal entry is merely a civil law violation.

While the civil nature of many immigration stipulations may not be of consequence to an officer when they have arrested an individual for a criminal offense (thereby already possessing probable cause for some other offense that is criminal in nature), this would be a matter of consequence for an officer who acted on the basis of a reasonable suspicion. As noted previously, the reasonable suspicion standard is based on the idea that the officer believes that the individual has been, is, or will be involved in criminal activity, not civil law violations. Thus, when an officer briefly detains a person suspected of illegal entry, and when it is likely that the offense is a civil law violation, the police officer is acting beyond the scope of authority intended with *Terry* stops. Though this may be a "fine line" difference, it is one that is very serious and can lead officers and/or police agencies into situations for which they may be subject to suit.

In nearly every police agency throughout the United States, the distinction between criminal issues and civil issues is clearly acknowledged. For instance, in child custody disputes, it is unusual for police to get involved with disputing parties unless there is probable cause to think that a criminal act has been committed by one of the parties. This usually goes beyond the simple act of not obeying a divorce decree (a civil judgment) and would require some type of criminal act such as assault and battery, criminal trespass, kidnapping, and so forth. Indeed, in *Gonzales v. City of Peoria*, the Ninth Circuit held that while Arizona could authorize the Peoria Police Department to enforce the criminal provisions of the immigration law, the Court noted that "we firmly emphasize that this authorization is limited to criminal violations" (*Gonzales v. City of Peoria*, 1983, p. 10). The Court did not support the Peoria Police Department's policy specifically because it obscured the difference between civil administrative violations and criminal violations of the immigration law, and the Court emphasized that the lack of documentation or an admission of illegal presence "does not, without more, provide probable cause of [any] criminal violation" of the immigration law (*Gonzales v. City of Peoria*, 1983). This obviously speaks in a direct manner to the problems associated with requiring officers to inquire about immigration status under the reasonable suspicion justification, since many of the immigration laws have a civil basis when enacted. Going further upon such suspicion to the point of arrest is even more problematic, since the arrest is based on probable cause of a civil law violation, not a criminal law infraction.

Lastly, as was noted earlier, the Court in *Gonzales v. City of Peoria* noted that city, county, and even state police are often untrained in federal immigration law. Thus, when these officers attempt to implement this type of arrest authority (obviously after they have completed their questioning and had their suspicions confirmed), their agencies will likely be legally liable for committing Fourth Amendment violations. Though the individual officer will not likely be held liable (because they are following agency policy in good faith and within the scope of their duty), the litigation process for agencies can be cumbersome and costly, even if the agency prevails. Also, we should consider that even federal immigration agents do not have the power to conduct warrantless arrests away from the border unless the agent can articulate specific reasons to believe the person was likely to escape before a warrant could be obtained. Therefore, SB 1070 gives broader powers to local police than are possessed by agents specifically tasked with immigration enforcement. Thus, it is unlikely that this law, and any attendant policies associated with it, will be upheld by federal courts who review its constitutionality and its consistency with other clearly established federal laws.

The Impact on Police Community Relations

Undoubtedly, if police are routinely questioning community members about their immigration status, there will be many more police–citizen contacts than would occur if they were not involved in this type of activity. While this may not be a serious problem for persons who are legal citizens, it can become a bit of an inconvenience. This is particularly true if persons who appear to be of Latino, Middle Eastern, or Asian origin are disproportionately questioned. This can lead to allegations of racial profiling that will be discussed later. Nevertheless, even if such persons, upon questioning, are found to be within U.S. borders legally, the experience is likely to be at least as inconvenient as it is to provide one's driver's license, proof of insurance, and automobile registration during a routine traffic stop. While this is considered a minor infringement on one's liberty, it can be a bit of a hassle nonetheless. Just this added inconvenience can add tension between police and citizens over time.

Also consider that most major urban areas throughout the nation consist of large immigrant communities. Indeed, in some communities, the immigrant population might be roughly 50% (or more) of the local population. Local police agencies are responsible for protecting the diverse members of their community, and this includes those who are legal and illegal. With this reality, local police agencies have implemented community policing approaches that facilitate trust and cooperation with these diverse populations, including those with high proportions of first- and second-generation immigrants. In most larger agencies, as well as agencies in midsized communities, officers who are specially qualified to work with immigrant groups and specific minority communities may be given duty assignments that are intended to maintain a positive relationship between these community members and the police agency.

These types of community policing initiatives often allow officers to become familiar with persons in a community, both those who are law abiding and those who are not. This then means that these officers will be accurate in determining which suspects have likely committed a type of crime within the community due to their informal connections in the community and the knowledge that they gain from resulting informal contacts. This also means that victims will be more comfortable reporting crimes to these officers, and witnesses will be more inclined to talk with officers who are routinely present in their community and have a reputation of being trustworthy and knowledgeable of the community and its problems. Lastly and just as important, officers who have developed this rapport will also have the ability to use their discretion (within legal and ethical bounds, of course) to resolve problems within the community. This may be especially important when incidents involve juvenile members of the community or persons who are related to respected families in the community. When complainants do not desire a formal criminal justice response, they will be hesitant to contact the police unless they know, in advance, that the responding officers are willing to consider other viable options as well (i.e., contacting parents, allowing individual citizens to work out petty issues, resolving disputes on the scene and deescalating the circumstances, or integrating the services of other agencies or organizations when a criminal justice response is not specifically required). All of this will be prefaced with months of dialog and discussion with community members who, during their contact with these officers (through informal talk, neighborhood watches, National Night Out programs, civic meetings, citizen police academies, and other formal and informal programs) will become more comfortable than they would be with a complete stranger responding to the call.

The ability for officers to better identify among suspects those who are guilty of specific crimes, gain more information from community members, and utilize informal means of response should not be underestimated. Whether an immigrant member of these communities is documented or undocumented, their cooperation can be invaluable to achieving clearance of a case. Community cooperation is needed to prevent and solve crimes and maintain public order, safety, and security in the whole community. The Major Cities Chiefs Immigration Committee also noted that positive contacts with immigrant communities are important for purposes of intelligence gathering to prevent potential terrorist attacks and as a means of strengthening homeland security. Naturally, this ties in with earlier points regarding the smuggling of terrorists into the country, but this intelligence gathering aspect can also improve law enforcement's ability to detect terrorist "sleeper" cells within the United States. In addition, if terrorist groups such as Al Qaeda or criminal gangs such as MS-13 are recruiting members within a given community, the cooperation of members living in the area is invaluable. This includes members who are legally in the country as well as those who are illegally within our borders. Obviously, immigration enforcement by local police would likely negatively affect and undermine the level of trust and cooperation between local police and immigrant communities, and this would then impair local police agencies' ability to gain valuable information to prevent crime or threats to public safety. The following excerpt from the Major City Chiefs Immigration Committee's list of recommendations explained that if immigrants fear deportation from local police, then

> Undoubtedly legal immigrants would avoid contact with the police for fear that they themselves or undocumented family members or friends may become subject to immigration enforcement. Without assurances that contact with the police would not result in purely civil immigration enforcement action, the hard won trust, communication and cooperation from the immigrant community would disappear. Such a divide between the local police and immigrant groups *would result in increased crime against immigrants* and in the broader community, *create a class of silent victims* and eliminate the potential for assistance from immigrants in solving crimes or preventing future terroristic acts. (Major City Chiefs Immigration Committee, 2006, p. 6)

The two areas that are italicized in this block quote is our own emphasis that we wish to provide to the reader. These statements provide a glimpse into the world of the immigrant, particularly the illegal immigrant, who comes into our country. In many cases, these populations are victimized by gangs and organized crime groups who are most often of the same racial group as the victim. This is particularly true of the Asian American community as well as the Latino American community.

In Chinatowns in New York and California, Asian gangs will usually know business owners and will also be aware of which community members have citizenship and those who do not. They will be more prone to victimize these individuals because those victims who are in the United States illegally are hesitant to report their victimization due to concerns with deportation. Further, business owners who have employed these illegal immigrants (often an illegal Asian immigrant has agreed to work for the business owner in exchange for the fee to get them into the country) are subjected to extortion and blackmail that occurs on a recurring basis. Further, Asian gangs most often target Asian families because they know that even legitimate immigrants will tend to not report due to past experiences (in their country of origin) where the police were corrupt, ineffective, or were themselves working in tandem with gangs or organized crime elements. Likewise, when a female member is sexual assaulted, the family will tend to avoid reporting due to the shame and dishonor that the family suffers within the broader Asian community. Lastly, when these families have members living among them or within their neighborhood who are themselves in the country illegally, they are again vulnerable to extortion and victimization and will not likely report crimes against them. As noted by the Major Cities Chiefs Immigration Committee (2006), these various dynamics create a class of silent victims within the Asian immigrant community.

Latino gangs are likewise prone to victimize other Latinos within their respective barrios (a lower socioeconomic Hispanic community). While Latino gangs will victimize persons who are not Latino, like their Asian counterparts, these criminals are aware of those members of their community who are legally vulnerable due to fear of deportation. In addition, they will also tend to sell drugs and/or have gang wars within their own communities, which leads to intraracial criminalization dynamics. The fact that criminal victimization tends to be intraracial is a commonly known tendency and naturally fits with Latino gangs. However, in the case of Latino immigrants who are illegally in the United States, these dynamics create a silent class of victims who tend to not report crimes against them. Latino gangs are aware of this and exploit these individuals on a routine basis.

Lack of Resources

Currently, many police agencies are feeling the crunch of budget cuts and the need for reduced spending due to the nation's current economic challenges. Without a doubt, most police agencies were challenged to provide optimal service delivery when they were tasked with fighting crime exclusive of concerns for the immigration status of day-to-day citizens. With this added responsibility, additional human resources will be required to process these cases. In some states, this expenditure will naturally be more costly than in others. Regardless, adding such an initiative will require additional time and effort from police officers. Consider also that with the creation of the Department of Homeland Security, federal funding for most police departments has been greatly reduced. This is despite the fact that police agencies have taken on additional responsibilities for fighting terrorism after 9/11.

This lack of funding also exists despite the fact that ICE has received increased funding during past years, which, as of 2010, was nearly $5.75 billion. Just as importantly, the "ICE Strategic Plan FY 2010–2014" specifically addressed three priorities that included the following:

(1) preventing terrorism and enhancing security,
(2) securing and managing our borders, and
(3) enforcing and administering our immigration laws.

Clearly, it is the purview of ICE to address issues related to immigration enforcement. It should also be clear that, given the emphasis of ICE's strategic plan on enforcing immigration laws, the use of technology, the need to crack down on employers who retain illegal workers, and the intent to prevent cross-border criminal activities, it is intended that ICE assume the role of immigration enforcement and serve as the coordinating authority on matters related to criminals illegally entering the United States. Indeed, consider the excerpt from this organization's strategic plan that reads as follows:

> ICE will engage in effective enforcement at the border and ports of entry by supporting the apprehension, detention and removal of newly arriving aliens seeking to enter illegally. Within the United States, ICE will pursue an effective worksite enforcement program to reduce the incentive for aliens to come to, enter and remain unlawfully. ICE also will prioritize the removal of convicted criminal aliens and gang members who undermine public security and reduce the quality of life in our communities. ICE will protect the integrity of the immigration system by enforcing final orders of removal and targeting fraud and abuse that undermine the sound administration of the nation's immigration laws. (Department of Homeland Security, 2010, pp. 5 & 6)

This directly indicates that the federal government expects ICE to address matters related to enforcement of immigrants who enter illegally. Just as interesting is the observation that this excerpt, as with the remainder of ICE's strategic plan, never mentions or even remotely alludes to the desire or intent to have local police agency assistance with this duty. Usually, in most strategic plans, the broad nature of these documents will make mention of any intent to cultivate innovations in operational approaches. The fact that no mention of partnerships with local police agencies is even briefly mentioned is a very clear clue that the federal government does not intend for resources to be allocated to local police for immigration enforcement. Rather, the federal government considers this a federal responsibility, and this is made clear in their funding decisions; additional monies are given to ICE, and no monies are allocated to local police for immigration enforcement activities.

In addition, many major police forces have noted that enforcement of federal immigration laws would result in a burden that goes beyond their ability given current resources possessed by these departments (Major City Chiefs Immigration Committee, 2006). These sources have noted that the cost in terms of personnel, facilities (both detention and transportation), equipment, and training for local agencies to address approximately 12 million illegal immigrants would be overwhelming. In their report, the Major City Chiefs Immigration Committee (2006) noted that local police agencies must meet their existing policing duties and cannot take on the added burden of immigration enforcement until federal assistance and funding are provided to support immigration enforcement. Adding to that concern is the fact that current notions of local police enforcement comes with no clear statement and no guarantee that adequate federal funding will be provided.

Lastly, the ability of the U.S. Border Patrol to meet its goals and objectives for border security have been largely unsuccessful. In a federal report prepared by the U.S. House of Representatives, the lack of a comprehensive border protection strategy has resulted in abject failure on the part of this agency. This lack of border strategy has caused inadequate staffing numbers along the nation's borders and has resulted in a failure to fully deploy state-of-the-art border security technology. It is clear that the House of Representatives do not believe that our borders are secure. This seems like a particularly problematic issue that is further exacerbated by the fact that only about $1.3 billion were allocated to this function in 2010, which is much less than that allocated to ICE. It would seem that securing our borders might provide a better preventive mechanism that would reduce the number of illegal immigrants in the country, and this would, in turn, reduce the need for local police to become involved with immigration enforcement. Regarding the lack of funding and resources allocated to these efforts, the Major Cities Chiefs Immigration Committee stated, in pointed terms, that the federal government "itself failed to provide the tremendous amount of resources necessary to accomplish such enforcement to its own agencies specifically charged with that responsibility" (Major Cities Chiefs Immigration Committee, 2006, p. 6). Thus it would seem that our first line of defense—Border Patrol—suffers from ineffective strategy setting and a lower priority budget. Further, it would seem that other federal agencies, such as ICE, are more fully funded and that they view immigration enforcement as their own unique jurisdiction. Given these logistical complexities, it is clear that there is dubious usage of federal resources, and it is also clear that additional resources have not been allocated for local police involvement in immigration enforcement. Therefore, it is unrealistic to think that local police agencies will have the capability to absorb this new enforcement responsibility.

States' Rights Versus Federal Rights in Responding to the Immigration Issue

Central to this issue is that fact that any responsibility over immigration begins and ends within the U.S. government, not state governments. Further, the United States may be in need of reexamining responses to migration, national status, and the rights of states to govern their own police resources within their borders. As it stands, states are entitled to exercise jurisdiction over criminal law and civil law within their borders as they see fit, so long as that activity ensures that no constitutional rights are violated in doing so. Further still, states are allowed to broaden rights of individuals within their borders beyond what the Constitution permits, but they cannot restrict those rights to less than what the U.S. Constitution provides. California is then within rights to extend protections of individuals within state borders, whether they are citizens or not.

The federal government is responsible for protecting the nation's borders and regulating international issues that impact those borders. However, it is very unlikely that the United States will be able to effectively counter the root causes of the illegal flow of immigrants. The reason is simple: citizens leaving Honduras, Guatemala, El Salvador, and Mexico are doing so because of the pervasive corruption inherent to these national governments. It is because of this simple fact that the United States is largely powerless to provide stability. In addition, there are resentments toward the United States among many Latin nations for past military involvement into the affairs of these nations (United Nations News Centre, 2013). It is clear that, for better or worse, many leaders of various Latin American countries have negative views of the United States.

It seems that the United States should take heed of what its neighbors are saying. This then means that Latin American nations will have to bail themselves out of the doldrums in which they find themselves. However, the nation of Bolivia has seen numerous gains by bringing people out of poverty, expanding its coverage for maternal health, boosting literacy, and investing in water and sanitation (United Nations News Centre, 2013). Indeed, President Evo Morales Ayma stated that "we live in sovereignty and dignity; no longer dominated by the North American empire ... no longer being blackmailed by the International Monetary Fund" (United Nations News Centre, 2013, p. 1). This example shows both that of these countries are capable of improving their condition, and, just as importantly, they tend to resent involvement by the United States. This is an important observation when trying to actually resolve this problem at its origin rather than simply attend to the symptoms of that problem.

Given that the current presidential administration has further polarized the United States from the remaining nations of the Americas, it does not seem that efforts to remedy illegal immigration will be in tandem with the priorities of many Latin American nations. While there is a possibility that these government leaders are themselves corrupt, this only serves to further restrict the United States in responding. Indeed, aside from some act of overt or covert warfare, there is little else that the United States can do to counter regimes of corruption, drug cartels that paralyze entire governments, and cultures that have developed around a "haves" and "have nots" mentality. Naturally, to engage in any form of armed intervention is both desperate and counterproductive, having the potential to further victimize and harm those persons whom the United States would be liberating so as to have better access to economic and social autonomy.

Though international issues that influence migration impacts individual states, it is primarily the state's job to regulate and respond to issues affecting its own jurisdiction. As long as this is done in a manner that does not contradict constitutionally protected civil rights, the state's responsibility therein begins and ends. Therefore, states have the right to adopt more liberal approaches within their own borders to the migration issue. Further, they may, ironically, have a better understanding of the complications involved with immigration issues within their borders than the federal government would like to admit.

This then means that, on the one hand, the U.S. government must grapple with the international considerations that impact migrant influxes (whether legal or illegal) within its borders, as federal resources are intended for such actions. On the other hand, the business of internal governance should be left to individual states to regulate. Should a state, as a whole, wish to engage in more vigorous expulsion of illegal migrants, then so be it. Should that state wish to not utilize their own resources for such efforts, so be that as well. In essence, part of the problem becomes a state rights versus federal rights issue. In this case, states have a right to determine their own codes, statutes, and laws on the matter, once the issue falls within their borders.

Legal Liabilities and Racial Profiling

Let us again consider the parameters of Section 287(g) in relation to police liability. Morawetz and Das (2010) noted that Section 287(g) agreements seem to provide legal protection over unlawful acts related to immigration enforcement. However, these agreements do not cover claims that are brought directly under constitutional guarantees distinct from torts under state law (Travis, 1982). In other words, liability under 42 U.S.C. § 1983 may still attach when the litigation alleges a civil rights violation rather than a tort suit. Further, these agreements do not cover discretionary activities or actions taken outside the scope of the officer's employment (Travis, 1982; Morawetz & Das, 2010). Therefore, some lawsuits will focus on whether an officer's actions were within the scope of the Section 287(g) agreement.

Likewise, Morawetz and Das (2010) pointed out that ICE has specified that Section 287(g) is not intended to allow state and local police to perform random street operations, nor is it intended to impact issues such as day labor activities among employers. Even more specifically, they contended that ICE guidelines have indicated that police are not permitted to randomly ask for a person's immigration status, nor may they conduct raids to uncover the existence of illegal immigrants. Lastly, Section 287(g) agreements do not provide legal protections for conduct that constitutes racial profiling. Because of this, Morawetz and Das (2010) concluded that "as a whole, Section 287(g) provides very limited protection to localities and their officers, and may even introduce new dangers in liability" (p. 79).

The issue of racial profiling has been an area of very particular concern when police agencies consider their role in immigration enforcement. However, the legal implications regarding potential liability for racial profiling have some interesting exceptions, particularly when one considers the Supreme Court precedent that has specifically addressed this issue. In 1975, the Court, in *United States v. Brignoni-Ponce*, identified six factors that Border Patrol agents are allowed to consider when determining who to stop during roving patrol stops. According to the Court, factors that can be considered are the area in which the stop occurs, the proximity to the border, the traffic patterns of the roadway where the stop occurs, the driver's behavior, the characteristics of the vehicle, and the appearance of the passengers themselves. These same factors would (presumably) be the parameters for local police who might be required to ask suspected illegal immigrants questions.

In clarifying how appearances may be used, the Court noted that agents could consider clothing and hairstyles when determining suspicion. However, Justice Lewis Powell further clarified by explicitly noting that agents could consider unchangeable physical characteristics when determining reasonable suspicion for questioning. He noted that "The likelihood that any given person of Mexican ancestry is an alien is high enough to make Mexican appearance a relevant factor, but standing alone it does not justify stopping all Mexican Americans to ask if they are aliens" (*United States v. Brignoni-Ponce*, 1975, pp. 886–887). This has resulted in an ambiguous guideline whereby, on the one hand, federal officers may question immigrants based on their Mexican appearance, but yet, on the other hand, this does not allow federal (not state or local) officers to question all Mexican-appearing individuals in the community. However, the law from SB 1070 does, in fact, require that officers question when upon a reasonable suspicion, and according to the caselaw in *United States v. Brignoni-Ponce*, appearance is sufficient grounds for questioning. Thus, it is likely that police officers in Arizona and other states that mandate their involvement in immigration enforcement will, in fact, be empowered to ask questions of all Mexican-appearing persons in their community; this means that the concerns of citizens that they may be targeted due to their racial appearance would seem to be founded.

Further, in *United States v. Martinez-Fuerte*, the Court discussed questions based on appearance of a suspect, though, at the time of this ruling (1976), the term *racial profiling* was not used. Justice Powell spoke for the Court by stating that "even if it be assumed that such referrals are made largely on the basis of apparent Mexican ancestry, we perceive no constitutional violation," (*United States v. Martinez-Fuerte*, 1976, pp. 884–885). The Court's decision has essentially allowed Border Patrol agents to be more suspicious of anyone who they think is of Mexican ancestry than of people who they think are not of Mexican ancestry (Hernandez, 2010).

While one could speculate that these same rules apply to local police acting in an immigration enforcement function, this is actually not likely to be the case for local police officers. The decisions in prior Supreme Court cases have centered on the role of Border Patrol agents acting in their official capacity. Further, these rulings address circumstances that are either on or somewhat near U.S. border regions. These situations are substantially different from cases that might occur within more interior areas of the United States and within a population, the proportion of illegal Mexican-appearing immigrants may be much less than when compared to other areas of the United States that are adjacent to Mexico. Morawetz and Das (2010) provided evidence that local police do not enjoy any special protections against racial profiling when engaged in immigration enforcement by stating that "under 287(g) agreements, localities have no protection from claims that they have engaged in racial profiling. The 287(g) agreements have specifically provided that officers exercising authority under the MOA are bound by all federal civil rights statutes and regulations" (p. 79). In fact, they point out that Section 287(g) makes reference to the DOJ's 2003 document entitled "Guidance Regarding the Use of Race by Federal Law Enforcement Agencies" that explicitly notes that reliance on race or ethnicity is only permitted when the officer is pursuing a specific individual or when persons are known to be identified criminal action. Thus, state and local agencies will need to avoid any practices that can be construed as racial profiling.

Concluding Comments:
Potential Reform and Likely Trends

From our discussion so far, it is clear that there are numerous questions yet to be answered when we have state and local police involved in immigration enforcement. Given that states, such as Arizona and California, have begun to enact more vigorous legislation related to immigrant enforcement, federal decision-makers have increased their efforts to demonstrate their ability to curb the influx of illegal immigrants within the nation's borders. To some extent, this is indeed the objective for California and Arizona as well as other states who, in desperation and in frustration, have created legislation to handle this issue, ignoring the possible legal ramifications that might ensue. This has caught the eye of the federal government, and this strategy has now placed this issue into the spotlight with the implication being made that it is the federal government's responsibility to now do something more tangible about this issue.

It is our recommendation that these issues be approached with the adage that "an ounce of prevention is worth a pound of cure," meaning that we should improve efforts at the earliest stage possible. This means that improvements in Border Patrol activities is where efforts should be focused. As we noted earlier, the CBP has been found wanting in achieving its goals, and this has been formally acknowledged by federal officials. Thus, we recommend that federal officials increase efforts on the border between the United States and Mexico, since this would produce immediately observable results and reduce the need for police enforcement of immigration laws; if illegal immigrants cannot get into the country, then there will be less need for enforcement within the nation's interior. This would also reduce the workload for ICE and would, therefore, reduce the need for additional funds to ICE. Thus, in the bluntest of terms, we recommend more focus on border protection efforts as a means of improving issues with illegal immigration.

In addition, we recommend that police agencies be discouraged from engaging in immigration enforcement. The role of police is one that is associated with crime fighting, and given the criminal and civil aspects of immigration law, this should not be an issue for police agencies to enforce. Rather, it is the federal government's responsibility, and it is they who have enforced legal mandates upon states regarding standards of care, the means by which states can enforce the law and so forth. Thus, it is the federal government who should "step up to the plate," so to speak, and absorb the cost of solving a national problem. This also prevents governors, police chiefs, and sheriffs from benefiting from political jockeying around this social issue. Thus, it is our recommendation and our prediction that federal officials will increase their efforts at immigration enforcement while, at the same time, downplaying the extent to which states are asked to assist. In our opinion, this is both the most ethically appropriate and legally sound remedy for this issue.

References

Barnes, R. (2012, June 25). Supreme Court rejects much of Arizona immigration law. *The Washington Post*. Retrieved from https://www.washingtonpost.com/politics/supreme-court-rules-on-arizona-immigration-law/2012/06/25/gJQA0Nrm1V_story.html?utm_term=.04831b6cec4e.

Capps, R. (2010). Local enforcement of immigration laws: Evolution of the 243(g) program and its potential impacts on local communities. In A. Khashu (Ed.), *The role of local police: Striking a balance between immigration enforcement and civil liberties*. Washington, DC: Police Foundation. Retrieved from https://www.policefoundation.org/publication/the-role-of-local-police-striking-a-balance-between-immigration-enforcement-and-civil-liberties/.

Department of Homeland Security (2010). ICE *U. S. Immigration and Enforcement Strategic Plan FY 2010–2014*. U. S. Immigration & Customs Enforcement.

Espenshade, T., Baraka, J., & Huber, G. (1997). Implications of the 1996 immigration and welfare reform acts for U.S. immigration. *Population and Development Review, 23*(4), 769–801.

Fry, W. (2017, December 28). How 2018 immigration law will affect local law enforcement. *NBC 7, San Diego*. Retrieved from https://www.nbcsandiego.com/news/local/California-Immigration-Law-SB-54-Affect-Local-Law-Enforcement-467064593.html.

Hanser, R. & Moran, N. (2008). Gang crimes: Latino gangs in America. In F. Shanty (Ed.), *Organized crime: From trafficking to terrorism* (pp. 120–125). Santa Barbara, CA: ABC-CLIO/Greenwood.

Hernandez, C. C. (2010). La Migra in the mirror: Immigration enforcement, racial profiling, and the psychology of one Mexican chasing another. *Albany Law Review, 72,* 891–897.

Major Cities Chiefs Immigration Committee (2006). *M.C.C. immigration committee recommendations: For enforcement of immigration laws by local police agencies.* Retrieved from http://majorcitieschiefs.org/pdfpublic/mcc_position_statement_revised_cef.pdf.

Markon, J., & Shear, M. D. (2010). Justice department sues Arizona over immigration law. *The Washington Post.* Retrieved from http://www.washingtonpost.com/wp-dyn/content/article/2010/07/06/AR2010070601928.html.

Morawetz, N. & Das, A. (2010). Legal issues in local police enforcement of federal immigration law. In A. Khashu (Ed.), *The role of local police: Striking a balance between immigration enforcement and civil liberties.* Washington, DC: Police Foundation. Retrieved from https://www.policefoundation.org/wp-content/uploads/2015/06/The-Role-of-Local-Police-Narrative.pdf.

Passel, J. S. (2006). *Size and characteristics of the unauthorized migrant population in the U.S.* Pew Research Center. Retrieved from http://www.pewhispanic.org/2006/03/07/size-and-characteristics-of-the-unauthorized-migrant-population-in-the-us/.

Travis, J. (1982). Rethinking sovereign immunity after Bivens. *New York University Law Review, 57,* 597.

UN News Centre. (2013). *Leaders of Latin American countries urge major push to promote social justice, end inequality.* Retrieved from http://www.un.org/apps/news/story.asp?NewsID=46022#.WdKS0cahfIU.

Ward, S. (2008). Illegal aliens on ICE: Tougher immigration enforcement tactics spur challenges. *Aba Journal.* Retrieved from http://www.abajournal.com/magazine/illegal_aliens_on_ice/.

Yardley, J. (2000, January 3). Some Texans say border patrol singles out too many blameless Hispanics. *The New York Times,* p. A17.

Cases Cited

Gonzales v. City of Peoria, 722 F. 2d 468 (1983)

Terry v. Ohio, 392 U.S. 1 (1968)

United States v. Brignoni-Ponce, 422 U.S. 873 (1975)

United States v. Martinez-Fuerte, 428 U.S. 543, 545 (1976)

Chapter 5

The Sentencing Revolution

Barbara Belbot

Introduction

The National Research Council's (2014) Committee on the Causes and Consequences of High Rates of Incarceration in the United States opened its 2014 report by emphasizing that the rate of incarceration in the United States quadrupled over the past four decades. The committee, composed of leading criminal justice scholars and practitioners, was charged by the prestigious National Research Council to examine what changes in society and public policy contributed to the rise of incarceration, the consequences those changes has had on crime rates, and the effect mass incarceration has had on communities. The committee found that the unprecedented growth in the rate of incarceration in the United States over the past 40 years can be attributed to a punitive political climate that developed during a period when crime rates were rising and society was undergoing social change. Policy choices were made across all levels of government that resulted in lengthier sentences, more severe sanctions for less serious offenses, and very severe sanctions for drug-related crimes. Importantly, the committee noted the considerable research, suggesting that the crime rate has not been significantly impacted by the increase in incarceration.

In 1973, the prison population in state and federal institutions in this country was about 200,000. By 2009, state and federal prison systems incarcerated 1.5 million people. Add an additional 700,000 prisoners held in local jails with the result that the United States has the largest prison/jail population in the world. With only 5% of the world's population, as of 2012, the United States held 25% of the world's prisoners (Gottschalk, 2006). Prison sentences in the United States are draconian compared to most European nations where, except for murder, the lengthiest prison sentence that can be imposed is 14 or 15 years. Sentences greater than one year are only 1% or 2% of all offenders who are incarcerated (Tonry, 2016). In his speech to the

American Bar Association (ABA) in 2003, U.S. Supreme Court Justice Anthony Kennedy addressed fundamental problems concerning criminal punishment in this country. He noted the large number of people incarcerated in the United States compared to other civilized nations and the disproportionate negative impact incarceration has had on minority communities. While prevention and incapacitation are legitimate goals in sentencing, he urged the public to recognize that rehabilitation must also be an important goal. He concluded by stating that "[o]ur resources are misspent, our punishments too severe, our sentences too long" (ABA, 2004, p. 4). In response to his challenge, the ABA formed a commission to recommend reforms to alleviate the bleak situation the Justice described (ABA, 2004).

This chapter looks at sentencing laws in the United States, keeping in mind Justice Kennedy's warnings. Sentencing, however, is a complicated topic that can be analyzed from a number of different directions. The public thinks of sentencing as the punishment imposed by a trial judge after a defendant has been convicted. The legislature enacts laws that detail which punishments judges can apply to different types of offenses. Habitual and repeat offender laws allow judges to enhance the punishment based on a defendant's prior criminal history. This is only one component of sentencing. Sentencing laws include parole laws that govern the back end of the process, addressing if and when offenders can be released from prison before their entire court-imposed sentence is served. Parole laws generally regulate good time or earned time. Sentencing laws also address what penalties should be applied when probationers and parolees violate their conditions of release. This chapter examines the dramatic shifts in sentencing from the 1970s through today. It addresses structured sentencing, abolishing discretionary parole, and the enactment of lengthy terms of incarceration—notably mandatory minimum penalties, truth in sentencing, and life with and without parole. Not all of these changes have been adopted in every state, but they have all been adopted in many. The chapter focuses on how these policies have impacted the growth of the nation's prison systems and concludes with observations about the future of sentencing. Extensive research and public debate concerning the failures of federal sentencing policy often overshadow what has been happening in the rest of the country (Weisberg, 2007). This chapter concentrates on state sentencing laws, referring only occasionally to the federal system. Finally, in order to understand the complete story of sentencing in the United States, readers are encouraged to explore the many important areas of sentencing policy outside the scope of this discussion.

The Sentencing Sea Change

The Indeterminate Sentencing Era

For most of the 20th century, the rehabilitative, or "medical," model dominated sentencing in both the federal and state criminal justice systems. The model assumes that fear of incarceration combined with rehabilitation can impact criminal behavior. Although proponents of the medical model acknowledge that some offenders require lengthy prison sentences, the primary emphasis is on rehabilitation (ABA, 2004). Therefore, sentences are to fit the individual offender, according to his or her risks and needs (Tonry, 2007). Rehabilitation programs include substance abuse counseling, job training, psychological counseling, and the like.

Before the mid-1970s, state and federal sentences could all be described as "indeterminate." In its broadest sense, indeterminate sentencing refers to both the discretion judges can exercise in imposing sentences during the front end of the process and the use of discretionary parole release on the back end (Reitz, 2001). In indeterminate sentencing jurisdictions, legislatures enact sentencing statutes that traditionally set wide ranges of punishment. Judges have almost unlimited discretion to sentence an offender anywhere within the maximum/minimum range of punishments created by statute, with few limits on the type of information they can use in making that decision (ABA, 2004).

In an indeterminate system, however, the sentence length an offender will actually serve is determined by a parole board, with the restriction that the board cannot keep an offender imprisoned beyond the sentence the judge imposed. Although the judge can sentence the defendant within the ranges provided by statute, the proportion of the term the defendant spends in prison is controlled by the jurisdiction's parole authority, usually an agency located in the executive branch of government (Stemen, Rengifo, & Wilson 2005). State and federal parole statutes outline at what point during a sentence an offender is eligible for parole consideration. Parole authorities generally have broad discretion to decide when a particular prisoner is ready for release, based on his or her progress toward rehabilitation. The discretion granted to both judges and parole boards is designed to promote individualized sentencing, tailored to the offender (Reitz, 2001).

The Determinate Sentencing Era

In the 1970s, the rehabilitative model was subjected to mounting criticism from both liberal and conservative fronts for a variety of reasons. Conservatives argued that crime was rising, and research showed that rehabilitation did not work (Martinson, 1974). They believed that indeterminate sentencing was soft on criminals. Critics also asserted that having parole boards assess a prisoner's progress toward reform, and risk if released, is inherently difficult and based primarily on in-prison behavior (Frase, 2005b). Liberals were concerned that indeterminate sentencing permitted unjust disparities among similarly situated offenders, disparities too frequently based on race, ethnicity, and gender. They argued that judges and parole boards had too much discretion, and individualized sentencing opened the door to arbitrary practices that negatively impacted minority offenders (Frankel, 1973). Prisoner groups argued that the uncertainty of indeterminate sentences was cruel (Irwin, 1980). According to the ABA's (2004) Justice Kennedy Commission, what resulted was the following:

> the determinate sentencing revolution, which has been characterized by (a) limitations on front end judicial sentencing discretion through passage of mandatory minimum sentences for certain offenses and sentencing guidelines that narrow the scope of unconstrained judicial sentencing discretion for all offenses, (b) elimination of or drastic limitations on parole or other forms of administrative early release authority, thus requiring defendants to serve a larger proportion of their judicially imposed sentences, and (c) in most places, increases in the statutory and/or guideline penalties for most serious crimes, particularly violent crimes involving firearms and drug offenses. (p. 16)

Michael Tonry (2016) described what followed as an implosion of indeterminate sentencing, leaving behind a system that today is fractured and fragmented. According to Tonry, the policy implosion was a shift away from the utilitarian goals of incapacitation and rehabilitation, replacing them with retributive goals based on proportional punishments and reduced disparity. Academicians began to speak in terms of "just deserts" and the "justice model." Sentences should not be individualized; rather, they should be based on the seriousness of the crime (Reitz, 2001).

Blumstein (2002) agreed that lost confidence in rehabilitation is the primary factor behind the shifts in sentencing policy occurring since the end of the 1970s. Importantly, he also noted that many experts who lost confidence never intended for criminal penalties to become more severe:

> It is ironic that the initial assault on the rehabilitation approach came from a de-incarceration perspective which argued that because there was so little the criminal justice system could do to change behavior, there should be less intervention with offenders. They also claimed

that those exercising the release authority—parole boards and their associated professionals—were engaged in an arbitrary exercise of power over individuals' liberty, and so declaimed the disparity of treatment that resulted. (p. 463–464)

The reformers' initial goal was to reduce incarceration, but according to Blumstein (2002), "this political shift transferred the emphasis away from rehabilitation to the more explicitly punitive deterrent and incapacitative effects of prison as the only means left to the criminal justice system to address the objective of reducing crime" (p. 464). Public pressure for harsher sentencing grew through the late 1970s and 1980s as the crime rate soared (Reitz, 2001). Sentencing reforms that were originally enacted to reduce disparity and temper the use of imprisonment ended up opening the door to longer prison sentences, mandatory minimums, additional restrictions on parole release in states that retain parole, the abolition of discretionary parole release in other jurisdictions, and more punitive probation and parole revocation regulations (Blumstein, 2002; Tonry, 2016).

Today, there is significant variation in sentencing laws across the country, much more so than prior to the determinate sentencing revolution. Getting a handle on sentencing law is challenging because it is a moving target; it is not static. State legislatures enact reforms just to abolish them or make significant revisions a few years later. Most states have adopted more than one type of sentencing reform, usually over a period of time, making it difficult to evaluate the impact of any single reform (Weisberg, 2007). Among states that have adopted similar reforms, there are substantial differences in how the reforms are structured and implemented (Stemen et al., 2005). Frase (2005a, p. 1191) commented that there is so much variation that "the approaches taken are as numerous as the jurisdictions adopting them." At times, the complexity has made it difficult to develop a cohesive national picture.

Structured Sentencing

Structured sentencing is perhaps the most significant approach to creating determinate sentencing. Proponents of structured sentencing maintain that it leads to more predictable and consistent sentencing, avoiding many of the problems critics had identified about indeterminate sentencing. According to Stemen and Rengifo (2011), between 1975 and 2004, 7 states adopted presumptive sentences and 22 states adopted either presumptive or voluntary guidelines. Presumptive sentences are enacted by state legislatures and provide a recommended prison term within the range of punishment detailed in the statute, based on the seriousness of the crime. Judges can legally depart from the statutorily mandated punishment only if they find aggravating or mitigating circumstances. In contrast, sentencing guidelines provide multiple recommended sentences within a system and a set of sentencing procedures the judge must follow to reach a sentencing decision. States with sentencing guidelines direct judicial discretion in determining the length of a prison term by proscribing either a fixed term or a narrow range of time within the broader sentencing range provided by the state's criminal statutes (Stemen et al., 2005). Sentencing decisions in guideline states are based on two factors: the seriousness of the offense and the offender's criminal history. There are, however, considerable variations among sentencing guideline jurisdictions. States differ in how they define and assign weight to an offender's criminal history. The sentencing ranges for offenses also vary, with some state guidelines having more distinct sentencing ranges than others (Frase, 2005a). Guidelines in 12 states and the federal system also regulate aspects of decisions about intermediate sanctions such as probation, house arrest, community service, and fines. Six states and the federal system have guidelines that include misdemeanor offenses (Frase, 2005a).

An important distinction among guideline states is how the guidelines are created and periodically revised. Minnesota was the first jurisdiction to enact guidelines that were developed by a permanent sentencing commission created by the legislature (Weisberg, 2007). In 1984, the U.S. Congress passed the Sentencing Reform Act, which created the U.S. Sentencing Commission, whose function was to develop sentencing guidelines for the federal system (ABA, 2004). Four guideline states do not have a permanent sentencing commission. In Alaska, the guidelines are written by the legislature (Frase, 2005a). In Florida, Michigan, Tennessee, and Wisconsin the guidelines were written by commissions that were eventually disbanded (Frase, 2005a; Tonry 2016).

The most critical difference among guideline states is how strictly the guidelines regulate judges. In 11 guideline states, they are presumptive, meaning judges are required by law to follow them or justify their reasons for departure on the record (Stemen and Rengifo, 2011). Depending on state statute or case law, some states with presumptive guidelines make it easy to seek appellate review of a judge's decision to depart, while others make it difficult to appeal a departure successfully (Frase, 2005a). In contrast, Utah, Maryland, Delaware, Virginia, Arkansas, Missouri, Wisconsin, and the District of Columbia enacted voluntary sentencing guidelines. The Ohio legislature revised the state's presumptive guidelines to be voluntary in 2006, and decisions by the Pennsylvania Supreme Court essentially revised the state's presumptive guidelines into voluntary guidelines (Tonry 2016). Voluntary guidelines are advisory; judges are encouraged to follow them but not legally required to do so. In some voluntary states, although judges are not required to adhere to the guidelines, they are required to explain a decision to depart from them. In Virginia, studies indicate judges generally comply with the guidelines, while in other voluntary states, compliance is uneven (Weisberg, 2007).

The federal sentencing guidelines were designed to be presumptive and severely limit sentencing discretion. For years they functioned in that manner despite mounting criticism that the loss of judicial discretion resulted in unduly harsh and unfair punishments. In its 2005 decision in *United States v. Booker*, the U.S. Supreme Court struck down provisions of the law requiring federal judges to impose sentences within the guideline range. The Court instructed federal judges to consider the guideline but to impose sentences based on factors that are broader than the factors covered by the guidelines. The federal guidelines are now effectively advisory (Weisberg, 2007).

Although 34 jurisdictions created sentencing commissions to evaluate the need for sentencing reform, not all commissions recommended guidelines (Barkow & O'Neill, 2006). Connecticut, Maine, Texas, Colorado, Nevada, and Montana considered but decided not to adopt the guidelines. Other commissions developed guidelines that were later rejected by the legislature (Barkow & O'Neill, 2006). Proposals to establish a sentencing commission in California have failed to make it through the legislative process (Weisberg, 2010).

Supporters of structured sentencing argue that it reduces the amount of discretion judges can exercise, making sentencing more fair and transparent. Structured systems, whether a product of guidelines or enacted by state statute, curtail opportunities for arbitrary sentencing decisions. Similarly situated convicted offenders are punished in a similar fashion (Reitz, 2001). Judges are not free to consider an offender's individual circumstances such as education and employment background, marital history, and medical and mental health (Stemen et al., 2005).

Abolishing Discretionary Parole Release

In 1976, Maine and California were the first states to abolish discretionary parole release (Stemen et al., 2005). Without discretionary parole, offenders are automatically released from prison after they serve the sentence imposed by the judge. That term can be reduced by earning good time if it is available under state law. Except for good time credits, the time served is determined by the length of the sentence imposed by a judge and not by a parole board's discretionary release decision. Between 1975 and 2003, 19 states abolished parole for most offenses, although two of those states reinstituted it for all offenses and one reinstated discretionary parole for first-time, nonviolent offenders (Stemen and Rengifo, 2011). Eleven sentencing guideline states, the District of Columbia, and the federal government have abolished discretionary parole release for all or most felons. When these 11 jurisdictions enacted guideline systems, abolishing parole was a major component of a reform package (Weisberg, 2007).

Long-Term Prison Sentences

During the tough on crime era that began in the late 1980s through the mid-1990s, every state in the country adopted severe sentencing laws. The laws varied from state to state, but they are primarily responsible for the massive buildup of our penal systems (Tonry, 2016a).

As of 2016, there were over 206,000 prisoners serving life sentences in U.S. prisons: 108,667 serving life with the possibility of parole (LWP); 53,290 serving life without the possibility of parole (LWOP); and 44,311 serving "virtual life" sentences of 50 years or more. In 2016, these three categories of inmates constituted 13.9% of the prison population: one in every seven prisoners (Nellis, 2017). The number of prisoners serving LWP sentences has quadrupled since 1984 (Ghandnoosh, 2017). In 1992, only 12,453 prisoners were serving LWOP sentences (Nellis, 2017). To put the increase in the population of lifers in historical perspective, until the 1970s, life sentences generally translated in most jurisdictions into 10 years and 6 months of incarceration (Gottschalk, (2013).

Nellis (2017) examined the crimes of conviction that result in life sentences, whether LWP, LWOP, or virtual. She found that 38% of prisoners serving life and virtual life sentences in the country's state prisons were convicted of first degree murder, 20.5% of second degree murder, and 33% of violent crimes other than murder. One in 12 lifers were sentenced for nonviolent crimes. In the Federal Bureau of Prisons, Nellis found that of the 1,517 prisoners serving LWP (117) and LWOP (1,400), two thirds were convicted of nonviolent crimes. Of the federal LWOP inmates, almost half were convicted of drug crimes. The explosion of life sentence statutes over the past few decades was fueled by the politics of the tough on crime movement, the War on Drugs, and opposition to the death penalty which often included support for LWOP as an alternative penalty (Gottschalk, 2013).

Ghandnoosh (2017) analyzed the stricter parole eligibility laws that have been enacted over the last three decades, making it much more difficult for LWP prisoners to parole. Many states have enacted laws that significantly delay parole eligibility for prisoners who are serving life with parole who committed violent offenses. Examples of these statutes include a Georgia law that increased the time lifers convicted of certain violent felonies need to serve before being parole eligible from 7 to 30 years and a Missouri law that increased the time lifers must serve before eligibility from 10 to 23 years. On average, LWP prisoners currently become eligible for parole after serving, on average, 25 years of their sentence (Nellis, 2017).

Further contributing to longer terms of incarceration are time-served requirements that were initially enacted in the 1984 Federal Sentencing Reform Act in which the U.S. Congress mandated that federal prisoners serve at least 85% of their sentence (Weisberg, 2007). Many states followed suit and enacted laws imposing specific time-served requirements for violent offenders. In 1994, Congress passed the Violent Crime Control and Law Enforcement Act that provided grant money to states to expand their prison capacity. In order to receive funding under the grant, states had to implement laws that required violent offenders to serve at least 85% of their sentence before being eligible for release. By 2002, 28 states had enacted truth in sentencing laws that qualified for federal funding (Stemen et al., 2005). As a result of the increased time-served requirements adopted across all jurisdictions, by 2002, offenders were required to serve an average of 93% of their sentence compared to serving an average of 70% in 1975 (Stemen et al., 2005).

Mandatory minimum sentencing statutes are another significant component of the trend toward longer terms of incarceration. At their most severe, they contribute to the increased use of life sentences. Some version of mandatory minimums has been enacted by all states and the federal government (ABA, 2004). They specify a minimum sentence a judge is required to impose on all convicted offenders who have committed crimes that a legislature determined deserves a mandatory minimum punishment. Although a judge can impose a sentence greater than the mandatory minimum, he or she has no discretion to impose a sentence below it, regardless of the circumstances surrounding the offense or the offender's prior criminal history. A parole board cannot release an offender serving a mandatory minimum sentence before the minimum sentence is completed. Sentencing commissions do not have the authority to revise sentences for mandatory minimum crimes (Reitz, 2001). Unlike sentencing schemes that attempt reform of an entire sentencing structure, mandatory minimums are determinate sentences that target specific crimes (Stemen et al., 2005).

Mandatory minimum sentences are not new to the criminal justice system, but not too long ago they were used sparingly. Before the push for determinate sentencing, in 1970 the U.S. Congress actually repealed federal mandatory minimum sentences that had been in enacted in the 1950s for drug crimes

(Weiman & Weiss, 2009). New York's Rockefeller Drug Laws, however, led the trend in the opposite direction in 1973, enacting severe mandatory sentences for drug offenses. Massachusetts's Bartley-Fox Amendment of 1974 requires a 1-year prison sentence for persons convicted of carrying an unlicensed firearm. In 1973, Michigan adopted a mandatory life sentence without parole for anyone delivering over 650 grams of cocaine or heroin (Weisberg, 2007). In 1977, Michigan enacted a mandatory 2-year prison term for possessing a firearm during the commission of a felony (Weisberg, 2007). Perhaps the most controversial mandatory minimum laws were the federal sentencing laws for cocaine crimes, which set a 5-year mandatory prison term for possession or sale of 5 grams of crack cocaine. In contrast, the law set a 5-year mandatory prison term for the sale of 500 grams of powder cocaine.

Many states have enacted mandatory minimum sentences that require 10-year, 20-year, or life sentences for violent, drug, and firearms offenses. Mandatory minimum sentences can be harsher than sentences for more serious violent or white collar crimes. They have been adopted by states with every type of sentencing structure: both determinate and indeterminate, sentencing commission guidelines states, and states that have rejected guidelines (Stemen et al., 2005). Mandatory minimum sentences have proven to be popular with the public and with legislators (Reitz, 2001; Tonry, 2007).

One of the most extreme cases of mandatory minimum sentences was California's three-strikes law, which, as it was enacted in 1994, required sentences from 25 years to life for any third felony, even a nonviolent felony (Zimring, Hawkins, & Kamin, 2001). Half of the states and the federal government have enacted some version of a three-strikes law since Washington state began the trend in 1993 (Blumstein, 2002). These laws impose lengthy prison sentences, sometimes life sentences, after a third conviction for a serious, generally violent, felony. In some jurisdictions, including California, a second serious felony conviction can also lead to a mandatory lengthy prison term (Zimring et al., 2001).

Summary of the Sentencing Revolution

Although there is a tremendous amount of variation, every jurisdiction in the country has moved toward reducing the use of discretion in the sentencing process. Some states adopted presumptive sentences and others, and the federal government adopted guidelines as a way to structure front end sentencing decisions, curtailing the use of judicial discretion. Every jurisdiction in the United States has adopted mandatory minimum sentences for certain categories of crimes. Many states currently impose severe mandatory penalties for two and three-strikes offenders, have harsh time-served requirements, or both.

There has been an explosion of life sentence statutes—LWP, LWOP, and virtual life sentences—that make it impossible or extremely difficult for prisoners to parole.

Discretion has also been curtailed on the back end of sentencing, parole release, and good time credit allowances. Some guideline states and the federal government have abolished discretionary parole release as a significant component of their sentencing reform initiatives. Like the federal system, several states impose severe restrictions on the amount of good time a prisoner can earn. In states that retain parole, discretionary parole release is limited by mandatory minimum sentences, mandatory two- and three-strikes sentences, and truth in sentencing statutes.

Despite a clear trend toward determinacy, many states continue to rely on indeterminate sentencing for some or many front end and back end sentencing decisions, so much so that according to Kevin Reitz (2001), indeterminate sentencing remains a dominant model used in the United States. As Tonry (2007) observed, since sentencing policies shifted in the 1970s, there is no coherent set of principles guiding sentencing. Every state, even those that continue to use some form of indeterminate sentencing, has adopted policies that cannot be reconciled with rehabilitative goals. There is currently a mix of indeterminate and determinate sentencing structures across the country, a mix that exists even within individual jurisdictions.

The Sentencing Sea Change Hits the Correctional System

Before the mid-1970s, the rate of incarceration in this country was relatively modest. The incarceration rate from 1933 to 1973 ranged from approximately 100 to 120 per 100,000 U.S. residents (Donohue, 2009). In 1980, the number of people incarcerated in state and federal prisons in the United States was 319,598 (Austin, 2010). By 2015, that number had climbed to 1,526,800, with an incarceration rate of 471 prisoners per 100,000 U.S. residents. The incarceration rate in 2015 for black adults was 1,745 per 100,000 U.S. residents; for Hispanic adults 860 per 100,000 U.S. residents; and for white adults 312 per 100,000 U.S. residents (Carson & Anderson, 2016).

Prisons are not the only sector of the correctional system that has experienced tremendous growth. According to Austin (2010), there was a 282% increase in the number of offenders on probation from 1980 to 2008, a 276% increase in parolees, and a 331% increase in the jail population. According to the Kaeble, & Glaze, (2015) 1 in every 37 adults in this country is under some form of correctional supervision, which includes persons incarcerated in federal and state prisons, local jails, and on probation and parole.

James Austin (2010) examined the relationship between rising crime rates and rising incarceration rates. The crime rate in the United States reached its peak by 1980. The following 10 to 15 years were marked by both increases and decreases, although there has been a steady decline in crime rates since 1994. Austin also documented a decline in arrest rates since the mid-1990s, with the exception of arrests for drug-related offenses. Between 1994 and 2004, however, the state prison population increased by 55%. The vast majority of experts agree that crime rates by themselves fail to explain the massive buildup in the correctional system since the mid-1970s (ABA, 2004). The growth of incarceration in the United States in the 1970s through 1980s was a response to rising crime rates. In the 1990s, however, crime rates began to fall, while rates of incarceration continued to rise. In the 2000s, crime rates stabilized at a low level, but incarceration rates reached their peak in 2007 (Tonry, 2016).

The Impact of Sentencing Reforms on Incarceration Rates

There is significant research exploring whether the sentencing reforms enacted over the past three decades explain the population growth in the U.S. correctional system. Although several factors influenced these tremendous increases, researchers agree that sentencing policies have had a substantial impact (Austin, 2010; Reitz, 2010). This consensus includes agreement that mandatory minimum sentences have played a significant role in the growth of America's prison population. Useem (2010) charts the impact the Rockefeller Drug Laws had on the number of drug offenders in New York's prisons. In 1980, New York incarcerated under 2,000 drug offenders, 9% of the prison population. By 1996, there were 23,500 drug offenders, 34% of the prison population. Penalties under the Rockefeller Drug Laws were eventually reduced in 1994, and by 2008, the drug offender population had fallen to 20% of the prison population. Piehl, Useem, and DiIulio (1999) conducted a cost/benefit analysis of incarceration policies in New York, New Mexico, and Arizona and concluded that mandatory minimum drug laws increased the prison population without increasing public safety. In their review of California's sentencing policies, Vitiello and Kelso (2004) concluded the research shows the state's three-strikes laws did not reduce crime and added to the prison population. Sorenson and Stemen (2002) explored the relationship between state sentencing policies and incarceration rates, concluding that states with three-strikes laws do not admit more violent offenders than states without such laws, but they do admit more drug offenders under these laws. In his speech before the ABA in 2003, Justice Kennedy rejected both the necessity and the wisdom of federal mandatory minimum sentences (ABA, 2004). The Justice Kennedy Commission recommended an end to mandatory minimum sentences in both the federal and state systems (ABA, 2004).

Research studies are mixed on whether abolishing discretionary parole release has increased the size of state prison populations. Kevin Reitz (2006) argued in favor of abolishing parole by noting that as of the end of 2004, 8 of the 10 states with the highest imprisonment rates retained discretionary parole release. Stemen et al.'s (2005) study found states that have combined abolishing discretionary parole with policies to control the costs of incarceration have been able to reduce growth.

Research looking at the impact of structured sentencing is also mixed. North Carolina is an example of a state where the legislature enacted a successful presumptive guideline scheme with the specific goal of reducing prison overcrowding. Prior to its guidelines, the state imprisoned 48% of convicted felons. After the guidelines, it has incarcerated between 28% and 34 % of convicted felons. Lower level property and drug offenders who are incarcerated serve less time than they did prior to the guidelines. The state has also diverted prison funds to develop more community sanction programs (Vitielo & Kelso, 2004). In contrast, one study looked at a determinate sentencing state that enacted guidelines but where prison growth has not been constrained. Bales, Gaes, Blomberg, and Pate (2010) analyzed the factors contributing to Florida's growing prison population over the last three decades. Their findings suggested that Florida's shift toward determinate sentencing with sentencing guidelines, abolishing parole, and requiring prisoners to serve 85% of their sentence was not responsible for the tremendous increase in state prisoners. Rather, the growth can be explained by the increase in the number of felony convictions, which, they determined, are proportionate to the rise in the state's population.

Using state-level data from 1978–2004, Stemen and Rengifo (2011) analyzed the impact on imprisonment rates of presumptive sentences, presumptive sentencing guidelines, voluntary guidelines, and abolishing parole along with several political and socioeconomic variables. Their findings showed that abolishing discretionary parole release alone can lower incarceration rates, regardless of the state's sentencing polices on the front end. They also found that presumptive sentencing and sentencing guidelines do not reduce incarceration rates if they are not combined with abolishing discretionary parole. Voluntary guidelines, even in states that abolished discretionary release, do not impact incarceration rates. Most importantly, their final model found that combining presumptive guidelines with abolishing parole has the most significant impact on lowering incarceration rates. Stemen and Rengifo (2011) examined data from across jurisdictions and compared the impact of several different sentencing models and their interactions on incarceration rates. They found that presumptive sentencing guidelines combined with ending discretionary parole release have helped control growth.

Concerning time-served statutes, Stemen et al. (2005) found that increasing the amount of prison time offenders must serve before they are eligible for release does not always lead to higher incarceration rates—if they apply to all incarcerated offenders. This is especially the case for states with presumptive sentencing guidelines and mandatory parole release. However, their research indicated that states with higher time-served requirements targeted to only violent offenders do have higher incarceration rates than other states. Spelman (2009) warned, however, although truth in sentencing laws have little immediate effect on incarceration rates, they have a substantial long-term impact. By increasing the length of incarceration, they reduce the number of prisoners released in future years. Their impact will occur after prisoners who are serving time under the old sentencing statutes are replaced by prisoners serving under truth in sentencing laws.

The Future of Sentencing Policy

Weisberg (2007) and Gottschalk (2006) believed that the time was, and still is, ripe for major changes in sentencing policy. States are crushed under the economic costs associated with incarceration. Legislatures have had to close prisons and lay off correctional staff. Because of the financial crisis, it is no longer political suicide for elected officials to promote reduced prison sentences and alternatives to incarceration. Rehabilitation is making a comeback, according to Tonry (2016). The success of drug courts and encouraging research about rehabilitation programs has led to the creation of other problem-solving courts. Tonry sees an emerging paradigm of restorative, community, and therapeutic justice gaining public support, undermining the shift toward punitive sentencing that has marked the last 30 years.

Many states have revised their sentencing laws. Some of those revisions have involved high profile and especially controversial statutes. New York reduced the severity of the Rockefeller Drug Laws in 2004 and again in 2009 (Useem, 2010). Michigan reduced its mandatory life sentence for possession of 650 grams of cocaine or heroin, a reform supported by the same governor who championed the mandatory life sentence in 1978 (Gottschalk, 2006). In 2012, California voters approved Proposition 36 that reformed the state's three-strikes law by restricting the felonies that could trigger the third strike to violent or serious crimes (Gottschalk, 2013). After abolishing discretionary parole in 1976, California enacted laws in 2016 that now allow parole for offenders who committed certain designated violent offenses. In 2010, the U.S. Congress passed the Fair Sentencing Act that reduced the disparity between the amount of crack cocaine and powder cocaine needed to trigger federal sentencing laws from a weight ratio of 100:1 to 18:1. Congress also eliminated the 5-year mandatory minimum sentence for possession of crack cocaine. The original 100:1 ratio and the 5-year minimum sentence were both enacted by the U.S. Congress in the Anti-Drug Abuse Act of 1986 (Tonry, 2016).

Sentencing reforms are not limited to only the high profile statutes that catch national attention. For example, Indiana, Louisiana, and Connecticut reduced sentences for certain drug crimes (Weisberg, 2007). Arizona, California, Michigan, and Ohio passed laws that divert drug offenders into treatment as opposed to prison (Gottschalk, 2006). In 2015, Maryland, Oklahoma, and North Dakota enacted laws that allow judges to depart from mandatory minimum sentences, and Connecticut reduced penalties for certain drug crimes. In 2016, Alaska expanded alternatives to incarceration, reduced jail time for misdemeanors, reclassified drug possession a misdemeanor, reduced presumptive sentencing ranges for some felonies, and expanded eligibility for discretionary parole. Delaware increased the number of convictions for certain offenses in order for an offender to be classified as habitual. Florida and Iowa restricted their mandatory minimum laws for certain offenses (The Sentencing Project, 2016).

The momentum for sentencing reform has been aided by the Justice Reinvestment Initiative, a partnership launched in 2006 involving the U.S. Bureau of Justice Assistance, Pew Charitable Trusts, the Council of State Governments Justice Center, the Crime and Justice Institute at Community Resources for Justice, and the Vera Institute of Justice, among other organizations. As of 2016, 27 states have participated in the initiative and have implemented reforms in their correctional systems and sentencing laws to reduce the use of incarceration in their jurisdictions. Participating states work with criminal justice experts and stakeholder groups to develop and implement evidence-based policies and practices to reduce the state's correctional population. The reforms vary across states, but the goals are the same: improve public safety, control costs, use prison space for serious and repeat offenders, and develop effective alternatives to incarceration for less serious offenders (Bureau of Justice Assistance, 2017).

In light of these developments, what does the future hold for sentencing in the United States? In 2007, Robert Weisberg described a "contemporary consensus on sentencing law," which espouses a moderately flexible set of presumptive guidelines enacted by a sentencing commission as the best sentencing model (p. 179). He believes this model is supported by most sentencing scholars and public officials. His claim is supported by the American Law Institute's (ALI) Model Penal Code: Sentencing project. The ALI is an organization composed of distinguished lawyers, judges, and professors producing influential work designed to modernize different areas of law, including the Model Penal Code (Reitz, 2009). The ALI Sentencing project makes several important recommendations, including the use of presumptive sentencing guidelines developed by state sentencing commissions that allow judges to depart for reasons that would be subject to appellate review (Reitz, 2009). Weisberg's claim is also supported by of the Justice Kennedy Commission (ABA, 2004), which recommended the creation of commissions to provide guidelines to judges making sentencing decisions. Recent empirical research supports the adoption of presumptive guidelines as a way to reduce prison growth, especially if they are combined with abolishing discretionary release (Stemen and Rengifo, 2011; Tonry, 2016).

Weisberg (2007) and his supporters championed guidelines created by commissions because sentencing commissions can fine tune sentencing rules in ways that legislatures cannot. Commission members are more insulated from political demagoguery than legislators and can make the tough and unpopular decisions with less fear of being replaced. Members can be appointed who can bring specific areas of expertise and experience to the process (ABA, 2004).

The current consensus favoring presumptive guidelines has not ignored concerns that restricting judicial discretion can lead to unfair and disproportionate sentences. After several decades of experience with limited discretion, some jurisdictions are exploring ways to increase the flexibility of presumptive sentences. Virginia created a risk assessment instrument to select 25% of the lowest risk drug and property offenders bound for prison for placement instead in nonprison community programs. Courts use the risk assessment instrument only for offenders who, under the sentencing guidelines, would be incarcerated. Low scoring offenders are recommended for nonprison alternative programs. Judges have the discretion to sentence offenders to prison under the guidelines or impose an alternative sanction (Kern & Farrar-Owens, 2004).

In 2005, Missouri adopted revisions to the state's voluntary guidelines that provide judges, defense attorneys, and prosecutors information about the offense (past sentencing practices and the commission's sentencing recommendations) and the offender (a risk factor score measuring the risk of recidivism based on prior criminal history, age, substance abuse history, education, and employment status at time of sentencing). Information is also provided about the parole board's release guidelines along with a management plan detailing how best to meet the offender's needs whether in prison or in the community.

There are studies indicating that guidelines help reduce racial sentencing disparities, although other studies indicate they have little or no impact (Engen, 2009; Tonry, 2007; Weisberg, 2007). Efforts to incorporate predictive risk and need assessment into presumptive guidelines attempt to reduce disparity but have not always been successful. According to the ABA's Justice Kennedy Commission (2004), disparities in sentencing are difficult to reduce because police and prosecutors exercise discretion at the arrest, charging, and plea bargaining stages. Limiting judicial discretion strengthens the discretion exercised by other actors in the criminal justice system, especially prosecutors (Engen, 2009; Richman, 2006). In many cases, judicial discretion is necessary to temper overzealous or arbitrary decisions made by law enforcement and prosecutors. Sentencing guidelines and mandatory minimum sentences make it difficult or impossible for judges to serve that function. Added to the shift in discretion are mandatory sentencing laws that appear race neutral but disproportionately impact minority offenders, such as the federal crack cocaine laws and laws that enhance penalties for drug crimes committed near schools and public housing (Mauer, 2007). Flexible presumptive sentencing guidelines that permit judges to consider factors in addition to offense severity and an offender's criminal record structure individualized sentencing decisions. Importantly, judges decide sentences according to factors that are the product of evidence-based research specific to that state. Using risk assessment to predict recidivism may be new to front end sentencing, but it is used by many state parole boards to guide conditional release decisions (Bergstrom & Mistick, 2010; Reitz, 2010; Tonry 2016).

Conclusion

This chapter focuses on research related to a few of the critical areas related to sentencing policy. Other important sentencing policies also impact the size of a state's prison population. For example, a 2007 study showed Texas's burgeoning prison population did not result from an increase in the state population or crime rates; it resulted from low parole grant rates, lack of in-prison and community treatment programs, and an increase in probation revocations. Texas embarked on reforms, including reducing the length of probation terms for property and drug offenders, grants to expand community sanctions for probation violators, and drug and specialty courts to divert offenders from prison (Fabelo, 2010). James Austin's (2010) research indicates that several key sentencing reforms would significantly impact the size of prison, jail, probation, and parole populations: reduce, overall, the length of prison terms, not limited to only abolishing mandatory minimums and time-served laws; divert technical parole and probation violators and victimless crime offenders from prison; reduce the length of probation and parole terms; reduce probationer and parolee revocation rates; and increase the use of fines and community service. The good and bad news is there are many opportunities to address the problems Justice Kennedy identified in 2003. If a particular policy reform is not feasible politically, there may be other ways to address a problem (Weisberg, 2010). What is central to all good policy development, however, is reliance on evidence-based research in design and implementation.

References

American Bar Association. (2004). *American Bar Association Justice Kennedy commission report with recommendations to the ABA House of Delegates.* Retrieved from http://www.abanet.org/crimjust/kennedy/JusticeKennedy CommissionReportsFinal.pdf.

Austin, J. (2010). Reducing America's correctional populations: A strategic plan. *Justice Research and Policy, 12*(1), 9–40.

Bales, W. D., Gaes, G. G., Blomberg, T. G., & Pate, K. N. (2010). An assessment of the development and outcomes of determinate sentencing in Florida. *Justice Research and Policy, 12*(1), 41–71.

Barkow, R. E., & O'Neill, K. M. (2010). Delegating punitive power: The political economy of sentencing commission and guideline regulation. *Texas Law Review, 84,* 1973–2022.

Bergstrom, M. H., & Mistick, J. S. (2010). Danger and opportunity: Making public safety job one in Pennsylvania's indeterminate sentencing system. *Justice Research and Policy, 12*(1), 73–88.

Blumstein, A. (2002). Prisons: A policy challenge. In J.Q. Wilson & J. Petersilia (Eds.), *Crime: Public policies for crime control* (pp. 451–482). Oakland, CA: Institute of Contemporary Studies Press.

Bureau of Justice Assistance (2017). *Justice Reinvestment Initiative.* Retrieved from https://www.bja.gov/programs/justicereinvestment/index.html.

Carson, E., & Anderson, E. (2016). *Prisoners in 2015.* Bureau of Justice Statistics. Retrieved on November 30, 2017 from https://www.bjs.gov/content/pub/pdf/p15.pdf.

Donohue, J. J. III. (2009). Assessing the relative benefits of incarceration: Overall changes and the benefits on the margin. In S. Raphael & M.A.

Stoll (Eds.), *Do prisons make us safer?: The benefits and costs of the prison boom* (pp. 269–341). New York, NY: Russell Sage Foundation.

Engen, R. L. (2009). Assessing determinate and presumptive sentencing: Making research relevant. *Criminology, 8*(2), 323–336.

Fabelo, T. (2010). Texas justice reinvestment: Be more like Texas? *Justice Research and Policy, 12*(1), 113–131.

Frankel, M. E. (1973). *Criminal sentences: Law without order.* New York, NY: Hill and Wang.

Frase, R. S. (2005a). State sentencing guidelines: Diversity, consensus, and unresolved policy issues. *Columbia Law Review, 105*(4), 1190–1232.

Frase, R. S. (2005b). Punishment purposes. *Stanford Law Review, 58*(1), 67–84.

Ghandnoosh, N. (2017). *Delaying a second chance: The declining prospects for parole on life sentences.* The Sentencing Project. Retrieved from http://www.sentencingproject.org/publications/delaying-second-chance-declining-prospects-parole-life-sentences/.

Gottschalk, M. (2006). Dismantling the carceral state: The future of penal policy reform. *Texas Law Review, 84*(7), 1693–1749.

Gottschalk, M. (2013). Sentenced to life: Penal reform and the most severe sanctions. *Annual Review of Law and Social Science, 9*, 353–382.

Kaeble, D & Glaze, L. (2015). *Correctional Populations in the United States, 2015.* Washington, DC: Bureau of Justice Statistics (2015). Retrieved on August 29, 2018 from https://www.bjs.gov/index.cfm?ty=pbdetail&iid=5870.

Kern, R. P., & Farrar-Owens, M. (2004). Sentencing guidelines with integrated offender risk assessment. *Federal Sentencing Reporter, 16*(3), 165–169.

Irwin, J. (1980). *Prisons in Turmoil.* Little, Brown and Company: Boston.

Martinson, R. (1974). What works? Questions and answers about prison reform. *Public Interest 35*(2), 22–54.

Mauer, M. (2007). Racial impact statements as a means of reducing unwarranted sentencing disparities. *Ohio State Journal of Criminal Law, 5*(1), 19–46.

National Research Council (2014). *The growth of incarceration in the United States: Exploring causes and consequences.* Retrieved on November 30, 2016 from http://doi.org/10.17226/18613.

Nellis, A. (2017). *Still life: America's increasing use of life and long-term sentences.* The Sentencing Project. Retrieved from http://www.sentencingproject.org/wp-content/uploads/2017/05/Still-Life.pdf.

Piehl, A. M., Useem, B., DiIulio, J. J. (1999). *Right-sizing justice: A cost-benefit analysis of imprisonment in three states.* Manhattan Institute for Policy Research. Retrieved December 17, 2010 from http://www.manhattan-institute.org/html/cr_8.htm.

Reitz, K. R. (2001). The disassembly and reassembly of U.S. sentencing practices. In M. Tonry & R.S. Frase (Eds.), *Sentencing and sanctions in western countries* (pp. 222–258). New York, NY: Oxford University Press.

Reitz, K. R. (2006). Don't blame determinacy: U.S. incarceration growth has been driven by other forces. *Texas Law Review, 84*(7), 1787–1802.

Reitz, K. R. (2009). Demographic impact statements, O'Connor's warning, and the mysteries of prison release: Topics from a sentencing reform agenda. *Florida Law Review, 61*(4), 683–707.

Reitz, K. R. (2010). Brandeis's laboratories of sentencing and corrections: Making better use of knowledge from the states. *Justice Research and Policy, 12*(1), 169–189.

Richman, D. (2006). Institutional coordination and sentencing reform. *Texas Law Review, 84*(7), 2055–2074.

Sorenson, J., & Stemen, D. (2002). The effect of state sentencing polices on incarceration rates. *Crime and Delinquency, 48*(3), 456–475.

Spelman, W. (2009). Crime, cash, and limited options: Explaining the prison boom. *Criminology and Public Policy, 8*, 29–77.

Stemen, D., Rengifo, A. F., & Wilson, J. (2005). *Of fragmentation and ferment: The impact of state sentencing policies on Incarceration Rates, 1975–2002.* National Criminal Justice Reference Service. Retrieved December 5, 2010 from http://www.vera.org/download?file=415/Of%2BFragmentation%2Band%2BFerment.pdf

Stemen, D., & Rengifo, A. F. (2011). Policies and imprisonment: The impact of structured sentencing and determinate sentencing on state incarceration rates, 1978–2004. *Justice Quarterly, 28*(1), 174–199.

The Sentencing Project (2016). *Policy Brief: State advances in criminal justice reform, 2016.* Retrieved on November 30, 2017 from http://www.sentencingproject.org/wp-content/uploads/2017/01/State-Advances-in-Criminal--Justice-Reform-2016-1.pdf

Tonry, M. (2007). Looking back to see the future of punishment in America. *Social Research, 74*(2), 353–378.

Tonry, M. (2016). *Sentencing fragments: Penal reform in America, 1975–2025.* New York, NY: Oxford University Press.

Useem, B. (2010). Right-sizing corrections in New York. *Justice Research and Policy, 12*(1), 89–112.

Vitiello, M., & Kelso, C. (2004). A proposal for a wholesale reform of California's sentencing practice and policy. *Loyola of Los Angeles Law Review, 38*(2), 903–966.

Weiman, D. F., & Weiss, C. (2009). The origins of mass incarceration in New York: The Rockefeller drug laws and the local war on drugs. In S. Raphael

& M.A. Stoll (Eds.), *Do prisons make us safer?: The benefits and costs of the prison boom* (pp. 73–116). New York, NY: Russell Sage Foundation.

Weisberg, R. (2007). How sentencing commissions turned out to be a good idea. *Berkeley Journal of Criminal Law, 12*(1), 179–230.

Weisberg, R. (2010). The not-so-Golden State of sentencing and corrections: California lessons for the nation. *Justice Research and Policy, 12*(1), 133–168.

Zimring, F. E., Hawkins, G., & Kamin, S. (2001). *Punishment and democracy: Three strikes and you're out in California.* New York, NY: Oxford University Press.

Cases Cited

United States v. Booker, 543 U.S. 220 (2005)

Chapter 6

Solitary Confinement

Scott Chenault and Benecia Carmack

Introduction

Solitary confinement has been part of the correctional system since its inception. The use of it goes back to the Auburn and Pennsylvania systems in the 19th century. The various reasons for its use include disciplinary segregation, administrative segregation, and protective custody. What is common to all systems of solitary confinement is the isolation the inmate feels once placed in these settings: limited time outside the cell, small amounts of interaction with others, and deprivation of sunlight, reading materials, or recreation. Inmates are placed in solitary confinement voluntarily or involuntarily. The use extends from felons awaiting capital punishment to pretrial detention, from violent offenders to juveniles, from inmates suffering from mental illness to gang affiliation. One can find solitary confinement in jails, prisons, military facilities, juvenile justice, and immigration detention facilities.

Common conditions to most of these facilities include one, sometimes two, persons to a cell, five hours a week of out-of-cell exercise alone in a small enclosed yard, cells with small or no windows, limited or no telephone access or social visits, limited reading materials, meals passed through doors, and possibly some programming activities, all of which may be eliminated as discipline if necessary. Nothing the prisoner does is private; everything is monitored (Ross, 2007). Isolation is the core component to solitary confinement.

Most believe the purpose of solitary confinement is for punishment or housing of dangerous and violent offenders, both of which increase the security of the institutions. The use of solitary confinement is broader than that. Its use is often for relatively minor infractions and disciplinary purposes (Shames, Wilcox, & Subramanian, 2015). Its use can also include protective custody for populations with mental illness, developmental disability, very young or old age groups, former members of gangs or law enforcement, sexually vulnerable or gender nonconforming inmates, use for medical treatment, or temporary confinement for victims of abuse in general populations (Shames et al., 2015).

At the end of 2015, the United States had 1,526,800 prisoners in custody within the state and federal prison systems (Carson & Anderson, 2016). In June 2016, the U.S. Department of Justice (DOJ) found that of the 148,227 inmates in the Federal Bureau of Prisons (BOP), 9,749 inmates, or 7%, were in some form of restricted housing (U.S. DOJ, 2017). Though estimates of inmates held in state solitary confinement on any given day are impossible to determine, the Vera Institute of Justice estimates it ranges from 5%–8% of total prisoners (Shames et al., 2015). That equates to a total of between 76,000 and 122,000 inmates held in solitary confinement.

Although solitary confinement in broad terms has always been present in corrections, the "tough on crime" era of criminal justice expanded the use of this technique and significantly altered its duration. Long-term solitary confinement practice goes by several names: restrictive housing, segregated housing, special or intensive management, special housing units, security housing, inmate segregation, and special management units. Regardless of the official terminology, the method represents a glaring example of failed correctional policy. The remainder of this chapter will examine the history of extended solitary confinement, its prevalence, the significant issues associated with it, the reasons we believe it is a failed policy, and a look forward at possible solutions.

Overview of Terms

There are almost as many reasons for the use of such confinement as there are terms for it. Probably the most commonly recognized use of solitary confinement is for disciplinary or punitive segregation. This is the use of solitary confinement when rules are broken within the prison system.

Another use is for administrative purposes. These are for purposes other than disciplinary and are used when someone is thought to be a threat to the facility and should be removed from the general population. This is most common among members of gangs who have been put in administrative solitary confinement for indefinite periods of time (Shames et al., 2015). The BOP defines this as nonpunitive, but necessary, for the "safety, security, and orderly operation of correctional facility, or protect the public" (Inmate Discipline and Special Housing Units, 2010). Other examples of this type of confinement can include new inmates pending classification or under review for reclassification, holdover status during transfer to a designated institution, and removal from general population because the inmate posed a threat to life, property, self, staff, or others (Inmate Discipline and Special Housing Units, 2010).

Another form of solitary confinement is protective custody. This segregation protects individual inmates thought to be at risk of harm in the general population. The inmates in most need of protection are "mentally ill, intellectually disabled, gay, transgender, or former law enforcement officers" (Shames et al., 2015, p.4). The BOP uses administrative detention for protection cases. Inmates in administrative detention as a protection case can include victims of inmate assault or threats, inmate informants, inmates refusing to enter general population because of alleged pressure or threats, or staff concerns (Inmate Discipline and Special Housing Units, 2010).

Facilities can also use solitary confinement for a short-term temporary basis when investigating an incident or during transfer situations (Shames et al., 2015). Table 1 developed by Minor and Parson provides a snapshot of the general differences between the three primary forms of solitary confinement used in American corrections (Minor & Parson, 2015), though the use of each of these and their terms by the various jurisdictions can overlap (Metcalf et al., 2013).

Any state or federal facility can use solitary confinement in the above-mentioned manner. However, there are specific facilities or wings of institutions built for the long-term total isolation of inmates for institutional security, commonly called supermax facilities. About two thirds of the states have their own version of a supermax facility. The federal government operates the U.S. Penitentiary Administrative Maximum Facility (ADX) in Florence, Colorado. An examination of supermax facilities, policies, issues, problems, and solutions follows.

Historical Development of Solitary

Solitary confinement has been around as long as American prisons have existed. Its use was meant for rehabilitation and to encourage offenders to repent for their sins (Hinds & Butler, 2015). The Pennsylvania model, which centered on the Quaker concept of the penitentiary, had solitary confinement as its defining characteristic. Quakers believed that through solitude, offenders would become repentant of their crimes and change their ways upon release (Morris & Rothman, 1995). Even the Auburn model, which is often referred to as the congregate system, initially confined offenders to one-person cells. Although America quickly moved away from the use of single-person cells (largely due to financial concerns), the use of isolation as a punishment became a staple of prison systems.

Table 1. Three Primary Forms of Solitary Corrections

Question	Disciplinary Segregation	Administrative Segregation	Protective Custody
Who typically assigns the prisoner to segregation?	A standing disciplinary committee or hearing officer	An ad hoc committee or single official	A standing classification committee
What is the process?	Formal hearing with some procedural protections (i.e., presentation of a defense) focused on the specific action, outcome is a deter-mination of guilt	Informal hearing or discussion often without the offender present; focus on general concerns, outcome is a finding of likelihood of what might occur if segregation is not imposed	Offenders may request PC placement, or officials may recommend the status, but offenders typically can waive the status
What is the length of segregation?	Definite or set period	Indefinite period	Indefinite period
Where is the prisoner segregated?	The disciplinary segregation unit "the hole"	Any of several secure units or facilities (i.e., supermax)	A separate protective custody unit, within the large segregation unit
Why is the prisoner segregated?	As punishment for a specific rule violation, which the offender admitted to or was proven guilty of	To disrupt or prevent an ongoing or potential security threat	For protection against victimization

(Minor & Parson, 2015).

Charles Dickens (1913) described solitary confinement after a visit to Cherry Hill in 1842:

> I believe that very few men are capable of estimating the immense amount of torture and agony which this dreadful punishment, prolonged for years, inflicts upon the sufferers; and in guessing at it myself, and in reasoning from what I have seen written upon their faces, and what to my certain knowledge they feel within, I am only the more convinced

that there is a depth of terrible endurance in it which none but the sufferers themselves can fathom, and which no man has a right to inflict upon his fellow creature. I hold this slow and daily tampering with the mysteries of the brain, to be immeasurably worse than any torture of the body: and because its ghastly signs and tokens are not so palpable to the eye and sense of touch as scars upon the flesh; because its wounds are not upon the surface, and it extorts few cries that human ears can hear; therefore I the more denounce it, as a secret punishment which slumbering humanity is not roused up to stay (p. 81).

Throughout the first half of the 20th century, nearly every prison in the country had a solitary confinement unit. These units were viewed as a "prison within prison" and were used as short-term punishment for recalcitrant offenders. The conditions in these units were stark, as described by Donald Clemmer (1940) in his landmark research:

> The 24 solitary cells are in a small building known as the yard office. It is set off by itself and is heavily barred and isolated. The cells themselves contain no furniture. The one window is small, and the iron bars of the door have another wooden door which keeps the light from entering. The cells are cold in winter and hot in summer. The inmate is given one blanket and must sleep on a wooden slab raised about two inches from the cement flooring. One piece of bread and a necessary amount of water is allowed each day.

Although some solitary units (such as Southern prison camp "hot boxes" or the dungeons found in several other prisons) were physically brutal, the punitive emphasis was primarily psychological (Irwin, 2005). Using the typology outlined above, solitary units during this period would be classified as disciplinary segregation. Although psychologically harmful, these units were used almost exclusively for short-term confinement as punishment for a specific infraction. In addition to solitary confinement in the form of disciplinary segregation, segregating offenders as a means of protective custody also emerged in the 1960s (Minor & Parson, 2015).

Throughout the 1970s and 1980s, the BOP and several large states had issues with increased violence within segregation units. Disciplinary segregation concentrated violent offenders but did not seem to deter them from their behavior. In 1973, the BOP created a control unit for troublesome offenders at the maximum security prison in Marion, Illinois (Irwin, 2005). In 1983, the federal maximum security prison in Marion, Illinois, experienced an inordinate amount of violence, culminating in the death of two correctional officers on the same day (Irwin, 2005). As a result, correctional officials pushed for new facilities specifically designed to hold "the worst of the worst" offenders. Arizona opened the first such supermax facility in 1986 (Lynch, 2010) and was quickly followed by California and other states (Reiter, 2012). These new facilities were developed to facilitate long-term total isolation of offenders. After 30 years of embracing the supermax model, there are now between 25 and 60 such facilities in the United States (Reiter, 2012). However, there has now been 30 years of research and data concerning the impact of long-term solitary confinement as a correctional management strategy. The chapter now turns to a review of long-term solitary confinement as correctional policy.

Solitary Confinement as Policy

Supermax prisons can be a specially designed institution, wing, or building connected to another institution. Supermax prisons are prisons for solitary confinement. Life in a supermax facility, in its most restrictive form, includes single-cell occupancy, meals received through thick metal doors, inmates shackled and escorted by two officers, limited privileges, exercise five hours a week alone in an enclosed room, limited personal items, and limited visitation. "Supermax prisons, once a novelty, have become common. In 1984, the U.S. Penitentiary in Marion, Illinois, was the only supermax prison in the country. By 1999, 34 states and the federal system had supermax prisons" (National Research Council, 2014, p.185). In 1983, a federal facility in Marion, Illinois, became a supermax institution after the fatal stabbing of two correctional officers by inmates that initiated a 23-hour-a-day lockdown (Ross, 2007). The ADX in Florence, Colorado, opened in November, 1994, and is also known as the Alcatraz of the Rockies (Ross, 2007). As of 2006, 40 states have at least 57 supermax facilities, and the BOP reports an increase of 17% in the use of solitary confinement between 2008 and 2013 (Church, 2014).

Supermax facilities grew out of incidents like the one in Marion. They also grew from the conservative political ideology coming from the Reagan Administration in the 1980s, continuing with George H.W. Bush into the 1990s (Ross, 2007). A change in punishment goals from rehabilitation to retribution helped to increase their numbers. This was also a period when the crime rate was rising. Politicians were elected by promising they are tough on crime, so legislation such as truth in sentencing, mandatory minimums, harsh sentencing guidelines, three-strikes laws, and determinant sentencing were all part of this ideology (Ross, 2007).

These facilities were originally built for the most dangerous, escape-prone, nothing-to-lose criminals. What we have seen in our recent history is the use of these facilities for persistent rule breakers, mafia and gang members, serial killers, and terrorists (Ross, 2007). Many of the inmates within supermax facilities are known for the events placing them there: the Oklahoma City bombing, the Unabomber, the 9/11 hijacking, the 1993 World Trade Center bombing, the American Airlines shoe bomber, the Centennial Olympic Park bombing, and other events.

Costs

Supermax facilities are expensive to build and operate. It is often estimated that the cost of building and operating solitary confinement units or a supermax prison is three times that of other facilities. Part of the operation cost is from the increased staff required to supervise the inmates at these facilities. The Urban Institute estimated the cost per cell of supermax prisons is three times as high as a cell in nonsupermax prisons (Ross, 2017). Costs of operating these facilities is one of the reasons states are reexamining their very existence. A recent report of the American Civil Liberties Union announced the closing of Tamms "Supermax" Correctional Center in Illinois (Fettig, 2013). The Illinois Department of Corrections cited one of the reasons for "closure is because it is by far the most expensive facility to operate" (Fettig, 2013). Fettig (2013) also mentioned other states were coming to the same conclusion regarding operational costs of supermax and solitary confinement:

- The Maine Department of Corrections cut its "supermax" population by over 50% and provided prisoners expanded access to programming and social stimulation.
- Over the last few years, Mississippi reduced the "supermax" population of one institution from 1000 to 150 and eventually closed the entire unit.
- In the last year, Colorado reduced the number of prisoners in solitary confinement by 36.9% and recently announced the closure of a 316-bed "supermax" facility, which is projected to save the state $4.5 million in Fiscal Year 2012–13 and $13.6 million in Fiscal Year 2013–14 (para. 6).

Violence

Most people believe the use of solitary confinement is limited to the worst of the worst, the most violent of inmates. The public thinks its use maintains prison safety for inmates, correctional officers, and visitors. In a May 2015 Vera Institute of Justice report, "Solitary Confinement: Common Misconceptions and Emerging Safe Alternatives," Shames et al. (2015) stated a sixth misconception that segregated housing helps keep prisons and jails safer. Shames et al. noted that there is very little evidence to suggest that the use of isolation increases prison safety. There is some evidence that solitary confinement may result in increased violence in prisons because the "distress of living and working in this environment actually causes violence between staff and prisoners" (Gordon, 2014, p. 515). Gordon also notes that in a study by Mears and Bales (2009) when nonsupermax and supermax prisoners were matched, there was not a statistical significance between the two groups regarding disciplinary records. The same study found that assignment to solitary confinement somewhat arbitrary, meaning those in isolation may not be the most violent prisoners.

Gordon (2014) also cited studies from Briggs et al. (2003), stating opening of supermax prisons did not decrease the amount of inmate-on-inmate violence. Prisoner-on-correctional staff violence does not seem to be affected by solitary confinement either (Gordon, 2014; Briggs et al., 2003). States implementing recent reforms to their solitary confinement policies, like allowing more socialization and time out of cell and lowering their solitary confinement populations, have not noticed an increase in violence and in some cases have seen violence reduced, as discussed below.

Mental Illness

Inmates are often placed in solitary confinement for rule breaking, and mentally ill inmates are especially susceptible to this. Placing mentally ill inmates in solitary confinement may not change their rule-breaking behavior. Mentally ill inmates are also assigned to solitary confinement for nondisciplinary reasons, including the safety of others and self. Once in solitary confinement, for whatever reason, the conditions are the same as if for a disciplinary reason (Hinds & Butler, 2015).

Prisons and jails dealing with the increased number of mentally ill inmates use solitary confinement as a way to control the inmate, ensure safety of the prison population and the mentally ill inmate, maintain order within the facility, and control the environment. As the statements below warn, the mental health of a healthy inmate can deteriorate within these conditions, and the mentally ill inmate can suffer deterioration of their condition, if not a complete breakdown. "Behavior that stems from mental illness is often used as a justification to place convicts with mental illness in the SHU [Security Housing Unit]" (Arrigo & Bullock, 2008, p. 628). To compound the problem, there are often limited resources to psychiatric services once in solitary confinement (Arrigo & Bullock, 2008). This has not gone unnoticed by the courts: "Texas' administrative segregation units are virtual incubators of psychoses-seeding illness in otherwise healthy inmates and exacerbating illness in those already suffering from mental infirmities" (*Ruiz v. Johnson*, 1999, p. 907).

A significantly high portion of inmates within solitary confinement already suffer from severe mental health problems, which was found in the SHU at Pelican Bay (*Madrid v. Gomez*, 1995). Inmates often suffer from confusion and impaired concentration, hallucination, paranoid episodes, depression and anxiety, problems with impulse control that can lead to violent reactions, self-mutilation, lethargy, and suicidal tendencies (Smith, 2006). The general health of inmates in solitary confinement can deteriorate rapidly.

Other concerns include the health, both physical and mental, of the inmate within these units or prisons. The Bureau of Justice Statistics reported one in seven state and federal prisoners and one in four jail inmates meet the threshold for serious psychological distress (Bronson & Berzofsky, 2017). Common physical complaints by inmates are severe headaches, heart palpitations, oversensitivity to stimuli, abdominal and muscle pains, digestive problems, diarrhea, weight loss, dizziness, and fainting (Smith, 2006). Death row inmates have also been known to "volunteer" or waive all appeals so their execution may proceed; one explanation for this is the time spent in solitary confinement (Rountree, 2014). The mental health of inmates is even more critical once they experience solitary confinement.

Half of the inmates in California's Pelican Bay State Prison are in general population, and the other half are in the SHU. Haney (1993), through interviews with inmates of the SHU, documented that [l]ong-term confinement under these conditions has several predictable psychological consequences" (p. 5). Haney noticed they lose the ability to conduct limit setting or initiate behavior of any kind, and a small of amount of freedom creates great discomfort. Haney (1993) also noted that profound despair and hopelessness is created, social withdrawal is increased (in fact, they become frightened of social contact), unreality sets in, and they start to live in a world of fantasy and experience intolerable levels of frustration. "This kind of environment is capable of creating clinical syndromes in even healthy personalities, and can be psychologically destructive for anyone who enters and endures it for significant periods of time" (Haney, 1993, p. 6). Arrigo and Bullock (2008) reviewed numerous studies on the psychological effect of solitary confinement and noted that Grassian (1983) and Kupers (1999) identified a condition known as SHU syndrome, "characterized by perceptual changes; affective disturbance; difficulty with thinking, concentration, and memory; disturbance of thought content; and problems with impulse control" (p. 628).

After noting the rise in jail and prison populations, prisoners with mental illness, and the increased use of prolonged solitary confinement, the American Psychiatric Association also promulgated the following statement in 2012:

> Prolonged segregation of adult inmates with serious mental illness, with rare exceptions, should be avoided due to the potential for harm to such inmates. If an inmate with serious mental illness is placed in segregation, out-of-cell structured therapeutic activities (i.e., mental health/psychiatric treatment) in appropriate programming space and adequate unstructured out-of-cell time should be permitted. Correctional mental health authorities should work closely with administrative custody staff to maximize access to clinically indicated programming and recreation for these individuals.

The July 2017 "Review of the Federal Bureau of Prisons' Use of Restrictive Housing for Inmates with Mental Illness" found the following:

- BOP policies do not adequately address the confinement of inmates with mental illness in Restricted Housing Units (RHUs), and the BOP does not sufficiently track or monitor such inmates.
- Mental health staff do not always document inmates' mental disorders, leaving the BOP unable to accurately determine the number of inmates with mental illness and ensure that it is providing appropriate care to them.
- Since the BOP adopted its new mental health policy, BOP data shows a 30 percent reduction in the number of inmates who receive regular mental health treatment.
- While the BOP has taken recent steps to mitigate mental health concerns for inmates in RHUs, additional actions can be taken (U.S. DOJ, 2017).

Because of the results found in this review, the BOP listed 15 recommendations for improvement when placing mentally ill prisoners in an RHU, which are discussed in the Future Considerations section.

Numerous studies show the harmful effects of solitary confinement on both healthy and mentally ill inmates. Smith (2006) noted some studies suggest inmates recover when solitary confinement is terminated (Grassian, 1983; Andersen et al., 1994; Kupers, 1999). In contrast, Smith (2006) lists other studies revealing the possibility of serious effects after the inmate is released from solitary confinement (Martel, 1999; Kock, 1982; Jorgensen, 1981). Some inmates experience social disablement and negative effects long after release from solitary confinement (Smith, 2006). These serious effects might quite possibly be the exact type of behaviors that would send them back to solitary confinement.

Civil Rights

Courts can review individual cases and decide if the specific practices meet or violate constitutional principles and rights. The holdings in these cases are usually narrow and written to address the specific concerns and facts of a given case. While this may be useful for the state and prison system involved in the case and potentially helpful to other states looking at their own correctional department policies, it doesn't usually provide for systemic change. There is an argument that structural change of solitary confinement is best accomplished through the executive and legislative branches of our governments (Hinds & Butler, 2015). We saw the beginning of an executive action for change with the January 2016 report ordered by President Barack Obama to review the government's use of restrictive housing. It produced over 50 guiding principles as best practices for all correctional institutions and is fully discussed below (U.S. DOJ, 2016).

A number of cases held prisoners still have rights within prison, as *Wolff v. McDonnell* (1974, p. 555–556) stated, "There is no iron curtain drawn between the Constitution and the prisons of this country." In *Wolff v. McDonnell*, the Supreme Court listed rights the Court has recognized, such as religious freedom, access to courts, equal protection, and due process, but also noting that these rights were subject to restrictions by the very nature of the prisoner's confinement (1974). Even though rights may be granted to prisoners, it's important to keep in mind the U.S. Supreme Court has stated that "the Constitution does not mandate comfortable prisons, and prisons … which house persons convicted of serious crimes, cannot be free of discomfort" (*Rhodes v. Chapman*, 1981, p. 349).

The federal courts are mindful of the difficult decisions made by prison officials in the operation and management of their facilities. Noting this in *Cruz v. Beto* (1972),

> Federal courts sit not to supervise prisons but to enforce the constitutional rights of all "persons," including prisoners. We are not unmindful that prison officials must be accorded latitude in the administration of prison affairs, and that prisoners necessarily are subject to appropriate rules and regulations. But persons in prison, like other individuals, have the right to petition the Government for redress of grievances (p. 321).

When the Eighth Amendment was written, the main form of punishment was public displays, and prisons were barely in existence (Hinds & Butler, 2015). Though inmates' rights may be restricted, they are not immune from the protections of the Eighth Amendment, as "Confinement in a prison or in an isolation cell is a form of punishment subject to scrutiny under Eighth Amendment standards" (*Hutto v. Finney*, 1978). In *Hudson v. McMillian* (1992), Justice Harry

Blackmun's concurring opinion was that the unnecessary pain prohibited by the Eighth Amendment could include psychological as well as physical pain.

To challenge under the Eighth Amendment, *Wilson v. Seiter* (1991) established a two-prong test to determine whether prison-related punishments are cruel and unusual. First, the objective component requires conditions to be sufficiently serious and pose a substantial risk of serious harm. The Court uses the rational basis test for this determination: "under this test, even if a prison regulation is found to infringe on an inmate's rights it is still valid if it bears a rational relationship to the legitimate governmental interest put forward to justify it" (Lyon & Cunningham, 2005, p. 12; *Turner v. Safley*, 1987). Next, the subjective component requires showing that prison officials were deliberately indifferent and knew of and disregarded harm to prisoners. *Farmer v. Brennan* (1994, p. 828) defined prison official's "deliberate indifference" by requiring that it be shown that the official was subjectively aware of the risk or something similar to criminal law recklessness.

The U.S. District Court for the Southern District of Texas case has held that the conditions of isolation violated the Eighth Amendment:

> The extreme deprivations and repressive conditions of confinement of Texas' administrative segregation units, however, have been found to violate the Constitution of the United States' prohibition against cruel and unusual punishment, both as to the plaintiff class generally and to the subclass of mentally ill inmates housed in such confinement (*Ruiz v. Johnson*, 1999, p. 861).

Eighth Amendment challenges have been brought against solitary confinement. One example is *Madrid v. Gomez* (1995), a Pelican Bay State Prison class action lawsuit involving the early existence of its SHU. The prison opened October of 1989 and was promoted by the governor of California as a model prison for the rest of the nation and the first supermax prison built solely for segregation (Hinds & Bulter, 2015, p. 334). The prisoners at Pelican Bay were held in solitary confinement for an average of 7.5 years; 89 had been there for at least 20 years, and one inmate had been there for 42 years (Church, 2014). The conditions at Pelican Bay were extremely harsh and isolative, even in comparison to other supermax facilities (Cockrell, 2012). The problems here included access to physicians, cruelty of guards, and deficient mental health treatment (Cockrell, 2012). The Court in *Madrid v. Gomez* held the following regarding healthy inmates:

> While a risk of a more serious injury is not non-existent, we are not persuaded, on the present record and given all the circumstances, that

the risk of developing an injury to mental health of sufficiently serious magnitude due to current conditions in the SHU is high enough for the SHU population as a whole, to find that current conditions in the SHU are per se violative of the Eighth Amendment with respect to all potential inmates (1995, p. 1265).

But with regard to mentally ill prison inmates the Court held the following:

We cannot, however, say the same for certain categories of inmates: those who the record demonstrates are at a particularly high risk for suffering very serious or severe injury to their mental health, including overt paranoia, psychotic breaks with reality, or massive exacerbations of existing mental illness as a result of the conditions in the SHU. Such inmates consist of the already mentally ill, as well as persons with borderline personality disorders, brain damage or mental retardation, impulse-ridden personalities, or a history of prior psychiatric problems or chronic depression. For these inmates, placing them in the SHU is the mental equivalent of putting an asthmatic in a place with little air to breathe. The risk is high enough, and the consequences serious enough, that we have no hesitancy in finding that the risk is plainly "unreasonable." (*Madrid v. Gomez*, 1995, p. 1265)

Injunctive relief was ordered to remedy the constitutional violations found in the lawsuit, but the Court did not find that prolonged isolation for nonvulnerable inmates violated the Eighth Amendment (*Madrid v. Gomez*, 1995).

Another class action lawsuit against Pelican Bay's SHU filed in 2012, *Ashker v. Governor of California*, alleged California Department of Corrections and Rehabilitation violated the due process clause of the Fourteenth Amendment and Eighth Amendment by placing, housing, managing, and retaining inmates designated as prison gang members and associates in the SHU. The settlement reached on September 1, 2015, reduces current and future solitary confinement with a review of all current gang-validated SHU inmates; ends solitary confinement for prisoners who have not violated rules meaning a change from status-based to a behavior-based system; caps the length of time a prisoner can be in solitary confinement; provides a step-down program for return to general population; provides a restrictive, but not isolating, alternative for prisoners who continue to violate rules with the creation of a new Restricted Custody General Population Unit (RCGP); and allows more out-of-cell time for prolonged solitary confinement inmates (Center for Constitutional Rights, 2015).

The U.S. Supreme Court considered the constitutionality of long-term solitary confinement in *Wilkinson v. Austin* (2005) that involved the Ohio state prison system and their classification of prisoners for placement in its supermax facility, the Ohio State Penitentiary (OSP). The OSP is extreme isolation in its most restrictive form of incarceration, more restrictive than the state's death row. Ultimately the Court held that Ohio's procedures provided sufficient protection to comply with the due process requirements of the Constitution. A classification review occurs upon entry to the prison or during incarceration, and with each step in the process a review occurs and notice is provided to the inmate. The inmate has an opportunity to attend the hearing or provide a written statement, and at any stage in the proceeding it can be determined that OSP is not recommended and the process stops (*Wilkinson v. Austin*, 2005). The Court held because of the duration and the fact that placement disqualifies an inmate for parole consideration, the inmates have a liberty interest in avoiding OSP. Once a liberty interest is established, the Court then considers what process is due the inmate. The policy established by Ohio provides a sufficient level of process for the inmate (*Wilkinson v. Austin*, 2005).

Though solitary confinement has not been squarely on issue in front of the Court, Justice Anthony Kennedy did make his thoughts known in *Davis v. Ayala* (2015) in a concurring opinion. The case was in front of the Court for a Batson challenge issue. Justice Kennedy wrote his opinion only to address death penalty defendant Hector Ayala and his more than 25 years of solitary confinement. Justice Kennedy not only cited previous cases but also quoted Charles Dickens, John Howard, Fyodor Dostoyevsky, Amnesty International, and several studies to make the point that it may be time for the Court to consider this type of lengthy segregated incarceration and the effects on prisoners. Justice Kennedy said, "There are indications of a new and growing awareness in the broader public of the subject of corrections and of solitary confinement in particular" (*Davis v. Ayala*, 2015, p. 2210). It is also not unheard of for the death row inmate to "volunteer" to waive all appeals and allow the execution to proceed or consider or commit suicide.

The most recent case is *Ruiz v. Texas* (2017). The Court denied a stay of execution of a death row inmate; however, Justice Stephen Breyer wrote a dissenting opinion stating the Court should consider the issue of if extended solitary confinement, in this case 22 years, violates the Eighth Amendment. Justice Breyer wrote that Ruiz had developed "anxiety and depression, suicidal thoughts, hallucinations, disorientation, memory loss and sleep difficulty," all common symptoms of solitary confinement (*Ruiz v. Texas*, 2017, p. 1247). This recently occurred again in *Smith v. Ryan* (2017) when Justice Breyer, denying the writ of certiorari, stated that Smith had been awaiting execution for 40 years, with most of those in solitary confinement. In his short opinion, he restated quotes from *In re Medley*, *Davis v. Ayala*, and *Glossip v. Gross*, urging the Court to consider the underlying constitutional question of capital punishment in an appropriate case.

Future Considerations

Recent policy debates focus on solitary confinement, with its sensory deprivation and social isolation, as torture (Hinds & Butler, 2015). In February 2010, the American Bar Association (ABA) approved the "ABA Standards for Criminal Justice: Treatment of Prisoners." The 83 standards were created with thoughtful consideration on both sides of the issue and are relied upon by judges, attorneys, legislatures, and governments (Marcus, 2009). As stated by Schlanger (2010), the standards use the Constitution, statutes and regulations, court decisions, and settlement negotiations between the U.S. DOJ to give the current state of the law and are consistent with good professional practices. These standards are discussed below.

"In 2015, the United Nations General Assembly, with US support, adopted the Mandela Rules, under which no person should be held in solitary confinement for more than 15 days" (Todrys, 2017). The new provisions define and restrict the use of solitary confinement to use as a last resort and only in exceptional circumstances; the rules also prohibit the reduction of food or water as punishment, indefinite or prolonged solitary confinement, and placement of prisoner in a dark or constantly lit cell (United Nations Office on Drugs and Crime, 2017). The above shows the state of the discussion internationally regarding solitary confinement but provides no mandates to American correctional policy.

The January 2016 report ordered by President Obama conducted a review of the government's use of restrictive housing and produced over 50 guiding principles as best practices for all correctional institutions (U.S. DOJ, 2016). Drawing from this report and other research, best practices for future use of solitary confinement have been developed in four key areas: duration of confinement, review of placement in segregation, adjustment in conditions of confinement, and provision of a transition program.

Duration of Solitary Confinement

The first clear takeaway from virtually every review of solitary confinement is the need to limit the duration. Although indeterminate segregation is currently common in the United States, research is clear that a relatively short and determinate time period is preferential. The May 2015 report from the Vera

Institute of Justice, "Solitary Confinement: Common Misconceptions and Emerging Safe Alternatives," found that the federal government and 19 states were allowed to hold inmates indefinitely in solitary confinement (Shames et al., 2015). The report proved to corrections officials that inmates were held in segregated housing for months, years, and decades. This information led officials in many states to change policies. The state of Washington changed the amount of days held in administrative segregation from 60 to 47 days without approval from a deputy director (Shames et al., 2015). Noting other states, Colorado and Pennsylvania now provide a multidisciplinary committee review, and Pennsylvania allows for release after completion of one half of the sanction (Shames et al., 2015). Arrigo and Bullock's (2008) recommendations for improvement specify placement as limited and emphasize that inmates should never be placed in a SHU setting for an indefinite period of time.

Days in Placement Before Review

When inmates are placed in restrictive housing pending an investigation of a disciplinary offense, the guiding principles from the 2016 U.S. DOJ report suggest a review within 24 hours, and time spent in investigative detention should be credited to the term determined for the disciplinary segregation. The suggestions also include ongoing regular review of those in restrictive housing.

ABA Standard 23-2.9(b) also states within 30 days of placement the authorities develop an individualized plan with an "assessment of the prisoner's needs, strategy for correctional authorities to assist the prison in meeting those needs, and statement of the expectations for the prisoner to progress toward fewer restrictions and lower levels of custody based on the prisoner's behavior" (ABA, 2010). It is recommended that the assessment be explained to the prisoner with a review of this plan every 30 days. Standard 23-2.9(f) goes on to state that correctional officials should facilitate the return of the prisoner to lower level security and should avoid releasing an inmate in segregated housing directly into the community (ABA, 2010).

Yale Law School's Arthur Liman Program joined with the Association of State Correctional Administrators to review 47 state and federal jurisdictions' administrative segregation and found some jurisdictions provide notice to inmates regarding reasons for segregation and an opportunity for a hearing, though the kind of notice and hearing vary greatly. Some jurisdictions mentioned no hearings at all (Metcalf et al., 2013). All policies provide for a review, but again in varying forms, and the decision-makers vary from warden, central office, committees, staff, or unit level supervisors. There was great variance on the presentation of evidence, assistance, or representation for the inmate as well as any review or appeal (Metcalf et al., 2013). Hinds and Butler (2017) also suggest that appropriately trained staff should review each case to determine if continued segregation is necessary once a week for the duration of the confinement.

The criteria for inmates remaining in segregation and returning to general population were even less defined, and this was suggested as a topic for further research (Metcalf et al., 2013). Best practices state a periodic review once an inmate is placed in segregation and once again, Metcalf et al. (2013) found this varied from seven days or less to six months or more.

Conditions of Confinement

The conditions of confinement also vary among jurisdictions. This can include issues, such as access to programs or visitors, which could eventually help the inmates return to general population. Arrigo and Bullock (2008) give five recommendations for improvements to life in an SHU, including an increased opportunity for social interactions and allowing for "congregate activity, such as dining, exercise, educational programming, or religious services, with other prisoners" (Arrigo & Bullock, 2008, p. 636). Hinds and Butler (2017) also suggest eliminating the use of extreme isolation, instead segregating dangerous prisoners only to the extent necessary without restricting access to social and sensory stimulation.

The 2016 U.S. DOJ report suggests increasing the minimal time allowed outside of the cell and to "include opportunities for recreation, education, clinically appropriate treatment therapies, skill-building and social interaction with staff and other inmates" (U.S. DOJ, 2016, p. 99). Other recommendations include increasing out-of-cell time as numbers of restricted housing inmates decrease, providing confidential psychological services, eliminating barriers to treatment, maintaining adequate environmental safety, and removing the practice of denying food and water as punishment. Arrigo and Bullock (2008) recommended that the SHU be clean, well ventilated and exposed to natural light and that the inmate have control of their cell's artificial light, access to personal belongings and reading materials, and sufficient space to exercise (Arrigo & Bullock, 2008).

Step-Down Programs

Of particular importance is the end-of-term placement guiding principles. Many inmates experience problems when returning to the general population after leaving solitary confinement. Even greater harm can occur when an inmate is released from solitary confinement into the community. The 2016 U.S. DOJ report states that absent any compelling reason, the inmate should not be placed directly into the community from restrictive housing (U.S. DOJ, 2016). Also, during the last 180 days of their term, restrictive housing should not be used, and if necessary, the facility should provide a targeted reentry program for the inmate to return to the community (U.S. DOJ, 2016). The Vera report (Shames et al., 2015) noted research is mixed, but one study has shown higher recidivism rates of those supermax participants released directly to the community as compared with participants that had three months between supermax and prison release (Lovell, Johnson, & Cain, 2007).

ABA Standard 23-8.9 addresses transition to the community. Standard 23-8.9(b) states the following:

> In the months prior to anticipated release of a sentenced prisoner confined for more than 6 months, correctional authorities should develop an individualized re-entry plan for the prisoner, which should take into account the individualized programming plan developed pursuant to Standard 23-8.2(b). In developing the re-entry plan, correctional authorities should involve any agency with supervisory authority over the prisoner in the community and, with the prisoner's permission, should invite involvement by the prisoner's family. Preparation for re-entry should include assistance in locating housing, identifying and finding job opportunities, developing a resume and learning interviewing skills, debt counseling, and developing or resuming healthy family relationships. (ABA, 2010)

Exiting segregation not only varied by jurisdiction but also was often undefined (Metcalf et al., 2013). Specific states have provided step-down programs within their reforms, and these are discussed below. Step-down programs created by prison officials and physicians, especially mental health providers, can offer additional opportunities for inmates to spend more time out of their cell and be resocialized with the general prison population (Hinds & Butler, 2017). These programs should be completed while serving in solitary confinement. If inmates are nearing the end of their sentences while in solitary confinement, a prerelease or resocialization program should be used to reintroduce the inmate to general population prior to release in the community (Hinds & Butler, 2017).

State Reforms

In states' recent past, the use of solitary confinement grew, often for governments to appear to be tough on crime. With this overuse, states realize that the consequences to prisoners can include lasting mental health and behavioral issues. In response, states have begun to implement changes to their policies and practices based on the best practice research reviewed above. Below is a limited review of some of the positive changes occurring nationwide.

In December 2015, New York State committed to reducing solitary, limiting the length of stay, and increasing rehabilitation (New York Civil Liberties Union, 2015). New York also committed to requiring de-escalation training for personnel, restricting the circumstances when solitary can be imposed, instilling maximum sentences of 30 days for first-time nonviolent offenders, allowing early release with good behavior and access to telephone and reading materials, abolishing the use of inedible food, and establishing a monitoring system to ensure compliance with the settlement from a lawsuit brought by the New York Civil Liberties Union (NYCLU) (NYCLU, 2015). Finally, as of January 1, 2016, the New York Department of Corrections banned the use of segregated housing of all in custody 21 years and younger (Vera Institute of Justice, 2017).

Due to a class action lawsuit, California began implementing the following changes to segregation in January of 2016: sending gang-validated prisoners to the SHU only if found guilty after a hearing on a rule violation and not simply because of their status as a gang member; allowing, after placement in SHU, gang affiliates to enter a 2-year (instead of a 4-year) step-down program to return to general population; reviewing all current gang-validated SHU prisoners within one year to determine release to general population; allowing prisoners to be immediately released to general population if prisoners have spent more than 10 years in solitary; creating a new RCGP as an alternative to solitary allowing more out-of-cell time, allowing contact visits, access to educational courses, small group recreation, leisure activities, programming, job opportunities, and phone calls; and limiting prolonged solitary confinement and increasing increased out-of-cell time for those in solitary (Center for Constitutional Rights, 2015).

Colorado has implemented changes such as lowering the total number of inmates in solitary confinement, eliminating the placement of inmates with mental illness, using an incentive system instead of solitary confinement, and preventing release from solitary directly to the community (Hinds & Butler, 2017). Colorado requires that inmates held in its Management Control Unit receive four hours of time outside their cell each day, and inmates spend 180 days in a transition unit prior to release to general population or the community (Shames et al., 2015).

Mississippi has made changes to solitary confinement including increasing time for social engagement by allowing inmates to spend multiple hours outside their cells daily, adding a basketball court and communal dining, and implementing a system of allowing prisoners to work their way toward more privileges (Church, 2014). Because of the prison reforms, violence has decreased, behavior has improved, the number of offenders in solitary confinement has declined, and the ultimate result, Unit 32 (a supermax unit) has closed, saving the state over $5 million (Church, 2014).

In addition to these general changes to segregation, step-down incentive programs have started in a number of states to provide increasing privileges like more time out of cell, group activities, television, and additional reading materials. These programs provide a structured course for leaving solitary confinement and help to reduce the number of inmates serving time in these conditions. Commonly called "Step-Down Programs," they are also known as "Intensive Management Programs" or "Behavioral Management Programs." These programs set goals for the inmate to successfully complete before returning to general population (Metcalf et al., 2013). Some states, such as Pennsylvania, Washington, and New Mexico, created specialized step-down programs for gang members (Shames et al., 2015). Other states are creating programs that allow segregated inmates to participate in group activities and therapy (Metcalf et al., 2013). Individualized plans created by prison officials and physicians can include increased out-of-cell opportunities while in solitary confinement to help the inmate resocialize with other inmates and the general population (Hinds & Butler, 2017). Step-down programs can now be found in Washington, Michigan, Virginia, Connecticut, and Missouri, among others.

Conclusion

"Over 150 years ago, Dostoyevsky wrote, 'The degree of civilization in a society can be judged by entering its prisons.' There is truth to this in our own time" (*Ayala v. Davis*, 2017, p. 2210). We do seem to be in a time of thoughtful review of the policies and procedures involving solitary confinement. Between the United Nations adoptions of the Mandela Rules, the guiding principles from the report ordered by President Obama, the ABA Criminal Justice standards, and dicta from recent U.S. Supreme Court cases, voices of thoughtful and humane experts are challenging us to rethink the purposes and uses of solitary confinement. There is a concern about training staff, providing medical and mental health treatment, and reintegration programs for the inmate transitioning back to general population.

The original purposes of solitary confinement—decreasing violence, segregating challenging mentally ill inmates, disciplining for rule breaking— are still in use today. The detrimental behaviors leading to placement in solitary confinement now seem to intensify instead of diminish once an inmate is placed there for even short periods of time. The flawed policy is that instead of solving problems, such as violence, rule breaking, and mental illness, solitary confinement is creating new problems and exacerbating existing ones.

Existing reforms have decreased the amount of prisoners and the time spent in solitary confinement. Certain types of inmates, such as mentally ill individuals and juveniles, have been excluded from further solitary confinement sentences in some jurisdictions. Those inmates in solitary confinement now have expressed reasons for their placement, systematic review of their placement, noted ways to lessen their stay, and step-down programs for reintegration. While in solitary confinement many find the conditions less restrictive than previously encountered, with more program opportunities, recreation, and chances to socialize with general populations. With the reforms proposed and enacted by states, the harmful effects of solitary confinement may attenuate, both physically and mentally, and entering our prisons now and in the future may show the degree of our current civilization, a more enlightened and compassionate one.

Appendix A
Office of the Inspector General
U.S. Department of Justice

Review of the Federal Bureau of Prisons' Use of Restrictive Housing for Inmates with Mental Illness
Evaluation and Inspections Division 17-05, July 2017
Available: https://oig.justice.gov/reports/2017/e1705.pdf
Recommendations

To ensure that inmates, including those with mental illness, are placed in restrictive housing under conditions of confinement that adhere to specific standards that are applied consistently and sustain appropriate mental health care, we recommend that the BOP:

1. Establish in policy the circumstances that warrant the placement of inmates in single-cell confinement while maintaining institutional and inmate safety and security and ensuring appropriate, meaningful human contact and out-of-cell opportunities to mitigate mental health concerns.
2. Define and establish in policy extended placement in measurable terms. To ensure that inmates receive appropriate mental health care and are

sufficiently tracked and monitored during their placement in restrictive housing, we recommend that the BOP:

3. Track all inmates in single-cell confinement and monitor, as appropriate, the cumulative amount of time that inmates with mental illness spend in restrictive housing, including single-cell confinement.

4. Identify all forms of restrictive housing utilized throughout its institutions and ensure that all local policies are updated to reflect standards for all inmates in restrictive housing consistent with established nationwide policies.

5. Evaluate and limit as appropriate the consecutive amount of time that inmates with serious mental illness may spend in restrictive housing.

6. Ensure that the Psychology Services staff documents inmates' mental illness diagnoses in the Bureau's Electronic Medical Record System and Psychology Data System.

7. Reassess the Mental Health Care Level system to ensure that it fully captures the mental health needs of inmates, including inmates in restrictive housing, and that classifications distinguish between inmates who have some form of mental illness and those who do not have any form of mental illness.

8. Regularly monitor, by institution and type of Restrictive Housing Unit, trends in inmates' designated Mental Health Care Levels to further assess the factors that affect the treatment of inmates with mental illness.

9. Determine what additional steps can be taken to prioritize and incentivize the hiring of mental health staff at institutions that have inmates with mental illness in long-term restrictive housing.

To improve the BOP's efforts to mitigate the placement of inmates with mental illness in traditional RHUs and enhance the effectiveness of secure residential mental health treatment programs, we recommend that the BOP:

10. Assess the scalability of secure residential mental health treatment programs and develop alternatives to address their potential limitations.

11. Develop and implement formal performance metrics sufficient to measure the effectiveness of secure residential mental health treatment programs.

12. Survey institutions and/or take other steps to identify alternative practices that reduce the frequency and duration of the placement of inmates with mental illness in restrictive housing, and implement such alternatives when appropriate.

13. Provide additional mental health training to correctional staff who are responsible for monitoring the behavior of inmates in restrictive housing.
14. Provide additional guidance and training to mental health staff on diagnosing mental illness, including guidance on documenting malingering behavior by inmates.

To address concerns regarding inmates with mental illness at USP Lewisburg's SMU, we recommend that the BOP:

15. Conduct a comprehensive review of U.S. Penitentiary Lewisburg's Special Management Unit that addresses the staffing, treatment, conditions of confinement, and performance metrics of the program.

References

American Psychiatric Association, (2012). *Position statement on segregation of prisoners with mental illness.* Retrieved from https://www.psychiatry.org/file%20library/about-apa/organization-documents-policies/policies/position-2012-prisoners-segregation.pdf.

American Bar Association. (2010). *ABA Standards for Criminal Justice: Treatment of Prisoners.* Retrieved from https://www.americanbar.org/publications/criminal_justice_section_archive/crimjust_standards_treatmentprisoners.html.

Andersen, H., Steen, T. Lillebæk, D. S., & Gorm, G. (1994). Isolationsundersøgelsen. Varetœgtsfængsling og psykisk helbred. Vols. 1–2. Copenhagen: Schultz.

Arrigo, B. A., & Bullock, J. L. (2008). The psychological effects of solitary confinement on prisoners in supermax units. *International Journal of Offender Therapy and Comparative Criminology, 52*(6), 622–640.

Briggs, C. S., Sundt, J. L., & Castellano, T. C. (2003). The effect of supermaximum security prisons on aggregate levels of institutional violence*. *Criminology, 41*(4), 1341–1376. Retrieved from https://login.cyrano.ucmo.edu/login?url=https://search-proquest-com.cyrano.ucmo.edu/docview/220703988?accountid=6143.

Bronson, J. & Berzofsky, M. (2017). *Indicators of mental health problems reported by prisoners and jail inmates, 2011–2012.* Bureau of Justice Statistics. Retrieved from https://www.bjs.gov/index.cfm?ty=pbdetail&iid=5946.

Carson, A. E., & Anderson, E. (2016). *Prisoners in 2015.* Bureau of Justice Statistics. Retrieved from https://www.bjs.gov/content/pub/pdf/p15.pdf.

Center for Constitutional Rights. (2015). *Summary of Ashker v. Governor of California: Settlement Terms.* Retrieved September 26, 2017 from https://ccrjustice.org/sites/default/files/attach/2015/08/2015-09-01-Ashker-settlement-summary.pdf.

Church, S. H. (2014). The depth of endurance: A critical look at prolonged solitary confinement in light of the Constitution and a call to reform. *Kentucky Law Journal, 103,* 639–656.

Clemmer, D. (1940). *The prison community.* New York, NY: Holt, Rinehart, and Winston.

Cockrell, J. F. (2012). Solitary confinement: The law today and the way forward. *Law and Psychology Review, 37,* 211–227.

Dickens, C. (1913) *American notes.* Mineloa, NY: Dover Publications, Inc.

Fettig, A. (2013). *Tamms "Supermax" prison, with its inhumane and ridiculously expensive solitary confinement practices, is officially a thing of the past!* American Civil Liberties Union. Retrieved from https://www.aclu.org/blog/mass-incarceration/tamms-supermax-prison-its-inhumane-and-ridiculously-expensive-solitary.

Gordon, S. E. (2014). Solitary confinement, public safety, and recidivism. *University of Michigan Journal of Law Reform, 47,* 495–527.

Grassian, S. (1983). Psychopathological effects of solitary confinement. American Journal of Psychiatry, 140(11), 1450–1454.

Haney, C. (1993). "Infamous punishment": The psychological consequences of isolation. *National Prison Project Journal, 8*(2), 3–7.

Hinds, M., & Butler, J. (2015). Solitary confinement: Can the courts get inmates out of the hole? *Stanford Journal of Civil Rights and Civil Liberties, 11*(2), 331–372.

Irwin, J. (2005). *The warehouse prison: Disposal of the new dangerous class.* Los Angeles, CA: Roxbury Press.

Jørgensen, F. (1981). "De psykiske følger af isolation." Ugeskrift for Lœger 143:3346–47.

Koch, I.E. (1982). "Isolationens psykiske og sociale følgevirkninger." Ma°-nedsskrift for Praktisk Lœgegerning 60(June):369–32.

Kupers, T. (1999). Prison madness: The mental health crisis behind bars and what we must do about it. San Francisco: Jossey-Bass.

Lovell, D., Johnson, L. C., & Cain, K. C. (2007). Recidivism of supermax prisoners in Washington State. *Crime and Delinquency, 53*(4), 633–656.

Lynch, M. (2010). *Sunbelt justice.* Stanford, CA: Stanford University Press.

Lyon, A., & Cunningham, M. D. (2005). "Reason not the need": Does the lack of compelling state interest in maintaining a separate death row make it unlawful? *American Journal of Criminal Law, 33,* 1–30.

Marcus, M., (2009). The making of the ABA criminal justice standards: Forty years of excellence. *American Bar Association Criminal Justice, 23*(4), 10–15.

Martel, J. (1999). Solitude and Cold Storage: Women's Journeys of Endurance in Segregation. Edmonton, Canada: ACI Communication.

Mears, D.P. & Bales, W. D. (2009). Supermax incarceration and recidivism. *Criminology, 47*(4), 1131–1166.

Metcalf, H., Morgan, J., Oliker-Friedland, S., Resnik, J., Spiegel, J., Tae, H., Work, A., & Holbrook, B. (2013). *Administrative segregation, degrees of isolation, and incarceration: A national overview of state and federal correctional policies* (Unpublished working paper). Yale Law School.

Minor, K., & Parson, S. (2015). Protective Custody. In P. Carlson (Ed.), *Prison and Jail Administration: Practice and Theory* (3rd ed.). Burlington, MA: Jones & Bartlett.

Morris, N., & Rothman, D. (1995). *The Oxford history of the prison.* New York, NY: Oxford University Press.

National Research Council. (2014). *The growth of incarceration in the United States: Exploring causes and consequences.* Washington, DC: National Academies Press.

New York Civil Liberties Union. (2015). *Historic settlement overhauls solitary confinement in Liberties Union Press Release.* Retrieved September 12, 2017 from https://www.nyclu.org/en/press-releases/historic-settlement-overhauls-solitary-confinement-new-york.

Reiter, K. (2012). Parole, snitch, or die: California's supermax prisons and prisoners, 1997–2007. *Punishment & Society, 14*(5), 530–563.

Ross, J. I. (2007). Supermax prisons. *Society, 44*(3), 60–64.

Rountree, M. M. (2014). Volunteers for execution: Directions for further research into grief, culpability, and legal structures. *UMKC Law Review, 82,* 295–333.

Schlanger, M. (2010). Regulating segregation: The contribution of the ABA criminal justice standards on the treatment of prisoners. *American Criminal Law Review, 47,* 1421–1440.

Shames, A., Wilcox, J., & Subramanian, R. (2015). *Solitary confinement: Common misconceptions and emerging safe alternatives.* Vera Institute of Justice. Retrieved from https://www.vera.org/publications/solitary-confinement-common-misconceptions-and-emerging-safe-alternatives.

Smith, P. S. (2006). The effects of solitary confinement on prison inmates: A brief history and review of the literature. *Crime and Justice, 34,* 441–528.

Todrys, K. (2017). *Fixing solitary confinement in New York State prisons.* Human Rights Watch. Retrieved from https://www.hrw.org/news/2017/05/02/fixing-solitary-confinement-new-york-state-prisons.

United Nations Office on Drugs and Crime. (2017). *The United Nations standard minimum rules for the treatment of prisoners (the Nelson Mandela Rules).* Retrieved from https://www.unodc.org/documents/justice-and-prison-reform/GA-RESOLUTION/E_ebook.pdf.

U.S. Department of Justice. (2016). *U.S. Department of Justice report and rec-ommendations concerning the use of restrictive housing.* Retrieved September 12, 2017 from https://www.justice.gov/archives/dag/file/815551/download.

U.S. Department of Justice. (2017). *Review of the Federal Bureau of Prisons' use of restrictive housing for inmates with mental illness.* Retrieved from https://oig.justice.gov/reports/2017/e1705.pdf.

Vera Institute of Justice. (2017). *Safe alternative to segregation initiatives.* Retrieved from https://www.vera.org/publications/safe-alternatives-segreg-ation-initiative-findings-recommendations.

Cases Cited

Cruz v. Beto, 405 U.S. 319 (1972)
Davis v. Ayala, 135 S. Ct. 2187 (2015)
Farmer v. Brennan, 511 U.S. 825 (1994)
Hudson v. McMillian, 503 U.S. 1 (1992)
Hutto et al. v. Finney et al., 437 U.S. 678 (1978)
Inmate Discipline and Special Housing Units, 28 C.F.R. §§ 541.21, 541.23, 541.27 (2010)
Madrid v. Gomez, 889 F. Supp. 1146 (1995)
Rhodes v. Chapman, 452 U.S. 337 (1981)
Ruiz v. Johnson, 37 F. Supp. 2d 855 (1999)
Ruiz v. Texas, 137 S. Ct. 1246 (2017)
Smith v. Ryan, 581 U.S. _____ (2017)
Turner v. Safley, 482 U.S. 89 (1987)
Wilkinson v. Austin, 545 U.S. 209 (2005)
Wilson v. Seiter, 501 U.S. 294 (1991)
Wolff v. McDonnell, 418 U.S. 539 (1974)

Chapter 7

The Death Penalty
Ultimate Punishment or
Failed Public Policy?

Scott Vollum

Introduction

Historically, the debate over the death penalty tends to be predominated by ideology and philosophy on the one hand and emotional reactions and outrage on the other. The question is often, "are you pro-death penalty or anti-death penalty?" And the answer is often supplied by ideology or visceral reaction. In the halls of academia, as well as among activists, we ask whether killing is a morally appropriate response to crime. The value and sanctity of life (even a defiled life) is debated. In the media and public, particularly brutal crimes are met with impassioned outrage and anger. Research on public opinion regarding the death penalty has revealed that death penalty attitudes are often more symbolic or value expressive than they are instrumental or rational (Bohm, 2017; Bohm, 1992; Bohm, Clark, & Aveni, 1991; Ellsworth & Gross, 1994; Lee, Bohm, & Pazzani, 2014; Tyler & Weber, 1982; Vollum, Longmire, & Buffington-Vollum, 2004; Vollum, Mallicoat, & Buffington-Vollum, 2009; Vollum & Buffington-Vollum, 2010). Specific examinations of public and media discourse surrounding the death penalty have offered further evidence of the level of emotion and outrage evoked in the wake of capital murder (Bandes, 2008; Lin & Phillips, 2014; Lynch, 2002; Vandiver, Giacopassi, & Gathje, 2002). Vandiver et al. (2002), for example, highlighted just how vitriolic and irrational death penalty support can become in citing one supporter yelling, "I hope someone murders your mother!" at death penalty protesters.

My own experience in Huntsville, Texas—the location where more executions are carried out than anywhere else in the country—provides ample examples of the emotion and public outrage on both sides of the death penalty debate. At executions of individuals who have received particularly heightened attention, the streets adjacent to the death house may become crowded with both protesters and what can only be described as celebrators (Lyons, 2000; Trow, 1998; Wheeler, 2000). This latter group often carries signs with clever quips about the impending execution of the condemned or impassioned proclamations of outrage and anger; in some cases, this group includes college students and others celebrating with beer and raucous yelling and chanting (Trow, 1998). Indeed, the death penalty brings out strong emotional and impassioned responses that include extreme levels of outrage. This outrage gives voice to the promotion of the death penalty and is a source of momentum for its continued use as public policy.

The question of whether or not the death penalty actually is good policy rarely enters the often heated and impassioned rhetoric surrounding the death penalty, and when it does, it is often supplied as a secondary rationale for an ideological position. It's not uncommon to hear something akin to "I'm against the death penalty because it's wrong to kill. Besides, it doesn't work," or "Of course I'm for the death penalty. It's an eye for an eye. Plus, it's the only way to stop evil people from killing again." Moreover, facts are often ignored or distorted by those with an emotional investment in their position on the death penalty. In this chapter, the death penalty will be considered as policy. As such, several key aspects of the death penalty—aspects associated with the instrumental value of the death penalty as policy—will be considered: deterrence, incapacitation, cost, and retribution. The first three aspects are relatively straightforward instrumental considerations. The last, retribution, is a bit more complex and encompasses multiple foci including proportionality/consistency of punishment (i.e., is it really applied to the worst of the worst?), "justice" for society and covictims (family and friends of the victim), and the issue of wrongful conviction and innocence that seems to plague the application of the death penalty. With each of these aspects of the death penalty, myths and public outrage play a significant role in perpetuating it as a solution to criminal violence. These factors, along with the evidence regarding these policy objectives, are considered.

Deterrence

The argument that the death penalty is a general deterrent is likely the oldest instrumental rationale for its use. Executions as "spectacles" were not uncommon prior to the 19th century in the United States, often drawing large crowds of citizens to witness this macabre event (Banner, 2002). These public spectacles were intended to reinforce the serious consequences of particularly egregious crimes and to "amplify the message of terror ... and to broadcast that message to the public" (Banner, 2002, p. 51). This ostensibly deterred spectators from committing crime. But such public executions are a thing of the past in the United States, and the notion of whether the death penalty effectively deters murder and violence has become much more contested. Today, scholars and policy makers have by and large abandoned general deterrence as a rational argument for the death penalty (Radelet & Akers, 1996; Radelet & Lacock, 2009; Robinson, 2008). Practitioners, too, seem to question the validity of any deterrent effect of the death penalty. Surveys of law enforcement officers, for example, reveal that those on the front lines in combating crime see little value in the death penalty as a general deterrent (Radelet & Akers, 1996). In fact, law enforcement officials from around the world gathered in Washington, DC, in 2011 to hold a summit on the death penalty and found general agreement that it was not an effective deterrent. An op-ed in the *San Jose Mercury Times* written by four of the attending officials proclaimed the following: "The deterrence argument is weak and it goes against our experience investigating serious crimes: the majority of offenders do not think through the consequences of their actions. In fact, they do not think they will ever be caught" (Abbott, Cluny, Denmark, & Hampton, 2011).

Though deterrence may have lost favor among academics, practitioners, and policy makers, it still carries some weight in public discourse (Donohue & Wolfers, 2009; Lynch, 2002; Whitehead, Blankenship, & Wright, 1999). A declining, but not insubstantial, proportion of the public continues to cite deterrence as a reason for supporting the death penalty (Gallup, 2014; Robinson, 2008). An examination of pro-death penalty websites further reveals that deterrence is still perceived as a tenable rationale for the death penalty (see, for example, www.prodeathpenalty.com and Wesley Lowe's pro-death penalty webpage at www.wesleylowe.com/cp.html). The simplistic logic of deterrence makes it an appealing rationale: it just seems to make sense that the threat of death would make people think twice about committing murder. Moreover, to call the deterrent effect of the death penalty into question seems to challenge a fundamental underpinning logic of all criminal sanctions and use of punishment. As Ernest Van den Haag (1982) stated, "[O]ur penal system rests on the proposition that more severe penalties are more deterrent than less severe penalties.... [Therefore,] the most severe penalty—the death penalty––would have the greatest deterrent effect" (pp. 326–327). This logical view is often reflected in public support for the death penalty, even if it's not often the primary rationale for its use (Bandes, 2008). What's more, it historically has been supplemented by political rhetoric and views expressed by public officials (Whitehead, 1998; Whitehead et al., 1999). For example, during the 2000 presidential election, both the republican and democratic candidates expressed their support for the death penalty based on grounds of general deterrence (Turow, 2003), and, more recently, the current U.S. president has cited deterrence as a primary reason for his unequivocal support for the death penalty for those who kill police officers (Ford, 2015).

In spite of the desire by some to hang on to this instrumental and historically popular rationale for the death penalty, the research has failed to provide solid evidence of any deterrent effect of the death penalty. For decades, researchers have been attempting to answer the question of whether the death penalty deters others from committing murder. Research on the deterrent value of the death penalty has taken a variety of forms over that time. Early studies attempted to assess the deterrent effect of the death penalty by comparing states that employed the death penalty with those that did not. These studies typically failed to find any apparent deterrent effect for those states that maintained the death penalty. In other words, murder rates were comparable across compared states regardless of whether or not they had the death penalty (Bohm, 2017; Peterson & Bailey, 2003; Sellin, 1967). What's more, in many cases, murder rates were higher in death penalty states than in nondeath penalty states (Peterson & Bailey, 2003). Other studies examined trends in murder rates before and after periods of abolition or moratoria (temporary stoppage) of the death penalty. One cross-national study found no consistent increase or decrease in murder during or after a stoppage of executions (Archer, Gartner, & Beittel, 1983). Some researchers have examined murder trends in more immediate proximity (both temporally and spatially) to executions, also examining the impact of publicity and media exposure for executions (Bailey, 1998; Cochran & Chamlin, 2000; Cochran, Chamlin, & Seth, 1994). These studies found that, paradoxically, executions led to both a decrease (deterrence effect) and increase (brutalization effect) in murders. Highly publicized executions were found to deter some forms of murder while catalyzing others (Bailey, 1998; Cochran & Chamlin, 2000).

The most recent research on deterrence and the death penalty centers around econometric analyses that purport to measure the specific impact of executions on homicides (i.e., identifying the number of murders averted for each execution). These studies revisit the controversial studies done in the 1970s by economist Isaac Ehrlich. Ehrlich (1975, 1977), through the use of multivariate econometric models to examine the death penalty during the 1950s and 1960s, concluded that each execution resulted in eight less murders. More contemporary econometric analyses have found that the death penalty deters anywhere from 3 to 18 additional murders (see, for example, Dezhbaksh, Rubin, & Shepherd,

2003; Liu, 2004; Mocan & Gittings, 2003; Shepherd, 2005; Zimmerman, 2004). However, documentation of methodological and statistical problems with these studies is legion (see, for example, Bowers & Pierce, 1980; Chalfin, Haviland, & Raphael, 2013; Donohue & Wolfers, 2005, 2009; Fagan, 2005). These econometric analyses and their conclusions have been discredited on a variety of grounds including failure to control for other causal factors, ignoring missing data, ignoring the effects of imprisonment (and particularly life imprisonment without parole) on murder rates, failure to account for population size, and faulty assumptions (Chalfin, Haviland, & Raphael, 2013; Donohue & Wolfers, 2005, 2009; Fagan, 2005; Robinson, 2008). Fagan (2005) captures the gravity of these flaws:

> These are serious flaws and omissions in a body of scientific evidence that render it unreliable, and certainly not sufficiently sound evidence on which to base laws whose application leads to life-and-death decisions. The omissions and errors are so egregious that this work falls well within the unfortunate category of junk science (p. 11).

Moreover, attempts at replicating some of these analyses have resulted in contradictory findings including that, in some cases, executions lead to an increase in murders (Donohue & Wolfers, 2005; Manski & Pepper, 2013). In any case, we are left only able to conclude that there is no sufficient evidence that, on balance, the death penalty either deters or encourages murder. Evidence of any marginal impact of the death penalty beyond that of life prison sentences or life without parole (LWOP) is inconsistent at best. Based on their own comprehensive examination of the research and data, Donohue and Wolfers (2005) support this conclusion: "We are led to conclude that there exists profound uncertainty about the deterrent (or antideterrent) effect of the death penalty; the data tell us that capital punishment is not a major influence on homicide rates" (p. 841).

Incapacitation

It's important to distinguish incapacitation from deterrence. In the context of the death penalty (and other criminal sanctions), incapacitation refers to physically removing the opportunity for an individual to engage in violent behavior. Though often confused with, and thus used as evidence of, deterrence (particularly specific deterrence), incapacitation is not deterrence. Deterrence refers to stopping behavior through the learning that occurs when one is punished. In the case of murder, this would mean that one experiences the pain of punishment in a way that would inhibit the same behavior in the future because one wishes to avoid again experiencing the punishment. This, for obvious reasons, does not apply to the death penalty. Rather, the death penalty serves as a form of incapacitation. In fact, execution is irrefutably the most effective form of incapacitation; death certainly physically prohibits one from being able to commit further acts of violence or murder.

Incapacitation—making certain that the offender is not able to hurt or kill again—is a cornerstone of public demand for the death penalty (Bohm, 2017; Sorensen & Marquart, 2003). Individuals for whom the death penalty is a possible punishment often have committed particularly heinous murders that evoke the greatest level of fear and outrage among citizens. These are murders for which a great amount of media coverage is likely and thus are imposed on the collective consciousness of society. These factors converge and result in a form of "moral panic" in which fear and danger overcome reason and more utilitarian considerations. For these reasons, public demand often centers on the need to remove these individuals from any opportunity to hurt anyone again. As Sorensen and Marquart (2003) noted, this demand has a very real impact on capital juries and the imposition of the death penalty: "Jurors caught up in a situation akin to a moral panic have little choice but to protect society by incapacitating these 'dangerous sociopaths'" (p. 298).

Though the incapacitation argument is based on a very real concern for public safety and the fact that death certainly prohibits an individual from being a future danger, it is also based on the often mistaken notion that there is no alternative means to effectively incapacitate an offender and ensure that he or she presents no further threat to society. More specifically, it is based on the mistaken belief that there is no real life imprisonment. The public and, by extension, juries have often held significant misperceptions about the reality of life sentences and parole eligibility in cases of murder (Bowers & Steiner, 1999; Vartkessian, Sorensen, & Kelly, 2017; Vollum, del Carmen, & Longmire, 2004). Moreover, people tend to substantially underestimate the actual amount of time spent incarcerated by those sentenced to life in prison (Bowers & Steiner, 1999). If the assumption is that murderers will eventually be released on parole (and, upon release, will present a heightened threat of committing additional violence), then the death penalty certainly has an incapacitative value as public policy. However, this assumption is a faulty one. Currently, all 31 death penalty states and all but one of nondeath penalty states have true LWOP sentences (Alaska is the only state that does not have an LWOP option).[1] Individuals con-

---

1. Currently, Alaska is the only state that does not have an LWOP option.

victed of capital murder who are not sentenced to death will receive the alternative sentence of life without parole and will remain incarcerated for the remainder of their life.

Of course, ensuring that an offender is incarcerated for the remainder of his or her life doesn't necessarily remove all threat of harm by that individual. There are opportunities within prison to harm other inmates, correctional officers, and other correctional staff. And there is always the possibility (remote as it might be) that an offender might escape and thus again present a potential threat to society. However, the modern advent of what's been termed *supermax* confinement virtually eliminates such dangers (Ross, 2007; Stickrath, Bucholtz, & Renfrow, 2003). Inmates under such confinement often have no physical contact with other people, and the mechanisms of control are such that escape is virtually impossible (Stickrath et al., 2003). Moreover, the research on future dangerousness of capital murderers indicates that it is exceedingly rare for murderers (and particularly capital murderers) to commit additional murders, whether in prison or after being released from prison (Buffington-Vollum, Edens, & Keilen, 2008; Edens, Buffington-Vollum, Keilen, Roskamp, & Anthony, 2005; Liem, Zahn, & Tichavsky, 2014; Marquart & Sorensen, 1988, 1989; Reidy, Cunningham, & Sorensen, 2001; Sorensen & Marquart, 2003). This fact, coupled with a heightened error rate (rate of wrongful convictions) in capital cases, calls into question any claim that the death penalty produces a marginal incapacitative value as public policy. Though there is no refuting that execution successfully incapacitates an offender (obviously), the evidence doesn't support the idea that the death penalty is necessary to achieve such incapacitation.

Cost

Recently, one of the most potent focal points regarding the death penalty as public policy, and one that spans the political spectrum, is the cost associated with its implementation. As states experience economic and budgetary hardships that demand cuts in the cost of housing the growing number of prison inmates, the cost of the death penalty has begun to take center stage in the discourse surrounding whether to maintain it as public policy. In fact, numerous states have recently taken the initiative to examine the costs associated with the death penalty amidst concern that other criminal justice components and programs are being sacrificed in lieu of maintaining the death penalty (Dieter, 2009; 2013). Historically, the cost-based rationale for the death penalty has been established on the reality that incarcerating offenders costs money in the way of housing, feeding, and providing for the basic needs of inmates. The perception, then, has commonly been that executing offenders would remove these costs and save taxpayers money. In spite of evidence to the contrary, this logical perception and rationale remains one to which many in the public subscribe (Bohm, 2003; Gallup, 2014; Robinson, 2008; Vogel, 2003; Vollum, Kubena, & Buffington-Vollum, 2004). Along these lines, the death penalty is perceived to reduce costs for the criminal justice system and alleviate prison crowding (Bohm, 2003; Vollum et al., 2004). A recent national poll reveals these to comprise the second most-cited reason (retribution being the most-cited reason) for death penalty support (Gallup, 2014).

Contrary to these perceptions, research has repeatedly revealed that the death penalty is not more cost effective than alternatives, including life sentences. In fact, the death penalty has been found to be substantially more expensive than alternatives and to produce what can only be characterized as extraordinary costs to taxpayers. For example, one study found that having the death penalty costs the taxpayers of North Carolina $11 million a year (Cook, 2009). A study of Maryland capital cases found that the cost per case is over a million dollars above what would have been incurred had the death penalty not been pursued (Roman, Chalfin, & Knight, 2009). The most recent study, analyzing the cost of the death penalty in Oregon, revealed that a death sentence costs the state, on average, between $800,000 to over $1,000,000 more than a capital life sentence (Kaplan, Collins, & Mayhew, 2016). One author conservatively estimates that, nationally, the death penalty in the modern era (since 1976) has cost over $2.5 billion (Dieter, 2009). More liberal estimates put it at 10 times that (Dieter, 2009). Whatever the estimated total cost, it has become abundantly clear that the death penalty presents a substantial financial burden on states that use it.

Of course, questions naturally arise about why the death penalty costs so much and what might be done to reduce it. Executions themselves are relatively cheap. For example, the drugs used in lethal injection typically cost anywhere from $70 to $700 (Bohm, 2017), with costs rising in some states as the drugs used in lethal injection have become scarce. Add the cost to employ the correctional employees who administer the execution and you're seeing only a minimal portion of the cost of the death penalty. It is the other aspects of the death penalty that bring the substantial financial costs. When the death penalty was, once again, declared constitutional by the Supreme Court in *Gregg v. Georgia* (1976), it was deemed allowable only with assurances of "super due process." Given the gravity and finality of the punishment of death (the commonly asserted notion that "death is different"), the Supreme Court declared that "heightened standards of reliability" were necessary to assure that the death penalty was imposed fairly and with great protection against wrongful conviction and execution (*Gregg v. Georgia*, 1976). Included among the provisions toward this end are a two-part (bifurcated) trial (with separate guilt and penalty phases), consideration of aggravating and mitigating circumstances that call for extensive investigation and expert involvement, and automatic appellate review. This has led to higher costs for pretrial, trial, and postconviction components of capital cases (Bohm, 2003; 2017). Moreover, the conditions of confinement required for condemned inmates are often heightened for safety concerns (after all, an inmate condemned to die has nothing left to lose).

If the lengthy and expensive trial and appellate processes that result from the currently required standards of "super due process" are alleviated, the death penalty may certainly cost less money to administer. What this fact fails to account for is the already substantial error rate in capital cases (more on this below). The fact that wrongful convictions and executions occur as they do, in spite of the current procedural safeguards, suggests that any attenuation of these safeguards would only increase the likelihood of such grave mistakes. Such mistakes (and any increase in the risk of their occurrence) are troubling for many reasons. Morally, it's unacceptable to knowingly make an allowance for greater levels of error in capital cases. Moreover, wrongful convictions also add another substantial financial burden on states in the way of compensation to those who have been exonerated, as well as costs of further investigation and trial of the actual offender who remained free while the wrong person was tried and punished for the crime.

Cost-based arguments for the death penalty, whether founded on the mistaken rationale that the death penalty saves money by reducing the number of inmates or on the rationale that eliminating the extensive procedural safeguards would make it cheaper, seem untenable given the current evidence. Legitimate concerns about wrongful convictions in capital cases coupled with the fact that life sentences without parole can be employed at a much lower cost suggest that, financially, the death penalty fails as public policy. In fact, it appears that states are recognizing this, as the focus seems to be shifting from using the death penalty to reduce costs to abolishing the death penalty to reduce costs.

Retribution

This leaves the rationale of retribution, which many have argued is (or should be) the real driving force surrounding the death penalty (Berns, 1982; Bohm, 1992; Davis, 2002; Radelet & Borg, 2000; Van den Haag, 1982, 1997, 2003). Retribution, in one form or another, is consistently the most-cited rationale for the death penalty (Gallup, 2014; Robinson, 2008). And, more than any other death penalty rationale, retribution is fueled by public outrage and anger in response to what are typically horrible and disturbing crimes. Often couched in terms of justice, revenge, and vindication, the death penalty supplies the ultimate response to intense public and personal hurt, anger, and fear. Given these acute emotions and reactions in the wake of capital murders, the public, and by extension prosecutors and juries, tends to look to the death penalty to "make things right" or offer a response that sufficiently acknowledges the gravity of the offense. One author goes so far as to refer to the desire for the death penalty in the face of these calls for justice as "terror management" (Kirchmeier, 2008). Quite simply, sometimes (especially in the immediate aftermath of horrendous acts of violence) retribution, in the form of killing and death, seems to be the only thing that adequately expresses the outrage and pain experienced by the public and by victims' family and friends (covictims).

So, what, exactly, is retribution, and can the death penalty attain it? In simple terms, retribution can be defined as an exchange of sorts that attempts to set things right or bring justice by rebalancing the scales that were thrown off balance by the offense (Cottingham, 1979; Finckenauer, 1988). Specifically, it can be looked at as a "repayment" that takes two divergent forms. The first constitutes an offender paying back a debt to society for the harm and destruction caused by his or her criminal actions. As such, the punishment accordingly counterbalances the harmful impact of the crime. The second constitutes delivering "payback" to an offender. In this form, retribution is presented as revenge or vengeance (Finckenauer, 1988). What this means in terms of the death penalty is that retribution calls for the death of an offender because of one of two reasons: 1) he or she has, by committing murder, forfeited his or her right to continue living and must lose his or her life in order to pay back society and make things right, or 2) society has a moral imperative on behalf of those harmed by the offender's actions, including those innocent individuals who lost their lives, to pay the offender back in a way that matches or exceeds the harm his or her crime caused. In the case of murder, this requires death of the offender. In either case, the death penalty is mandated to maintain a balance of justice and order in society.

This warrants some consideration, as an argument can be made for the death penalty if the retributive ideal can be met. There are three key criteria that can be considered when determining whether the death penalty actually meets the objectives of retribution. First, it must be proportionate in that the offenders who receive the death penalty represent a relatively homogenous group of those most deserving of death. Second, it must produce social catharsis or a righting of the wrongs created by the offense. Finally, it must be administered with as little error as is possible. In other words, those receiving their "just deserts" must be those who actually committed the crime and thus deserve the punishment. Close examination of each of these components of the death penalty sheds light on whether the death penalty achieves retributive justice or whether retribution is just another myth about the death penalty.

Proportionality

One of the retributive foundations of the death penalty is that it is the ultimate punishment for the ultimate crime. This suggests that it is a punishment to be equitably applied to those most deserving of the most severe possible sanction. This is the lex talionis, eye for an eye, rationale much touted by death penalty supporters (Robinson, 2008; Bohm, 2017). This ideal calls for pro-portionality in the application of the death penalty, a notion also supported by the U.S. Supreme Court in assessing the constitutionality of the death penalty (*Gregg v. Georgia*, 1976). What this means is that the death penalty is applied equivalently based on the nature (heinousness) of the offense and that those who commit like crimes receive like punishments and those who commit the worst possible crimes receive the death penalty. Conversely, it means that it is reserved only for those who commit the worst possible crimes.

Is the death penalty reserved for, and applied to, only the worst of the worst? Are the only factors determining who gets a death sentence and who gets a lesser punishment the heinousness of the offense and malevolence of the offender? To answer the first question, one need not go to great lengths. Factors, such as geographical location, prosecutorial discretion and predilection, and jury discretion, all contribute to the fact that those who get sentenced to death is not based solely on the seriousness and nature of the offense or on who most "deserves" the sanction. Where one commits the crime appears to be much more determinative of who receives the death penalty than any consideration of proportionality. Death sentences and executions tend to be highly concentrated geographically. Only five states account for about two thirds of executions in the United States. Moreover, within states, death sentences tend to predominantly come from a small proportion of jurisdictions. A recent analysis of death sentences by county between 2004 and 2009 revealed that only 1% of counties imposed, on average, at least one death sentence per year (Smith, 2012). Dif-ferences in the predilections of prosecutors also often play a role in which capital murderers get sentenced to death. In Virginia, for example, prosecutors in rural jurisdictions are significantly more likely to seek the death penalty than are their urban counterparts (Bohm, 2017). Prosecutorial discretion also plays out in more specific ways. Some offenders may receive less than a death sentence due to plea bargaining in exchange for a confession, information, or willingness to testify against a codefendant. It's not uncommon for one codefendant to receive a life sentence while the other receives death. It's hard to maintain the "worst of the worst" standard in the face of such practical realities in the legal process.

Prosecutorial discretion, along with jury discretion, also play a significant role in disparities in the application of the death penalty based on characteristics of the offender and/or victim. The earliest research examining extralegal factors that bear on possible disparity in sentencing in capital cases focused on racial discrimination (Baldus, Pulaski, & Woodworth, 1983, 1986). Though a disproportionate number of racial minorities receive the death penalty, when controlling for the proportion represented among capital murderers (or murders with the appropriate level of aggravation) there appears to be little or no disparity (Baldus & Woodworth, 2003). However, there does appear to be a disparity in the victim's race. Offenders who murder a black victim are far less likely to receive the death penalty than offenders who murder a white victim (Baldus & Woodworth, 2003). In Texas, for example, of the 544 executions since 1976, less than 1% (five) have been of a white offender who killed a black victim. On the other hand, there have been 112 executions in Texas of black offenders who killed white victims. In Florida, there were no executions of a white offender who murdered a black victim until this year , and he killed both a white and black victim (Death Penalty Information Center, 2017). Additionally, social class and gender of offender and victim appear to play significant roles in determining who gets the death penalty (Bohm, 2017; Tomsich, Richards, & Gover, 2014). Women are substantially underrepresented on death rows and among those executed. And there is no debating that death rows are populated by predominantly poor offenders.

In short, some offenders who "deserve" the death penalty more than others do not receive the death penalty, and some offenders who don't "deserve" it as much as others do receive it. Retribution fails if only a select few (on both the offender and victim side) are granted retributive justice. "Justice" fails to be delivered in a manner that comports with the notion that it be provided to those who most deserve it. And those who have suffered as victims or covictims are often left without the justice and catharsis promised to them in the form of retribution via the death penalty. Of course, the very notion that the death penalty even has the capacity to provide such justice and catharsis is debatable.

Justice & Social Catharsis

The death penalty is often perceived to be a way (perhaps the only way) in which society can achieve justice and catharsis in the wake of murder (and especially particularly brutal murders that capture the attention of the public). The public response to such horrifying and brutal acts of violence often leads to a call for retribution in terms of revenge or vengeance (Garland, 2012; Lynch, 2002; Vandiver et al., 2002; Vollum et al., 2004; Vollum, 2008). This is not about proportionality in punishment; it's about something much more visceral. It's about striking back at those who cause such harm and anger, asserting with the strongest sanction available that such offenses (and offenders) will not be tolerated. It's also about attempting to balance the scales, and thus attempting to produce social catharsis, by meeting particularly offensive and harmful criminal acts with a punishment of equal gravity. Others see the death penalty in these terms as the only way to uphold the sanctity of law and honor the lives lost and those harmed at the hands of capital murderers (see, for example, Berns, 1982; Van den Haag, 2003). In this way, the death penalty is perceived as a moral imperative both in terms of the sanctity of human life and of maintaining an orderly society.

One of the strongest calls for the death penalty in the wake of murder (and especially particularly brutal murders) is "justice" for the victim and covictims. As I have written elsewhere, "The claim that we have a duty to deliver justice and retribution for the victims and covictims is one of the most dominant and emotionally powerful arguments for the death penalty" (Vollum, 2008, p. 47). It is a popular sentiment that we must somehow avenge these victims' and cov-ictims' loss and suffering. The death penalty is often held out as the only official mechanism that can possibly offer an opportunity to do so. It is not uncommon for prosecutors to use such rhetoric to secure death sentences or for politicians and policy makers to use it to appeal to the public. And it's hard for the public to deny murder victims and covictims in light of the suffering they have endured. Underneath this rhetoric, however, is the reality that covictims and their needs go largely ignored or neglected in the wake of both the murder and the capital trial process (Eaton & Christensen, 2014; Freeman, Shaffer, & Smith, 1996; Magee, 1983; Vollum, 2008). Very little, if anything, is offered to covictims of murder toward healing and managing grief and loss. In fact, the way they are often treated in the days and years following the murder, as they experience not only the personal aftermath of the crime but also the trauma of the inves-tigation and legal processes, are often counterproductive in regard to these needs (Dicks, 1991; King, 2003; Lifton & Mitchell, 2000; Vollum, 2008). Moreover, it is unclear whether the death penalty actually produces the catharsis it promises. Though the death penalty certainly provides solace to some covictims, many covictims indicate that execution failed to deliver the healing, closure, or justice that was hoped for, and some victims contend that the death penalty only extends or exacerbates their grief and suffering (Dicks, 1991; King, 2003; Vollum, 2008). For retribution to stand on the basis of social catharsis and justice, the full range of experiences, needs, and desires of those most directly harmed by the crime must be attended to. The death penalty, though often presented as a mechanism for providing justice and catharsis for these victims and covictims, seems to instead be a prime example of a retributive criminal justice system that neglects victims and covictims and their very real needs in the wake of crime.

Innocence and Wrongful Conviction

Retribution requires that justice is served to those who actually deserve it. The retributive ideal cannot bear a system that results in substantial errors in the form of wrongful conviction, imprisonment, and perhaps even execution. Unfortunately, such errors seem to plague the death penalty system in the United States. Since 1973, 160 death row inmates have been exonerated (see Death Penalty Information Center's (DPIC) database of all exonerees here: https://deathpenaltyinfo.org/innocence), some of whom have come within hours of execution. What is perhaps more disturbing is the evidence that a number of those who have been executed were innocent (Acker, 2009; Baumgartner, De Boef, & Boydstun, 2008; Bedau & Radelet, 1987; Radelet & Bedau, 2003; Liebman, Fagan, & West, 2000). The case of Cameron Willingham, who was executed in Texas in 2004, provides one of the most cogent examples of this reality. Willingham was executed for killing his three children by burning his house down with them inside. He was convicted based on the results of an arson investigation that has since been discredited. In fact, since Willingham's execution, another defendant sentenced to death based on nearly identical evidence has been exonerated and released from death row (Grann, 2009). Willingham's is not an isolated case. There are numerous cases in which there are compelling reasons to believe an innocent person was executed (Bohm, 2017). However, obtaining definitive proof is difficult, given that states are under no obligation to either maintain or release evidence after an execution. Cameron Willingham's case came closest to reaching an official conclusion. The Texas Forensic Science Commission prepared a report attesting that the forensic conclusions were faulty and that the fire had not been intentionally started (Grann, 2009). However, before the commission could officially report its findings, Governor Rick Perry disbanded the commission and the report was never released.

Obviously, those who are wrongfully convicted, imprisoned, or executed are no more deserving of the death penalty than any other innocent citizen. This has become a real Achilles' heel for the retributivist death penalty rationale; the legitimacy of the death penalty as retribution is seriously challenged by such errors. Execution of an innocent person is the gravest possible error that can be made in our criminal justice system. Not only do these errors bring retribution against an individual who clearly does not deserve it, but they also create a situation in which there is a failure to bring retribution against the person actually responsible for the crime. This failure of retribution leads to an innocent person suffering greatly (or even possibly being killed) and to a guilty, and potentially dangerous, individual remaining free.

Of course, errors happen throughout the criminal justice system, not just in death penalty cases. Indeed, given that humans administer criminal justice, such errors are inevitable. The question then is, are errors more likely in capital cases? There are many reasons to believe that the answer to this question is yes. There are several unique characteristics of capital cases that contribute to an increased likelihood of innocent individuals being convicted and, in some cases, potentially executed. First, capital murders are, by nature, particularly brutal crimes that evoke horror and outrage on the part of the public. This heightened outrage produces a situation in which there is great pressure on police to make an arrest and on prosecutors to secure a conviction. This pressure creates a situation ripe for overzealous investigation and prosecution, which in turn exacerbates a lot of the already common factors that contribute to wrongful convictions (e.g., false confessions,[2] faulty eyewitness testimony, inadequate defense council, prosecutorial misconduct) (Bedau & Radelet, 1987; Liebman et al., 2000). Police officers under great pressure to make an arrest are more likely to take shortcuts or circumvent rigorous investigative due diligence. They are also more likely to pursue a confession beyond normal bounds. A prosecutor under great pressure to secure a conviction is more likely to ignore exculpatory evidence or engage in questionable legal practice surrounding evidence and witnesses. The horrific nature of the crime and associated public outrage that puts such pressure on police and prosecutors also spills over to capital juries who may be driven toward findings of guilt in part by a strong desire to see justice done in such cases (Eisenberg, Garvey, & Wells, 2001; Haney, 1997). These are not simply hypothetical suppositions; they are well-documented realities in capital cases, which contribute to a heightened

---

2. A related problem, not directly considered here, is the fact that the threat of death sentence is often used to get suspects to plea bargain for a life sentence by cooperating with law enforcement and confessing to the crime. In situations in which an innocent suspect is made to believe that they have no hope of overcoming what appears to be evidence that will convict them and lead to a death sentence, a false confession may be perceived as the only way to spare their lives. This does not directly result in a wrongful capital conviction but is another example of how the presence of the death penalty increases error in the criminal justice system.

risk of error (see, for example, Acker, 2009; Bedau & Radelet, 1987; Eisenberg et al., 2001; Gross, 1996; Gross, Jacoby, Matheson, Montgomery, & Patil, 2005; Gross, O'Brien, Hu, & Kennedy, 2014; Haney, 1997; Liebman et al., 2000).

A second factor contributing to the uniquely heightened risk of error in capital cases is the way in which capital cases are tried. As previously mentioned, capital trials are bifurcated or conducted in two parts. There are two phases, one in which guilt is determined and another in which sentence is determined. This alone is not a problem in terms of increasing risk of wrongful conviction (in fact, it's intended to enhance the reliability of capital cases). It is the resulting jury selection process that seems to create a heightened risk of error. A key component of jury selection in capital cases is referred to as "death qualification," a process by which potential jurors who oppose the death penalty are excluded from serving on the jury (see Supreme Court case *Lockhart v. McCree*, 1986). The logic of this is that such potential jurors are unable to uphold the law by sentencing a defendant to death if that is, in fact, what the evidence calls for. Though this makes legal sense, it also "stacks the deck" in terms of the composition of capital juries leading to a greater likelihood of a death sentence but also to a greater likelihood that the jury finds the defendant guilty in the first place (Bowers, 1996; Bowers, Sandys, & Steiner, 1998; Sandys & McCelland, 2003; Springer & Lalasz, 2014). Particularly salient to the capital jury's inclination to find the defendant guilty is the fact that the death qualification process includes engaging prospective jurors in a presumption of guilt during voir dire. Because death qualification concerns the ability of prospective jurors to sentence a defendant to death, they are essentially asked to assume a determination of guilt in responding to questions about whether or not they could vote for a sentence of death. Such presumption of guilt occurring before the trial even begins produces a subtle, but potent, conviction proneness among capital juries (Gross, 1996; Sandys & McClelland, 2003; Springer & Lalasz, 2014). This bias, along with the natural horror and outrage over a particularly brutal murder, undoubtedly impacts capital juries in a way that increases the likelihood that innocent defendants are found guilty of capital murder and subsequently sentenced to death.

These realities, in terms of the excessive numbers of individuals who have been wrongfully convicted and executed in our current death penalty system, are well documented. Recently, Gross et al. (2014) analyzed all contemporary capital cases in which the defendants were sentenced to death, revealing an error rate of 4.1%; for every 25 death sentences, one was imposed on an innocent defendant. Such an error rate and the associated consequences of the death penalty system must make one seriously question the retributive ideal that underpins its use. Indeed, these are realities that call into question the use of the death penalty for any reason or rationale.

The Decline of the Death Penalty and Lessons Learned

By all accounts, the death penalty seems to be on the decline in the United States. The combination of growing concern about the financial cost of the death penalty, news of gruesome "botched" lethal injection executions, growing knowledge about wrongful convictions and executions, and growing availability and awareness of LWOP seems to be catalyzing a change in public opinion and political will. For the first time in the post-Furman era, some public opinion polls are revealing that death penalty support has fallen below 50% (Oliphant, 2016). Over the last decade, we have also seen polls indicate that, when presented with the option of LWOP, a majority of the public does not support the death penalty (Gallup, 2014; DPIC, 2010). Polls also reveal that a majority of the public supports replacing the death penalty with more cost-effective criminal justice policies including crime prevention measures (DPIC, 2010). In the last 10 years, seven states have repealed the death penalty, and several others are considering doing so. Moreover, prosecutors and juries appear to be less likely to pursue the death penalty. The annual number of death sentences have declined to their lowest point since the death penalty was reinstated in 1976. In Virginia, the state that has carried out the second greatest number of executions in the modern era, has not seen a death sentence in over five years.

These trends suggest that the death penalty is increasingly becoming perceived as faulty or failing public policy. As indicated in this chapter, it is a perception that is supported by the evidence on numerous grounds. The death penalty fails to achieve deterrence, incapacitation, cost savings, or retribution beyond what less severe and terminal alternatives can provide. Just as Beccaria (1764/1963) argued centuries ago, the death penalty does not provide enough marginal benefit to outweigh the destructiveness inherent in such an extreme punishment.

So, if the death penalty is failed public policy, what can be done instead? For example, the following question is commonly asked in the face of possible abolition of the death penalty: what do we do with people who simply cannot live in free society without hurting others, who need to be incapacitated for the remainder of their lives? The simple answer to this is LWOP. And, indeed, LWOP is being used instead of the death penalty in many states and jurisdictions in the United States already, as well as in many countries around the world. And this is a very logical and feasible option when faced with such incorrigible individuals. However, I do not want to overemphasize this punishment or suggest its wholesale use as a panacea applicable to all murderers or cases of murder. Those referenced above, those who will indefinitely continue to harm others if they remain free, are rare even among murderers (Marquart & Sorensen, 1988, 1989). Widespread use of LWOP and supermax confinement potentially presents as many problems as does the use of the death penalty. Capricious application of LWOP would undoubtedly result in the same injustices and unreasonable outcomes as has capricious application of the death penalty. Moreover, it would simply replace one policy based on emotion instead of reason, fear instead of logic, and resignation instead of hope with another. Instead of falling back on a policy that simply repeats the mistakes of the death penalty, we should attend to the lessons learned from these mistakes and heed the associated warnings as future public policy is considered.

There are valuable lessons that can be learned from the failure of the death penalty, lessons that suggest more enlightened criminal justice policies and practices. First, attention needs to be given to policies that address the roots of violence before individuals get to the point of committing murder. We quite simply cannot afford to either execute or incarcerate for life all those who commit these crimes. Instead, we should attempt to reduce the prevalence with which these crimes occur through preemptive action, including building a better understanding of the factors that contribute to violent criminal action or high rates of violent crime. Policies and programs founded on such knowledge and understanding are certain to be wiser investments than spending millions to simply eliminate individuals deemed beyond redemption without any attempt to understand how they came to such an irredeemable point. Resources currently spent on capital cases and the disposition of capital defendants could be shifted toward policies that work to prevent criminality and violence. There are signs that such shifts may be occurring. In 2008, the California Commission on the Fair Administration of Justice (CCFAJ) published a comprehensive report asserting that the death penalty system in California is "dysfunctional" and "broken" (CCFAJ, 2008). In a letter to the commission, 30 practitioners, including prosecutors, police officers, and correctional employees, asked that, instead of spending money on the death penalty, money be spent on measures to solve open homicide cases, enhance law enforcement and investigative capabilities, modernize crime labs, and develop violence prevention programs. Likewise, the Illinois state legislature passed a bill in 2011 that abolished the death penalty but also included provisions that reallocated funds to training for law enforcement and services for murder covictims (Wilson & Long, 2011). On the national level, U.S. Senator Jim Webb, though not addressing the death penalty specifically, proposed similar criminal justice reforms. In sponsoring the National Criminal Justice Commission Act, Senator Webb called for programs and policies that would focus on violence prevention, reentry for those released from prison, and adequate assessment and care for those with mental illness

(Webb, 2009). It seems the tide has turned from a predominantly retributive approach exemplified by the death penalty to a multi-faceted approach that attempts to reduce the crime and violence that otherwise lead to a call for such an extreme and nonredemptive punishment.

Another important lesson we can learn from the failure of the death penalty is that we can do much better in meeting the needs of covictims and the community of all who are harmed (directly or indirectly) by such violent acts. In the current retributive system, crime victims and covictims are often marginalized, their needs and desires being secondary to the state's attempt to apprehend and punish criminals. If we're really sincere about the desire to provide justice to crime victims and covictims, then more than just lip service needs to be paid to this aspect of crime and criminal justice. One author has gone so far as to suggest a dual criminal justice system that she refers to as "parallel justice" (Herman, 2010). In such a system, there would be one aspect that focuses on the traditional retributive path in which an offender is tried and, if convicted, punished, and another aspect focuses on attending to the needs of victims and covictims. Simple processes, such as having specially trained individuals who communicate with victims and covictims, providing counselors and therapeutic resources, and facilitating social support networks, would go a long way toward truly helping those who suffer at the hands of the criminals we condemn.

From a broader perspective, principles of restorative justice offer additional avenues toward healing for not only victims and covictims but also others who are harmed by acts that undoubtedly have ripple effects that extend far beyond just those directly impacted by it. This would include opening up dialog within communities and drawing together individuals who share the pain and suffering that results from acts of violence. It would include developing opportunities for apology and forgiveness. It might also include offering opportunities to gain information and perspective by talking to the offender. Some have even suggested that family members of both the offender and victim can benefit from communication and dialog (Arrigo & Fowler, 2001; Eschholz, Reed, Beck, & Leonard, 2003). Whatever the future prospects are for such ideals and initiatives, the death penalty is certainly an impediment to any restorative processes that may offer real opportunities for much needed healing in the wake of murder.

These lessons, if heeded, offer a public policy shift from a path of resignation and pessimism to a path of transformation and hope. The death penalty has proven to be an untenable public policy that does not live up to the rationale on which it was based. It fails to provide cost savings, deterrence, or any marginal incapacitative value. It further fails to rise to the lofty ideals of retribution through its inequitable provision of "justice" and the inevitable and fatal mistakes that it generates. The current decline in the use of the death penalty in the United States reflects these realities, but more importantly, this decline provides an opportunity to learn from the failures of the death penalty and embrace more enlightened and socially productive policies in the future.

References

Abbott, J., Cluny, A., Denmark, B., & Hampton, R. (2011, January 8). Police officials argue death penalty doesn't make us safer. *San Jose Mercury Times.* Retrieved from http://www.mercurynews.com/ci_17040923?IADID=Search-www.mercurynews.comwww.mercurynews.com&nclick_check=1.

Acker, J. R. (2009). Actual innocence: Is death different? *Behavioral Sciences and the Law, 27,* 297–311.

Archer, D., Gartner, R., & Beittel, M. (1983). Homicide and the death penalty: A cross-national test of a deterrence hypothesis. *Journal of Criminal Law and Criminology, 74,* 991–1013.

Arrigo, B. A., & Fowler, C. R. (2001). The "death row community": A community psychology perspective. *Deviant Behavior, 22,* 43–71.

Bailey, W. C. (1998). Deterrence, brutalization, and the death penalty: Another examination of Oklahoma's return to capital punishment. *Criminology, 36*(4), 711–733.

Baldus, D. C., Pulaski, C., & Woodworth, G. (1983). Comparative review of death sentences: An empirical study of the Georgia experience. *Journal of Criminal Law and Criminology, 74,* 661–753.

Baldus, D. C., Pulaski, C., & Woodworth, G. (1986). Arbitrariness and discrimination in the administration of the death penalty: A challenge to state supreme courts. *Stetson Law Review, 15,* 133–261.

Baldus, D. C., & Woodworth, G. (2003). Race discrimination and the death penalty: An empirical and legal overview. In J. R. Acker, R. M. Bohm, & C. S. Lanier (Eds.), *America's experiment with capital punishment: Reflections on the past, present, and future of the ultimate penal sanction* (2nd ed., pp. 501–551). Durham, NC: Carolina Academic Press.

Bandes, S. A. (2008). The heart has its reasons: Examining the strange persistence of the American death penalty. *Studies in Law, Politics, and Society, 42,* 21–52.

Banner, S. (2002). *The death penalty: An American history.* Cambridge, MA: Harvard University Press.

Baumgartner, F. R., De Boef, S. L., & Boydstun, A. E. (2008). *The decline of the death penalty and the discovery of innocence.* New York, NY: Cambridge University Press.

Beccaria, C. (1963). *Of crimes and punishment (H. Paolucci, Trans.).* Indianapolis, IN: Bobbs Merrill. (Original work published 1764).

Bedau, H. A., & Radelet, M. L. (1987). Miscarriages of justice in potentially capital cases. *Stanford Law Review, 40,* 21–179.

Berns, W. (1982). The morality of anger. In H. A. Bedau (Ed.), *The death penalty in America* (3rd ed., pp. 333–341). New York, NY: Oxford University Press.

Bohm, R. M. (1992). Retribution and capital punishment: Toward a better understanding of death penalty opinion. *Journal of Criminal Justice, 20,* 227–236.

Bohm, R. M. (2003). The economic costs of capital punishment: Past, present, and future. In J. R. Acker, R. M. Bohm, & C. S. Lanier (Eds.), *America's experiment with capital punishment:Reflections on the past, present, and future of the ultimate penal sanction* (2nd ed., pp. 573–594). Durham, NC: Carolina Academic Press.

Bohm, R. M. (2017). *Deathquest: An introduction to the theory and practice of capital punishment in the United States* (5th ed.). New York, NY: Routledge.

Bohm, R. M., Clark, L. J., & Aveni, A. F. (1991). Knowledge and death penalty opinion: A test of the Marshall hypotheses. *Journal of Research in Crime and Delinquency, 28*(3), 360–387.

Bowers, W. J. (1996). The capital jury: Is it tilted toward death? *Judicature, 79*(5), 220–223.

Bowers, W. J., & Pierce, G. L. (1980). Deterrence or brutalization: What is the effect of executions? *Crime and Delinquency, 26*(4), 453–484.

Bowers, W. J., Sandys, M., & Steiner, B. D. (1998). Foreclosed impartiality in capital sentencing: Jurors' predispositions, guilt-trial experience, and premature decision making. *Cornell Law Review, 83,* 1474–1556.

Bowers, W. J., & Steiner, B. D. (1999). Death by default: An empirical demonstration of false and forced choices in capital sentencing. *Texas Law Review, 77,* 605–717.

Buffington-Vollum, J. K., Edens, J. F., & Keilen, A. (2008). Predicting institutional violence among death row inmates: The utility of the Sorensen and Pilgrim model. *Journal of Police and Criminal Psychology, 23*(1), 16–22.

California Commission on the Fair Administration of Justice. (2008, June 30). *Report and recommendations on the administration of the death penalty in California.* Retrieved from www.ccfaj.org/documents/reports/dp/official/FINAL%20REPORT%20DEATH%20PENALTYpdf.

Chalfin, A., Haviland, A. M., & Raphael, S. (2013). What do panel studies tell us about a deterrent effect of capital punishment? A critique of the literature. *Journal of Quantitative Criminology, 29*(1), 5–43.

Cochran, J. K., Chamlin, M. B., & Seth, M. (1994). Deterrence or brutalization? An impact assessment of Oklahoma's return to capital punishment. *Criminology, 32*, 107–134.

Cochran, J. K., & Chamlin, M. B. (2000). Deterrence and brutalization: The dual effects of executions. *Justice Quarterly, 17*(4), 685–706.

Cook, P. J. (2009). Potential savings from abolition of the death penalty in North Carolina. *American Law and Economics Review, 11*(2), 498–529.

Cottingham, J. (1979). Varieties of retribution. *Philosophical Quarterly, 29*(116), 238–246.

Davis, M. (2002). A sound retributive argument for the death penalty. *Criminal Justice Ethics, 21*, 22–26.

Death Penalty Information Center. (2010). *The death penalty in 2010: Year-end report.* Retrieved from https://deathpenaltyinfo.org/documents/2010YearEnd-Final.pdf.

Death Penalty Information Center. (2017). *Execution Database.* Retrieved on October 22, 2017, from http://www.deathpenaltyinfo.org/executions.

Dezhbakhsh, H., Rubin, P., & Shepherd, J. M. (2003). Does capital punishment have a deterrent effect? New evidence from post-moratorium panel data. *American Law and Economics Review, 5*, 344–376.

Dicks, S. (1991). *Victims of crime and punishment: Interviews with victims, convicts, their families, and support groups.* Jefferson, NC: McFarland & Company, Inc.

Dieter, R. C. (2009). *Smart on crime: Reconsidering the death penalty in a time of economic crisis.* Death Penalty Information Center. Retrieved from https://deathpenaltyinfo.org/documents/CostsRptFinal.pdf.

Dieter, R. C. (2013). *The 2% death penalty: How a minority of counties produce most death cases at enormous costs to all.* Death Penalty Information Center. Retrieved from https://deathpenaltyinfo.org/documents/TwoPercentReport.pdf.

Donohue, J. J., & Wolfers, J. (2005). The ethics and empirics of capital punishment: Uses and abuses of empirical evidence in the death penalty debate. *Stanford Law Review, 58*, 791–845.

Donohue, J. J., & Wolfers, J. (2009). Estimating the impact of the death penalty on murder. *American Law and Economics Review, 11*(2), 249–309.

Eaton, J., & Christensen, T. (2014). Closure and its myths: Victims' families, the death penalty, and the closure argument. *International Review of Victimology, 20*(3), 327–343.

Edens, J. F., Buffington-Vollum, J. K., Keilen, A., Roskamp, P., & Anthony, C. (2005). Predictions of future dangerousness in capital murder trials: Is it time to "disinvent the wheel"? *Law and Human Behavior, 29*(1), 55–86.

Ehrlich, I. (1975). The deterrent effect of capital punishment: A question of life and death. *American Economic Review, 65*, 397–417.

Ehrlich, I. (1977). Capital punishment and deterrence: Some further thoughts and additional evidence. *Journal of Political Economy, 85*, 741–788.

Eisenberg, T., Garvey, S. P., & Wells, M. T. (2001). The deadly paradox of capital jurors. *Southern California Law Review, 74*, 371–391.

Ellsworth, P., & Gross, S. (1994). Hardening of the attitudes: Americans' views on the death penalty. *Journal of Social Issues, 50*, 19–52.

Eschholz, S., Reed, M. D., Beck, E., & Leonard, P. B. (2003). Offenders' family members' responses to capital crimes: The need for restorative justice initiatives. *Homicide Studies, 7*(2), 154–181.

Fagan, J. (2005, January 21). *Deterrence and the death penalty: A critical review of new evidence.* Death Penalty Information Center. Retrieved from https://deathpenaltyinfo.org/node/59.

Finckenauer, J. O. (1988). Public support for the death penalty: Retribution as just deserts or retribution as revenge? *Justice Quarterly, 5*(1), 81–100.

Ford, M. (2015, December 18). Donald Trump's racially charged advocacy of the death penalty. *The Atlantic.* Retrieved from https://www.theatlantic.com/politics/archive/2015/12/donald-trump-death-penalty/420069/.

Freeman, L. N., Shaffer, D., & Smith, H. (1996). Neglected victims of homicide: The needs of young siblings of murder victims. *American Journal of Orthopsychiatry, 66*(3), 337–345.

Gallup (2014). *Death Penalty.* Retrieved October 21, 2017, from http://news.gallup.com/poll/1606/death-penalty.aspx.

Garland, D. (2012). *Peculiar institution: America's death penalty.* New York, NY: Belknap Press.

Grann, D. (2009, September 7). Trial by fire: Did Texas execute an innocent man? *The New Yorker.* Retrieved from www.newyorker.com/reporting/2009/09/07/090907fa_fact_grann.

Gross, S. R. (1996). The risks of death: Why erroneous convictions are common in capital cases. *Buffalo Law Review, 44*, 469–500.

Gross, S. R., Jacoby, K., Matheson, D. J., Montgomery, N., & Patil, S. (2005). Exonerations in the United States 1989 through 2003. *Journal of Criminal Law & Criminology, 95*(2), 523–560.

Gross, S. R., O'Brien, B., Hu, C., & Kennedy, E. H. (2014). Rate of false conviction of criminal defendants who are sentenced to death. *Proceedings of the National Academy of Sciences, 111*(20), 7230–7235.

Haney, C. (1997). Violence and the capital jury: Mechanisms of moral disengagement and the impulse to condemn to death. *Stanford Law Review, 49*, 1447–1486.

Herman, S. (2010). *Parallel justice for victims of crime.* Washington, DC: The National Center for Victims of Crime.

Kaplan, A. B., Collins, P. A., & Mayhew, V. L. (2016, November 16). *Oregon's death penalty: A cost analysis.* Oregon Justice Resource Center. Retrieved from http://ojrc.info/oregons-death-penalty-a-cost-analysis/.

King, R. (2003). *Don't kill in our names: Families of murder victims speak out against the death penalty.* New Brunswick, NJ: Rutgers University Press.

Kirchmeier, J. L. (2008). Our existential death penalty: Judges, jurors, and terror management. *Law and Psychology Review, 32,* 55–107.

Lee, G. M., Bohm, R. M., & Pazzani, L. M. (2014). Knowledge and death penalty opinion: The Marshall hypothesis revisited. *American Journal of Criminal Justice, 39*(3), 642–659.

Liebman, J. S., Fagan, J., & West, V. (2000). *A broken system: Error rates in capital cases, 1973–1995.* The Justice Project. Retrieved from www.thejusticeproject.org.

Liem, M., Zahn, M. A., & Tichavsky, L. (2014). Criminal recidivism among homicide offenders. *Journal of Interpersonal Violence, 29*(14), 2630–2651.

Lifton, R. J., & Mitchell, G. (2000). *Who owns death? Capital punishment, the American conscience, and the end of executions.* New York, NY: William Morrow.

Lin, J., & Phillips, S. (2014). Media coverage of capital murders: Exceptions sustain the rule. *Justice Quarterly, 31*(5), 934–959.

Liu, Z. (2004). Capital punishment and the deterrence hypothesis: Some new insights and empirical evidence. *Eastern Economic Journal, 30*(2), 237–258.

Lynch, M. (2002). Capital punishment as moral imperative: Pro-death penalty discourse on the internet. *Punishment and Society, 4*(2), 213–236.

Lyons, M. C. (2000, June 23). High-profile killer dies by injection. *The Huntsville Item,* pp. 1A, 5A.

Magee, D. (1983). *What murder leaves behind: The victim's family.* New York, NY: Dodd, Mead and Company.

Manski, C. F., & Pepper, J. V. (2013). Deterrence and the death penalty: Partial identification analysis using repeated cross sections. *Journal of Quantitative Criminology, 29*(1), 123–141.

Marquart, J. W., & Sorensen, J. R. (1988). Institutional and postrelease behavior of Furman commuted inmates in Texas. *Criminology, 26*(4), 677–693.

Marquart, J. W., & Sorensen, J. R. (1989). A national study of the Furman-commuted inmates: Assessing the threat to society from capital offenders. *Loyola of Los Angeles Law Review, 23*(1), 5–28.

Mocan, H. N., & Gittings, R. K. (2003). Getting off death row: Commuted sentences and the deterrent effect of capital punishment. *Journal of Law and Economics, 46,* 453–478.

Oliphant, B. (2016). *Support for death penalty lowest in more than four decades.* Pew Research Center. http://www.pewresearch.org/fact-tank/2016/09/29/support-for-death-penalty-lowest-in-more-than-four-decades/.

Peterson, R. D., & Bailey, W. C. (2003). Is capital punishment an effective deterrent for murder? An examination of social science research. In J. R. Acker, R. M. Bohm, & C. S. Lanier (Eds.), *America's experiment with capital punishment: Reflections on the past, present, and future of the ultimate penal sanction* (2nd ed., pp. 251–282). Durham, NC: Carolina Academic Press.

Radelet, M. L., & Akers, R. L. (1996). Deterrence and the death penalty: The views of the experts. *Journal of Criminal Law and Criminology, 87*(1), 1–16.

Radelet, M. L., & Bedau, H. A. (2003). The execution of the innocent. In J. R. Acker, R. M. Bohm, & C. S. Lanier (Eds.), *America's experiment with capital punishment: Reflections on the past, present, and future of the ultimate penal sanction* (2nd ed., pp. 325–344). Durham, NC: Carolina Academic Press.

Radelet, M. L., & Borg, M. J. (2000). The changing nature of death penalty debates. *Annual Review of Sociology, 26*, 43–61.

Radelet, M. L., & Lacock, T. L. (2009). Do executions lower homicide rates?: The views of leading criminologists. *Journal of Criminal Law and Criminology, 99*(2), 489–508.

Reidy, T. J., Cunningham, M. D., & Sorensen, J. R. (2001). From death to life: Prison behavior of former death row inmates in Indiana. *Criminal Justice and Behavior, 28*(1), 62–82.

Robinson, M. B. (2008). *Death nation: The experts explain American capital punishment.* Upper Saddle River, NJ: Pearson Prentice Hall.

Roman, J. K., Chalfin, A. J., & Knight, C. R. (2009). Reassessing the cost of the death penalty using quasi-experimental methods: Evidence from Maryland. *American Law and Economics Review, 11*(2), 530–574.

Ross, J. I. (2007). Supermax prisons. *Society, 44*(3), 60–64.

Sandys, M., & McClelland, S. (2003). Stacking the deck for guilt and death: The failure of death qualification to ensure impartiality. In J. R. Acker, R. M. Bohm, & C. S. Lanier (Eds.), *America's experiment with capital punishment: Reflections on the past, present, and future of the ultimate penal sanction* (2nd ed., pp. 385–411). Durham, NC: Carolina Academic Press.

Sellin, T. (1967). *Capital punishment.* New York, NY: Harper & Row.

Shepherd, J. M. (2005). Deterrence versus brutalization: Capital punishment's differing impacts among states. *Michigan Law Review, 104*(2), 203–256.

Smith, R. J. (2012). The geography of the death penalty and its ramifications. *Boston University Law Review, 92*, 227–289.

Sorensen, J., & Marquart, J. (2003). Future dangerousness and incapacitation. In J. R. Acker, R. M. Bohm, & C. S. Lanier (Eds.), *America's experiment with capital punishment: Reflections on the past, present, and future of the ultimate penal sanction* (2nd ed., pp. 283–300). Durham, NC: Carolina Academic Press.

Springer, V., & Lalasz, C. B. (2014). Death-qualified jurors and the assumption of innocence: A cognitive dissonance perspective on conviction-prone verdicts. *Social Science Journal, 51*(2), 287–294.

Stickrath, T. J., Bucholtz, G. A., & Renfrow, N. (2003). *Supermax prisons: Beyond the rock.* Lanham, MD: American Correctional Association.

Tomsich, E. A., Richards, T. N., & Gover, A. R. (2014). A review of sex disparities in the "key players" of the capital punishment process: From defendants to jurors. *American Journal of Criminal Justice, 39*(4), 732–752.

Trow, L. (1998, February 4). Scene of execution resembles carnival. *The Huntsville Item*, pp. 1A, 4A.

Turow, S. (2003). *Ultimate punishment: A lawyer's reflection on dealing with the death penalty.* New York, NY: Farrar, Straus and Giroux.

Tyler, T. R., & Weber, R. (1982). Support for the death penalty: Instrumental response to crime, or symbolic attitude? *Law & Society Review, 17*(1), 21–45.

Van den Haag, E. (1982). In defense of the death penalty: A practical and moral analysis. In H. A. Bedau (Ed.), *The death penalty in America* (3rd ed., pp. 323–333). New York, NY: Oxford University Press.

Van den Haag, E. (1997). The death penalty once more. In H. A. Bedau (Ed.), *The death penalty in America: Current controversies* (pp. 445–456). New York, NY: Oxford University Press.

Van den Haag, E. (2003). Justice, deterrence and the death penalty. In J. R. Acker, R. M. Bohm, & C. S. Lanier (Eds.), *America's experiment with capital punishment: Reflections on the past, present, and future of the ultimate penal sanction* (2nd ed., pp. 233–249). Durham, NC: Carolina Academic Press.

Vandiver, M., Giacopassi, D. J., & Gathje, P. R. (2002). "I hope someone murders your mother!": An exploration of extreme support for the death penalty. *Deviant Behavior: An Interdisciplinary Journal, 23*, 385–415.

Vartkessian, E. S., Sorensen, J. R., & Kelly, C. E. (2017). Tinkering with the machinery of death: An analysis of juror decision-making in Texas death penalty trials during two statutory eras. *Justice Quarterly, 34*(1), 1–24.

Vogel, B. L. (2003). Support for life in prison without the possibility of parole among death penalty proponents. *American Journal of Criminal Justice, 27*(2), 263–275.

Vollum, S. (2008). *Last words and the death penalty: Voices of the condemned and their covictims.* New York, NY: LFB Scholarly Press.

Vollum S., & Buffington-Vollum, J. K. (2010). An examination of social-psychological factors and support for the death penalty: Attribution, moral disengagement, and value-expressive functions of attitudes. *American Journal of Criminal Justice, 35*(1), 15–36.

Vollum, S., del Carmen, R. V., & Longmire, D. R. (2004). Should jurors be informed about parole eligibility in death penalty cases? An analysis of Kelly v. South Carolina. *Prison Journal, 84*(3), 395–410.

Vollum, S., Kubena, J., & Buffington-Vollum, J. (2004, March). *Attitudes about the death penalty: An examination of underlying bases of support for the "ultimate punishment."* Paper presented at the annual meetings of the Academy of Criminal Justice Sciences, Las Vegas, NV.

Vollum, S., Longmire, D. R., & Buffington-Vollum, J. (2004). Confidence in the death penalty and support for its use: Exploring the value-expressive dimension of death penalty attitudes. *Justice Quarterly, 21*(3), 521–546.

Vollum, S., Mallicoat, S., & Buffington-Vollum, J. (2009). Death penalty attitudes in an increasingly critical climate: Value-expressive support and attitude mutability. *Southwest Journal of Criminal Justice, 5*(3), 221–242.

Webb, J. (2009, March 29). What's wrong with our prisons? *Parade*. Retrieved from https://parade.com/104227/senatorjimwebb/why-we-must-fix-our-prisons/.

Wheeler, M. (2000, June 23). Protesters declare war on Gov. Bush. *The Huntsville Item*, pp. 1A, 3A.

Whitehead, J. T. (1998). "Good ol' boys" and the chair: Death penalty attitudes of policy makers in Tennessee. *Crime and Delinquency, 44*(2), 245–256.

Whitehead, J. T., Blankenship, M. B., & Wright, J. P. (1999). Elite versus citizen attitudes on capital punishment: Incongruity between the public and policymakers. *Journal of Criminal Justice, 27*(3), 249–258.

Wilson, T., & Long, R. (2011, January 11). Illinois death penalty ban sent to Gov. Pat Quinn. *Chicago Tribune*. Retrieved from http://newsblogs.chicagotribune.com/clout_st/2011/01/illinois-death-penalty-ban-a-step-closer-to-governors-desk.html.

Zimmerman, P. R. (2004). State executions, deterrence, and the incidence of murder. *Journal of Applied Economics, 7*, 163–193.

Cases Cited

Gregg v. Georgia, 428 U.S. 153 (1976)

Lockhart v. McCree, 476 U.S. 162 (1986)

Chapter 8

Faulty Sex Offender Policies

Alissa R. Ackerman and Karen J. Terry

Introduction

Over the last two decades, policy makers have enacted a myriad of laws to protect the public from sex offenders by increasing prison sentences, permitting involuntary civil commitment, and enacting broad residence restrictions. These policies are widely accepted as providing safety and security from dangerous recidivist offenders who repeatedly commit horrendous acts against young children. Many of these laws are named after the tragic, though not typical, sexual crime against a child. Since the early 1990s, federal legislation has been enacted in the attempt to streamline state level policies, though state and local jurisdictions can, and often do, enact supplementary policies to further enhance community protection. The major federal laws created to protect communities and regulate behavior include the Jacob Wetterling Crimes Against Children and Sexually Violent Offender Registration Act,[1] Megan's Law,[2] and the Adam Walsh Child Protection and Safety Act of 2006.[3] There have been few evaluation studies assessing the effectiveness of these laws, but those studies have provided mixed results.

This chapter will discuss the many policies designed to enhance community protection that may prove to be ineffective and potentially dangerous. Some of these policies include broad community notification, residency restrictions, civil commitment, and GPS tracking. We will address both federal and state policies.

---

1. 42 U.S.C. § 14071.
2. 42 U.S.C. § 14071(e).
3. Pub. L. 109-248, § 501(1)(A), 120 Stat. 587, 623 (July 27, 2006).

The Emergence of Current Sex Offender Laws

After a few highly publicized and high-profile cases in the late 1980s and early 1990s committed by strangers against young children, public policies began focusing on the issue of stranger danger. Wesley Alan Dodd and Earl Shriner were two such individuals. Dodd murdered three young boys after molesting and torturing them, and Shriner kidnapped a seven-year-old boy, sexually assaulted him, cut off his penis, and left him to die. Both men had previously served prison terms for sexually based offenses, but because they had served their time, the state of Washington could do nothing but release them. These cases prompted Washington to pass comprehensive legislation to prevent these types of events from occurring again.

In 1990, Washington became the first state to enact registration and community notification laws. The Community Protection Act of 1990 contained 14 provisions for ensuring community safety against predators. These provisions provided the impetus for other states and the federal government to enact similar legislation, including sexually violent predator legislation and registration and community notification. Table 1 shows a summary of the key laws related to the supervision and management of sex offenders.

Registration and Community Notification Laws

In 1989, 11-year-old Jacob Wetterling was abducted at gunpoint while riding his bike with his brother and their friend. The masked gunman ordered all three boys to lie face down on the ground and, after asking their ages, told Jacob's brother and friend to run into the woods without looking back. The two boys looked back in time to see the gunman take Jacob by the arm, but by the time they returned to the woods, Jacob and the gunman were gone. Jacob's body was discovered in 2016. In 1994, Congress passed the Jacob Wetterling Crimes Against Children and Sexually Violent Offender Registration Act (herein referred to as the Jacob Wetterling Act), which mandates each state to create a central registry of offenders convicted of sexual and other specific crimes against children. States were provided an allotted amount of time to comply with the law, and if they did not comply, would forfeit 10% of federal funding under the Omnibus Crime Control and Safe Streets Act of 1968.

In 1994, Megan Kanka, a seven-year-old girl was raped and killed by a repeat sex offender living across the street from her New Jersey home. The assailant, Jesse Timmendequas, had twice been convicted of sexual offenses against children and lived with two other child molesters. Timmendequas was able to

Table 1. Key Federal and State Statutes

Name of Statute	Federal or State	Brief Description
Community Protection Act of 1990	Washington State	America's first Community Notification statute. Allowed law enforcement to notify the public about released sex offenders in the community.
Jacob Wetterling Crimes Against Children and Sexually Violent Predator Program (1994)	Federal	Required each state to create a registry for offenders convicted of sexual offenses against and other certain other offenses against children. States that do not comply risk losing 10% of federal funding.
Megan's Law (1996)	Federal	Subsection of the Jacob Wetterling Act. Together, these are referred to as Registration and Community Notification Laws (RCNL). The two acts required all states to implement RCNL by the end of 1997 or risk losing federal funding for state and local law enforcement. States that do not comply risk losing 10% of federal funding.
Pam Lychner Sexual Offender Tracking and Identification Act of 1996	Federal	Subsection of the Jacob Wetterling Act. Established a national database at the Federal Bureau of Investigation (FBI) to track the whereabouts of all those who have been convicted of an offense against a minor or a sexually violent offense. States that do not comply risk losing 10% of federal funding.
Jimmy Ryce Involuntary Civil Commitment for Sexually Violent Predators Treatment and Care Act (1998)	Florida	There are a small number of extremely dangerous sexually violent predators who do not have a mental disease or defect but who have antisocial personality features that make them unamenable to existing treatment. This law allows for long-term civil commitment of such offenders.
Jessica Lunsford Act (2005)	Florida	State law that increased penalties for sexually based offenses against minors and required fingerprinting and identification of all individuals working at schools. Florida was the first state to pass this law, but other states have "Jessica's Laws" that are very similar to the Florida Law.

Name of Statute	Federal or State	Brief Description
Adam Walsh Child Protection and Safety Act (2006)	Federal	The Act sets national standards on the following measures: registration and notification, civil commitment, child pornography prevention, Internet safety, and makes failure to register as a sex offender a deportable offense. It is one of the most comprehensive acts ever created to supervise and manage sex offenders. States that do not comply risk losing 10% of federal funding.

Source: Terry and Ackerman (2009).

lure Megan into his house to see his puppy and subsequently raped and murdered her. Megan's parents and many community members did not understand how a dangerous sex offender could be living in the community among them without their knowledge. Maureen Kanka, Megan's mother, campaigned to change the current law, stating that registration alone could not protect children. She further stated that if she had known about the dangerous individual living across the street, she could have warned Megan, who would still be alive today. New Jersey legislators passed Megan's Law 89 days after Megan's death, and President Bill Clinton enacted a federal version of the law, to streamline state statutes, in 1996 (Terry & Furlong, 2008). The federal version of Megan's Law amended the Jacob Wetterling Act, and together these laws are referred to as Registration and Community Notification Laws (RCNL). Like the Jacob Wetterling Act, Megan's Law mandated state compliance by 1997 and threatened the loss of federal funding for law enforcement for noncompliance. Every state complied with the mandate, though there were certainly discrepancies in how states drafted Megan's Law statutes. Today there is greater consistency, but variation does exist.

Making Our Communities Safer for Children

Since the inception of RCNL statues, policy makers have examined more stringent ways to keep offenders away from children and to monitor them in the community. At the state and local level, enacted policies now include GPS monitoring, special identifiers on licenses, and residence restrictions. For example, Florida requires all sex offenders and predators to obtain a driver's license indicating their offense.[4] Alabama requires a similar sanction where sex offenders must obtain a driver's license upon which a special designation shall be placed.[5] The premise, upon which license designation is based, is that law enforcement can quickly identify a criminal sex offender. GPS monitoring became a popular method of supervision in the community after the kidnapping, rape, and murder of Jessica Lunsford. In February of 2005, nine-year-old Jessica was taken from her bedroom in the middle of the night by a recidivist sex offender living nearby. Months passed by the time her body was discovered in a shallow grave less than 200 feet from her home, and she had been buried alive. Florida law was quickly amended by the enactment of the Jessica Lunsford Act or Jessie's Law. Among other things,[6] Jessie's Law requires that any person who commits a crime against a minor will, after release from incarceration, be subject to GPS monitoring for the remainder of his or her life. Several states have adopted a version of Jessica's Law, often including provisions for GPS monitoring. In California, Jessica's Law was voted into law by 70% of California voters and required paroled sex offenders and high-risk sex offenders to be fitted with a GPS monitoring device. High-risk sex offenders would be monitored for life. There are many proponents of GPS monitoring because it alerts law enforcement when an offender, who is wearing the tracking device, enters an off limits zone. These devices also allow law enforcement to decipher where an individual was at the time of the occurrence of an offense. Despite the growing popularity of GPS monitoring, the most common of the aforementioned policies is residence restrictions. Under the assertion that geographical proximity to opportunities fosters one's likelihood of reoffending, residence restriction limits where sex offenders can live, work, or loiter. The legislation is often vague, stating that sex offenders cannot live within a certain distance from where children congregate. Of course, such places and the distance restriction vary by jurisdiction. Most restrictions prevent offenders from living 1,000 to 2,500 feet from schools, parks, or day care centers (Nieto & Jung, 2006) but may also include bus stops, malls, and other places densely populated by children. There are currently 22 states with some type of restriction, but this is a misleading count because most restrictions are executed at the local level (Nieto & Jung, 2006). It is also possible for a state to enact a specific restriction, with a jurisdiction within the state enacting a local, and more stringent, ordinance.

---

4. F.S. 322.141(3)(a)(b) and 322.141(4).
5. A.S. Section 15-20-26.2.
6. Florida Department of Law Enforcement (2005).

The Civil Commitment of Sexually Violent Predators

The emotionally charged and cyclical nature of policy implementation today, where a high-profile case occurs and new policies reflect public sentiments regarding being tough on sex offenders, is not a new phenomenon. After a few highly publicized cases in the early 1930s, severe forms of legislation were passed that were similar to the policies of today. One such case involved Albert Fish, who claims to have sexually assaulted more than 400 children. Fish's case was not, and is not, typical. His interest in sadism and masochism, the sheer number of alleged offenses, and his practice of cannibalism point to Fish as an outlier, not the norm. Nevertheless, his cases, and others like his, lead to the support of the incapacitation of "sexual defectives" (see "Isolation Advised for Sex Criminals," 1937). At the time, the number of sexually based offenses was decreasing, yet the number of arrests increased sharply. The arrests reflected changes in policing practices and crackdowns on minor crimes, such as homosexual acts in public, and the offenders became known as habitual sexual offenders and sexual psychopaths (Karpman, 1954; Jenkins, 1998; Tappan, 1950).

At the time, sexual deviancy and sexual psychopathy were thought to be diagnosable and treatable, and as such, states began enacting policies to incapacitate sexual psychopaths in mental hospitals indefinitely. Michigan first adopted mentally disordered sex offender (MDSO) legislation in 1937, and 28 states followed (Schwartz, 1999). Alexander (1993) notes that MDSO laws allowed states to incapacitate individuals until they were cured. To be held under an MDSO statute, the individual had to meet two criteria: mental illness and danger to oneself or others. Once the individual was no longer dangerous, he was to be released. Unfortunately, no consistent method of evaluating dangerousness existed, and diagnoses were often subjective. The notion of dangerousness typified the mores and values of the time, and as such, homosexual men were often considered dangerous. Instead of incapacitating the truly dangerous people like Albert Fish, states were committing homosexual men along with exhibitionists and other individuals convicted of nuisance sexual behaviors. The use of MDSO statutes continued through the early 1950s when many of the offenders committed had been accused of acts such as peeping or lewdness. Researchers and medical professionals began opposing the use of MDSO laws because of the premises on which they were based. First, professionals did not know enough about the etiology of sexual offending to warrant indefinite commitment. Tappan (1950) argued that this type of legislation was precarious because it allowed for the civil adjudication of individuals with no due process. In addition, individuals often committed under these laws were not mentally ill or impaired in any way. Finally, Tappan argued that many offenders were indefinitely held until cured but were not being provided the treatment necessary to cure them. The laws fell into disrepute, and by the early 1990s, only 13 states had MDSO statutes written into law.

Despite the numerous issues with MDSO laws, under the Community Protection Act, Washington State enacted new civil commitment statutes in 1990. The new Sexually Violent Predator (SVP) legislation is very similar to its predecessor, with a few changes. The main goal of the new SVP legislation is to civilly commit criminally convicted and dangerous sex offenders who suffer from a mental abnormality or personality disorder and who are a danger to themselves or others after their incarceration. Civil commitment is not a replacement for one's incarceration. After the completion of the criminal sentence, certain sex offenders are committed to a mental hospital until rehabilitated. These high-risk sex offenders will remain incapacitated until they are rehabilitated and no longer a risk to the community (Seling, 2000). To date, 20 states have enacted some type of SVP legislation. Similar to the enactment of RCNL statutes, many states enacted SVP legislation after heinous crimes against children. In Florida, the rape and murder of Jimmy Ryce by Juan Carlos Chavez led to the implementation of SVP legislation. Jimmy's parents lead the fight to pass civil commitment legislation, and almost three years after his death, Governor Lawton Chiles signed the Jimmy Ryce Involuntary Civil Commitment for Sexually Violent Predators' Treatment and Care Act (Jimmy Ryce Act).

Faulty Policy

The first portion of this chapter provided a brief introduction to current sex offender policies. The second half of the chapter will discuss why and how the logic on which these policies are based is faulty. This section will also discuss legal challenges and case law regarding sex offender policies. It is important to note that the original premise upon which the various sex offender policies were enacted was community protection against recidivist, high-risk sex offenders. Over the last 20 years our policies have become broader in focus and have widened the net of individuals sanctioned under the laws. Additionally, the sanctions under which offenders have been mandated have become harsher and more difficult to follow. Not surprisingly, RCNL policies have been challenged on numerous constitutional grounds, including violations of ex post facto, due process, cruel and unusual punishment, equal protection, and search and seizure. Other items dealing with the vague nature of these policies have been brought to the courts and include failure of the state to notify the offender of his duty to register, including registerable offenses that are not sex crimes (e.g., kidnapping a child with no sexual offense); failure to register as a criminal offense; application of RCNL to homeless and juvenile offenders; and the broad nature of Internet notification. Notably, the challenges that have been met with success only further define previously written policies, and the courts have continually decided that the sanctions of RCNL are not punishment and are not overly burdensome. The Supreme Court has even upheld challenges to the most broad notification systems.

The Jacob Wetterling Act and Megan's Law provide that states must create RCNL statutes as they see fit. One issue with state level statutes and registries is that it hinders one's ability to identify dangerous offenders at the national level. In an attempt to streamline information sharing across agencies, Congress passed the Pam Lychner Sexual Offender Tracking and Identification Act of 1996, another amendment to the Jacob Wetterling Act. This Act established a national database at the FBI that attempted to track the whereabouts of individuals convicted of certain offenses against children or sexually violent offenses. Today, anyone can search the Dru Sjodin National Sex Offender Public Website (NSOPW) to determine the address of any sex offender subject to public notification. While this is an important step, there are still many issues regarding information sharing. The data provided on the NSOPW is derived from each state database. If a state does not update current information, the national registry is incorrect.

Additional issues with having state level RCNLs include each state determining the level of risk to the community, which offenders to subject to public notification, and the length of time an offender is subject to notification. States often utilize varying risk assessment protocols. For example, some states utilize the STATIC-99 (Hanson & Thornton, 1999), while others rely on the Mn-SOST-R (Epperson, Kaul, Huot, Goldman, & Alexander, 2003), a tool that assesses both dynamic and static factors related to risk. Other states have created their own risk assessment guidelines. Without uniformity in assessing danger-ousness and without cross-validation among the various assessment tools, it is not possible to know much about the average risk posed by the population of registered offenders. States also decide which offenders will be subject to public notification. While some states, such as Nebraska and Minnesota, only publicly notify communities about high-risk (Level 3) sex offenders, other states have broad sweeping notification policies designed to notify the public about all individuals convicted of a sexually based offense. Certain states have found middle ground where their public registries provide information about moderate- and high-risk offenders. California provides public information including address disclosure on certain offenders, while providing public information, but no address disclosure, on separate class of sex offenders. Finally, California has an additional registry of sex offenders subject to notification but not registration. States also legislate the amount of time an individual will be subject to public notification.

In an attempt to bring all states into unison, the federal government passed the Adam Walsh Child Protection and Safety Act of 2006 (H.R. 4472), otherwise known as the Adam Walsh Act. The Act sets national standards for registration and notification, civil commitment, child pornography prevention, Internet safety, and it makes failure to register as a sex offender a deportable offense for immigrants. Probably the most significant item of the Act is that it attempts to enhance the current national registry by creating one with common factors for all sex offenders, regardless of the state they reside in. Some of the key features of the registry include the following:

- Tier 3, or the highest risk offenders, will be registered on a national database for life.
- Tier 2 (moderate risk) and Tier 1 (low-risk) offenders will be required to register for 25 and 15 years, respectively.
- Failure to register or update home and work information can result in felony charges, punishable by 10 years in prison.
- In-person verification of registry information will be 12 months for Tier 1 offenders, 6 months for Tier 2 offenders, and 3 months for Tier 3 offenders.
- All state registry websites must include information for all sex offenders in their database—not just that of high-risk (Tiers 2 and 3) offenders.
- DNA samples will be required of all registrants.
- All juvenile sex offenders will be required register, and those who are least 14 years of age at the time of the offense and who have been adjudicated for aggravated sexual abuse or some comparable offense will be subject to community notification provisions.

Unfortunately, many states have failed to comply with the Adam Walsh Act. There is growing concern over the efficacy of many of sex offense policies, including the broad sweeping Adam Walsh Act. For instance, Minnesota has elected not to comply with the Act, as the state embraces an evidence-based policy model. It is their approach that, until there is research finding that the Adam Walsh Act is effective in its pursuit of community safety and reduced recidivism, no law will be enacted to follow the legislation. Because the law is so broad and the long-term consequences are unknown, states fear compliance more so than the risk of losing federal funding for noncompliance.

Civil Commitment

The efficacy of SVP statutes and the use of civil commitment have also been called into question. To be civilly committed one must generally (1) be convicted of a sexually violent offense and (2) suffer from a mental abnormality or personality disorder that is likely to put the person at high risk of committing a future act of sexual violence. SVP legislation is meant to target a small, but dangerous, group of offenders that "renders them appropriate for involuntary treatment" (Kansas SVPA §59-29a). The civil commitment process takes several steps that lead to a civil commitment trial. First, the offender must be referred to the course prior to release from incarceration. Next, a hearing is held to determine whether there is probable cause to believe the offender meets the criteria for commitment. If there is probable cause, the offender is subject to a risk assessment evaluation and, if deemed dangerous, a trial is held within 45 days. Like RCNL laws, states differ on certain factors. With SVP laws, states differ on their burden of proof necessary at trial to determine if the offender is an SVP; some states require proof beyond a reasonable doubt, but others merely require clear and convincing evidence. Given this difference, it is difficult to determine, at the national level, whether the most dangerous offenders are being targeted for commitment. In addition to the inability of researchers to make certain cross-state comparisons, the practice of indefinitely committing someone after the end of a criminal sentence is highly controversial. Actuarial risk assessment tools do not always properly assess risk. Human behavior is dynamic, and the ability to accurately predict it depends on the assessor, the quality of the assessment, and the individual being assessed (Lidz & Mulvey, 1995).

The type of facility utilized in each state also differs. While some states utilize state hospitals (Arizona, California, North Dakota, and Wisconsin), mental health hospitals (Minnesota, Missouri, and Wisconsin), and mental health facilities (Kansas, New Jersey, and Washington) to confine SVPs, other statues utilize "secure facilities" (South Carolina and Illinois), maximum security prisons (Iowa), and even private (for profit) maximum security facilities (Florida). For example, the Florida Civil Commitment Center is run by Liberty Behavioral Health, a private corporation contracted by the state to run the facility.

While most states provide for indefinite commitment, some mandate review at specific time intervals. These reviews are typically biennial or annual reviews. Further, states differ in the length of time the individual can be confined, the most common being indefinite/indeterminate commitment. However, many states mandate review of the commitment at specific time intervals. Texas mandates biennial review, whereas Florida requires an annual review. California allows for a 2-year confinement at which time a petition must be filed to extend that time period. By 2006, almost 5,000 individuals had been civilly committed in the United States (4,534). Only 494 has been discharged or released, and most were released on technicalities rather than having been deemed as rehabilitated. As most individuals held under SVP statues will never be released, many criticize the expensive nature of the policy. While incarceration costs, on average, $26,000 a year, civil commitment is almost four times the cost at approximately $94,000 (Gookin, 2007).

The intended purpose of SVP legislation was to incapacitate dangerous sex offenders who suffered from some type of mental disease or abnormality until they are rehabilitated. Rehabilitation requires some type of treatment protocol; however, in *Kansas v. Hendricks* (1997) 521 U.S. 346, 117 S.Ct. 2072, 138 L.Ed.2d 501, the Court ruled that civil commitment is constitutional even if treatment is not available as long as it may become available at some point in the future. It is possible that in many places, civil commitment is nothing more than expensive incapacitation. Indeed, an investigative report by Jason Grotto (2005), a journalist at the *Miami Herald*, found that at the Florida Civil Commitment Center, drug use is rampant, treatment does not work, and often the "inmates run the asylum."

The Management of Sex Offenders in the Community—Moving Beyond Registration

The most recent policy set in place is the use of residence restrictions. These policies mandate where certain sex offenders can live and make it difficult for people to find secure housing. Residency restrictions have been challenged in court, but in 2005, the Eighth Circuit Court of Appeals upheld an Iowa statute that prohibited sex offenders from living within 2,000 feet of designated places where children congregate [(*Doe v. Miller*, 418 F.3d 950 (2005)]. In doing so, the Court stated that residency restrictions are not, on their face, unconstitutional. The Association for the Treatment of Sexual Abusers (ATSA) (2005), in a petition to the Supreme Court, argued that residency restrictions may deprive sex offenders of housing options, force offenders to move from supportive environments and employment opportunities, and, subsequently, could increase, rather than decrease, recidivism risk. A recent study of registered sex offenders shed light on the stance taken by ATSA. To assess whether sex offender policies put undue strain or stress on sex offenders, Ackerman (2009) surveyed offenders in three states. The study showed that offenders who reported a lack of supportive environments (e.g., having to move away from family and friends or move from a home and a lack of prosocial ties to the community) and increased levels of stress or strain increased the likelihood that the offender reported a subsequent offense. Interestingly, these subsequent offenses were less likely to be sexually based offenses and more likely to include drugs or violence.

Few other empirical studies have thus far addressed the outcome of this legislation, and the empirical studies that do exist have produced conflicting results. In 2003, the Minnesota Department of Corrections found that residency restrictions created a shortage of available housing alternatives for sex offenders, which may force them into isolated areas that lack services, employment opportunities, and/or adequate social support. Similarly, the Colorado Department of Public Safety (2004) found that the use of residency restrictions in urban areas leaves few areas available for sex offenders to reside. Wartell (2007) found that only 27% of available living space within the city of San Diego was available to sex offenders. Some studies find that sex offenders still live within sex offender "buffer zones," with higher risk offenders living closer to places where children congregate. Walker, Golden, and VanHouten (2002) mapped the addresses of 170 sex offenders in a metropolitan Arkansas county and found that a higher percentage of child sex offenders (48%) lived within 1,000 buffer zones around schools, day care centers, and parks than did nonchild sex offenders (26%). Weiner (2007) found that 85% of New York City's highest risk offenders lived within five blocks of a school. A few studies have found that, even with restrictions in place, there are still places for offenders to find adequate housing. Grubesic, Murray, and Mack (2007) found that 63% of residential space remained available after 1,000 feet residency restrictions were put in place in Hamilton County, Ohio. Tewksbury and Mustaine (2006), however, found that fewer than one quarter of sex offenders reside near a park or playground, while less than one in seven live near a school, community center, or library.

There is an area of research that indicates destabilization caused by residency restrictions. Levenson and Cotter (2005) found that 57% of offenders reported that they found it difficult to locate affordable housing, 48% reported having suffered financially, and another 60% reported having suffered emotionally as a result of residency restrictions. Mercado and Alvarez (2007) reported that 35% of the offenders in their sample were unable to live with supportive family members and that 40% of the offenders reported that they had to live further from employment as a result of residency restrictions in New Jersey. Levenson and Hern (2007) found that offenders frequently reported housing instability and difficulties accessing employment, social services, and other community supports. Ackerman (2009) found that 54.7% of her sample had been denied a place to live and 65.2% reported experiencing financial hardships as a result of sex offender policies. In addition, 55.4% of the sample reported losing a job and 63.2% reported losing several friends. Unfortunately, the inconsistent findings from research and the lack of large scale studies makes it difficult to assess the usefulness of sex offender laws.

Little research has been conducted on the use of GPS tracking to monitor sex offenders, but from what has been studied, we know that such policies often fall short of their purpose because of lack of communication and collaboration between organizations and jurisdictions. States spend substantial resources on GPS tracking on a broad scale but have yet to conduct evaluations of the effectiveness of the policy. If local and state level organizations do not communicate, the use of GPS tracking will be an expensive and ineffective program.

Efficacy of the Sex Offender Laws

The premise on which our sex offender policies are based is that of community safety. It is still unclear as to whether the implementation of these policies has accomplished this goal. Research findings are mixed, and much more needs to be conducted to determine whether our laws are effective. A second goal, which we often lose sight of, should be reentry and reintegration of sex offenders into the community. While offenders are reentering the community every day, it is not known whether our laws are reintegrative. Before implementing any more such laws, it is necessary to thoroughly evaluate the policies currently in place. Many of our current laws are reactionary and are thought of as "feel good" legislation. These knee jerk reactions may not be the most effective for all offenders. Sex offenders constitute a heterogeneous group of individuals who offend for a variety of reasons, but the overall recidivism rate for sex offenders is low. There are, of course, some very serious sex offenders who are repeat offenders with many victims. It is important to identify those individuals and make all efforts to keep them from committing future offenses that might have been preventable. However, it is important to assess whether sex offender laws appropriately target those very serious offenders to protect the community from them or if they cast such a wide net that the dangerous offenders are lost among the low- to moderate-risk offenders subject to the same legislation.

The public loathes sex offenders because of the fear that they will inevitably commit new sex crimes. Many state legislatures and sex offender registry websites have stated in their laws that sex offenders pose a high risk of reoffending. Sex offender legislation is based on the assumption that sex offenders will recidivate with new sexual offenses, but research findings tell a different story. Hanson and Morton-Bourgon (2005) conducted a meta-analysis and found a 13.7% recidivism rate for a new sex crime over five years, and the Bureau of Justice Statistics (BJS) found a 5.3% recidivism rate for sex offenders over three years (BJS, 2003). Sex offenses are among the least reported of all crimes. It is always best to use caution when interpreting official statistics because of the low reporting rates. Research in the field of criminology provides some support for the official numbers on sex offender recidivism. Interestingly, these studies consistently find that when sex offenders do reoffend, they are more likely to commit a nonsexual offense than a sexual one (see Lussier, LeBlanc, & Proulx, 2005; Miethe, Olson, & Mitchell, 2006; Simon, 2000; Smallbone & Wortley, 2004; Soothill, Francis, Sanderson, & Ackerley, 2000; and Zimring, Piquero, & Jennings, 2007).

The aim of all sex offender legislation is to protect the community. However, much of the legislation is based upon flawed assumptions about sex offenders, or it is based upon the rare occurrence where someone abducts and murders a child. It is true that this legislation might have prevented certain tragic cases. Had the Kanka's known that Timmendequas lived across the street, Megan would have been instructed not to go near his house. However, our current legislation is severely flawed and will likely not prevent most cases. It may actually increase the amount of risk in a community. Listed below are five basic flaws in our current policies:

- Sex offenders have low recidivism rates.
- When registered sex offenders do recidivate, it is often with a nonsexual offense.
- Victims of sexual offenses are likely to know the perpetrator.
- Most sexual abuse occurs within the home of the perpetrator and/or victim.
- Local and state laws do not account for offenders committing crimes in locations outside their communities.

Legislation targeting sex offenders has been described as a "one size fits all" policy that could never properly address the etiology of offending for a very heterogeneous population. Yet, community members often report feeling safer because of the implementation of such laws (Anderson & Sample, 2008; Lieb & Nunlist, 2008; Phillips, 1998). Further, research shows that the public agrees that community notification, registration, as well as various other laws (residency restrictions and GPS monitoring), will deter people from committing sex offenses (Katz, Levenson, & Ackerman, 2008; Levenson, Brannon, Fortney, & Baker, 2007; Philips, 1998; Redlich, 2001). The wide support for sex offense legislation does not equate to what the public perceives to be true about sexual offending and offenders. In 2007, Levenson and her colleagues found that 80% of respondents in a survey of Florida residents believed that 80% of sex offenders will reoffend and that many child victims of sexual assault do not know their assailant. In addition, most respondents questioned whether sex offenders could be rehabilitated (Levenson et al., 2007). In a second analysis, the research compared public opinion data with published research on recidivism, assault, and rehabilitation and found statistically significant differences (Fortney, Levenson, Brannon, & Baker, 2007). These data suggest that the public will continue to support the broad use of sex offense legislation while harboring a false sense of security regarding the effectiveness of the legislation at keeping their families safe. Unfortunately, it is possible that the laws and the false sense of security only increases, rather than decreases, risk to the community. Complying with harsher legislation and increased sanctions might cause offenders to abscond. Bedarf (1995) suggested that this can be seen when comparing compliance rates across states, as states with more restrictive policies have lower rate of compliance.

Current policies also influence the broader criminal justice system. Alleged offenders may be less likely to accept a plea bargain when they are aware that doing so will subject them to the harsh realities of registration and the various other requirements. This may cause a backup in the court system, where more alleged individuals will risk a trial and a harsher sentence to avoid the inevitable requirements by pleading guilty. As more states fully implement and comply with the Adam Walsh Act, it is possible that fear of such consequences will rise, overwhelming the court system.

While our laws should be implemented to keep people safe from dangerous offenders, our interest in the sex offending population is spurred by cases that are uncommon and least likely to occur. We see all sex offenders as "monsters," in part because of the heinous cases described above but also because of offenses involving people of trust (e.g., clergy members, coaches, and teachers). As sensationalized cases come to the forefront, we continue to broaden our laws, and it does not appear that any major benefits will occur. All sexually based offenses are harmful to victims and their families, and no sex offense should be dismissed as anything less than tragic. However, the goals of legislation should be prevention, reduction in recidivism, and community protection while balancing the rights of victims, offenders, and the community. We offer the three "Es" as to accomplish this:

- evaluation
- effectiveness
- education

First and foremost, all potential legislation should be fully evaluated prior to being written into law. Prior to the enactment of RCNL, little research was conducted to determine if these laws would be effective in reducing recidivism (Thomas, 2003). Terry (2003) maintains that legislators never asked the questions that were "essential to understand whether such legislation would be effective in its goal of community protection" (p. 57). Since that time, researchers have begun to assess the effectiveness of the laws, but most studies seeking to determine whether RCNL are effective find limited support (see Adkins, Huff, & Stageberg, 2000; Walker, Maddan, Vasquez, VanHouten, & Ervin-Mclarty, 2005; Zevitz, 2006). Certain states have research bodies that evaluate policy and then use the findings to make programmatic and evidence-based decisions. For instance, two state-sponsored studies on residency restrictions found that they would not be effective in reducing recidivism (Colorado Department of Public Safety, 2004; Minnesota Department of Corrections, 2007). Both states elected to not utilize residency restrictions (at the state level) as a community sanction. Additionally, both states have elected not to follow the Adam Walsh Act until there is evidence to suggest that the Act is effective in its aim of community protection.

After policy evaluations are conducted, states should make evidence-based decisions regarding the implantation of laws. Policies that are found to be ineffective should be reevaluated. Potential legislation should never be used to obtain community support when the premise upon which it is based is inherently flawed. Finally, educating the public is crucial. The public is ill-informed regarding sexual offending, and the best strategy to prevent future offending is to inform communities about actual risk. Research shows that over 90% of child sexual abusers are well known to their victims (Berliner, Schram, Miller, & Milloy, 1995; BJS, 2000); about 34% are family members and 59% are acquaintances (BJS, 2000). While teaching children not to talk to strangers is important, parents must understand and convey to their children that the greatest risk of victimization is within a much closer network of people. Other research suggests that many people do not utilize state sex offender registries to access information on offenders (Anderson & Sample, 2008); however, state registry websites often provide a frequently asked question section to answer basic questions about sex offenders and their offenses. If this information were more readily available, it might broaden community understanding of offending patterns.

It is not known what the future of sex offender legislation will be, but by most accounts it appears to be broadening quickly. New legislation should be targeted at specific offenders, sanctioned on an individual basis. The Adam Walsh Act, meant to streamline state legislation, does not account for this heterogeneity. Questions remain as to what policies will be most effective, but until such time, legislators should proceed with caution.

References

Ackerman, A. (2009). *Registered sex offenders in the community: A test of Agnew's general strain theory* (Unpublished doctoral dissertation). City University of New York, NY.

Adkins, G., Huff, D., & Stageberg, P. (2000). *The Iowa Sex Offender Registry and recidivism.* Des Moines, IA: Iowa Department of Human Rights.

Alexander, R. (1993.) The civil commitment of sex offenders in light of Foucha v. Louisiana. *Criminal Justice and Behavior, 20,* 371–387.

Anderson, A. L., & Sample, L. (2008). Public awareness and action resulting from sex offender community notification laws. *Criminal Justice Policy Review, 19,* 371–396.

Bedarf, A. R. (1995). Examining Sex Offender Notification Laws. *California Law Review, 83*(3), 885–939.

Berliner, L., Schram, D., Miller, L., & Milloy, C. D. (1995). A sentencing alternative for sex offenders: A study of decision making and recidivism. *Journal of Interpersonal Violence, 10*(4), 487–502.

Bureau of Justice Statistics. (2000). *Sexual assault of young children as reported to law enforcement: Victim, incident, and offender characteristics.* Retrieved from https://www.bjs.gov/content/pub/pdf/saycrle.pdf.

Bureau of Justice Statistics. (2003). *Recidivism of sex offenders released from prison in 1994.* Retrieved from https://www.bjs.gov/content/pub/pdf/rsorp94.pdf.

Colorado Department of Public Safety. (2004). *Report on safety issues raised by living arrangements for and location of sex offenders in the community.* Denver, CO: Colorado Department of Public Safety, Division of Criminal Justice, Sex Offender Management Board.

Epperson, D. L., Kaul, J. D., Huot, S., Goldman, R., & Alexander, W. (2003). *Minnesota Sex Offender Screening Tool-Revised (MnSOST-R) technical paper: Development, validation, and recommended risk level cut scores.* St. Paul, MN: Minnesota Department of Corrections.

Florida Department of Law Enforcement (2005). *Highlights from the Jessica Lunsford Act.* Retrieved March 31, 2008, http://www3.fdle.state.fl.us/sopu/citizeninfo.asp

Fortney, T., Levenson, J. S., Brannon, Y., & Baker, J. (2007). Myths and facts about sex offenders: Implications for practice and public policy. *Sex Offender Treatment, 2*(1), 1–17.

Gookin, K. (2007). *Comparison of state laws authorizing involuntary commitment of sexually violent predators: 2006 update.* Washington State Institute for Public Policy. Retrieved from http://www.wsipp.wa.gov/ReportFile/989/Wsipp_Comparison-of-State-Laws-Authorizing-Involuntary-Commitment-of-Sexually-Violent-Predators-2006-Update-Revised_Full-Report.pdf.

Grotto, J. (2005) Predators among us (4-day series 1/29/05–2/2/06). *Miami Herald.*

Grubesic, T. H., Murray, A. T., & Mack, E. A. (2007, March). *Geographic exclusion: Spatial analysis for evaluating the implications of Megan's Law.* Presented at the National Institute of Justice's Ninth Annual Crime Mapping Conference held in Pittsburgh, PA.

Hanson, R. K., & Morton-Bourgon, K. (2005). The characteristics of persistent sexual offenders. *Journal of Consulting and Clinical Psychology, 73*, 1154–1163.

Hanson, R. K., & Thornton, D. M. (1999). *STATIC-99: Improving actuarial risk assessments of sexual recidivism.* Ottawa, ON: Office of the Solicitor General of Canada.

Isolation advised for sex criminals; Dr. Lichtenstein would keep defectives off the streets and out of prison. (1937, October 14). *New York Times.*

Jenkins, P. (1998). *Moral panic: Changing concepts of the child molester in modern America.* New Haven, CT: Yale University Press.

Karpman, B. (1954). *The sexual offender and his offenses: Etiology, pathology, psychodynamics and treatment.* New York, NY: Julian Press.

Kansas SVPA § 59-29a.

Katz, S. M., Levenson, J. S., & Ackerman, A. R. (2008). Myths and facts about sexual violence: Public perceptions and implications for prevention. *Journal of Criminal Justice and Popular Culture, 15*, 291–311.

Levenson, J. S., Brannon, Y., Fortney, T., & Baker, J. (2007). Public perceptions about sex offenders and community protection policies. *Analyses of Social Issues and Public Policy, 7*, 1–25.

Levenson, J. S., & Cotter, L. P. (2005). The effect of Megan's Law on sex offender reintegration. Journal of Contemporary Criminal Justice, *21*, 49–66.

Levenson, J. S., & Hern, A., 2007. Sex offender residence restrictions: Unintended consequences and community re-entry. *Justice Research and Policy, 9*, 60–73.

Lidz, C. W., & Mulvey, E. P. (1995). Dangerousness: From legal definition to theoretical research. *Law and Human Behavior, 19*, 41–48.

Lieb, R., & Nunlist, C. (2008). *Community notification as viewed by Washington's citizens: A ten-year follow-up* (No. 08-03-1101). Olympia, WA: Washington State Institute for Public Policy.

Lussier, P., LeBlanc, M., & Proulx, J. (2005). The generality of criminal behavior: A confirmatory factor analysis of the criminal activity of sex offenders in adulthood. *Journal of Criminal Justice, 33*, 177–189.

Mercado, C. C., & Alvarez, S. (2007). *The impact of community notification and residency restrictions on sex offender community reintegration.* Paper presented at the Off the Witness Stand: Using Psychology in the Practice of Justice conference, New York, NY.

Miethe, T. D., Olson, J., & Mitchell, O. (2006). Specialization and persistence in the arrest histories of sex offenders: A comparative analysis of alternative measures and offense types. *Journal of Research in Crime and Delinquency, 43,* 204–229.

Minnesota Department of Corrections (2007). *Residential proximity & sex offense recidivism in Minnesota.* St. Paul, MN: Minnesota Department of Corrections.

Nieto, M., & Jung, D. (2006). *The impact of residency restrictions on sex offenders and correctional management practices: A literature review.* Sacramento, CA: California Research Bureau.

Phillips, D. M. (1998). *Community notification as viewed by Washington's citizens.* Olympia, WA: Washington State Institute for Public Policy.

Redlich, A., (2001). Community notification: Perceptions of its effectiveness in preventing child sexual abuse. *Journal of Child Sexual Abuse, 10,* 91–116.

Schwartz, B. K. (1999). The case against involuntary commitment. In Schlank, A., & Cohen, F. (Eds.), *The Sexual Predator: Law, Policy, Evaluation and Treatment, Vol. 2.* Kingston, NJ: Civic Research Institute.

Seling, M. (2000). *A treatment program overview.* Steilacoom, WA: Special Commitment Center.

Simon, L. M. J. (2000). An examination of the assumptions of specialization, mental disorder, and dangerousness in sex offenders. *Behavioral Sciences and the Law, 18,* 175–308.

Smallbone, S. W., & Wortley, R. K. (2004). Criminal diversity and paraphilic interests among adult males convicted of sexual offenses against children. *International Journal of Offender Therapy and Comparative Criminology, 48,* 175–188.

Soothill, K., Francis, B., Sanderson, B., & Ackerley, E. (2000). Sex offenders: Specialists, generalists—or both? *British Journal of Criminology, 40,* 56–67.

Tappan, P. W. (1950). *The habitual sex offender: Report and recommendation of the commission on the habitual sex offender.* Trenton, NJ: Commission on the Habitual Sex Offender.

Terry, K. J. (2003). Sex offenders: Editorial introduction. *Criminology and Public Policy, 3,* 57–59.

Terry, K., J. & Ackerman, A. R. (2009) A history of sex offender registration. In R. G. Wright. (Ed.), *Sex offender laws: Failed policies new directions.* New York, NY: Springer.

Terry, K. J., & Furlong, J. (2008). *Sex offender registration and community notification: A "Megan's Law" sourcebook*. Kingston, NJ: Civic Research Institute.

Tewksbury, R., & Mustaine, E. E. (2006). Where to find sex offenders: An examination of residential locations and neighborhood conditions. *Criminal Justice Studies, 19*, 61–75.

Thomas, T. (2003). Sex offender community notification: Experiences from America. *Howard Journal of Criminal Justice, 42*, 217–228.

Walker, J. T., Golden, J. W., & VanHouten, A. C. (2001). The geographic link between sex offenders and potential victims: A routine activities approach. *Justice Research and Policy, 3*(2), 15–33.

Walker, J. T., Maddan, S., Vasquez, B. E., VanHouten, A. C., & Ervin-McLarty, G. (2005). *The influence of sex offender registration and notification laws in the United States*. Retrieved November 20, 2008, from http://www.acic.org/statistics/Research/SO_Report_Final.pdf.

Wartell, J. (2007, March). *Sex offender laws: Planning for an election*. Paper presented at the National Institute of Justice Ninth Annual Crime Mapping Research Conference, Pittsburgh, PA.

Weiner, A. D. (2007, January). *Sex offenders near schools: A review of the sex offender database*. Retrieved June 22, 2007, from http://www.house.gov/weiner/report39.htm.

Zevitz, R. G. (2006). Sex offender community notification: Its role in recidivism and offender reintegration. *Criminal Justice Studies, 19*, 193–208.

Zimring, F. E., Piquero, A. R., & Jennings, W. G. (2007). Sexual delinquency in Racine: Does early sex offending predict later sex offending in youth and young adulthood? *Criminology and Public Policy, 6*, 507–553.

Cases Cited

Kansas v. Hendricks (1997) 521 U.S. 346, 117 S.Ct. 2072, 138 L.Ed.2d 501.

Chapter 9

"Getting Tough" and the Adultification of Juvenile Justice

Frances P. Reddington

Introduction

Among all of the policy areas affecting vulnerable children and families, juvenile justice has probably suffered the most glaring gaps between best practice and common practice, between what we know and what we most often do. Perhaps because it serves an unpopular and powerless segment of our society—behaviorally troubled, primarily poor, mostly minority teenagers—juvenile justice policy has been too long shaped by misinformation, hyperbole, and political prejudices (Nelson, 2008).

The American juvenile justice system presents an interesting and often cyclical history. Much of what has impacted recent policy associated with juvenile justice is based on flawed public perception fueled by the media. In fact, perhaps this happens more in the juvenile system than in the criminal justice system because, in an effort to protect troubled children from scrutiny, the rehabilitative juvenile court system created in the late 1800s was a closed system, one that the public and the media did not have access to, and thus, did not—and still do not—fully understand.

This chapter contends that this lack of understanding contributed to a high reliance by the public and the legislature on the media to provide them with their understanding of how juvenile justice worked, or perhaps, did not work. The reliance on information that was not accurate, combined with a changing juvenile crime rate and a fear of the juvenile "super predators," resulted in some very questionable juvenile policy.

This chapter will briefly examine the history of the juvenile justice system, including information about the philosophy that inspired the first juvenile court in the United States. The chapter will also examine the influence that the Civil Rights Movement and subsequent legal and congressional responses had in shaping American juvenile justice. Also included is an in-depth examination of the "get tough" movement of the 1990s, a movement that helped to create a very different juvenile justice system and resulted in changes in both philosophy and process in the treatment of juvenile offenders. The chapter will then focus on the process of transfer—treating juveniles as adult offenders, which is perhaps the most significant policy changed during the get tough agenda of the recent past (Zimring, 2010). The following pages will examine the changes in breadth of transfer, changes in the transfer process, and frequency of use following the policy changes. The process of transfer will also be examined regarding effectiveness. Finally, this chapter will ask, where do we go from here? The chapter will conclude with suggestions for future juvenile justice policy to be based on sound scientific evidence-based research and proven best practices.

A Brief History of Juvenile Justice

Juvenile crime and misbehavior was not an issue in America until the 1830s when industrialization, immigration, and urbanization changed the traditional way of life and children were left unsupervised with idle time on their hands. As the only system in place to deal with misbehavior was the criminal justice system, most juveniles who committed crimes came through the criminal courts and were placed in prisons. At that time, the crimes could range from serious crimes to being homeless or loitering in public. Many young people were placed into prisons for nothing more than not being cared for. The maltreatment of juveniles in the prison system led reformers to think that perhaps there was a better way to deal with troubled children.

Instead of a separate court system for young offenders, reformers believed that separate housing for juveniles would be the best solution. New York City opened the first House of Refuge in 1825, an institution opened to house young offenders who had the potential to reform, and soon the house of refuge movement spread. In 1838, *Ex Parte Crouse*, decided in the Pennsylvania Supreme Court, gave these houses of refuge (and thus the state) the legal authority to raise children in these institutions when their parents failed to do so in the home (Sheldon & Macallair, 2008). Eventually, local governments became strong and big enough to begin to take over the housing of troubled and delinquent children. The houses of refuge gradually changed into state-run reformatories and reform schools. Allegations of abuse and concern of the effectiveness of these institutions led reformers to consider alternative approaches to dealing with troubled and delinquent children (Shelden & Maacallair, 2008).

The first juvenile court was created in Chicago, Illinois, and opened in 1899. Although Chicago is considered the home of the first juvenile court, in Denver, Colorado, the courts' approach to dealing with troubled and delinquent youth is often noted as being a major contributor to the philosophies of the first juvenile courts. Judge Julian Mack, a major force in the philosophy of the first juvenile court, summed it up well when he said, "(T)he focus of the juvenile court was not to decide if the child committed a specific wrong … but what had best be done in his interest and in the interest of the state to save him from a downward career" (Deitch, 2009, p. 6). With a court designed to replace in-effective parents (otherwise the child would never have been referred to court) and to operate in the best interests of the child, it did not seem as if the legal rights and procedures of the adult court needed to be afforded to juveniles. However, shortcomings in the system and the failure of the juvenile courts to live up to their lofty ideals soon led to the question of whether juvenile offenders deserved, and in fact were constitutionally entitled to, the same legal rights as adults in criminal courts were afforded. These questions were formally addressed in the 1960s.

The 1960s brought with them the massive Civil Rights Movement, and part of that movement included the rights of those accused of committing a crime and those housed in correctional institutions, including juveniles. The twin focus on the rights of juveniles in the court process and surfacing allegations of abuse within juvenile facilities led to a number of changes designed to better the juvenile justice system and afford juveniles due process rights. In 1968, the Juvenile Delinquency Prevention and Control Act (JDPCA) was passed. This has been referred to as the four Ds of juvenile justice: **diversion, decriminalization, deinstitutionalization, and due process** (Bell & Ridolfi, 2008).

Diversion refers to creating and placing juveniles in programs that bypass the formal juvenile court process. **Decriminalization** refers to the system addressing that those children who committed status offenses (those acts only defined as against the law for juveniles such as running away from home and truancy) should not be labeled as delinquent and institutionalized in a youth correctional system. **Deinstitutionalization** refers to the movement to reserve youth correctional institutions for those who really need incapacitation and to remove inappropriate placements and those who could be better served in other types of correctional programming. Some states closed or debated closing some of their institutions. **Due process**, however, may have been the biggest movement of the 1960s and 1970s when it came to shaping juvenile justice procedure and policy. After years of not taking cases involving juvenile justice, the Supreme Court accepted a number of cases involving the juvenile court and the rights of youth accused of a criminal act. The following major cases will be discussed below: *Kent, Gault, Winship,* and *McKeiver.*

Kent: *The Case That Opened the Door*

In September of 1961, 16-year-old Morris Kent was taken into custody and charged with breaking into a house, robbery, and rape. Morris was currently on juvenile probation for several home invasions and an attempted purse snatching. Kent's attorney asked for a hearing on whether Kent should be transferred to the adult court and for access to Kent's records. There was no hearing in the case, yet the judge, stated that he had made a "full investigation" and waived the jurisdiction of the case to the criminal court. The judge gave no reasons for his decision to send the case to the adult court. After the case was sent to the adult system, a grand jury indicted Kent. Kent went to trial and was found "not guilty by reason of insanity" on the rape charges, and he found guilty on numerous counts of breaking and entering and robbery. He was sentenced to a total of 30 to 90 years in prison (*Kent v. United States,* 1966).

The question that the Supreme Court addressed from the Kent case was whether juveniles who are being transferred to adult court have any due process rights during that waiver process. In 1966, the Supreme Court held that juveniles facing transfer to the adult criminal courts did, in fact, have certain due process rights that were to be upheld in the transfer process. These rights afforded in *Kent* are the following:

- a transfer hearing
- an attorney for the hearing
- access to the records that the juvenile court holds about the juvenile
- a statement of reasons for an affirmative transfer decision (*Kent v. US,* 1966)

These rights are very significant, as they signaled the first time that juveniles were afforded constitutional rights by the Supreme Court. However, the case dealt only with juveniles who might be transferred to the adult system, thus not a large percentage of juveniles were impacted by the decision. However, perhaps of most significance was the forewarning that the Supreme Court gave the juvenile court. The Court was not done accepting juvenile justice cases, as it certainly did not hold great faith in the practice of juvenile justice in the United States.

> While there can be no doubt of the original laudable purpose of the juvenile courts, studies and critiques of recent years raise serious questions as to whether actual performances measures well enough against purpose to make tolerable the immunity of the process from

the reach of constitutional guarantees applicable to adults. There is much evidence that some juvenile courts ... lack the personnel, facilities and techniques to perform adequately as representatives of the State in a *parens patriae* capacity, at least with respect to children charged with law violation. There is evidence, in fact, that there may by grounds for concern that the juvenile receives the worst of both worlds: that he gets neither the protections accorded to adults nor the solicitous care and regenerative treatment postulated for children. (*Kent v. US*, 1966)

Notice that while this court granted juveniles in the process of being transferred some basic fundamental rights, the Court commented on the continued failure of the facilities, programs, and institutions to rehabilitate troubled youth.

Gault: *The Case of Major Significance*

On June 8, 1964, mid-morning, a 15-year-old named Gerald Gault and his friend, Ronald Lewis, were taken into custody for reportedly making an obscene phone call to a female neighbor, Mrs. Cook. In the words of the Court, "it will suffice, for purposes of this opinion, to say that the remarks or questions put to her were of the irritatingly offensive, adolescent, sex variety" (*In re Gault*, 1967). Supposedly, the lewd comments consisted of "are your cherries ripe today" and "do you have big bombers" (Snyder & Sickmund, 2006, p.100). Gault was already on probation for being with a boy who had taken a wallet out of a woman's purse.

No one informed the Gaults of their son's arrest. Later that evening, after investigating his whereabouts, his mother learned that he was being held in detention. She traveled to the detention center, only to be told that Gault was to have a hearing the next day. The next day, Gault, his mother, brother, and the superintendent of the detention center were all present in the judge's chamber. They were the only people present. Apparently at the hearing, there was some confusion about whether Gault had made the offensive statements at all or only some of the statements. The judge sent him back to detention while he pondered the case. Six days later, there was another hearing. This time Gault, his codefendant, and parents were present. There was, again, general discussion about the role that Gault played in the alleged offense. The neighbor who had made the allegation was not present at this hearing either (*In re Gault*, 1967).

After the hearing, the judge committed Gault to the State Industrial School. The court order stated, as was common practice, that he was to remain there until the age of majority, which was 21 at that time. In essence, Gault, 15 years old, had just received a possible 6-year sentence for making a lewd phone call. If he had been an adult, the maximum punishment for a lewd phone call would have been two months in the local jail or a maximum $50 fine (*In re Gault*, 1967).

After the hearing, Gault's parents obtained an attorney who filed a writ of habeas corpus on the grounds that several of Gault's basic constitutional rights had been violated. In reality, the writ was asking the Supreme Court to hold that juveniles in juvenile court, in fact, did have constitutional rights, and as such, this child had been denied his.

The Supreme Court held in 1967 in an 8–1 decision that juveniles who are in an adjudication hearing where an affirmative finding of guilt could result in institutionalization do have certain due process rights. These rights are the following:

- the right to receive notice of the charges
- the right to counsel
- the right to confront and cross-examine
- the right to remain silent—the right against self-incrimination (*In re Gault*, 1967)

The Gault case was, and perhaps still is, the single most important juvenile case ever heard by the Supreme Court. By giving juveniles due process rights, the Supreme Court was tinkering with a juvenile system that had specifically not given due process rights to juveniles for 68 years, because children needed no due process protection against a system designed to protect them. What the High Court believed about the juvenile justice system was found in the majority opinion.

> We do not mean by this to denigrate the juvenile court process or to suggest that there are not aspects of the juvenile system relating to offenders which are valuable. But the features of the juvenile system which its proponents have asserted are of unique benefit will not be impaired by constitutional documentation. For example, the commendable principles relating to the processing and treatment of juveniles separately from adults are in no way involved or affected by the procedural issues under discussion.... It would be extraordinary if our Constitution did not require the procedural regularity and exercise of care implied in the phrase "due process." Under our Constitution, the condition of being a boy does not justify a kangaroo court." (*In re Gault*, 1967)

Winship: *The Case About Burden of Proof*

Twelve-year-old Samuel Winship was adjudicated delinquent of the theft of $112 out of a woman's purse that he had removed from a locker (*In re Winship*,

1970). As was New York juvenile law at the time, Winship was found guilty on a preponderance of the evidence. Winship was committed to the state system of juvenile corrections. He was sent to the facility for an initial 18 months and then could be subjected to extensions up until his 18th birthday, which would be six years total. The judge who presided over the case acknowledged that there might not have been enough evidence for an adjudication if the burden of proof in juvenile court was "beyond a reasonable doubt," but the burden in juvenile court was the much lower standard of "preponderance of the evidence" (*In re Winship*, 1970).

The single question that the Supreme Court decided in 1970 was "whether proof beyond a reasonable doubt is among the 'essential of due process and fair treatment' required during the adjudicatory stage when a juvenile is charged with an act which would constitute a crime if committed by an adult" (*In re Winship*, 1070). Were juveniles accused of committing a delinquent act entitled to the same burden of proof as adults accused of committing a crime? The Supreme Court decided, in a split 5–3 decision, that juveniles were entitled to proof beyond a reasonable doubt in a juvenile adjudication hearing. Furthermore, the Supreme Court said, "We conclude, as we concluded regarding the essential due process safeguards applied in *Gault*, that the observance of the standard of proof beyond a reasonable doubt 'will not compel the states to abandon or displace any of the substantive benefits of the juvenile process'" (*In re Winship*, 1970). In this case, the Supreme Court specifically mentions that an accused child deserves the highest burden of proof to determine guilt in juvenile court when that finding could result in institutionalization (*In re Winship*, 1970).

McKeiver: *The Case That Changed Direction*

In 1968, 16 year old Joseph McKeiver was charged with robbery, larceny, and receiving stolen goods. A group of many youth, including McKeiver, pursued three other children and robbed them of 25 cents. McKeiver requested that he be given a jury trial. His request was denied; he was adjudicated delinquent by a juvenile court judge and placed on juvenile probation. The case that was decided in 1971 by the Supreme Court answered the question of whether juveniles were entitled to a trial by jury in a juvenile adjudicatory hearing. In a 6–3 decision, the Supreme Court held that juveniles were not constitutionally entitled to a trial by jury during an adjudication hearing. In the words of the court, the "requiring of a jury trial might remake the juvenile proceedings into a fully adversarial process, with the attendant delay, formality, and clamor of such process, and would effectively end the juvenile system's idealistic prospect of an intimate, informal, protective procedure" (*McKeiver v. Pennsylvania*, 1971). However, the Supreme Court added, states could grant the right to trial by jury to juvenile adjudication hearing through their state constitutions, were they so inclined.

Federal Intervention

In addition to the four Ds of reform, diversion, decriminalization, deinstitutionalization, and due process, the concerns about juvenile justice in the United States prompted action by Congress. By the 1960s, a series of congressional hearings took place addressing the juvenile justice system and, in particular, the conditions of confinement. Many employees and clients of the juvenile justice system testified to mistreatment and even abuse within the system, especially within the institutions. As previously mentioned, in 1968 Congress passed the Juvenile Delinquency and Control Act, which encouraged states to develop community-based delinquency prevention programs combined with a promise of federal funding for approved programs (Bell & Ridolfi, 2008).

By the early 1970s, with a national momentum to address juvenile justice, and close to six years of research by a senate subcommittee designated to study juvenile justice, Congress passed a stronger piece of legislation that replaced the Juvenile Delinquency and Control Act. This was the Juvenile Justice and Delinquency Prevention Act of 1974 (JJDPA). JJDPA held a broader mandate aimed at prevention, rehabilitation, and improving the juvenile justice system (Act 4 Juvenile Justice, 2007). There are four major requirements that the JJDPA is known for, though the last two were added in later years through amendments. In 1974, the primary focus of the Act called for the deinstitutionalization of status offenders and the separation of adult and juvenile offenders. In 1980, the Act was amended to include the removal of juveniles from adult jails and lockups; in 1988, the Act called for the study of disproportionate minority confinement (DMC); and in 2002, the Act expanded the study of DMC to all areas of the juvenile justice system process, not just confinement (Snyder & Sickmund, 2007). The compliance with these mandates affected the level of federal funding for juvenile programming within individual states.

Reforms Follow

The preceding cases afforded juveniles many due process rights that were never guaranteed in juvenile court before. These procedural differences had to change the face of juvenile justice. In addition, federal intervention and the JJDPA prompted changes in the process of juvenile justice. States removed status offenders from delinquency proceedings and juveniles from adult jails, and they reexamined institutionalization practices for delinquents. Some truly good programs were created during this time of change. However, the sentiment driving these progressive reforms soon began to waiver. It appears that during this time, the main goal of juvenile reform was to reserve juvenile institution for those children who truly needed to be locked away from society and to find alternative placements, such as diversion programs, status offender programs, mental health programs, and drug treatment programs, for those who didn't need to be in secure custody.

However, despite the strong push for deinstitutionalization, federal intervention, and the rhetoric of reform, the movement was not successful. Yes, many states took status offenses out of the juvenile delinquency statutes, many states invested in diversion programs, and some states even closed juvenile facilities. However, despite these movements and a falling juvenile crime rate, the numbers of children in juvenile institutions still increased, and inappropriate placements still found their way into the institutions. In the late 1970s, something else began to affect the juvenile justice process in the United States. The general sentiment toward juvenile offenders and the appropriate action to take with them began to shift. The public, influenced by the media, began to look at juvenile offenders less as troubled children needing to be treated fairly and rehabilitated and more as serious offenders who needed to be punished.

Winds of Change:
Getting Tough on Juvenile Offenders

The more conservative political shift of the late 1970s and 1980s made a significant impact on the juvenile justice system. Monies for new and innovative juvenile programming dried up during the Regan/Bush eras and forced the system to again rely primarily on institutionalization as a standard response to serious and repeat juvenile offending (Krisberg, 1990). The media fueled public sentiment that juvenile crime was getting out of control and that rehabilitation did not work. According to Yanich (2005), crime, including juvenile crime, is the most covered of all types of news stories. When juvenile crime is overrepresented in the news or unfairly represented, the result is the creation of public fear (Yanich, 2005). The result of this growing fear led the public to demand a tougher juvenile justice system, one that relied more on punishment and sending a tough message to would-be offenders (Merlo & Benekos, 2010). The belief that more serious and punitive adultlike sanctions would deter juvenile crime became widespread (Redding, 2010). In addition, the juvenile justice system, was created as a closed system to protect juveniles from public scrutiny. This protection, however, also left the system, and juvenile crime "shrouded in myths" (Krisberg, 1990, p. 901). Krisberg called this an information disconnect which makes "juvenile justice policy easy prey for demagogues of every political stripe" (1990, p. 901).

When the juvenile crime and arrest rate began to rise in the late 1980s and early 1990s, including, and in particular, violent juvenile crime associated with guns, the sentiment to get tough on juvenile offenders became even stronger (Hinton, Sims, Adams, & West, 2007). Scholars warned of juvenile crime rates doubling, the impending juvenile "super predator," and an unsalvageable generation of youth (Krisberg, 2005). People feared an epidemic of ruthless juvenile offenders putting society as risk (Deitch, Barstow, Lukens, & Reyna, 2009). The federal government and state legislatures responded accordingly. The major results of the get tough movement were a renewed reliance on juvenile institutions and the overall adultification of juvenile justice, including a very real discussion of the death penalty for juvenile offenders. However, perhaps the most significant change in the juvenile justice process was an increased use of and numerous legislative changes to judicial waiver, the process used to transfer youths into the adult system. Following is a detailed discussion on the policies of transfer as this process truly represents the best example of the adultification of the juvenile justice system that was taking place during this time frame.

Transfer to Adult Court

Transferring (also known as waiving) juveniles into the adult system has existed as long as there has been a juvenile court (Shepherd, 2008). It was a safety valve left in the first juvenile court as a means to handle those juveniles that were not amenable to rehabilitation in the juvenile justice system. A mostly unused process in the early juvenile court, transfer was the area in juvenile justice that was most dramatically changed during the get tough agenda. Every state has some form of transfer in their juvenile codes (Adams & Addie, 2010). During the get tough years in juvenile justice, transfer laws were changed in many ways, including breadth of statutes, changing the transfer process by changing the major decision-maker in the process, and an expansion of eligible offenses resulting in more frequent use. Overall, 40 states changed their laws, making it easier to transfer juveniles to adult court (Krisberg, 2005). The following paragraphs will examine these three areas, changing the breadth of transfer, changing the transfer process, and the increasing frequency of use.

Breadth of Transfer

Transfer laws were changed substantially in the 1980 and the 1990s, even after the juvenile crime rate began to decline. States began to rapidly expand the list of crimes that could result in transfer by expanding criteria, such as the age or criminal history, that could result in transfer (Redding, 2010). They also started to expand offender eligibility. "Between 1992 and 1999, 27 states extended the reach of judicial waiver laws, lowered age requirements, or otherwise broadened eligibility" in their transfer laws (Adams & Addie, 2010, p. 2). The result of this is that currently, 23 states still have no **minimum** age requirements for transferring juveniles into adult court, and of the other states, the **minimum** age for transfer eligibility ranges from 10 to 15 years old (Hartney, 2006).

Changing the Transfer Process

In 2010, almost every state had the process of discretionary **judicial waiver** in their state juvenile codes (Adams & Addie, 2010). Judicial waiver is the process by which the juvenile court judge is the major decision-maker in the court process. The case comes to the attention of the juvenile court, and before being adjudicated delinquent (found guilty) in juvenile court, the judge makes the decision to transfer the case up to the criminal courts. Most states have spelled out criteria for transfer, including age, offense, criminal history, and amenability to treatment. In fact, in *Kent v. US* in 1966, the Supreme Court listed the eight criteria that judges could look at to determine transfer. These criteria are listed as follows:

1. the seriousness of the alleged offense to the community and whether the protection of the community requires waiver;
2. whether the alleged offense was committed in an aggressive, violent, premeditated, or willful manner;
3. whether the alleged offense was against persons or against property, greater weight being given to offenses against persons, especially if personal injury resulted;
4. the prosecutive merit of the complaint, i.e., whether there is evidence upon which a Grand Jury may be expected to return an indictment (to be determined by consultation with the United States Attorney);
5. the desirability of trial and disposition of the entire offense in one court when the juvenile's associates in the alleged offense are adults who will be charged with a crime in the U.S. District Court for the District of Columbia;

6. the sophistication and maturity of the juvenile as determined by consideration of his home, environmental situation, emotional attitude and pattern of living;
7. the record and previous history of the juvenile, including previous contacts with the Youth Aid Division, other law enforcement agencies, juvenile courts and other jurisdictions, prior periods of probation to this Court, or prior commitments to juvenile institutions; and
8. the prospects for adequate protection of the public and the likelihood of reasonable rehabilitation of the juvenile (if he is found to have committed the alleged offense) by the use of procedures, services and facilities currently available to the Juvenile Court" (*Kent v. US*, 1966, Appendix).

Recent changes in judicial waiver include presumptive waiver laws, where the waiver is presumed if the juvenile meets general criteria—usually age and offense. This is used in 15 states; basically, in this process, the burden of proof shifts from the prosecutor to the juvenile offender to show the court why he or she should not be transferred. In addition, in 15 other states, there is a mandatory judicial waiver where the judge basically becomes a fact checker of transfer criteria and carries no decision-making authority in the decision to process the juvenile as an adult (Adams & Addie, 2010).

In addition, concern about the "leniency" of juvenile judges and their faith in the juvenile system clouding their judgment led to a rapid increase in other methods used to transfer youth. These methods basically take the decision to transfer out of the hands of juvenile judges and pass it on to others. One method is called **prosecutorial discretion** or **direct file**. In this process, prosecutors are given the authority to file cases directly into juvenile or criminal court; this is called concurrent jurisdiction. In this process, the juvenile court can be completely bypassed in the process (Sickmund, 1994).

The third most significant way that a juvenile can end up in criminal court is through **statutory exclusion** or what some call **mandatory transfer**. In this method, state legislatures can transform the law to exclude certain ages from juvenile court; for example, they can declare all people as adults at any age under age 18. While most states set 18 as the age to reach adulthood for justice purposes, a handful of states go lower—some as low as age 16. But more significantly, perhaps, the legislature can exclude violent crime from juvenile court jurisdiction. This is usually done in conjunction with age criteria and may include something similar to the three-strikes concept that exists in criminal justice sentencing (Sickmund, 1994).

It is important to note that, after the practices of both prosecutorial discretion and statutory exclusion were put into place, some states created a reverse waiver process, a process for transferring the offender into juvenile court from criminal court. Obviously these new transfer laws were affecting some children who did not belong in adult court, and thus there had to be a safety value created in the adult court system to waive the inappropriate cases back down to the juvenile system.

Frequency of Use

It is estimated that the number of juvenile cases transferred to criminal court by judicial waiver peaked in 1994 with 12,100 cases being waived (Puzzanchera, 2001). This number represents a 51% increase of transfers reported in 1989 (Puzzanchera, 2001). Between 1988 and 1992, there was a 68% increase in judicially waived cases. This represents a 101% increase in the number of youth being transferred for crimes against person, a 42% increase for crimes against property, a 91% increase for drug related offenses, and a 91% increase in transfer for crimes against public order (Sickmund, 1994). In 1995, the numbers of cases being waived to criminal court began to decrease. By 2007, 48% of judicially waived cases involved crimes against people, 5% were for drug related offenses, and 53% were for property crimes (Adams & Addie, 2010).

This only tells us part of the story. It is not really possible to determine the number of juveniles who were directly filed through prosecutorial discretion into the criminal justice system, especially during the high peak years of judicial waiver transfer. Limited data available suggests that the numbers of juveniles transferred by direct file is likely higher than the number transferred through judicial waiver (Sickmund, 1994). Some early research suggested that at least in one state, two cases were direct filed for every case judicially waived in the early 1980s. However, during the peak of transfer use, that number may increase from 2:1 to 6:1 (Sickmund, 1994). In addition, there exists no data on the number of juveniles who may have been transferred by statutory exclusion (Sickmund, 1994). Some estimates suggests that there are about 250,000 juveniles each year who end up in adult courts (Benekos & Merso, 2008).

Though research cannot determine an exact number of juveniles transferred during the peak years of transfer, an increasing number of juveniles were transferred to criminal court, convicted of a crime, and sentenced to adult sanctions (Redding, 2010). Some research indicates that many of the juveniles transferred were incarcerated in adult penitentiaries and jails. In fact, some sources state that since the 1990s, the number of transferred juveniles sent to adult jail has increased 208% (Hartney, 2006).

Provisions to protect juveniles from adult prisoners, the "sound and sight separation" mandated by the JJDPA, do not apply to transferred juveniles.

Though state laws vary, 66% of the youth who are transferred to adult court spend time in an adult jail. Arya (2011) stated that about one half of these youth would never be convicted in adult court (either having charges dropped or being transferred back to juvenile court) and would spend one month or longer in an adult jail, while 20% would have spent longer than half a year incarcerated in an adult jail. Sickmund and Snyder stated that in 2002, about 1.1% of all new prisoners in state prisons were under the age of 18—about 4,100 in total (as cited in Benekos & Merlo, 2008).

Research has attempted to answer the question of, how effective are these tougher transfer laws? If this get tough approach was, in fact, the result of a get tough movement to punish young offenders and keep us safer from them both now and in the future, we must examine how effective this get tough movement was. Did transferring more juveniles into the adult system incapacitate serious juvenile offenders for longer periods or deter future crime by other would-be juvenile offenders?

An Evaluation of Transfer

Is public safety increased by transferring youth into the criminal justice system? Research suggested (Bishop, 2000; Kupchik & Liberman, 2003; Kane et al., 2002; Lanza-Kandace et al., 2005) that youth transferred do get longer sentences than they would in the juvenile system (as cited in Redding, 2010). However, according to Myers (2005), some youth may come back into the community on bail pending court action (as cited in Redding, 2010). As a result, Bishop (2000), Fritsch et al. (1996), and Myers (2001) found that they would then not serve the entire sentence and might end up serving the same amount of time as they would have had they not been transferred (as cited in Redding, 2010). In addition, some research suggests that the majority of youth transferred are not convicted on the crimes for which they were transferred (Juszkiewicz, 2000).

Moreover, "there is no evidence that locking up more youth will definitely improve public safety," whether that lockup be in adult or juvenile facilities (Justice Policy Institute, 2009, p. 10). Some research, in fact, has suggested that juvenile institutionalization in an adult prison has a long-term negative impact on public safety, as the incarcerated youth receive reduced or no educational or vocational services while institutionalized. In addition, most youth "age out" of criminal activity. However, the influence of adult career criminals on those most likely to age out may delay or negate that process all together, thus creating a negative impact on public safety (Justice Policy Institute, 2009).

Furthermore, a 2007 report from the Centers for Disease Control (CDC), which analyzed the available research, concluded that youth who are transferred into the adult system are 34% more likely to be rearrested than youth who were kept in the juvenile justice system. In fact, the report strongly concluded that "the use of transfer laws and strengthened transfer policies is counterproductive to reducing juvenile violence and enhancing public safety" (Shepherd, 2008, p. 42).

Redding (2010) questioned whether general or specific deterrence goals are met by transferring juveniles to criminal court. General deterrence is the effect that getting tough would have on the general juvenile population, and specific deterrence refers to the juvenile who was punished and his future criminality (Hahn et al., 2007). Redding argued that many big research projects have suggested that juveniles who are sanctioned as adults will actually have higher recidivism rates when compared to like juveniles kept in the juvenile system; thus, the evidence is strong that the goal of general deterrence is not being met by transfer (2010). Moreover, the CDC also concluded that, in their review of the available research, there is "sufficient evidence that the transfer of youth to the adult criminal justice system typically results in greater subsequent crime, including violent crime" (Hahn et al., 2007, p. 8).

Redding did suggest that the conclusions get more complicated when you look at general deterrence. Do tough adult sanctions on juvenile offenders make other juveniles think twice before offending? The research results are mixed and contradictory (Redding, 2010). The CDC's recent report found essentially the same results. Citing too few studies and inconsistent findings among the studies examined, the CDC could offer no definitive conclusion about general deterrence. However, the authors did feel that "little evidence supports the idea that transfer laws defer juveniles in the general population from violent crime" (Hahn et al., 2007, p. 10).

Other Concerns About Transfer Policies

Other criticisms of the change in transfer policies, in addition to the effectiveness of these policies, tend to question the philosophical change in focus that these policy changes represent. Some note that the new transfer methods are at odds with the historical roots of the juvenile justice system (which was designed to seek individualized justice), overlook the psychological differences between children and adults, promote future crime by housing juvenile with harsher and wiser offenders, place youth in danger of victimization, and do not diminish the concern with disproportionate minority contact (Shepherd, 2008). In addition, once youth were transferred to adult court, they were, until quite recently, subjected to all adult sanctions up to and including Life Without Parole (LWOP) and the death penalty (Merlo & Benekos, 2010).

Where Do We Go from Here?

There had been a movement to systematically reform juvenile justice, which includes addressing the policies of the last 30 years, many of which have adultified juvenile offenders and juvenile justice systems across the United States. With support of the public, there seems to be a movement "back" to the rehabilitation of juvenile offenders (Merlo & Benekos, 2010). According to the Justice Policy Institute (2007), in a publication, "[A]fter a decade shaped by myths of juveniles 'superpredators' and the ascendency of harsh penalties and adult treatment for minors, momentum for systematic reform is growing" (p. 3). The publication discusses the trends of large scale institutional reforms in five states, including the return of juvenile offenders to juvenile court jurisdiction, strengthening aftercare or parole services, focusing on mental health treatment, returning to community services rather than institutionalization, improving indigent defense for juvenile offenders, and improving the conditions of juvenile institutions (Ziedenberg, 2006). The report suggests that over half of the states are involved in one or more of the above stated reforms (Ziedenberg, 2006).

According to Arya (2011), there have been recent changes to many state statures regarding transferring juvenile to the adult system. As mentioned in a released report (Arya, 2011), there are four trends emerging since 2005 regarding transfer that the Campaign for Youth Justice found significant. The first trend refers to some states, as well as some local policies, which remove juveniles from both adult prisons and local jails. Maine, Virginia, Pennsylvania, and a local jurisdiction in Oregon changed laws to reflect that youths should be allowed, or even required in some instances, to be held in juvenile facilities although they are officially in the adult system. Colorado reexamined and changed the criteria to determine the placement of youth into adult or juvenile facilities, and New York City officials have requested that research be conducted about the dangers that juveniles face when incarcerated in adult facilities (Arya, 2011).

The second trend is that some states have raised the age of jurisdiction in the juvenile court. In most states, citizens become adults at age 18 and face criminal sanctions for illegal acts. However, 13 states have a lower than 18 age of criminal responsibility. In these states, 16 and/or 17 years olds who commit offenses are automatically prosecuted through the adult courts. Recently, three states, Connecticut, Illinois, and Mississippi, have risen the ages that their juvenile courts hold jurisdiction over, while four more states are contemplating similar moves (Arya, 2011).

The third trend involves legislative changes to modify transfer laws to keep more children in the juvenile justice system. Ten states have made significant changes in the past few years. Three states, Arizona, Colorado, and Nevada, have changed the age requirements in their transfer statutes. Connecticut, Delaware, Illinois, and Indiana have either decreased the number of crimes that mandate transfer or have modified the adult court prosecution presumptions. Indiana, Virginia, and Washington all made changes to their "once an adult, always an adult" statutes (Arya, 2011). These statues had indicated that youth who are transferred to criminal court will be handled in adult court for all subsequent offenses (Ghatt & Turner, 2008). In addition, many other states are currently reexamining their transfer statues and contemplating making legislative changes to those laws (Arya, 2011).

The final trend that report discussed by Arya (2011) is that many states are examining their juvenile sentencing laws. Historically, there were no provisions in sentencing guidelines for transferred juvenile offenders, despite mounting evidence that juvenile offenders are developmentally different from adult offenders. In 2005, Supreme Court held in a 5–4 decision in *Roper v. Simmons* that the death penalty for anyone under the age of 18 at the time of the crime is unconstitutional. Thus, they abolished the juvenile death penalty. In 2010, in *Graham v. Florida*, the U.S. Supreme Court again used maturity and development of the adolescent mind as rationale when they abolished LWOP for offenders under age 18 at the time of crime for youths not convicted of homicide (Arya, 2011).

The Supreme Court examined research evidence about recidivism, brain development, adolescent competency, and juvenile justice programs that worked effectively to render their holdings in *Roper* and *Graham* (Ghatt & Turner, 2008). The research the Court examined was not available when state and local legislatures began to make the changes to get tough on juvenile offenders. Particularly unknown was the full impact of treating juvenile as adults in criminal court (Ghatt & Turner, 2008). Several states are in the process of examining their sentencing laws and determining if the developmental information relied on by the Supreme Court in these two paramount decisions are reflected in their own juvenile and sentencing laws (Arya, 2011).

Conclusion

It would appear that what the public wants is an effective juvenile justice system based on rational and informed policies and procedures (Ziedenberg, 2006). Public opinion matters. What the public thinks about, and wants, for youthful offenders will impact legislative action (Merlo & Benekos, 2010). The trend appears to be turning away from a focus on punitive sanctions and turning to a support of rehabilitative services designed on evidence-based research, scientific evidence about the development of the adolescent brain, and best practices research results (Ziedenberg, 2006). Examining the literature suggests that states are making reforms and legislative changes, which are based on research and empirical examination. What will make a difference now will be if this path is continued or if there will be another knee-jerk reaction should the juvenile crime rate increase (Loughran, 2011). Have we come far enough along to have learned our lessons about the best practices of treating juvenile offenders, or are we vulnerable to future actions based on quick fixes that don't work? We must continue to educate people, including the media, legislators, and the public, about the realities and myths of juvenile crime and juvenile justice. That way, we can be confident that we are moving forward—both in the effective and enlightened treatment of juvenile offenders and in keeping the public safe.

References

Act 4 Juvenile Justice. (2007). *The juvenile justice and delinquency prevention act: A handbook.* Retrieved from http://www.act4jj.org/media/factsheets/factsheet_27.pdf.

Adams, B., & Addie, S. (2010). *Delinquency cases waived to criminal court, 2007.* Washington, DC: Office of Juvenile Justice and Delinquency Prevention.

Arya, N. (2011). *State trends: Legislative changes from 2005 to 2010 removing youth from the adult criminal justice system.* Washington, DC: Campaign for Youth Justice.

Bell, J., & Ridolfi, L. (2008). *Adoration of the question: Reflections on the failure to reduce racial and ethnic disparities in the juvenile justice system.* San Francisco, CA: W. Haywood Burns Institute.

Benekos, P., & Merlo, A. (2008). Juvenile justice: The legacy of punitive policy. *Youth Violence and Juvenile Justice, 6*(1), 28–46.

Deitch, M., Barstow, A., Lukens, L., & Reyna, R. (2009). *From time out to hard time: Young children in the adult criminal justice system.* Austin, TX: University of Texas at Austin, LBJ School of Public Affairs.

Ghatt, R., & Turner, S. (2008) New report highlights the impact of incarcerating youth in adult facilities and strategies for reform. *Sheriff, 60*(1), 60–66.

Hahn, R., McGowan, A., Liberman, A., Crosby, A., Fullilove, M., Johnson, R., Moscicki, E., Price, L., Snyder, S., Tuma, F., Lowy, J., Briss, P., Cory, S., & Stone, G. (2007). Effects on violence of laws and policies facilitating the transfer of youth from the juvenile to the adult justice system: A report on recommendations of the Task Force on Community Preventive Services. *MMWR Recommendations and Reports, 56*(RR-9), 1–11.

Hartney, C. (2006). *Youth under age 18 in the adult criminal justice system.* Oakland, CA: National Council on Crime and Delinquency.

Hinton, W., Sims, P., Adams, M., & West, C. (2007). Juvenile justice: A system divided. *Journal of Criminal Justice Policy Review, 18*(4), 466–483.

Justice Policy Institute. (2009). *The costs of confinement: Why good juvenile justice policies make good fiscal sense.* Washington, DC: Justice Policy Institute.

Juszkiewicz, J. (2000). *Youth crime/adult time: Is justice served? Building blocks for youth.* Retrieved from http://njjn.org/uploads/digital-library/resource_127.pdf.

Krisberg, B. (1990). The politics of juvenile justice: Then and now. *Law and Social Inquiry, 15*(4), 893–905.

Krisberg, B. (2005). *Juvenile justice: Redeeming our children.* Thousand Oaks, CA: Sage.

Loughran, E. (February, 2011). The cycle of reform and retrenchment in juvenile justice. *Corrections Today, 73*(1), p. 6.

Merlo, A., & Benekos, P. (2010). Is punitive juvenile justice policy declining in the United States? A critique of emergent initiatives. *Youth Justice, 10*(1), 3–24.

Nelson, D. W. (2008). A road map for juvenile justice reform. In *The 2008 KIDS COUNT Data Book* (pp. 6–27). Baltimore, MD: Annie C. Casey Foundation.

Puzzanchera, C. (2001). *Delinquency cases waived to criminal court, 1989–1998.* Washington, DC: Office of Juvenile Justice and Delinquency Prevention.

Redding, R. (2010). *Juvenile transfer laws: An effective deterrent to delinquency?* Washington, DC: Office of Juvenile Justice and Delinquency Prevention.

Shelden, D., & Macallair, D. (2008). *Juvenile justice in America: Problems and prospects.* Long Grove, IL: Waveland Press.

Shepherd, R. (2008). Evidence mounts on wisdom of trying juveniles as adults. *Criminal Justice, 22*(1), 12–15.

Sickmund, M. (1994). *How juveniles get to criminal court.* Washington, DC: National Center for Juvenile Justice.

Snyder, H. N., & Sickmund, M. (2007). *Juvenile offenders and victims: 2006 national report.* Washington, DC: Office of Juvenile Justice and Delinquency Prevention.

Yanich, D. (2005). Kids, crime, and local television news. *Crime and Delinquency, 51*(1), 103–132.

Ziedenberg, J. (2006). *Models for change: Building momentum for juvenile justice reform.* Washington, DC: Justice Policy Institute Report.

Zimring, F. (2101). The power politics of juvenile court transfer: A mildly revisionist history of the 1990s. *Louisiana Law Review, 71*(1), 1–15.

Cases Cited

Ex Parte Crouse, 4 Wharton (Pa.) 9 (1838)
In re Gault, 387 U.S. 1 (1967)
Kent v. United States, 383 U.S. 541 (1966)
In re Winship, 397 U.S. 358 (1970)
McKeiver v. Pennsylvania, 403 U.S. 528 (1971)
Roper v. Simmons, 543 U.S. 551 (2005)
Graham v. Florida, 560 U.S. 48 (2010)

Chapter 10

Deliberate Indifference?
Individuals with Mental Illness
in the Criminal Justice System

Jacqueline Buffington and Natalie Perron

Introduction

Every year, hundreds of thousands of individuals with serious mental illness are arrested and jailed, the majority for petty crimes (Clark, McHugo, & Ricketts, 1999; Primm, Osher, & Gomez, 2005). Although the criminal justice system is not the place or the system that can best serve this particular population, since the 1980s, it has been the criminal justice system—the system that can't say "no"—that has been increasingly called upon to manage these individuals and the situations in which they find themselves. Indeed, the three institutions in the United States that hold the largest populations of people with mental illness are not psychiatric facilities but large urban jails: L.A. County Jail, Cook County Jail in Chicago, and New York City's Riker's Island (Torrey, 1999; Torrey, Kennard, Eslinger, Lamb, & Pavle, 2010). L.A. County Jail has an entire tower devoted to holding inmates with mental illness, holding more individuals with mental illness than any state hospital or mental health institution in the United States (Council of State Governments, 2002a). Altogether, jails and prisons in the United States hold approximately three to five times more individuals with mental illnesses than state psychiatric hospitals do across the country (Leifman, 2001; Lerner-Wren, 2000). Although the general public might be surprised to learn this, most criminal justice professionals are not surprised, as this is the reality they live with every day in their jobs.

This chapter focuses on this population of offenders. It will begin with an overview of statistics on the overrepresentation of individuals with serious mental illness in the criminal justice system. Reasons for these high numbers will be discussed. Finally, efforts to manage this dilemma, with an emphasis on innovative strategies, will be described.

Definitions and Prevalence of Serious Mental Illnesses in the Criminal Justice System

Members of the lay public often mistakenly believe that anyone who commits a crime or engages in behavior to which the perceiver cannot relate personally is mentally ill. However, in fact, most crimes are not committed by people with major mental illness. Moreover, although anxiety disorders, substance use disorders, and personality disorders are prominent within the criminal justice system, just as they are in the general public, these are not included under the category of "serious mental illness," which is the focus of this chapter. It is important to first define this category of illnesses.

"Serious mental illness" pertains to disorders of thought, perception, or mood that significantly impair an individual's functioning. This includes such mental illnesses as schizophrenia-spectrum disorders, bipolar disorders, and severe depression. Sometimes, borderline personality disorder (BPD) and post-traumatic stress disorder (PTSD) are included in this category.

Schizophrenia primarily involves a disturbance of thought and perception, or psychosis, typically characterized by hallucinations (i.e., false sensory experiences, such as hearing voices or noises), delusions (i.e., false beliefs that are held despite impossibility, such as paranoid delusions or delusions of grandeur/grandiosity), and severe disorganization (e.g., incoherent speech, bizarre behavior). Individuals with schizophrenia also tend to exhibit social withdrawal and inappropriate social behavior and/or emotions. Bipolar disorder involves periods of opposing moods: i.e., mania and depression. Mania refers to episodes of extreme energy; reduced need for sleep; elevated and/or irritable mood; racing thoughts, distractibility, and talkativeness; and excessive involvement in pleasurable, and often dangerous, activities. Depression, conversely, involves depressed mood, characterized by diminished interest in things that typically bring them pleasure, feelings of worthlessness and guilt, sometimes irritability, and often recurrent suicidal ideation; cognitive problems, such as difficulty concentrating; and physical symptoms, including lack of energy and disturbed sleep patterns and appetite. Whereas schizophrenia is the prototypical psychotic disorder, severe mania and depression can also involve psychosis. The thought disorder, hallucinations and delusions, mood disturbance, and erratic behavior involved with these disorders are not un-commonly present among people who commit offenses.

Rates of these disorders are approximately 2.5 to 10 times higher in criminal justice settings as they are in the general U.S. population (Kessler, Chiu, Demler, & Walters, 2005). Specifically, in any given year, approximately 1% of the general population will be diagnosed with schizophrenia, 3% with bipolar disorders, and 7% with depressive disorders (Kessler, Berglund, et al., 2005; Kessler, Chiu, et al., 2005). In jails and prisons, however, a conservative estimate of the rate of these serious mental illnesses is 16% (Ditton, 1999[1]; Steadman, Osher, Robbins, Case, & Samuels, 2009), with 14.5% of men and 31% of women afflicted (Steadman et al., 2009).[2]

In recent years, some have recognized BPD and PTSD as conditions that qualify as serious mental illnesses. Severe BPD, unlike most personality disorders, is often considered a serious mental illness due to the severity of the symptoms and their vast effects on an individual's life. It is characterized by extreme and reactive emotions and difficulty controlling these emotions; feelings of personal emptiness; intense and volatile relationships; impulsivity, anger, and aggressiveness; and engagement in risky, maladaptive behaviors (e.g., risky sexual behaviors, substance abuse, excessive financial spending) in unsuccessful efforts to "feel better."[3] People with PTSD—as a result of trauma they have experienced—have recurrent intrusive thoughts and nightmares about their trauma (usually abuse experienced during childhood and/or adulthood); experience chronic anxiety, hypervigilance about their safety, and, at times, irritability and/or aggression; develop pervasive distrust and other negative

---

1. A 2006 Bureau of Justice Statistics report (James & Glaze, 2006) suggested mental illness afflicts over 50% of inmates in the jail and prison system. However, the study has been criticized on methodological grounds (e.g., using self-report only, looking only at single symptoms to define mental illness rather than the constellation of symptoms it takes for adequate diagnosis, not taking into account the effects of substance abuse) and is believed to be an overestimate.

2. This is consistent with the percentage of people on probation and parole who are believed to have mental illness (Ditton, 1999; Louden & Skeem, 2011; Lurigio, Cho, Swartz, Johnson, Graf, & Pickup, 2003; Prins & Draper, 2009) and the percentage of clients that defense attorneys question their competency to stand trial (Hoge, Bonnie, Poythress, & Monahan, 1992; Poythress, Bonnie, Hoge, Monahan, & Oberlander, 1994).

3. The most common personality disorder within the criminal justice system is antisocial personality disorder (APD). APD is characterized by a failure to conform to social norms with respect to lawful behavior (i.e., criminality), reckless disregard for the rights and safety of others, impulsivity, irresponsibility, deceitfulness, and lack of remorse. People with APD alone, however, unlike some people with psychotic disorders, understand what they are doing and that their actions are wrong by legal and moral standards. As such, this diagnosis is not particularly useful in the context of the criminal justice system, as virtually all individuals in this context could be so diagnosed.

thoughts and feelings about themselves and others; and go to extremes to avoid memories of their traumas. People with BPD and PTSD may experience sensations that situations are unreal, which in extreme cases can temporarily cross into psychosis. These episodes of derealization/psychosis and difficulty controlling their extreme emotions involved in both disorders not uncommonly result in people acting out impulsively and criminally. The rates of these disorders in the general U.S. population are approximately 2% for BPD (Lenzenweger, Lane, Loranger, & Kessler, 2007) and 4% for PTSD (Kessler, Berglund, et al., 2005; Kessler, Chiu, et al., 2005). As many as 30% of inmates are estimated to have BPD (Black et al., 2007; Jordan, Schlenger, Fairbank, & Caddell, 1996; Trestman, Ford, Zhang, & Wiesbrock, 2007) and 46% have PTSD (Gosein, Stiffler, Francoia, & Ford, 2016). Given the high prevalence of these disorders among offenders in the criminal justice system, they have been increasingly recognized as important for professionals working in criminal justice settings to consider.

A large proportion of individuals with serious mental illness, particularly those found in the criminal justice system, also struggle with substance use disorders. Approximately 75%–80% of jail inmates with serious mental illness also have co-occurring chemical dependency issues (Abram & Teplin, 1991; Steadman et al., 2009). This comorbidity happens with such regularity, in fact, that substance abuse completes what Steadman, Morrissey, and Parker (2016) refer to as the *trifecta* for justice-involved persons with serious mental illness: serious mental illness, physical and/or sexual abuse (often leading to PTSD), and substance abuse.

Reasons for the Overrepresentation of Individuals with Mental Illness in the Criminal Justice System

There are a variety of converging factors that account for the overrepresentation of people with mental illness in the criminal justice system. The lay public tends to assume that the large number of people with mental illness in our criminal justice system is due to characteristics intrinsic to the individuals themselves (e.g., that they are inherently unpredictable and violent). However, because of the wide variability in the presentation of mental illnesses, individual-level factors are among the least influential reasons for the overrepresentation of individuals with mental illness in the criminal justice system. Instead, it is the historical events (e.g., deinstitutionalization) and societal-level factors (e.g., attitudes regarding mental illness and criminality), coupled with the nature of the criminal justice system, that have resulted in the system-level difficulties with—and problematic policies of—managing offenders with mental illness. Each is discussed below.

Historical Events

Attitudes about individuals with mental illness and their treatment have operated on a pendulum swing since the founding of the United States. Specifically, this swing has consisted of alternating periods of, on the one end, massive institutionalization and, at the other, periods of deinstitutionalization (Johnson, 2011). As Grob (1995) outlined in his book on the history of America's care of the mentally ill, prior to the 1840s, people with mental illness were either cared for by relatives or were imprisoned. The conditions in which they lived in jails were brutal and inhumane, characterized by exceedingly tight quarters (e.g., "closets"), freezing temperatures with no heat, hay for bedding, and a few scraps of rags for clothing. It was not until the efforts of Dorothea Dix, who spent two decades traveling state-to-state exposing to the public the abuses that the mentally ill were enduring in jails and prisons, that the treatment of the mentally ill changed. She was responsible for convincing 30 states to build asylums, as they were called, whereby people with mental illness could be removed from jails and provided treatment. This marked the first deinstitutionalization movement (Johnson, 2011).

By 1900, every state had a psychiatric institution (Earley, 2006). However, these institutions were just as problematic as the jails before them. Getting someone admitted to one of these facilities was simple, requiring merely the concern of a family member, a process that was sometimes abused. The cause of mental illness was unknown, and the only available treatments—electric shock, insulin injections, and other seizure-inducing medications and eventually lobotomies—were merely effective in halting disruptive behavior by permanently damaging the brain. Thus, these facilities essentially became warehouses of humans at the furthest margins of society. Fueled by the Not In My Backyard (NIMBY) mentality, these facilities were built in the most remote areas of the country, far away from the love, support, and oversight of their families and friends. By 1950, approximately a half million people were institutionalized in these asylums (Earley, 2006).

In 1952, the drug Thorazine was discovered to be successful in treating some of the symptoms of schizophrenia (Earley, 2006). Touted as a "wonder drug" and "cure" for mental illness, Thorazine was prescribed to more than two million patients in the first eight months it was on the market. In 1961, the

Joint Commission on Mental Illness and Health released a report recommending a reduction in dependence on institutions and movement toward a system of community mental health centers. The report argued that these community centers were cheaper, more humane, and allowed for reintegration of people with mental illness into the fabric of society (Slate, Buffington-Vollum, & Johnson, 2013). These events, coupled with the personal experience of having a sister who was institutionalized with mental illness for most of her life (Kessler, 1996), led President John F. Kennedy to adopt mental illness as a priority of his administration (Earley, 2006). Kennedy signed into law the Community Mental Health Centers Construction (CMHC) Act in 1963, just before his assassination. With more pressing public concerns, such as Vietnam and Watergate, the money was never allocated. Most CMHCs were never constructed; the system of CMHCs was never realized.

Nevertheless, the impetus had been set into motion, and several social movements fueled the fire (Earley, 2006). An antipsychiatry movement—initiated by critical academic writings such as Thomas Szasz's *The Myth of Mental Illness* (1961), the release of Kesey's (1962) popular book, and the 1975 film *One Flew Over the Cuckoo's Nest*—spread throughout the nation. Moreover, the Civil Rights Movement championed this sentiment by bringing lawsuits against state hospitals, fighting on behalf of people with mental illness to ensure better treatment and recognition of their rights. They also fought to make civil commitment, or the process of treating people with mental illness against their will, more difficult. By the mid-1970s, most states had adopted the "imminent danger to self or others" standard (i.e., the individual must present an imminent danger to harm him/herself or others before he/she could be committed), an exceedingly rigorous standard to meet. Although an act of respect toward people with mental illness, these revised standards sometimes legally hindered much needed treatment.

All of these events converged to bring about the second deinstitutionalization movement involving the mentally ill (Johnson, 2011), which is generally regarded as being responsible for the current overrepresentation of people with mental illness in the criminal justice system. During this period of deinstitutionalization, hundreds of thousands of psychiatric inpatients were released from the state hospitals into the nation's communities. Specifically, the number of psychiatric inpatients dwindled from 559,000 in 1955 to approximately 59,000 in 2000 (Lamb & Weinberger, 2005)—a 95% decrease. Without the treatment system that was supposed to have been constructed, many deinstitutionalized patients rapidly decompensated into acute mental illness. And with the more restrictive civil commitment criteria, it became practically impossible to get treatment for those who needed it (Earley, 2006).

Many became homeless, resorted to substance use to dampen their symptoms, and became increasingly embroiled in the criminal justice system (Earley, 2006). In an effort to "clean up the streets," the homeless mentally ill were charged with minor nuisance crimes (e.g., loitering, trespassing) (Clark et al., 1999). Others are detained on "mercy bookings"—such as arresting a homeless, mentally ill woman on a bogus misdemeanor charge in order to protect her from potential sexual assault on the streets—by well-intentioned police who perceive there to be no suitable treatment alternatives available (Lamb, Weinberger, & DeCuir, 2002). In an effort to subsist, many were charged with misdemeanor shoplifting and minor theft charges. Others were charged with felonies when their behavior escalated, often in response to paranoia, hallucinations, and/or mania.

Coinciding with the deinstitutionalization movement, U.S. society shifted its attitudes about criminal justice in the 1980s. The criminal justice system moved from a rehabilitative model to a more retributive, punitive model. U.S. jail and prison populations soared. Between 1978 and 2000—i.e., in half the time period as the 95% decline in state hospital populations cited earlier— the number of jail and prison inmates increased approximately 400%, from just under 475,000 to nearly two million (Lamb & Weinberger, 2005).

These generally punitive attitudes with regard to criminal justice extended to people with mental illness and especially to those within the criminal justice system. Despite an overall better understanding of the basis and treatment of mental illness, fear of individuals with mental illness has grown since the 1950s. Likely due to highly publicized and sensationalized acts of violence in the media, the proportion of U.S. society that believes people with mental illness are dangerous, violent, and/or frightening increased by 250% between 1950 and 2000, with 75% of the public currently holding such beliefs (Phelan, Link, Stueve, & Pescosolido, 2000). This is particularly noteworthy, as decades of research have revealed that mental illness alone is not predictive of violence (Elbogen & Johnson, 2009).[4] Moreover, people in the lay public tend to believe

---

4. Although a complete discussion of the relationship between mental illness and violence is beyond the scope of this chapter, it is necessary to summarize the basic findings of the research, considering the pivotal role that this mistaken belief has on attitudes and policy involving this population. First, most violent offenses are not committed by individuals with mental illness. The risk of being assaulted by someone with serious mental illness, at 3%–5%, is seven times less than being violently victimized by someone abusing substances without mental illness (Friedman, 2006). Moreover, the vast majority of people with mental illness will never commit an act of violence (Choe, Teplin, & Abram, 2008; McCampbell, 2001); it tends to be concentrated in a fraction of the overall population of those with mental illness, and it is usually related to co-occurring substance abuse during periods of noncompliance with medications (Elbogen & Johnson, 2009; Swartz et al., 1998). Moreover,

other myths about mental illness such as persons with mental illness being responsible for causing their illness (Corrigan et al., 2000).

Thus, coinciding with the general move away from rehabilitation by the general public, people with mental illness in particular were seen as worthy of arrest and unworthy of treatment in the criminal justice system (Lamb & Weinberger, 1998). By the 1980s, the mentally ill began arriving in jails and prisons in such numbers that the term "transinstitutionalization" has been used in replacement of "deinstitutionalization" (Barr, 2003). People with mental illness who were released from state hospital institutions were merely being deposited into the jail/prison institutions.

System Failures: Traditional Approaches to Working with Offenders with Mental Illness

Deinstitutionalization, an inadequate mental health system, and negative societal attitudes toward people with mental illness are but a few reasons why people with mental illness have been propelled into the criminal justice system. Lack of preparation by the criminal justice system to respond to this population and, again, an inadequate mental health system is what keeps people with mental illness revolving through the door to our jails and prisons. The various breakdowns in both the mental health and criminal justice systems will be summarized below.

An Inadequate Mental Health System

In 2009, the National Alliance on Mental Illness (NAMI), the best-known advocacy group for people with mental illness in the country, published the "Grading the States 2009" report. The group researched and conducted a thorough analysis of 65 specific criteria related to the availability of services, funding, etc., and assigned grades to each state and the country as a whole. The nation's mental health system received a dismal "D," consistent with the D it had received in 2006. Across the country, systems were failing to provide adequate "services that are the lynchpins of a comprehensive system of care, such as … integrated mental health and substance abuse treatment, and hospital

---

even when an individual with mental illness does become violent, contrary to the popular image propagated by the media, most do not target strangers; instead, it is usually the people most involved in the person's care, such as family members, who are the target (Steadman et al., 1998).

based care when needed" (NAMI, 2009, p. xi). Few public health insurance plans adequately met the needs of people with serious mental illnesses, and private insurance plans lacked sufficient coverage. Consumers were not feeling respected, and services were not provided in a culturally competent way. Few states were developing plans or investing resources to address long-term housing needs for people with serious mental illness. And effective diversion from the criminal justice system was "scattershot without state-level leadership" (NAMI, 2009, p. xi). Since that time, mental health system budgets have continued to be cut.

The current state of community mental health systems is one of poor funding, lack of resources, shortage of mental health providers (especially psychiatrists who can prescribe medications), inadequate treatment, and long waiting lists. There is often a lack of integrated mental health and chemical dependency treatment services, even though such services have been recognized as best practices for decades. Many citizens cannot receive care because of insurance issues or have other life circumstances, such as homelessness and poverty, that overshadow the need for mental healthcare.

While only a partial indicator of the state of the mental health system, it is a relevant indicator regarding the availability of services for our most seriously mentally ill, many of whom end up embroiled with the criminal justice system as a result. Specifically, hospital beds in the mental health system continue to decline from the days of deinstitutionalization, which has an effect on all aspects of the criminal justice system. Specifically, following the 95% decrease in state psychiatric beds from 1955 to 2000, the number of state psychiatric beds decreased another 15% from 2000 to 2005 and yet another 14% between 2005 and 2010, and this rate shows no signs of stopping (Torrey, Fuller, Geller, Jacobs, & Ragosta, 2012). Perhaps most striking, per capita state psychiatric bed populations have declined to 1850 levels (e.g., 14 beds per 100,000 persons in the general population); experts advise that the "minimally adequate" number of beds to meet the needs of the population should be 50 beds per 100,000 (Torrey et al., 2012).

Due to a lack of hospital beds, more and more people with serious mental illness and substance abuse issues are receiving care in medical emergency rooms. As of 2007, one in eight ER patients had a mental health or substance abuse condition, a number that has been increasing for over a decade (Owens, Mutter, & Stocks, 2010). ERs are "boarding" these patients and for longer and longer periods of time. In a briefing before Congress, the National Association of State Mental Health Program Directors Research Institute (NASHMHPDRI) reported that 70% of more than 6,000 emergency departments nationwide indicated they boarded individuals in psychiatric crisis for "hours or days," and 10% boarded such patients for several weeks (Glover, Miller, & Sadowski,

2012). The alternative is to release or "street" psychiatric patients, even those worthy of civil commitment—e.g., releasing them from custody because there are no state psychiatric beds available, and/or the emergency custody order expires before an order for a full evaluation can be obtained from the court (Huffman, 2011).

Individuals with Mental Illness and Law Enforcement

Arrest by law enforcement is all too common for people with mental illness. Between 25% and 50% of persons with mental illness have been arrested at least once (Frankle et al., 2001; Livingston, 2016; Solomon & Draine, 1995; Walsh & Bricourt, 1997). This is despite the fact that less than 1%, according to some estimates, ever become violent (McCampbell, 2001).[5] Most are being arrested due to nonviolent misdemeanors and felonies associated with their illnesses (e.g., "nuisance crimes," such as loitering/trespassing, panhandling/ petty theft, public disturbances; mercy bookings, and subsistence offenses) (Primm, Osher, & Gomez, 2005).

Early research on the subject found that individuals with mental illness were significantly more likely to be arrested than individuals without mental illness. In the seminal study on this issue, Teplin (1984) found that 47% of suspects who exhibited signs of mental illness were arrested, compared to 28% of suspects of who did not exhibit such signs. This difference equated to a 67 times greater likelihood of arrest for mentally ill suspects than suspects without mental illness. Fortunately, since that time, the situation appears to have changed somewhat (Engel & Silver, 2001).

Looking at the data from the perspective of law enforcement, recent research suggests that approximately 1% (Livington, 2016) to 10% (Rosenbaum, Tinney, & Tohen, 2017) of police calls involve people with mental illness, and such encounters are on the rise. One study found a 48% increase in police mental health calls over the past five years (Rosenbaum et al., 2017). This only reflects the mere number of calls; it does not account for the significantly greater amount of time each mental health call takes. Suffice it to say, responding to calls involving people with mental illness in crisis consumes a great deal of law enforcement's time.

---

5. The rate of violence among individuals with severe mental illness varies widely, depending on the definition of mental illness and the methodology of the study. For example, a review article of all studies examining violence among individuals with severe mental illness, defined by psychotic disorders and major affective disorders, found rates to vary from 2%–13% among outpatients and from 17%–50% among inpatients (Choe et al., 2008).

Given the number of mentally ill individuals with whom law enforcement comes into contact, coupled with the power officers hold, they have an extremely important role. Law enforcement officers operate under two common law powers: police power, or that which enables them to do what is necessary to protect the welfare and safety of the community, and the power of *parens patriae*, which they are able to invoke when the paternalistic protection of an individual is warranted (e.g., an individual is threatening to attempt suicide) (Lamb et al., 2002). As first responders to an increasing number of mental health crises, police officers have been referred to as "street-corner psychiatrists" (Teplin, 1984), providers of "psychiatric first aid" (Lamb et al., 2002), "de facto mental health providers" (Patch & Arrigo, 1999), and the "primary gatekeepers" of both the criminal justice and mental health systems. These labels have been validated by a recent research analysis looking at data across 48 studies, which found that 10% of individuals have police involved in their pathway to mental healthcare (Livingston, 2016).

Law enforcement officers have a great amount of latitude in determining how to resolve situations involving individuals with mental illness. They can choose to handle the situation formally, in the form of arrest or transport to a hospital in pursuit of civil commitment, or they can resolve the situation informally, such as providing a verbal warning or referring the individual to services in the community (Cooper, McLearen, & Zapf, 2004; Sellers, Sullivan, Veysey, & Shane, 2005). Which route an officer takes is determined by a combination of personal, situational, and systemic factors. For example, less experienced officers tend to be more likely to arrest than more seasoned officers (Watson & Angell, 2007). Officers who believe individuals are responsible for their mental illness are less willing to provide assistance and are more likely to arrest (Watson, Ottati, Lurigio, & Heyrman, 2005). Moreover, the more public an event is, the higher the likelihood of arrest over informal resolution or transfer to a psychiatric facility (Patch & Arrigo, 1999).

Citizen injuries and fatalities related to police use of force have always been scrutinized, and have been increasingly so in recent years, due to increased publicity on police use of force against minorities, people with mental illness, and other marginalized populations. Research confirms that persons with mental illness are four times more likely to be killed by police than vice versa (Cordner, 2006) and even more likely to be injured. Rossler and Terrill's (2017) study revealed that officers do in fact use higher levels of force on persons with mental illness, and these individuals are at slightly higher risk for injury (approximately 33%) than those without mental illness (approximately 25%). Such use of force by police is likely due in part to officers' unconscious biases or implicit associations (Greenwald, Banaji, & Nosek, 2015) about people with mental illness, including the stereotype that they are violent. Ultimately, however, Livingston et al. (2014) found that most people with mental illness they surveyed reported that officers acted in a procedurally just manner (e.g., treating the individual with respect and dignity).

Even when it is recognized that a situation involves mental illness, law enforcement's (and by extension, the rest of the criminal justice system's) hands are tied. When called to a scene involving a person with mental illness—whether it is by a family member or a friend seeking assistance in obtaining treatment for the individual or as the result of an individual with mental illness having committed a crime—law enforcement cannot say "no" (Lamb et al., 2002). Unlike the mental health system, which may not accept an individual on grounds that there are no hospital beds available, the individual does not have health insurance,[6] or the individual has co-occurring substance abuse, the criminal justice system must act. The ultimate irony is that with the strict civil commitment statutes described previously, an individual must become dangerous to oneself or others to be civilly committed; yet, when a mentally ill individual does become violent, the mental health system may refuse to accept him or her.

When law enforcement officers, who are tasked with keeping the streets safe, run out of treatment options for people with mental illness, they may believe they have no option but to arrest the individual (Lamb et al., 2002). It is usually more expedient for police officers to arrest and take the person to jail than to wait at the hospital for the individual to undergo the cumbersome and time-consuming process of psychiatric evaluation for civil commitment (DuPont & Cochran, 2000). If the individual is found to not constitute a sufficient danger from a legal standpoint, he or she is released within hours, only to return to the streets where the officer might have to deal with the individual again (DuPont & Cochran, 2000). After having witnessed this scenario repeatedly, law enforcement officers sometimes choose to arrest due to the perception that the individual will receive better mental health treatment in jail than from the underfunded mental health system and/or that jail is safer than the streets, where the individual is vulnerable (i.e., "mercy bookings") (Lamb et al., 2002).

Individuals with Mental Illness in Jails and Prisons

Prevalence of mental illness in jails and prisons has been studied extensively. Since the 1980s, the numbers of people with mental illness in jails has steadily risen, with a 154% increase in the number of between 1980 and 1992 alone (Watson, Hanrahan, Luchins, & Lurigio, 2001). As mentioned previously, it has

---

6. As of 1997, two thirds of U.S. hospitals refused patients with mental illness who are unable to pay (Coleman, 1997).

been recently estimated that approximately 16% of inmates in U.S. jails and prisons (Ditton, 1999; Steadman et al., 2009)—or approximately 500,000 inmates (James & Glaze, 2006)—have a serious mental illness, and this is a conservative estimate. Moreover, these numbers include people with serious mental illness who have no charges against them (Ellis & Alexander, 2017). Twenty-nine percent of U.S. jails are holding people while the individual awaits either psychiatric evaluation, availability of hospital beds, transportation to a psychiatric facility, or all of the above (James & Glaze, 2006; Minton & Zeng, 2015). Without significant changes in the mental health system, these numbers will continue to rise.

Having such large numbers of people with mental illness in jails and prisons poses significant challenges, not only for the individuals themselves but also for the jail and prison staff responsible for managing them. As a result, the duration of imprisonment for persons with mental illness tends to be longer than for inmates without mental illness.[7] For example, in Fairfax, Virginia, psychotic misdemeanants stayed in jail six-and-one-half times longer than nonmentally ill offenders (Axelson & Wahl, 1992). Moreover, people with serious mental illness in Pennsylvania prisons in 2000 were three times more likely to serve their maximum sentence (Council of State Governments, 2002c). In some cases, inmates with mental illness end up serving more time in prison than their allotted sentence. For example, one individual profiled in the PBS documentary, *Frontline: The New Asylums* (Navasky & O'Connor, 2005), served 13 years on a 3-year sentence in Ohio. The heightened rate of arrest and detention, coupled with longer lengths of stay in jails, results in a backlog of individuals with mental illness in U.S. jails and prisons.

Acute Psychopathology

Not only is the number of inmates with mental illness growing, but more persons whose illnesses fall at the most severe end of the mental illness spectrum are being incarcerated (Human Rights Watch, 2003). Severe, untreated, acute mental illness is especially prevalent in jails, where individuals with mental illness have just been delivered from the community—often, literally, from the streets—after weeks, months, and even years of being off their medications. Moreover, a majority has also been abusing alcohol and/or drugs while in the community, often just prior to their arrests. Abusing substances not only complicates mental illness (e.g., makes existing symptoms worse) but also can make behavior in the jail more erratic, impulsive, and aggressive, to both self and

---

7. Not all research bears this out, however (e.g., Draine, Blank Wilson, Metraux, Hadley, & Evans, 2010).

others. Finally, with any inmate, withdrawal from substances in the early hours of detention in jail can lead to delirium (e.g., cognitive confusion, erratic behavior), if not posing life-threatening complications (e.g., seizures, alterations in blood pressure or other heart functioning, respiratory depression), that must be monitored closely.

Conditions of Incarceration

Although few individuals thrive while incarcerated, persons with mental illness function particularly poorly under these conditions (Human Rights Watch, 2003). The crowded and/or unsanitary environment, excessive sensory stimulation (e.g., noise, lack of privacy, lights being on all day and night), and disruptions in eating and sleeping patterns are especially detrimental for individuals with mental illness, whose senses tend to be enhanced and who have fewer psychological resources with which to cope with the chaos. Moreover, the intake process, which usually consists of a strip search and other degrading rituals, and victimization by other inmates and even staff can re-activate prior traumas and, accordingly, post-traumatic symptoms. Any and all of these circumstances can trigger a psychiatric episode or exacerbate an existing episode of psychosis, mania, or depression.

Disciplinary Infractions

Individuals with mental illness often have a hard time following the strict rules and regimen of the institution and, thus, accrue disciplinary infractions and, accordingly, punishment in the form of days in segregation, refusal of parole, and/or additional time in prison (Human Rights Watch, 2003; Matejkowski, Caplan, & Wiesel Cullen, 2010). Individuals with disorganized cognitive symptoms of psychosis or mental retardation may not understand and/or be capable of complying with strict rules and unfamiliar regimens. Similarly, rules do not mean much when one is hearing voices and having impulses to kill oneself. For others, symptoms of mental illness render it difficult to control their behavior and/or manifest in disruptiveness, belligerence, paranoia, and aggression (Human Rights Watch, 2003). Regardless of the reason, noncompliance with institutional rules and disruptive behavior is usually punished by security staff, often in the form of segregation or new charges and, thus, increased time. In short, individuals with serious mental illness commit more rule infractions, spend more time in segregation, and ultimately are less likely to be released (Slate et al., 2013). Because of rule violations, the average length of stay in the New York City jail system for inmates with mental illness is 215 days, versus 42 days for inmates without mental illness (Council of State Governments, 2002b).

Use of Segregation

A policy in many jails is to segregate people with mental illness in order to place them in a location where treatment can be conveniently administered, to protect them from assault or exploitation by other inmates, and/or to protect other inmates from mentally ill inmates who might become assaultive. In other circumstances, individuals with mental illness and/or intellectual disabilities are placed in segregation because they break the institution's rules. Segregation, which is characterized by stressors, such as being stripped and being forced to wear a thin paper smock in a cold and barren cell, sensory deprivation, and lack of social interaction, is known to have detrimental effects on mental health, but the effects are particularly pronounced for individuals with existing mental health issues (Haney, Weill, Bakhshay, & Lockett, 2016; Human Rights Watch, 2003). At the mild end, individuals might experience anxiety, headaches, lethargy, trouble sleeping, oversensitivity to stimuli, and difficulties with concentration and memory. At the extreme end, even short periods of isolation can cause confusion, perceptual distortions (e.g., hallucinations), paranoia, and motor excitement (e.g., "lashing out"). Ironically, although aggression is often the very thing that this punishment is intended to eliminate (Haney, 2003), segregation can often precipitate aggression in a previously nonaggressive mentally ill inmate, leading to further disciplinary action, extended periods in segregation, and lengthier sentences.

Segregation is also used regularly for inmates who are at risk of committing suicide, either by direct threats or history of suicide attempts. Ironically, while suicide reduction is a key consideration for jails and prisons due to liability issues, the common practice of placing inmates at risk for suicide in isolation merely sets them up for further deterioration of their mental health and/or progression of their suicidal ideation (Haney, 2003). Although jail and prison staff have policies and procedures to monitor inmates in segregation, removal from general population inadvertently eliminates one of the staff's greatest assets for preventing suicide: peer supervision. Research consistently shows that self-mutilation and suicide risk is increased in conditions of segregation, social isolation, and psychosocial deprivation (e.g., being placed in single cells with little supervision) (Haney, 2003). For example, 30%–50% of suicides in New York State prisons occurred within the 8% of inmates confined in 23-hour isolation, and the three supermax prisons in California accounted for one third of all prison suicides in the state (Human Rights Watch, 2003).

Lack of Services

Inmates in jails and prisons have a legal right to mental health treatment, grounded in the Eighth Amendment's prohibition of cruel and unusual punishment and upheld by the U.S. Supreme Court case of *Estelle v. Gamble* (1976). However, this right is quite narrow (Honberg, 2008) to the point that services in many jails and prisons are virtually nonexistent. A federal government report of statistics provided by jails and prisons themselves indicated that only 17.5% of local jail inmates who needed mental healthcare received hospital care, medications, or therapy (James & Glaze, 2006). Mental health services in correctional institutions are mainly reactive, rather than proactive, focusing on responding to mental health crises and managing symptoms rather than improving coping skills and quality of life for its prisoners. From a management perspective, this alone is likely to be inefficient and ineffective, sometimes with dire consequences (e.g., suicide).

Due to the current punitive philosophy and budget constraints on the correctional system, mental health services are severely understaffed, both in terms of quantity and quality (Human Rights Watch, 2003). In prisons, the vast majority of services are provided by "counselors," who typically are not required to have mental health training (Human Rights Watch, 2003). In terms of quantity, Humans Rights Watch (2003) uncovered prisons in states like Arkansas operating with one psychiatrist to serve 14,000 inmates; this is in stark contrast to the American Psychiatric Association's (2000) recommended inmate-to-psychiatrist ratio of 150:1. Similarly, in Wyoming, one psychiatrist is on the prison premises two days per month; and in California, a psychiatrist being paid for full-time work sees inmates only 36 hours per month (Human Rights Watch, 2003). In many jails, the only form of mental health treatment is psychotropic medications, if that.

Medications

In a further attempt to cut costs, many state legislatures impose on jails and prisons restrictive drug formularies (Council of State Governments, 2002a) or lists of medications—usually generic and/or the cheapest—that the system will pay for (Koyanagi, Forquer, & Alfano, 2005). In so doing, many institutions will switch an inmate's medications from what he or she was taking in the community to medications that are ineffective for the individual. Although an appeals process might be available, appeals are often denied and usually require a "fail first" policy (Koyanagi et al., 2005). This practice has inconvenient, if not dangerous, and often expensive implications (Slate et al., 2013). First, psychiatric medications often take weeks to build up in an individual's body before having a therapeutic effect. More importantly, changing an individual's medications from those that work for the individual to those that could be ineffective can result in decompensation and potentially even more severe, and unexpected, symptoms. After such decompensation, even the medication that was previously effective may no longer work in alleviating symptoms, and the attending psychiatrist must set out on the potentially long process of finding an alternative medication that does in fact work. This process renders this practice more expensive, rather than less, not to mention the complication it adds to the jobs of both jail officers and mental health staff. Medications can also have side effects that are harmful—and even deadly—especially if combined with certain other medications and/or illicit substances that might not have cleared the individual's system (Slate et al., 2013). These side effects must be closely monitored, which is hard to do given the significant lack of psychiatric services available at most jails and prisons.

Even when medications are provided, however, individuals with mental illness may be distrustful, to the point of clinical paranoia, about accepting medication from jail or prison staff. This frequently leads to medication noncompliance and/or further psychiatric deterioration. Just as inmates have a limited right to treatment, they also have a right to refuse that treatment, based on due process protecting the fundamental right of individuals to make autonomous medical decisions (Honberg, 2008). This has detrimental consequences, not only to themselves but also to the institution and even to the court system in which incompetency to stand trial is at issue (see below).

Individuals with Mental Illness in the Courts

In the traditional court system, mental illness is only formally considered when questions about a defendant's competency to stand trial or mens rea (e.g., diminished capacity or the insanity defense) are raised or as a mitigating factor at sentencing. There are surprisingly few studies on the frequency with which these issues arise. The studies that do exist, albeit dated, found rates of mental illness consistent with those previously discussed in the context of jails and prisons; e.g., defense attorneys doubted their clients' competency to stand trial in 8%–15% of cases (Hoge, Bonnie, Poythress, & Monahan, 1992; Poythress et al., 1994).

Incompetency to Stand Trial and Competency Restoration

Competency to stand trial, or whether the individual is able to work with his or her attorney and to understand the proceedings against him/her, both factually and rationally (*Dusky v. United States*, 1960), is required for all defendants to stand trial. Typically, questions of competence are raised by the individual's defense attorney, and the court will order a psychological evaluation (Honberg, 2008). However, by definition, "incompetent" individuals are incapable of defending themselves legally. Thus, in acute psychiatric states, individuals with mental illness are unlikely to contact their defense attorneys to solicit their assistance in seeking bail or diversion or in planning a legal defense. They frequently lack insight into their symptoms and/or are paranoid about their attorney's intentions. Many, due to the same symptoms, are vehemently resistant to having their competency questioned and/or being evaluated. Thus, too often, acutely mentally ill individuals languish in their jail cells alone, making no progress toward going to court and resolving their charges.

If an individual is evaluated and found incompetent to stand trial, he or she will be ordered to undergo treatment to restore competency. This process is controversial for various reasons. First, in most states, this occurs in a state inpatient psychiatric facility, as opposed to the least restrictive alternative (Miller, 2003). Also, the quality of these services varies widely from facility to facility. Usually, the individual is stabilized on psychotropic medication and receives psychoeducation about his or her charges, the court system, and the legal proceedings. Sometimes, however, the focus is purely on rote memorization of the proceedings, and the individual is taken to trial without a rational understanding of what he/she will face (Earley, 2006). Moreover, individuals are often treated only to the point of being well enough (i.e., "restored") to the standard defined above; regardless of whether their psychiatric condition is fully stabilized, they are returned to jail to await trial. Finally, even those who had been previously found incompetent to stand trial are allowed to refuse their medications once they return to jail (Honberg, 2008), only to decompensate yet again. Some decompensate to the point of again becoming incompetent and needing to be returned to the hospital for restoration. This process of revolving through the competency restoration system has earned the euphemism *riding the bus*, i.e., traveling back and forth, ostensibly by bus, between the jail and the state hospital (Earley, 2006). For some, this process can go on for years — even for misdemeanors — before they are put on trial to resolve their charges (Earley, 2006; Miller, 2003).

The Not Guilty by Reason of Insanity Plea and the Guilty but Mentally Ill Verdict

The not guilty by reason of insanity (NGRI) defense, or the insanity defense, is even more controversial. Defendants found NGRI are legally regarded as not responsible for their crimes due to mental illness and are sent to a state psychiatric facility for indefinite treatment. Much of the American public opposes the NGRI defense primarily because they believe it is too frequently raised and is a way to evade justice (Borum & Fulero, 1999; Lamb & Weinberger, 1998). In fact, however, studies reveal that the defense is actually used in less than 1% of felony cases and is successful in only 15%–25% of the cases in which it is raised (Borum & Fulero, 1999). Moreover, persons found NGRI frequently spend much longer periods of time in the hospital, sometimes twice as long, than those who are found guilty for similar crimes spend in prison (Borum & Fulero, 1999).

Nevertheless, due to public outcry, in an effort to reduce the number of insanity acquittals, several states enacted guilty but mentally ill (GBMI) legislation (Borum & Fulero, 1999). Defendants found GBMI, instead of being sent to a state hospital, are imprisoned in the state correctional system with a stipulation for mental health treatment. However, research has found that GBMI laws have been largely unsuccessful: they have not significantly reduced the overall rate of NGRI acquittals; there are no additional treatment accommodations in the prisons beyond the meager services described earlier; and, unlike NGRI acquittees who are monitored closely after release from the hospital, many of those found GBMI are released without discharge services (Borum & Fulero, 1999).

Individuals with Mental Illness and Discharge Planning From Jail & Prison

Discharge planning involves developing a plan for the continuation of treatment after discharge from an institution—in this case, from jail or prison. Discharge planning is generally recognized to be critical in preventing an individual with mental illness from decompensating and recycling through the criminal justice system. Indeed, individuals with mental illness—especially those who do not receive necessary community services—are known to have an extremely high rate of recidivism. For example, in L.A. County, 90% of jail inmates with mental illness are repeat offenders, 31% of which have been incarcerated 10 times or more (Council of State Governments, 2002b). Moreover, one survival analysis (Cloyes, Wong, Latimer, & Abarca, 2010) revealed that after release from prison, those with serious mental illness returned to prison nearly a year sooner than those without SMI (385 versus 743 days, respectively).

The importance of discharge planning is apparent when looking at locations that have discharge planning and intensive community-based services. In these areas, criminal recidivism decreases substantially. The Thresholds Jail Program in Cook County, Illinois, is a useful illustration. Among the first 24 individuals with mental illness who participated in the program, there was a reduction of approximately 90% in the number of days in jail in a year's time (e.g., from an average of 107.1 days in jail in the year preceding the program to 7.8 days in the year after beginning the program) (McCoy, Roberts, Hanrahan, Clay, & Luchins, 2004).

Lack of Adequate Discharge Planning

Despite clear successes of some programs, discharge planning remains the least often provided mental health service by the criminal justice system (Steadman & Veysey, 1997). Mental health treatment in jails and prisons has been mandated by the U.S. Supreme Court, and discharge planning has been included as "treatment" because the process of discharge planning should begin as early after entry into jail and prison as possible (Barr, 2003). However, discharge planning—particularly timely discharge planning—remains largely ignored. One study revealed that only 19% of jail inmates with serious mental illness were released through mechanisms that had release dates that allowed adequate time for discharge planning (Draine et al., 2010).

To maximize the success of persons with mental illness being released from jails and prison, discharge planning must also include assistance with the basic necessities of life: housing, reinstating insurance and other benefits, transportation, assistance with finding employment, etc. (Blank Wilson, 2013; Cuddeback, Morrissey, & Domino, 2016). From the perspective of offenders, housing (identified by 63% of offenders) and financial assistance (identified by 35%) were their two most important service needs, whereas only 12% selected treatment services. These findings reflect Maslow's long-recognized theory of a hierarchy of needs (1943), that the most basic level of needs must be met before the individual can focus motivation upon the secondary or higher level needs.[8]

---

8. This is compounded by a lack of social support in the community (what would fall under Maslow's need, belonging). This is a situation many inmates—especially those with mental illness—find themselves in upon release from (especially, long) stays in jail or prison. Individuals with mental illness often end up serving their entire sentence in jail or prison, only to be returned to the streets with little or no resources. Social support is important to the success of an offender's reintegration into society, and this is especially so for an individual with mental illness. However, the stress of caring for an individual with mental illness—particularly if he or she frequently becomes noncompliant with treatment, abuses substances, blames or becomes hostile towards those who try to help during periods of decompensation, and/or puts oneself in danger—takes its toll on relationships, sometimes becoming too

Perhaps the most well-known example of a system's failure to provide adequate discharge services—at least, of those that brought to the attention of the public—occurred in New York City in the 1990s. It had become a New York City Department of Corrections practice to drop off individuals with mental illness who had completed their jail time at Queens Plaza with $1.50 in cash and a $3 MetroCard (Barr, 2003; Parish, 2007). This drop occurred between 2 a.m. and 6 a.m., ostensibly to avoid detection by the public. Discharge planning, such as assistance with obtaining treatment in the community, locating housing, or applying for social assistance, was not provided. Twenty-five thousand mentally ill inmates per year were left to fend for themselves.

As a result of this irresponsible treatment, a class action lawsuit—named after a 44-year-old homeless man with schizophrenia, *Brad H.*—was brought against the city (Barr, 2003). Brad H. had been in jail 26 times without ever receiving discharge services. On grounds of cruel and unusual punishment and violation of a New York state law that mandated providers of inpatient mental health treatment services to provide discharge planning, the parties settled in 2003, with the city agreeing to provide an adequate supply of medication, at least a shelter with a bed, access to mental health services, and reinstatement of benefits like Medicaid and food stamps without a 45-day waiting period (Barr, 2003).[9]

Lack of (Easy Access to) Community Services

Providing even a basic level of discharge services is often a challenge because it is dependent on the availability of services in the community. There are frequently months-long waiting lists for treatment services, especially psychiatric care (i.e., prescribing medications), due to a lack of community resources. And this is for those without a criminal history. Once an individual is labeled a "criminal" or "offender," it becomes more difficult to obtain treatment in the community; if identified as a "violent offender," it is practically impossible. Moreover, even if medications are made available, it is common practice in most areas to terminate Medicaid benefits upon entry into jail, even though federal law does not require it (Substance Abuse and Mental Health Services Administration, 2002), and the process of reapplying for such benefits can

---

much for friends and family to cope with. Especially when an individual has served a long sentence, ties to family and friends have often been severed long ago (Earley, 2006).

9. Compliance with the agreement was to be monitored for five years by the plaintiffs' attorneys and two special court-appointed monitors. Notably, however, as of 2007, four years into the settlement, the City had yet to provide reliable data documenting their compliance (Parish, 2007).

take months. When single medications cost hundreds, if not thousands, of dollars per month, an individual is on multiple medications, and/or he or she is unemployed, disabled, and/or homeless, paying for medications out of pocket is not an option; instead, the individual often must do without. Thus, without adequate assistance and case management connecting them to necessary mental health and social services in the community, justice-involved individuals with mental illness are doomed for almost certain failure. If the services are not available, however, which is often the case and is likely to increase as mental health budgets continue to shrink nationally, there are no linkages to be made or staff to assist in making those linkages.

Lack of Communication Between the Agencies Providing Services

Furthermore, even when discharge services are provided, there is frequently a lack of communication between the systems (and agencies within the systems) involved and no follow-up component to ensure that individuals are actually engaging with the treatment that is arranged (Slate et al., 2013). Such was the case in Blacksburg, Virginia, prior to the Virginia Tech massacre in 2005. After expressing suicidal ideation to a roommate, Seung Hui Cho was ordered by a special mental health magistrate into involuntary outpatient commitment (i.e., to undergo mental health treatment in the community against his will). The judge believed that the court's responsibility ended there, assuming that the community mental health agency would honor its statutorily mandated obligation to "recommend a specific course of treatment" and to "monitor the person's compliance" (Schulte & Jenkins, 2007, p. A01). However, according to the mental health agency, these referrals were never communicated to them. Cho did not follow through with treatment. He fell through the cracks, and a national tragedy resulted.

Probation and Parole

The best most people with mental illness get in terms of discharge planning from jails and prisons is supervision by the criminal justice system in the form of probation and parole. Surprisingly, probation and parole supervision of persons with mental illness has only recently begun to be studied. Rates of probationers and parolees with serious mental illness, again, hover around the 16% mark—ranging from 13% of parolees in California (Louden & Skeem, 2011) to 19% in Illinois (Lurigio et al., 2003). This percentage would perhaps be higher if, as some studies suggested, inmates with mental illness were not being rejected for parole at a disproportionate level. Hannah-Moffat (2004), for example, found that 94% of inmates without a mental illness were paroled, compared with 71% of inmates with a mental illness. Likewise, inmates with a history of psychiatric hospitalization while incarcerated were 30 times less likely to be granted parole than inmates with a history of psychiatric hospitalization (Feder, 1994). However, more recent research discovered that inmates with mental illness were not less likely to be released on parole (Matejkowski, Draine, Solomon, & Salzer, 2011), so this practice of rejecting inmates with mental illness for parole might be changing.

There is some research finding that supervision for offenders with mental illness does have some positive results. Ostermann and Matejkowski (2012) found that, while those with mental illness were at an increased risk of recidivism, parole supervision decreased the likelihood that they would recidivate. Specifically, being released to parole supervision for offenders with mental illness was associated with both a decreased rearrest rate and a decreased reconviction rate of 29%.

Ultimately, however, this level of "discharge planning" in the form of probation and parole is less than optimal. Probation/parole supervision planning does not usually begin until the individual is already released (or close to it). Inmates with mental illness need their medications, housing, and assistance with other needs immediately upon release. Moreover, probation/parole officers usually include treatment among a long list of requirements of an offender's supervision, leaving it to the offender to find services. This is not unexpected, as officers are criminal justice professionals, not mental health case managers. However, most individuals with serious mental illness—even many without serious mental illness—need assistance to navigate the often confusing, disjointed mental health system.

Recommendations for Policy and Practice Involving Offenders with Mental Illness

Fortunately, the growing crisis involving the overrepresentation of people with mental illnesses in the criminal justice system has been recognized, and concerted efforts to identify solutions have been forged in the past two decades. The pioneering Criminal Justice/Mental Health Consensus Project was an unprecedented, 2-year bipartisan collaboration of key stakeholders in the criminal justice and mental health systems, organized by the Council of State Governments, to improve the response to individuals with mental illness who are involved with (or at risk of involvement with) the criminal justice system (Thompson, Reuland, & Souweine, 2003). This collaboration culminated in a 453-page report of policy recommendations that spanned all phases of the criminal justice system, all of which were informed by research, program examples, and the expertise of dozens of practitioners (Council of State Governments, 2002a).

Simultaneously, Mark Munetz and Patricia A. Griffin, along with Henry J. Steadman, were developing the Sequential Intercept Model (SIM). The SIM was developed as a conceptual model to illustrate and guide community-based responses to the criminalization of people with mental illness (Abreu, Parker, Noether, Steadman, & Case, 2017). The authors explained that, if the mental health and criminal justice systems were working properly, the rate of mental illness in the criminal justice system would be equivalent to the prevalence of mental illness in the community. They asserted and built the SIM around the premise that the solution can only occur through a multi-systematic response; no one system (mental health, addiction, or criminal justice) is solely responsible. (Munetz & Griffin, 2006).

According to the SIM, there are numerous intercept points within the criminal justice system that represent opportunities for identifying, diverting, and linking justice-involved people with mental illness to services and for preventing further penetration into the criminal justice system (Steadman et al., 2016). Specifically, Munetz and Griffin (2006) identified five intercepts:

- Intercept 1: Law Enforcement and Emergency Services;
- Intercept 2: Initial Hearings and Initial Detention;
- Intercept 3: Jails and Courts;
- Intercept 4: Reentry from Jails, Prisons, and Hospitals; and
- Intercept 5: Community Corrections and Community Support Services.

Recently, Abreu et al. (2017) have proposed a slight reconfiguration of the model with the addition of "Intercept 0: Community Services," consisting of the early intervention and prevention points for people with mental and substance use disorders before they are arrested and thrust into the criminal justice system.

Ultimately, these six intercepts are intended to serve as a guide for communities to develop systematic responses to reduce criminalization of people with mental and substance use disorders (Munetz & Griffin, 2006). For over a decade, the GAINS (Gather, Assess, Integrate, Network, and Stimulate) Center for Behavioral Health and Justice Transformation, the research and training agency of the federal government's Substance Abuse and Mental Health Services Administration (SAMHSA), has been offering SIM (sometimes referred to as "cross-systems mapping") trainings to communities. In the SIM workshops, local community stakeholders come together to develop a map of their local systems, including the various intercept points; identify resources, gaps in services, and opportunities at each intercept in their community; and develop priorities to improve their systems' response to individuals with mental illness.

Indeed, given the failings of the past, the possibilities for improving the way the criminal justice system—and by extension, society—react to and handle mental illness in the future are endless. A comprehensive discussion of recommended strategies is beyond the scope of this chapter. Therefore, the most common themes, categorized into criminal justice-specific innovations, criminal justice–mental health collaboration, and societal recommendations, are discussed below. As noted by Steadman et al. (2016), strategies need to move "upstream" (on the SIM)—i.e., communities should work to find approaches that intercept persons with mental illness before they even enter the criminal justice system —to make adequate gains.

Criminal Justice-Specific Innovations

Beginning in the late 1980s, recognizing the need to do something about the increasing number of persons with serious mental illness entering the criminal justice system, sheriffs, police chiefs, judges, and the associations to which they belong began to stand up collectively to stop the revolving door to the criminal justice system for this population. It is largely the criminal justice system that has developed innovative programs to better serve this population. Most grants to fund such programs for justice-involved persons with mental illness are spearheaded by criminal justice entities.

Diversion

Criminal justice and mental health professionals alike tend to agree that diversion is an important, useful strategy for stopping, or at least slowing, the revolving door for people with mental illness in and out of the criminal justice system. There are two broad types of diversion programs for individuals with mental illness, differentiated by the point at which diversion takes place. Pre-booking, or police-based, diversion occurs prior to charges being entered by law enforcement, and post-booking diversion, such as early release to pretrial community supervision or mental health courts, occurs after an individual has been booked into jail with charges entered (Steadman, Deane, Borum, & Morrissey, 2000). For post-booking programs, screening individuals as early as possible is emphasized; it allows pretrial services, mental health providers, and court personnel to determine whether continuation through the criminal justice system is the most appropriate avenue for the individual, and/or whether the needs of all involved can best be served in the community versus the institution (Council of State Governments, 2002a).

In a study comparing three of each pre- and post-booking diversion programs, it was found that, overall, (1) individuals with mental illnesses who were diverted from the criminal justice system spent more time in the community without a corresponding increase in arrest, and (2) these individuals enjoyed greater access to mental health services—both crisis services (emergency room and hospitalization) and noncrisis services (medication and counseling)—than did people who were not (Steadman & Naples, 2005). Moreover, it conserved valuable criminal justice resources (Steadman et al., 1999). Ideally, localities would have a combination of both pre- and post-booking types of jail diversion (Steadman & Morrissette, 2016), and this is becoming more and more common throughout the country.

Crisis Intervention Teams: Training and Beyond

Likely the most well-known and widely adopted criminal justice program to respond to the needs of people with mental illness is the pre-booking diversion program, CIT.[10] Initially developed in 1987 by the Memphis Police Department in Tennessee following a fatal shooting of a mentally ill individual, the program involves 40 hours of training for law enforcement officers on recognizing the characteristics of mental illness, skills to de-escalate situations rather than resorting to physical force, and information about local community mental health services and resources (DuPont & Cochran, 2000). While many localities have developed an extensive training course and call it CIT, the true Memphis model of CIT is more than training. Central to the name CIT, when a call is registered as a mental health crisis, a team of officers who have gone through the extensive training are dispatched and respond, armed with their skills in de-escalation. Moreover, a central component is the availability of a centralized, around-the-clock, "drop off" mental health treatment facility with a no-refusal policy, where officers can easily and safely transfer custody of the individual in crisis to mental health professionals. Ultimately, though, the key is strong collaboration between law enforcement and the local mental health system.

---

10. Although CIT is the most well known, there are a variety of other models of police-based diversion programs (Steadman et al., 2000). Examples include mobile crisis teams in which interdisciplinary mental health teams operate in partnership with law enforcement and community service officers in which an officer of a police department functions as a broker for social services for individuals with mental illness.

As Steadman and Morrissette (2016) noted, CIT is about inclusive collaboration by community mental health, chemical dependency, and criminal justice professionals; cross-discipline training; and a coordinated community response. The ultimate goal of a well-functioning community in terms of behavioral health would be to avoid police involvement when it is unnecessary (Steadman & Morrissette, 2016).

Currently implemented in more than 1,000 localities nationwide (Ritter, Teller, Munetz, & Bonfine, 2010; Steadman & Morrissette, 2016), CIT has been found to result in increased knowledge and decreased stigma about mental illness by law enforcement officers (Bahora, Hanafi, Chien, & Compton, 2008; Compton, Esterberg, McGee, Kotwicki, & Oliva, 2006). Accordingly, arrests have gone down in cities that have implemented CIT—e.g., arrest rates as low as 1% (Reuland, 2004) and up to 5% (Steadman et al., 2000) of people with mental illness. Even the number of calls for the special tactical team in Memphis decreased by almost 50% (Dupont & Cochran, 2000). Furthermore, the referral and/or transport to psychiatric emergency services increased by 42% in the first four years after CIT was implemented (Dupont & Cochran, 2000). Other cities have seen similar results (Teller, Munetz, Gil, & Ritter, 2006).

The success of CIT has been recognized by the broader criminal justice system and has been adapted for use within jails, prisons, and probation/parole departments (Hodges, 2010). Only recently has the important role of correctional officers in the institution's mental healthcare continuum been recognized, but officers' attitudes can influence whether inmates seek and/or receive mental health services (Appelbaum, Hickey, & Packer, 2001). Indeed, officers can be invaluable in observing and providing essential information to mental health staff about inmates' behavior (including medication noncompliance), and when balanced between firmness and sensitivity, officers can even serve as "treatment extenders," providing necessary structure, support, and responsiveness to inmates' mental health needs.

The prototype for jail-based CIT programs—and the most widely researched —was implemented in numerous jurisdictions in Maine. Encompassing both the training and team-based approach of CIT, jail-based CIT programs exist in an increasing number of locales (Cattabriga, Deprez, Kinner, Louis, & Lumb, 2007; NAMI of Ohio, 2009; Buffington-Vollum, 2009), with results comparable to its street law enforcement-based counterpart. These programs have been so well received, in fact, that the National Institute of Corrections offered a training, initially broadcast in March 2012, entitled "Crisis Intervention Teams: A Frontline Response to Mental Illness in Corrections," designed to build an agency's capacity to implement locally owned and administered jail-based CIT programs (National Institute of Corrections, 2012).

Specialized Mental Health Units in Criminal Justice Agencies

Law enforcement agencies, while the first to implement such an approach, are not the only criminal justice agencies to establish specialized units within their departments to better respond to the needs of offenders with mental illness. Specialty courts—or what have been referred to as problem-solving courts or, now, treatment courts—a type of post-booking diversion program are a prime example of this. Mental health courts are just one of the many types of treatment courts that employ teams of specially trained professionals that focus on the unique needs of particular populations (e.g., veterans, homeless, domestic violence perpetrators, prostitutes, individuals reentering society after incarceration). Similarly, in recent years, we have witnessed the advent of units of specially trained probation/parole officers to work with distinct groups of offenders—e.g., domestic violence offenders, sex offenders, and now, offenders with mental illness.

Mental Health Courts

Finding that the traditional adversarial approach to the law was not effective at deterring drug offenders, many of whom had an illness that was propelling their criminal behavior, the first "problem-solving" drug court was created in Dade County, Florida, in 1989 (Denckla & Berman, 2001).[11] In 1997, Florida's Broward County Mental Health Court developed as a derivative of drug courts to better meet the needs of defendants with serious mental illness (Denckla & Berman, 2001). Since that time, mental health courts have been gaining in popularity. Composed of court staff, probation officers, and community mental health treatment providers, these specialized court teams provide direct supervision to defendants with serious mental illness in the community, in lieu of traditional court processing (Redlich, Steadman, Monahan, Robbins, & Petrila, 2006). Modeled on principles of therapeutic jurisprudence, if participants remain compliant with community-based treatment and attend regular judicial status review hearings, they might have their charges suspended or dismissed, thereby diverting them out of the criminal justice system.

Research on mental health courts has yielded positive results. A multisite study found that mental health courts were associated with lower arrest rates

---

11. It is noteworthy how close in time this occurred relative to the development of the first CIT program in Memphis. It appears that criminal justice professionals from a variety of disciplines—law enforcement, the courts—were simultaneously realizing that what was then being done to deal with people with mental illness in the criminal justice system was not working.

and reduced number of days of incarceration for participants (Steadman et al., 2011). Likewise, participants in select mental health courts required fewer inpatient treatment days and less crisis interventions, and they showed decreased abuse of substances and improved psychosocial functioning (Slate et al., 2013). While mental health courts are still in their infancy—e.g., there are approximately 300 mental health courts (Council of State Governments, 2018) versus approximately 2,500 drug courts—these promising outcomes will undoubtedly lead other jurisdictions to create their own.

Specially Trained Probation/Parole Officers

Slate, Roskes, Feldman, and Baerga (2003) were the first to discuss in the literature the idea of probation officers specially trained to work with offenders with mental illness. They recommended that federal probation offices have designated officers who would receive 40 hours of training on mental illness annually and maintain specialized caseloads of only probationers with mental illness. When implemented, they found positive results, specifically that such specialty caseloads reduced the risk of probation violations (Slate, Feldman, Roskes, & Baerga, 2004).

While the exact number of localities that have specially trained mental health probation and parole officers is unknown, it is clear that they are on the rise as evidenced by an increase in research on the topic. What researchers have discovered is that, in addition to training and a caseload made up solely of clients with mental illness, specialty mental health probation/parole officers have reduced caseload size, have collaborated with community mental health agencies to assist those they supervise with more easily accessing mental health treatment and supportive services, and have strived to maintain high quality-low conflict (e.g., work on problem-solving, minimize conflict, apply less negative pressure and coercion) in their working relationships with their clients (Epperson, Canada, Thompson, & Lurigio, 2014; Matejkowski, Severson, & Manthey, 2015; Skeem, Emke-Francis, & Louden, 2006). Supervision officers who use this approach are more successful at promoting treatment involvement and reducing violations of supervision conditions and jail days (Manchak, Skeem, Kennealy, & Louden, 2014; Skeem & Louden, 2006; Wolff et al., 2014).

Use Evidence-Based Practices

To be most effective, practices must be evidence based. This requires team members to remain abreast of the research literature on best practices with offenders with mental illness. For example, there are several research discoveries in the past decade in the field of mental health courts and specialty probation—e.g., the risk-needs-responsivity (RNR) model applies to offenders with mental illness, the need for trauma-informed services—that should have changed the way teams approach their work. However, without knowledge of these developments in evidence-based practices, teams continue operate in the same way they always have (or change slowly), not meeting the obligations they have to their clients or to the taxpayers supporting these programs.

For example, in an attempt to better understand the supervisory practices of specially trained probation/parole officers, including whether they are operating under best practices, Matejkowski et al. (2015) surveyed 90 specially trained officers throughout the nation. They discovered that there are currently three common approaches that are utilized among these probation/parole officers to address the needs of offenders with serious mental illness. The first, the mental health approach, targets the reduction and management of psychiatric symptoms under the premise that this will reduce criminal involvement (Skeem et al., 2011). The primary strategy used by officers who employ this approach is requiring treatment as a special condition of supervision. While this approach is intuitively appealing given the clientele being served (i.e., offenders with serious mental illness)—and historically has been (and likely continues to be) the predominant approach of many mental health court teams—research has shown that mental health services alone are not particularly successful at reducing criminal involvement of offenders with serious mental illness (Matejkowski et al., 2015; Skeem et al., 2011). In fact, even evidence-based practices with regard to improving mental health outcomes (e.g., reducing psychiatric symptoms, reducing psychiatric hospitalizations) do not translate to reductions in criminal behavior (Peterson, Skeem, Hart, Vidal, & Keith, 2010).

The other two supervision approaches used by specially trained probation/ parole officers are those commonly used in offender rehabilitation in general, not specifically with offenders with mental illness, but that are also applicable to those with mental health issues (Matejkowski et al., 2015). The strengths promotion approach, operationalized in the Good Lives Model (GLM) (Ward & Marshall, 2004) of offender rehabilitation, is somewhat related to the mental health approach in that it is person centered and recovery focused (e.g., emphasizes the importance of individuals leading a self-directed life and striving to reach their full potential). As the name suggests, it focuses on helping offenders to identify, develop, and utilize prosocial skills to achieve their personally valued goals, to improve their quality of life, and in so doing, to reduce their likelihood of resorting to crime (Ward & Marshall, 2004). While based in research, this approach too falls short in addressing all the needs of offenders with mental illness.

The approach that most specialty officers employ in supervising their mentally ill clients is the risk reduction approach (Matejkowski et al., 2015). This is hopeful, given that this is the most empirically supported approach, not only for offenders in general but also for offenders with serious mental illness. Based on the RNR model (Andrews & Bonta, 2010), the risk reduction approach assumes that an offender's level of risk for criminal behavior can be assessed by a validated risk assessment instrument (such as the level of services/case management inventory) and that those risks can be specifically targeted by supervision. Backed by a substantial amount of research spanning two decades, this model articulates quite clearly a model for reducing offenders' risk and, thus, changing behavior. Specifically, the RNR model (Andrews & Bonta, 2010) identifies eight central risk factors known to be most predictive of criminal behavior: (1) lack of attachment to family/marital supports, (2) school/employment problems, (3) lack of prosocial leisure or recreational activities, (4) antisocial peers, (5) antisocial attitudes, (6) antisocial personality, (7) substance abuse, and (8) history of antisocial behavior. After assessing these risks, treatment services must be titrated to target these risks at an intensity proportional to the severity of that risk. Put otherwise, research has shown that individuals with a high number of these risk factors should be targeted, as they will yield the greatest reductions in recidivism, whereas targeting low-risk offenders with the same interventions can actually increase their likelihood of recidivism (Fisler, 2015). Thus, the risk principle of the RNR model identifies who to target. The need principle of the model identifies what to target. What dynamic (i.e., changeable) risk factors—or criminogenic needs—can a supervision officer target with treatment? Finally, the responsivity principle of the model addresses how to tailor treatments to the specific abilities and learning styles of the individual (Fisler, 2015).

A long-held, common misconception—even among criminal justice professionals specially trained on mental illness—is that mental disorder is a risk factor for criminality and recidivism. This misunderstanding remains despite the fact that research since the mid-1990s has shown that mental illness alone has little direct relationship to criminal behavior (Bonta, Law, & Hanson, 1998; Gendreau, Little, & Goggin, 1996; Quinsey, Harris, Rice, & Cormier, 1998; Swartz & Lurigio, 2007). Instead, the evidence shows that mental illness is a responsivity factor; it affects an individual's ability to benefit from interventions. As such, treatment for mental illness is still important—not for the purpose of reducing recidivism directly but for improving an individual's ability to respond to interventions that do target criminal behavior (Fisler, 2015).

As discussed throughout this chapter, there is a revolving door in which people with mental illness are escorted in and out of the criminal justice system.

People with mental illness recidivate and are reincarcerated at a higher rate than those without mental illness. Perhaps surprisingly—especially to those who adhere to the belief that mental disorder is the main risk factor contributing to criminality and recidivism—what is actually propelling this revolving door is that offenders with serious mental illness have significantly more of the central eight risk factors than offenders without serious mental illness (Matejkowski et al., 2011). Specifically, over 80% of offenders with mental illness had a substance use disorder and were eight times more likely than those without mental illness to have chemical dependency issues (Matejkowski et al., 2011). They were twice as likely to have an antisocial personality, as well as more likely to engage in antisocial behaviors, than offenders without mental illness (Matejkowski et al., 2011). Likewise, offenders with serious mental illness have as great or greater levels of criminal thinking and criminal attitudes than offenders without mental illness (Morgan, Fisher, Duan, Mandracchia, & Murray, 2010; Wolff, Morgan, & Shi, 2013). Half of Matejkowski et al.'s (2011) sample lacked a high school education. Thus, it is their criminogenic risk levels that are associated with recidivism for offenders with mental illness, not their psychiatric condition per se.

Ultimately, it is important for professionals working in this field to stay current with the empirical research and evidence-based best practices. Without knowledge of the RNR model, for example, mental health courts and probation/parole officers might be using the mental health approach (e.g., focusing on reducing symptoms of mental illness) to the neglect of criminogenic needs that form the real basis for their clients' recidivism.

Program Evaluation

Program evaluation is essential for the success and longevity of any program. Not only does solid evaluation research monitor the effectiveness of a program, but it also illuminates the strengths of the program as well as areas that need improvement. In addition, it is merely reality that program evaluation is necessary to justify the existence and continuation of a program from a resource perspective (e.g., funding, staffing, time invested). Frequently, the outcome of greatest interest to the community is cost savings.

Two examples of model program evaluations have come out of San Antonio, Texas, between 2013 and 2015. In the first, Cowell, Hinde, Broner, and Aldridge (2013) examined the cost savings of a single jail diversion program. They found that, due to reduced utilization of criminal justice resources, the jail diversion program saved taxpayers $2,800 (over a 2-year period) per offender with mental illness that was diverted. As such, there were immediate cost savings. Moreover, they predicted longer term cost savings associated with a four-time greater access to treatment for these individuals, as compared to those offenders with mental illness who were not diverted out of the criminal justice system. The authors explained this on grounds that treatment might reduce offenders' symptoms, reduce the number of future offenses, and thus reduce subsequent arrests and incarceration.

In 2015, Cowell, Hinde, Broner, and Aldridge reported on another program evaluation, comparing three types of diversion programs in San Antonio: a pre-booking police diversion program, a post-booking bond program, and a post-booking court docket program. The pre-booking diversion program— a CIT program with a centralized crisis facility, which provides medical and psychiatric assessment, short-term monitoring, treatment planning, short-term treatment, and linkage to treatment in the community—cost the most, with $370 per person. Ninety percent of these costs were incurred by community mental health agencies. The post-booking bond program (e.g., a jail diversion program focused on early identification and release to intensive pretrial probation) cost $238 per person, and the post-booking court docket (e.g., judicial order for conditional release, contingent upon compliance with community-based treatment) cost the least, with $205 per person. With the latter two programs, the majority of costs were incurred by the courts.

In both program evaluations, while examining different aspects of a number of programs, the researchers distilled the data into comprehensible statistics that are of interest to their local community (e.g., cost savings). The evaluations also provide useful information to other cities that might be interested in developing similar programs. In particular, the second evaluation provided a simple, yet cogent, comparison of the costs of three types of diversion programs. This provided other communities with concrete information to consider in their own decision-making.

Criminal Justice–Mental Health Collaboration

Most efforts by the criminal justice system to respond to and manage individuals with mental illness are only as effective as the mental health services available (Slate et al., 2013). These are reliant on the adequacy of the mental health system itself as well as successful collaboration between the two systems. Thus, policies to improve responses to mentally ill offenders must be broader in scope—indeed, cross-system in nature—to be effective (Council of State Governments, 2002a).

Intercept 0: Community Services

As mentioned previously, Steadman and colleagues (Abreu et al., 2017) recently proposed revising the 12-year-old, highly regarded SIM of the criminal justice system to add Intercept 0: Community Services. This is a commentary on how critically important the field recognizes an adequate mental health system to be. No criminal justice program for offenders with mental illness can be successful without it. On the other hand, if a community's mental health system were functioning optimally, such criminal justice programs would be unnecessary.

Steadman and Morrissette (2016) described a continuum of crisis response services that a community needs to function well, noting that not all crises need to, or should, lead to emergency room visits. These range from (1) *prevention* (e.g., supported housing and education, peer and family supports), to (2) *early intervention* (e.g., hotlines, mobile crisis outreach), to (3) *intervention and stabilization* (e.g., 23-hour crisis stabilization centers, detox centers, short-term crisis residential settings, inpatient settings), and to (4) *"postvention"* (e.g., assessment and reassessment of services and supports, case management to assist with transition back into the community).

Fast and Easy Access to Mental Healthcare

Individuals with mental illness, particularly during psychiatric crises, often lack the wherewithal to actively seek out and navigate the inherently complicated mental health system. Thus, in order to successfully engage justice-involved individuals with mental illness, access to mental healthcare must be easy and straightforward. For example, probation and parole supervision of offenders with mental illness has been found to be optimized by using a forensic assertive community treatment (FACT) team. Such teams are multidisciplinary in nature, typically consisting of a psychiatrist, nurse, social worker, substance abuse specialist, occupational therapist, vocational rehabilitation specialist, and peer specialist as well as the individual's probation or parole officer. They provide mental health services designed to respond to the special needs of an offender with mental illness. Specifically, FACT mental health services are (a) mobile, where FACT team workers actively engage the client by going to the client rather than requiring the client to come to a mental health clinic; (b) provided 24/7; and (c) comprehensive, involving not only medication but also case management as well as substance abuse treatment, nonpsychiatric medical care, education, employment, and housing assistance (Lamberti, Weisman, & Faden, 2004). Such teams have been found to assist individuals with functioning in the community as well as reduce forensic outcomes, such as number of arrests, rearrests, and incarcerations (Marquant, Sabbe, Van Nuffel, & Goethals, 2016).

Without prompt, accessible, and consistent mental health treatment, such as medications and social support and fulfillment of basic needs of living such as housing, individuals with mental illness are bound to decompensate and recycle into the criminal justice system. Thus, at a minimum, adequate discharge services should include assistance in obtaining mental health treatment, including access to at least a month of medication, housing, and expedited reinstatement of public benefits (Barr, 2003). Medicaid should be suspended, rather than terminated, when an individual with mental illness is jailed so that they can be quickly restored upon release (Council of State Governments, 2002). Other important community services include treatment for co-occurring disorders, life skills training, employment services, transportation arrangements, and peer involvement (Haimowitz, 2002). A last, but integral and commonly neglected, component of community services for justice-involved individuals with mental illness is creating a follow-up mechanism for ensuring an individual's attendance and engagement in the mental health services arranged (Slate et al., 2013).

Facilitating Release of Information

An important aspect of providing appropriate responses to individuals with mental illness in the criminal justice system is obtaining records of their mental health history. For example, for the sake of expedience, screening conducted at booking is usually based on an inmate's self-report. However, such self-reports are notoriously unreliable, especially for those with mental illness who may be too cognitively disorganized and/or paranoid to provide valid information about their history. Thus, corroborating information on past symptoms, treatment (both that which did and did not work) and involvement with the criminal justice system can be invaluable, and this information should follow the individual throughout both the criminal justice and mental health systems (Council of State Governments, 2002a).

As such, a mechanism by which criminal justice agencies can gain access to mental health information is invaluable. One useful—and easy, as it bypasses bureaucracy—method by which access to historical information about an individual's mental health can be achieved is by encouraging and/or supporting the involvement of family members (Council of State Governments, 2002a). Moreover, developing a formal agreement with the local mental health system by which records of justice-involved individuals can be shared is recommended (Council of State Governments, 2002a). Although such an agreement is commonly met with resistance by mental health agencies, who are typically protected by confidentiality laws, what many mental health agencies don't realize is that the federal confidentiality law, the Health Information Portability and Accountability Act (HIPAA), permits certain disclosures to criminal justice agencies without the individual's consent (Petrila, 2007). In particular, HIPAA allows release of information, limited to the "minimal necessary" to accomplish the following criminal justice purposes:

> [For] judicial and administrative proceedings; law enforcement purposes; [and] disclosures necessary to avert a serious threat to health or safety ... [as well as sharing] with a correctional institution or law enforcement official with custody of the individual, if the information is necessary for the provision of healthcare; the health and safety of the inmate, other inmates, or correctional officials and staff (Petrila, 2007, p. 2).

Thus, mental health agencies can in fact provide information to the criminal justice system without bureaucratic red tape, at least according to federal laws.[12] Nevertheless, even if mental health agencies are resistant to disclosing records, merely developing the means of cross-referencing the names of individuals detained by the criminal justice system with the names of mental health system clients can be useful by keeping both systems "in the know" (Council of State Governments, 2002a).

Preparation and Communication

Any successful collaboration—in this case, between the criminal justice system and the mental health system—requires both active preparation and communication. Unfortunately, as is seen in too many cases of the mentally ill both harming and being harmed by others, such preparation and communication is often not a reality. In particular, for any of the innovative programs mentioned above (e.g., CIT, FACT teams), the involved agencies must explicitly define their separation of duties, make everyone involved aware of resources, and formalize agreements so as to avoid confusion and to ensure appropriate action (Council of State Governments, 2002a).

---

12. Of course, disclosing information can risk the mental health system's therapeutic relationship with the client. Thus, the benefit of disclosure must be weighed against the risk.

Cultural, Social, and Economic Reform

Increase Funding for Mental Healthcare

Of course, none of the above recommendations are possible without increasing funding for the mental health system. Unfortunately, this is unlikely in the foreseeable future given the current political climate of the United States. State budgets for already poorly funded mental health systems have been repeatedly cut. Specifically, according to a 2008 survey of the National Association of State Mental Health Program Directors, 32 state mental health agencies reported budget cuts on average of 5% for fiscal year 2009; one state reported a cut as high as 17.5% (National Association of State Mental Health Program Directors Research Institute, 2008). Moreover, the states expected an average budget cut of 8% (up to 25% in some states) in 2010 and in excess of 9% (again, up to 25% in some states) in 2011. In total, approximately $2.1 billion were cut from state mental health budgets between 2008 and 2011 (Lacey, Sack, & Sulzberger, 2011). The most commonly affected programs are adult inpatient services and adult clinic services.

Unlike the past several decades of seemingly limitless funding for the criminal justice system, corrections budgets are currently facing similar cuts. Specifically, a 2009 report by the Vera Institute revealed that at least 26 states cut their corrections budgets (Scott-Hayward, 2009). Of course, among the first expenses to be reduced by the correctional system is healthcare services, which includes mental healthcare. Moreover, as a result of prison budget cuts, experts predict that states will begin to increase the number of inmates released under supervision in the community, thereby increasing the number of offenders with mental illness who will be in need of treatment in the community (Johnson, 2011). Whether it will comprise America's third deinstitutionalization movement remains to be seen.

Federal monies, although striking optimism, are frequently only short-term fixes. For example, the 2004 Mentally Ill Offender Treatment and Crime Reduction Act (MIOTCRA) authorized federal grant monies to fund the development and implementation of mental health courts and other criminal justice diversion projects, as well as correctional treatment and community reentry programs. However, the concern with any external funding sources is that they do not continue indefinitely. Although MIOTCRA has been extended, the reliability of federal grant funds is uncertain, depending on fluctuations in the economy.

Political and economic pressures have grave implications for those with mental illness. Both those with preexisting mental illness who are losing treatment as a result of ailing state budgets, as well as those who are just beginning to experience mental health issues due to unemployment and other economic stressors for whom appropriate treatment is unavailable, are suffering. Without necessary services, both groups are vulnerable to entanglement with the criminal justice system. As such, the criminal justice system will be hit hard by the mental health system's cuts, as law enforcement, jails, and prisons continue to be put in the role of responding to the mentally ill. Likewise, the mental health system will be severely impacted by the cuts in the criminal justice system's budgets, as increasing numbers of persons with mental illness are released from prisons into the community. Thus, it would behoove both systems to work together.

Decrease Stigma

Stigma toward mental illness is longstanding and pervasive in U.S. culture. Stigmatizing attitudes, in turn, lead to discriminatory behavior. People who endorse myths about individuals with mental illness (e.g., people with mental illness are responsible for their disease, people with mental illness are dangerous) tend to respond to individuals with mental illness with greater avoidance, as well as endorsement of coercive treatment (Corrigan, Markowitz, Watson, Rowan, & Kubiak, 2003). People with mental illness are also more likely to face employment discrimination (Bordieri & Drehmer, 1986), housing discrimination (Page, 1977), and even to be falsely charged with violent crimes (Steadman, 1981), all of which affect their involvement with the criminal justice system and successful reintegration into the community. Such discrimination can also be seen on a structural level, whereby public institutions restrict opportunities for persons with mental illness (Corrigan & Kleinlein, 2005), and there is reason to believe that this trend is increasing, not declining. For example, Hemmens, Miller, Burton, and Milner (2002) found that, between 1989 and 1999, state laws became increasingly restrictive of civil rights for the mentally ill, including familial rights such as marriage and parenting. Furthermore, comparatively fewer public financial resources are being allocated to the mental health system than to the physical health medical system (Corrigan & Watson, 2003).

Thus, persons with mental illness are left to struggle with not only the symptoms of their disease but also with the repercussions of "a largely uninformed, misinformed and apathetic public" (Slate et al., 2013, p. 347). The stress of discrimination undoubtedly exacerbates an individual's mental illness. Moreover, many people with mental illness internalize the common prejudices against them (i.e., self-stigma). This frequently manifests in refusal to pursue much needed services, which hinders successful functioning in society (Corrigan &

Kleinlein, 2005). This further contributes to the public and structural stigma against them. The self-perpetuating nature of this cycle is obvious.

Many experts have advocated public education as a means to address social stigma against persons with mental illness. And research reveals that educational programs can in fact be effective in reducing negative attitudes and fears about individuals with mental illness, if conducted properly. For example, Corrigan, Watson, Warpinski, and Gracia (2004) found that people enrolled in a brief educational program focusing on the stigma related to mental illness, compared to those in a control group, were less likely to believe that people with mental illness were dangerous, to fear people with mental illness, to endorse social avoidance, or to favor segregation and coercive treatment. They were also more likely to help an individual with mental illness and to support putting money into rehabilitative services. Moreover, when individuals were provided accurate information about the relative risk of violence by people with mental illness, perceptions of dangerousness were reduced (Penn, Kommana, Mansfield, & Link, 1999). Research also suggests that, when individuals have greater familiarity with mental illness, they are less likely to fear or to advocate social distance from individuals with such an illness (Angermeyer, Matschinger, & Corrigan, 2004; Corrigan, Green, Lundin, Kubiak, & Penn, 2001). Therefore, opportunities for contact with mentally ill individuals should be included as part of educational programs (Rusch, Angermeyer, & Corrigan, 2005).

Conclusion

There is no denying that individuals with mental illness make up a significant and growing proportion, not to mention an often challenging segment, of our country's criminal justice population. This group of offenders and their needs can no longer be ignored; they must be brought out of the shadows of not only the criminal justice and mental health systems but also of society. As outlined in this chapter, there are many varied reasons for the overrepresentation of individuals with mental illness in the criminal justice system—in particular, decades of failed mental health and criminal justice policy propelled by misconceptions about mental illness and mental health treatment. Fortunately, there are currently countless opportunities to implement new and more enlightened policies. Among these are innovative criminal justice strategies, such as pre- and post-booking diversion programs and development of specialized units in criminal justice agencies, to respond to this unique population.

However, improvements in responding to offenders with mental illness will not result from reforms limited to the criminal justice system. First, any criminal justice program targeting this special population is only as successful as the mental health resources offered in the community; thus, improved collaboration between the criminal justice and mental health systems is essential. Nor will criminal justice and mental health reforms, whatever their merits, be successful without shifts in the prevailing cultural, social, and economic forces in our country. Indeed, such reforms are contingent upon more well-informed and empathic citizens, policy makers, and policies. The futility of continuing to imprison individuals on whom the goals of punishment are often wasted must be acknowledged, and the will must be formed to put the money and resources into halting the revolving door for those with mental illness.

References

Abram, K. M., & Teplin, L. A. (1991). Co-occurring disorders among mentally ill jail detainees Implications for public policy. *American Psychologist 46,* 1036–1045.

Abreu, D., Parker, T. W., Noether, C. D., Steadman, H. J., & Case, B. (2017). Revising the paradigm for jail diversion for people with mental and substance use disorders: Intercept 0. *Behavioral Sciences & the Law, 35,* 380–395.

American Psychiatric Association. (2000). *Psychiatric services in jails and prisons* (2nd ed.). Washington, DC: Author.

Andrews, D. A., & Bonta, J. (2010). *The psychology of criminal conduct* (5th ed.). New Providence, NJ: Routledge.

Angermeyer, M. C., Matschinger, H., & Corrigan, P. W. (2004). Familiarity with mental illness and social distance from people with schizophrenia and major depression: Testing a model using data from a representative population survey. *Schizophrenia Research, 69,* 175–182.

Appelbaum, K. L., Hickey, J. M., & Packer, I. (2001). The role of correctional officers in multidisciplinary mental health care in prisons. *Psychiatric Services, 52,* 1343–1347.

Axelson, G. L., & Wahl, O. F. (1992). Psychotic versus nonpsychotic misdemeanants in a large county jail: An analysis of pretrial treatment by the legal system. *International Journal of Law and Psychiatry, 15,* 379–386.

Bahora, M., Hanafi, S., Chien, V. H., & Compton, M. T. (2008). Preliminary evidence of effects of crisis intervention team training on self-efficacy and social distance. *Administration and Policy in Mental Health and Mental Health Services Research, 35,* 159–167.

Barr, H. (2003). Transinstitutionalization in the courts: Brad H. v. City of New York and the fight for discharge planning for people with psychiatric disabilities leaving Rikers Island. *Crime and Delinquency, 49,* 97–123.doi:10.1177/00111287022.

Blank Wilson, A. (2013). How people with serious mental illness seek help after leaving jail. *Qualitative Health Research, 23*(12), 1575–1590.

Bonta, J., Law, M., & Hanson, K. (1998). The prediction of criminal and violent recidivism among mentally disordered offenders: A meta-analysis. *Psychological Bulletin, 123,* 123–142.

Bordieri, J. E., & Drehmer, D. E. (1986). Hiring decisions for disabled workers: Looking at the cause. *Journal of Applied Social Psychology, 16,* 197–208.

Borum, R., & Fulero, S. M. (1999). Empirical research on the insanity defense and attempted reforms: Evidence toward informed policy. *Law and Human Behavior, 23,* 375–394.

Buffington-Vollum, J. K. (2009). *Assessing the impact of and responding to the mentally ill in the criminal justice system.* Harrisonburg, VA: Commonwealth of Virginia Health Planning Region I.

Cattabriga, G., Deprez, R., Kinner, A., Louie, M., & Lumb, R. (2007, December). Crisis Intervention Team (CIT) training for correctional officers: An evaluation of NAMI Maine's 2005–2007 Expansion Program. The Center for Health Policy, Planning and Research. Retrieved from http://www.pacenterof excellence.pitt.edu/documents/Maine%20NAMI%20CIT-3.pdf

Choe, J. Y., Teplin, L. A., & Abram, K. M. (2008). Perpetration of violence, violent victimization, and severe mental illness: Balancing public health concerns. *Psychiatric Services, 59,* 153–164.

Clark, R. E., Ricketts, S. K., & McHugo, G. J. (1999). Legal system involvement and costs for persons in treatment for severe mental illness and substance use disorders. *Psychiatric Services, 50,* 641–647.

Cloyes, K. G., Wong, B., Latimer, S., & Abarca, J. (2010). Time to prison return for offenders with serious mental illness released from prison: A survival analysis. *Criminal Justice and Behavior, 37*(2), 175–187.

Coleman, B. C. (1997, December 10). Study: Most hospitals dump mental patients. *The Ledger,* p. A4.

Compton, M. T., Esterberg, M. L., McGee, R., Kotwicki, R. J., & Oliva, J. R. (2006). Crisis intervention team training: Changes in knowledge, attitudes, and stigma related to schizophrenia. *Psychiatric Services, 57,* 1199–1202.

Cooper, V. G., McLearen, A. M., & Zapf, P. A. (2004). Dispositional decisions with the mentally ill: Police perceptions and characteristics. *Police Quarterly, 7,* 295–310.

Cordner, G. (2006). *People with mental illness. Problem-oriented guides for police, guide no. 40.* Washington, DC: Office of Community-Oriented Policing Services.

Corrigan, P. W., Green, A., Lundin, R., Kubiak, M. A., & Penn, D. L. (2001). Familiarity with and social distance from people with serious mental illness. *Psychiatric Services, 52,* 953–958.

Corrigan, P. W., & Kleinlein, P. (2005). The impact of mental illness stigma. In P. W. Corrigan (Ed.), *On the stigma of mental illness: Practical strategies for research and social change* (pp. 11–44). Washington, DC: American Psychological Association.

Corrigan, P. W., Markowitz, F., Watson, A., Rowan, D., & Kubiak, M. A. (2003). An attribution model of public discrimination towards persons with mental illness. *Journal of Health and Social Behavior, 44,* 162–179.

Corrigan, P. W., River, L. P., Lundin, R. K., Wasowski, K. U., Campion, J., Mathisen, J., & Kubiak, M. A. (2000) Stigmatizing attributions about mental illness. *Journal of Community Psychology, 28,* 91–103.

Corrigan, P. W., & Watson, A. C. (2003). Factors that explain how policy makers distribute resources to mental health services. *Psychiatric Services, 54,* 501–507.

Corrigan, P. W., Watson, A. C., Warpinski, A. C., & Gracia, G. (2004). Implications for educating the public on mental illness, violence, and stigma. *Psychiatric Services, 55,* 577–580.

Council of State Governments. (2002a). *Criminal Justice/Mental Health Consensus Project Report.* New York, NY: Author.

Council of State Governments. (2002b). *Fact sheet: Mental illness and jails.* New York, NY: Author.

Council of State Governments. (2002c). *Fact sheet: People with mental illness in the criminal justice system: About the problem fact sheet.* New York, NY: Author.

Council of State Governments. (2018). *Mental health courts.* New York, NY: CSG Justice Center. Retrieved from https://csgjusticecenter.org/mental-health-court-project/.

Cowell, A. J., Hinde, J. M., Broner, N., & Aldridge, A. P. (2013). The impact on taxpayer costs of a jail diversion program for people with serious mental illness. *Evaluation and Program Planning, 41,* 31–37.

Cowell, A. J., Hinde, J. M., Broner, N., & Aldridge, A. P. (2015). The cost of implementing a jail diversion program for people with mental illness in San Antonio, Texas. *Evaluation and Program Planning, 48,* 57–62.

Cuddeback, G. S., Morrissey, J. P., & Domino, M. E. (2016). Enrollment and service use patterns among persons with severe mental illness receiving expedited Medicaid on release from state prisons, county jails, and psychiatric hospitals. *Psychiatric Services, 67*(8), 835–841.

Denckla, D., & Berman, G. (2001). *Rethinking the revolving door: A look at mental illness in the courts.* New York, NY: Center for Court Innovation/ State Justice Institute. Retrieved from http://www. courtinnovation.org/ pdf/mental_health.pdf.

Ditton, P. M. (1999). *Mental health and treatment of inmates and probationers.* Bureau of Justice Statistics: Special Report.

Draine, J., Blank Wilson, A., Metraux, S., Hadley, T., & Evans, A. C. (2010). The impact of mental illness status on the length of jail detention and the legal mechanism of jail release. *Psychiatric Services, 61*(5), 458–462.

DuPont, R., & Cochran, S. (2000). Police response to mental health emergencies —Barriers to change. *Journal of the American Academy of Psychiatry and the Law, 28,* 338–344.

Earley, P. (2006). *Crazy: A father's search through America's mental health madness.* New York, NY: Putnam.

Elbogen, E. B., & Johnson, S. C. (2009). The intricate link between violence and mental disorder: Results from the National Epidemiologic Survey on Alcohol and Related Conditions. *Archives of General Psychiatry, 66,* 152–161.

Ellis, H., & Alexander, V. (2017). The mentally ill in jail: Contemporary clinical and practice perspectives for psychiatric mental health nursing. *Archives of Psychiatric Nursing, 31,* 217–222.

Engel, R. S. & Silver, E. (2001). Policing mentally disordered suspects: A reexamination of the criminalization hypothesis. *Criminology, 39*(2), 225–252.

Epperson, M., Canada, K., Thompson, J., & Lurigio, A. (2014). Walking the line: Specialized and standard probation officer perspectives on supervising probationers with serious mental illnesses. *International Journal of Law and Psychiatry, 37*(5), 473–483.

Feder, L. (1994). Psychiatric hospitalization history and parole decisions. *Law and Human Behavior, 18,* 395–410.

Fisler, C. (2015). When research challenges policy and practice: Toward a new understanding of mental health courts. *The Judges Journal, 54*(2), 8–13.

Frankle, W. G., Shera, D., Berger-Hershkowitz, H., Evins, A. E., Connolly, C., Goff, D. C., & Henderson, D. C. (2001). Clozapine-associated reduction in arrest rates of psychotic patients with criminal histories. *American Journal of Psychiatry, 158,* 270–274.

Friedman, R. A. (2006). Violence and mental illness—How strong is the link? *New England Journal of Medicine, 355,* 2064–2066.

Gendreau, P., Little, T., & Goggin, C. (1996). A meta-analysis of the predictors of adult offender recidivism: What works! *Criminology, 34,* 575–608.

Glover, R. W., Miller, J. E., & Sadowski, S. R. (2012). *Proceedings on the state budget crisis and the behavioral health treatment gap: The impact on public substance abuse and mental health systems.* Washington, DC: National Association of State Mental Health Program Directors.

Gosein, V. J., Stiffler, J. D., Frascoia, A., & Ford, E. B. (2016). Life stressors and post-traumatic stress disorder in a seriously mentally ill jail population. *Journal of Forensic Sciences, 61*(1), 116–121.

Greenwald, A. G., Banaji, M. R., & Nosek, B. A. (2015). Statistically small effects of the Implicit Association Test can have societally large effects. *Journal of Personality and Social Psychology, 108*(4), 553–561.

Grob, G. E. (1995). *The mad among us: A history of the care of America's mentally ill.* Cambridge, MA: Harvard University Press.

Haimowitz, S. (2002). Can mental health courts end the criminalization of persons with mental illness? *Psychiatric Services, 53*(10), 1226–1238.

Haney, C. (2003). Mental health issues in long-term solitary and "supermax" confinement. *Crime and Delinquency, 49,* 124–156.

Haney, C., Weill, J., Bakhshay, S., & Lockett, T. (2016). Examining jail isolation: What we don't know can be profoundly harmful. *The Prison Journal, 96*(1), 1–26.

Hannah-Moffat, K. (2004). Losing ground: Gendered knowledge, parole risk, and responsibility. *Social Politics, 11,* 363–385.

Hemmens, C., Miller, M., Burton, V. S., Jr., & Milner, S. (2002). The consequences of official labels: An examination of the rights lost by the mentally ill and mentally incompetent ten years later. *Community Mental Health Journal, 38,* 129–140.

Hodges, J. (2010, October). Crisis intervention teams adapted to correctional populations. *Corrections Today,* 106–107.

Hoge, S. K., Bonnie, R. J., Poythress, N., & Monahan, J. (1992). Attorney-client decision-making in criminal cases: Client competence and participation as perceived by their attorneys. *Behavioral Sciences & the Law, 10,* 385–394.

Honberg, R. (2008). The intersection of mental illness and criminal law. In R. N. Slate and W. W. Johnson (Eds.), *Criminalization of mental illness: Crisis and opportunity for the justice system* (pp. 321–346). Durham, NC: Carolina Academic Press.

Huffman, M. (2011, December). Legal and ethical challenges in mental health law: A primer for Virginia lawyers. *Virginia Lawyer, 60,* 32–35.

Human Rights Watch. (2003). *Ill-equipped: U.S. prisons and offenders with mental illness.* New York, NY: Author.

James, D. J., & Glaze, L. E. (2006, September). *Mental health problems of prison and jail inmates.* Washington, DC: Bureau of Justice Statistics.

Johnson, W. W. (2011). Rethinking the interface between mental illness, criminal justice and academia. *Justice Quarterly, 28,* 15–22.

Jordan, B. K., Schlenger, W. E., Fairbank, J. A., & Caddell, J. M. (1996). Prevalence of psychiatric disorders among incarcerated women: Convicted felons entering prison. *Archives of General Psychiatry. 53,* 513–519.

Kessler, R. (1996). *The sins of the father: Joseph P. Kennedy and the dynasty he founded.* New York, NY: Warner Books.

Kessler, R. C., Berglund, P., Demler, O., Jin, R., Merikangas, K. R., & Walters, E. E. (2005). Lifetime prevalence and age-of-onset distributions of DSM-IV disorders in the National Comorbidity Survey Replication (NCS-R). *Archives of General Psychiatry, 62,* 593–602.

Kessler, R. C., Chiu, W. T., Demler, O., & Walters, E. E. (2005). Prevalence, severity, and comorbidity of twelve-month DSM-IV disorders in the National Comorbidity Survey Replication (NCS-R). *Archives of General Psychiatry, 62,* 617–627.

Kesey, K. (1962). *One flew over the cuckoo's nest.* New York, NY: Marion Boyars Publishers.

Koyanagi, C., Forquer, S., & Alfano, E. (2005). Medicaid policies to contain psychiatric drug costs. *Health Affairs, 24,* 536–544.

Lacey, M., Sack, K., & Sulzberger, A. G. (2011, January 20). States' budget crises cut deeply into financing for mental health programs. *The New York Times.* Retrieved from https://www.nytimes.com/2011/01/21/us/21mental.html.

Lamb, H. R., & Weinberger, L. E. (1998). Persons with severe mental illness in jails and prisons: A review. *Psychiatric Services, 49,* 483–492.

Lamb, H. R., & Weinberger, L. E. (2005). The shift of psychiatric inpatient care from hospitals to jails and prisons. *Journal of the American Academy of Psychiatry and the Law, 33,* 529–534.

Lamb, H. R., Weinberger, L. E., & DeCuir, W. J., Jr. (2002). The police and mental health. *Psychiatric Services, 53,* 1266–1271.

Lamberti, J. S., Weisman, R., & Faden, D. I. (2004). Forensic assertive community treatment: Preventing incarceration of adults with severe mental illness. *Psychiatric Services, 55,* 1285–1293.

Leifman, S. (2001, August 16). Mentally ill and in jail. *Washington Post,* p. A25.

Lenzenweger, M. F., Lane, M. C., Loranger, A. W., & Kessler, R. C. (2007). DSM-IV personality disorders in the National Comorbidity Survey Replication. *Biological Psychiatry, 62*(6), 553–564.

Lerner-Wren, G. (2000). Broward's mental health court: An innovative approach to the mentally disabled in the criminal justice system. *Community Mental Health Report, 1*(1), 5–6, 16.

Livingston, J. D. (2016). Contact between police and people with mental disorders: A review of rates. *Psychiatric Services, 67*(8), 850–857.

Livingston, J. D., Desmarais, S. L., Greaves, C., Parent, R., Verdun-Jones, S., & Brink, J. (2014). What influences perceptions of procedural justice among people with mental illness regarding their interactions with the police? *Community Mental Health Journal, 50,* 281–287.

Louden, J. E., & Skeem, J. L. (2011). Parolees with mental disorder: Toward evidence-based practice. *UC Irvine Center for Evidence-Based Corrections: The Bulletin, 7*(1).

Lurigio, A. J., Cho, Y. I., Swartz, J. A., Johnson, T. P., Graf, I., & Pickup, L. (2003). Standardized assessment of substance-related, other psychiatric, and comorbid disorders among probationers. *International Journal of Offender Therapy and Comparative Criminology, 47*(6), 630–652.

Manchak, S. M., Skeem, J. L., Kennealy, P. J., & Louden, J. E. (2014). High-fidelity specialty mental health probation improves officer practices, treatment access, and rule compliance. *Law and Human Behavior, 38,* 450–461.

Marquant, T., Sabbe, B., Van Nuffel, M., & Goethals, K. (2016). Forensic assertive community treatment: A review of the literature. *Community Mental Health Journal, 52,* 873–881.

Maslow, A. H. (1943). A theory of human motivation. *Psychological Review, 50*(4), 370–396.

Matejkowski, J., Caplan, J. M., & Wiesel Cullen, S. (2010). The impact of severe mental illness on parole decisions: Social integration within a prison setting. *Criminal Justice and Behavior, 37*(9), 1005–1029.

Matejkowski, J., Draine, J., Solomon, P., & Salzer, M. S. (2011). Mental illness, criminal risk factors and parole release decisions. *Behavioral Sciences & the Law, 29,* 528–553.

Matejkowski, J., Severson, M. E., & Manthey, T. J. (2015). Strategies for postrelease supervision of individuals with serious mental illness: Comparing specialized community corrections officers to those not serving on a specialized team. *Journal of Offender Rehabilitation, 54,* 520–537.

McCampbell, S. W. (2001). Mental health courts: What sheriffs need to know. *Sheriff, 53,* 40–43.

McCoy, M. L., Roberts, D. L., Hanrahan, P., Clay, R., & Luchins, D. J. (2004). Jail linkage assertive community treatment services for individuals with mental illnesses. *Psychiatric Rehabilitation Journal, 27,* 243–250.

Miller, R.D. (2003). Hospitalization of criminal defendants for evaluation of competence to stand trial or for restoration of competence: Clinical and legal issues. *Behavioral Sciences and the Law, 21,* 369–391.

Minton, T. D., & Zeng, Z. (2015). *Jail inmates at midyear 2014*. Washington, DC: Bureau of Justice Statistics.

Morgan, R. D., Fisher, W. H., Duan, N., Mandracchia, J. T., & Murray, D. (2010). Prevalence of criminal thinking among state prison inmates with serious mental illness. *Law and Human Behavior, 34*, 324–336.

Mumola, C., & Karberg, J. (2006). *Drug use and dependence, state and federal prisoners, 2004*. Washington, DC: Bureau of Justice Statistics.

Munetz, M. R., & Griffin, P. A. (2006). Use of the sequential intercept model as an approach to decriminalization of people with serious mental illness. *Psychiatric Services, 57*, 544–549.

NAMI. (2009, March). *Grading the states: A report on America's Health Care System for Adults with Serious Mental Illness*. Arlington, VA: Author.

NAMI of Ohio. (2009, March). An interview with Hancock County Sheriff Michael Heldman and Jail Administrator Ryan Kidwell. *The Stigma Buster: A Monthly Publication by the National Alliance on Mental Illness of Ohio*. Retrieved from http://www.namiohio.org/web_pub/NAMINewsMar09.html.

National Institute of Corrections. (2012, March 12). *Crisis Intervention Teams: A frontline response to mental illness in corrections*. Retrieved from http://nicic.gov/Training/12B3203.

Navasky, M., & O'Connor, K. (Producers). (2005, May 10). *Frontline: The New Asylums* [Television broadcast]. Boston, MA: PBS/WGBH Educational Foundation.

Ostermann, M., & Matejkowski, X. (2012). Exploring the intersection of mental health and release status with recidivism. *Justice Quarterly, 31*(4), 596–618.

Owens, P., Mutter, R., & Stocks, C. (2010, July). *Mental health and substance abuse-related emergency department visits among adults, 2007. HCUP Statistical Brief #92*. Rockville, MD: Agency for Healthcare Research and Quality.

Page, S. (1977). Effects of the mental illness label in attempts to obtain accommodation. *Canadian Journal of Behavioral Sciences, 9*, 85–90.

Parish, J. J. (2007, April 30). *New York City Council Hearing testimony: Status of the implementation of the Brad. H. settlement*. Retrieved from http://www.urbanjustice.org/pdf/publications/BradHTestimony.pdf.

Patch, P. C., & Arrigo, B. A. (1999). Police officer attitudes and use of discretion in situations involving the mentally ill: The need to narrow the focus. *International Journal of Law and Psychiatry, 22*, 23–35.

Penn, D. L., Kommana, S., Mansfield, M., & Link, B. G. (19999). Dispelling the stigma of schizophrenia: The impact of information on dangerousness. *Schizophrenia Bulletin, 25*(3), 437–446.

Peterson, J., Skeem, J., Hart, E., Vidal, S., & Keith, F. (2010). Analyzing offense patterns as a function of mental illness to test the criminalization hypothesis. *Psychiatric Services, 61*(12), 1217–1222.

Petrila, J. (2007, February). *Dispelling the myths about information sharing between the mental health and criminal justice systems.* Delmar, NY: GAINS Center.

Phelan, J. C., Link, B. G., Stueve, A., & Pescosolido, B. A. (2000). Public concepts of mental illness in 1950 and 1996: What is mental illness and is it to be feared? *Journal of Health & Social Behavior, 41,* 188–207.

Poythress, N. G., Bonnie, R. J., Hoge, S. K., Monahan, J., & Oberlander, L. B. (1994). Client abilities to assist counsel and make decisions in criminal cases: Findings from three studies. *Law and Human Behavior, 18,* 437–452.

Primm, A. B., Osher, F. C., & Gomez, M. B. (2005). Race and ethnicity, mental health services and cultural competence in the criminal justice system: Are we ready to change? *Community Mental Health Journal, 41*(5), 557–569.

Prins, S. J. & Draper, L. (2009). *Improving outcomes for people with mental illnesses under community corrections supervision: A guide to research-informed policy and practice.* Council of State Governments Justice Center: New York, New York.

Quinsey, V. L., Harris, G. T., Rice, M. E., & Cormier, C. A. (1998). *Violent offenders: Appraising and managing risk.* Washington, DC: American Psychological Association.

Redlich, A. D., Steadman, H. J., Monahan, J., Robbins, P. C., & Petrila, J. (2006). Patterns of practice in mental health courts: A national survey. *Law and Human Behavior, 30,* 347–362.

Reuland, M. (2010). Tailoring the police response to people with mental illness to community characteristics in the USA. *Police Practice and Research, 11*(4), 315–329.

Ritter, C., Teller, J. L. S., Munetz, M. R., & Bonfine, N. (2010). Crisis Intervention Team (CIT) training: Selection effects and long-term changes in perceptions of mental illness and community preparedness. *Journal of Police Crisis Negotiations, 10,* 133–152.

Rosenbaum, N., Tinney, M., & Tohen, M. (2017). Collaboration to reduce tragedy and improve outcomes: Law enforcement, psychiatry, and people living with mental illness. *American Journal of Psychiatry, 174*(6), 513–517.

Rossler, M. T., & Terrill, W. (2017). Mental illness, police use of force, and citizen injury. *Police Quarterly, 20*(2), 189–212.

Rusch, N., Angermeyer, M. C., & Corrigan, P. (2005). Mental illness stigma: Concepts, consequences, and initiatives to reduce stigma. *European Psychiatry, 20,* 529–539.

SAMHSA. (2002). *Fact sheet: Maintaining Medicaid benefits for jail detainees with co-occurring mental health and substance use disorders.* Delmar, NY: GAINS Center.

Schulte, B., & Jenkins, C. L. (2007, May 7). Cho didn't get court-ordered treatment. *Washington Post,* p. A01.

Scott-Hayward, C. (2009). *The fiscal crisis in corrections: Rethinking policies and practices.* New York, NY: Vera Institute of Justice.

Sellers, C. L., Sullivan, C. J., Veysey, B. M., & Shane, J. M. (2005). Responding to persons with mental illnesses: Police perspectives on specialized and traditional practices. *Behavioral Sciences and the Law, 23,* 647–657.

Skeem, J., Emke-Francis, P., & Louden, J. E. (2006). Probation, mental health, and mandated treatment: A national survey. *Criminal Justice and Behavior, 33*(2), 158–184.

Skeem, J. L., Polaschek, D., & Lilienfeld, S. (2011). Psychopathic personality: Bridging the gap between scientific evidence and public policy. *Psychological Science in the Public Interest, 12,* 95–162.

Skeem, J. L., & Louden, J. E. (2006). Toward evidence-based practice for probationers and parolees mandated to mental health treatment. *Psychiatric Services, 57,* 333–342.

Slate, R. N., Buffington-Vollum, J. K., & Johnson, W. W. (2013). *Criminalization of mental illness: Crisis and opportunity for the justice system* (2nd ed.). Durham, NC: Carolina Academic Press.

Slate, R. N., Feldman, R., Roskes, E., & Baerga, M. (2004). Training federal probation officers as mental health specialists. *Federal Probation, 68,* 9–15.

Slate, R. N., Roskes, E., Feldman, R., & Baerga, M. (2003). Doing justice for mental illness and society: Federal probation and pretrial service officers as mental health specialists. *Federal Probation, 67,*13–19.

Solomon, P., & Draine, J. (1995). Issues in serving the forensic client. *Social Work, 40,* 25–33.

Steadman, H. J. (1981). Critically reassessing the accuracy of public perceptions of the dangerousness of the mentally ill. *Journal of Health & Social Behavior, 22,* 310–316.

Steadman, H. J., Deane, M. W., Borum, R., & Morrissey, J. P. (2000). Comparing outcomes of major models of police responses to mental health emergencies. *Psychiatric Services, 52,* 219–222.

Steadman, H. J., Deane, M. W., Morrissey, J. P., Westcott, M., Salasin, S., & Shapiro, S. (1999). A SAMHSA research initiative assessing the effectiveness of jail diversion programs for mentally ill persons. *Psychiatric Services, 50,* 1620–1623.

Steadman, H. J., & Morrissette, D. (2016). Police responses to persons with mental illness: Going beyond CIT training. *Psychiatric Services 67*(10), 1054–1056.

Steadman, H. J., Morrissey, J. P., & Parker, T. W. (2016). When political will is not enough: Jails, communities, and persons with mental health disorders. *Prison Journal, 96*(1), 10–26.

Steadman, H. J. & Naples, M. (2005). Assessing the effectiveness of jail diversion programs for persons with serious mental illness and co-occurring substance use disorders. *Behavioral Science Law, 23*(2), 163–170.

Steadman, H. J., Mulvey, E. P., Monahan, J., Robbins, P. C., Appelbaum, P. S., Grisso, T., Silver, E. (1998). Violence by people discharged from acute psychiatric inpatient facilities and by others in the same neighborhoods. *Archives of General Psychiatry, 55*, 393–401.

Steadman, H. J., Osher, F. C., Robbins, P. C., Case, B., & Samuels, S. (2009). Prevalence of serious mental illness among jail inmates. *Psychiatric Services, 60*, 761–765.

Steadman, H. J., Redlich, A., Callahan, L., Robbins, P. C., & Vesselinov, R. (2011). Effect of mental health courts on arrests and jail days: A multisite study. Archives of General Psychiatry, *68*, 167–172.

Steadman, H. J., & Veysey, B. (1997, January). *Providing services for jail inmates with mental disorders (Research in brief)*. Washington, DC: National Institute of Justice.

Swartz, J. A., & Lurigio, A. J. (2007). Serious mental illness and arrest: The generalized mediating effect of substance use. *Crime and Delinquency, 53*, 581–604.

Swartz, M. S., Swanson, J. W., Hiday, V. A., Borum, R., Wagner, H. R., & Burns, B. J. (1998). Violence and severe mental illness: The effects of substance abuse and nonadherence to medication. *American Journal of Psychiatry, 155*, 226–231.

Szasz, T. (1961). *The myth of mental illness: Foundations of a theory of personal conduct*. New York, NY: Dell Publishing.

Teller, J. L. S., Munetz, M. R., Gil, K. M., & Ritter, C. (2006). Crisis intervention team training for police officers responding to mental disturbance calls. *Psychiatric Services, 57*(2), 232–237.

Teplin, L. A. (1984). Criminalizing mental disorder: The comparative arrest rate of the mentally ill. *American Psychologist, 39*, 794–803.

Thompson, M. D., Reuland, M., & Souweine, D. (2003). Criminal justice/ mental health consensus: Improving responses to people with mental illness. *Crime & Delinquency, 49*, 30–51.

Torrey, E. F. (1999). Reinventing mental health care. *City Journal, 9*, 4.

Torrey, E. F., Fuller, D. A., Geller, J., Jacobs, C., & Ragosta, K. (2012, July 19). *No room at the inn: Trends and consequences of closing public psychiatric hospitals.* Arlington, VA: Treatment Advocacy Center.

Torrey, E. F., Kennard, A. D., Eslinger, D., Lamb, R., & Pavle, J. (2010). *More mentally ill persons are in jails and prisons than hospitals: A survey of the states.* Arlington, VA: Treatment Advocacy Center.

Trestman, R. L., Ford, J., Zhang, W., & Wiesbrock, J. (2007). Current and lifetime psychiatric illness among inmates not identified as acutely mentally ill at intake in Connecticut's jails. *Journal of the American Academy of Psychiatry and the Law, 35*, 490–500.

Walsh, J., & Bricourt, J. (1997). Services for persons with mental illness in jail: Implications for family involvement. *Families in Society: The Journal of Contemporary Human Services, 78*(4), 420–428.

Ward, T., & Marshall, W. (2004). Good lives, aetiology and the rehabilitation of sex offenders: A bridging theory. *Journal of Sexual Aggression, 10*(2), 153–169.

Watson, A. C., & Angell, B. A. (2007). Applying procedural justice theory to law enforcement's response to persons with mental illness. *Psychiatric Services, 58*, 787–792.

Watson, A. C., Hanrahan, P., Luchins, D., & Lurigio, A. (2001). Mental health courts and the complex issue of mentally ill offenders. *Psychiatric Services, 52*, 477–481.

Watson, A. C., Ottati, V., Lurigio, A., & Heyrman, M. (2005). Stigma and the police. In P.W. Corrigan (Ed.), *On the stigma of mental illness: Practical strategies for research and social change* (pp. 197–217). Washington, DC: American Psychological Association.

Wolff, N., Epperson, M., Shi, J., Huening, J., Schumann, B. E., & Sullivan, I. R. (2014). Mental health specialized probation caseloads: Are they effective? *International Journal of Law and Psychiatry, 37*(5), 464–472.

Wolff, N., Morgan, R. D., & Shi, J. (2013). Comparative analysis of attitudes and emotions among inmates: Does mental illness matter? *Criminal Justice and Behavior, 40*, 1092–1108.

Court Cases

Dusky v. United States, 362 U.S. 302 (1960)
Estelle v. Gamble, 429 U.S. 97 (1976)

Chapter 11

Concealed Carry on College Campuses

Amy M. Memmer and Patricia P. Dahl

Introduction

Americans have had a somewhat tumultuous relationship with guns. A culture has developed that embraces guns and gun violence as a commonplace occurrence in movies, video games, and even everyday life. Yet, we find ourselves constantly caught trying to balance the right to bear arms with the need or desire for gun control laws. For some, the only answer is to put more guns in the hands of the "good guys" to defend us; for others, the only solution is to limit access to guns and reduce the number of guns present in our society. For years, this debate was focused on individuals' right to bear arms to defend themselves and their homes. However, in recent years, the arguments and legislation have found their way onto the campuses of colleges and universities. In this chapter, we will explore how the issue of concealed carry on campus emerged, what the current landscape of this legislation looks like, arguments for and against such legislation, and policy concerns and public opinion. At this point, it may be too soon to analyze evidence and determine the effect of such legislation. However, we will also discuss the necessity of accurate reporting and tracking of crime statistics on campuses as we move forward with the goal of being able to analyze such data in the near future.

Background Information

The tension between the constitutionally protected right to bear arms and the ever-present interest in gun control and safety regulations has a long history in American culture. In the days of the Wild West, it was common to see individuals openly carrying firearms in public. They did not rely on constitutional protections, but rather the fact that it was socially acceptable and no one was challenging the practice, so there was no need to defend it as a constitutionally protected right. However, what is not often focused on in western films and recitations of the history of gun culture is that these frontier towns also had gun control laws in place. For example, "[t]own ordinances in the famous havens of the West, places like Tombstone, Arizona, and Dodge City, Kansas, required newcomers to hand their guns over to the sheriff or leave them with their horses at the stables on the outskirts of town" (Winkler, 2011). It seems that as long as guns have been part of American culture, so has the struggle to balance gun rights with gun control.

By the 1930s, many states had adopted laws to regulate the possession and sale of guns. Initially, some states drafted statutes prohibiting the practice of concealed carrying entirely, with no exemptions even for law enforcement while on duty (Cramer & Kopel, 1995). After recognizing that some individuals, even civilians, might have a legitimate need for the concealed carrying of a handgun, most states began adopting provisions allowing individuals to conceal carry only after receiving a permit. These statutes were very broad and had a great deal of discretion surrounding the minimum standards for obtaining a permit and the ultimate decision of whether a permit should be granted (Cramer & Kopel, 1995). However, even these regulatory statutes were based on a state's perception of need rather than a Second Amendment right to bear arms. In fact, in 1939, the U.S. Supreme Court issued an opinion, in *United States v. Miller*, limiting the Second Amendment protections to weapons useful to militias, and did not extend the right to individuals.

That interpretation of the Second Amendment by the U.S. Supreme Court, in *Miller*, was allowed to stand for nearly 70 years without much interference by the Court. Over this span of years, both the federal government and states continued to adopt laws increasing the regulations on guns. For example, the federal government passed the Gun-Free School Zones Act of 1990 (GFSZA), making it a federal offense for any individual to knowingly possess a firearm in a place that individual believes or has reasonable cause to believe is a school zone. However, that legislation was later held to be unconstitutional, in *United States v. Lopez*, not based on a Second Amendment argument but based on a finding that the law exceeded Congress's Commerce Clause authority. In essence, the Court merely held that the act was criminal in nature and had nothing to do with interstate commerce. Following the ruling in *Lopez*, Congress reenacted the GFSZA in 1996, correcting the defects identified by the U.S. Supreme Court and adding language that required the government to prove that the firearm had affected interstate or foreign commerce. However, the GFSZA does not apply to people licensed by a state or locality to possess a gun and has further exceptions if the firearm is unloaded and "in a locked container, or a locked firearms rack that is on a motor vehicle" or is possessed for use in a program approved by a school.

Recognizing that this legislation was not likely to provide enough protection to combat the growing levels of gun violence in schools, Congress also adopted the Gun-Free Schools Act of 1994 (GFSA), penalizing students with expulsion in hopes of deterring them from bringing firearms to school and threatening to take away the educational institution's ability to receive federal funding if they did not report the incident to law enforcement and follow through with the expulsion of the student for at least one year. However, the GFSA was repealed in 2015.

At a time when federal and state legislation regulating guns was expanding in light of the increased number of public mass shootings, gun control legislation seemed to be aimed entirely at keeping the public safe and increasing restrictions on an individual's ability to possess firearms. It wasn't until 2008 when the U.S. Supreme Court took a more thorough review of the Second Amendment, in *District of Columbia v. Heller*, that the Court considered expanding the Second Amendment protections to include an individual's right to possess handguns for self-defense in their homes. At the time, provisions of the District of Columbia Code made it illegal to carry an unregistered firearm and prohibited the registration of handguns, with the exception that the chief of police could issue 1-year licenses for handguns. The code also contained provisions that required such owners of lawfully registered firearms, under these 1-year licenses, to keep them "unloaded and disassembled or bound by a trigger lock or similar device" unless they were located in a place of business or were being used for lawful recreational activities.

Dick Heller was a D.C. special police officer authorized to carry a handgun while on duty. He applied for a 1-year license to allow him to keep a handgun at home, but his application was denied. Heller sued the District of Columbia, arguing that the Code violated his Second Amendment right to keep a functional firearm in his home without a license. The district court dismissed the complaint. The U.S. Court of Appeals for the District of Columbia reversed and held that the Second Amendment protects the right of an individual to keep firearms in their home for self-defense. The U.S. Supreme Court granted review in the case to consider whether the ban on registering handguns and the requirement to keep guns in the home disassembled or nonfunctional violated the Second Amendment.

The language in the Second Amendment that has been so often debated reads: "A well regulated Militia, being necessary to the security of a free State, the right of the people to keep and bear Arms, shall not be infringed." Since its ratification, Americans have been arguing over what the language in this Amendment means and how the commas and clauses should be interpreted. Gun activists interpret the Amendment to provide every individual citizen the right to own and possess a gun, free of federal regulations, to defend themselves. Proponents of gun control argue the Amendment only gives each state the right to maintain militia, like the National Guard, and the right to bear arms should only be given to the militia (Winkle, 2011). They believe that the federal government cannot abolish state militias but can, and should, place restrictions on who is able to possess what type of firearm where. Both groups argue the language in the Second Amendment clearly supports their version of the debate; yet, the only thing that is clear is that the language of the Second Amendment is ambiguous.

So, in 2008, when the U.S. Supreme Court finally decided to weigh in on the issue, in *Heller*, the public anxiously awaited some resolution to this debate. When the opinion was released, the public got a narrow answer to one question, but an onset of additional questions would soon emerge. In *Heller*, the U.S. Supreme Court decided in a 5–4 majority decision to agree with Heller and overturn the district's handgun ban. The conservative Justice Antonin Scalia wrote the opinion in narrow, but unprecedented terms, and for the first time in the history of this debate, the U.S. Supreme Court explicitly affirmed the individual's right to own and possess a firearm at home for self-defense. The majority reasoned that the first clause of the Second Amendment that references a "militia" is a prefatory clause that does not limit the operative clause of the Amendment, guaranteeing individuals the right to possess and carry weapons in case of confrontation.

Washington, DC, is a federal jurisdiction; however, the Court's holding in *Heller* established a narrow precedent. It took one more case, *McDonald v. Chicago*, to be decided by the U.S. Supreme Court, in 2010, to clearly extend the Court's ruling in *Heller* to all states. In another 5–4 opinion, a majority of the Court found that the individual right set out in the holdings of *Heller* was incorporated by the Fourteenth Amendment and should be fully applicable to every state.

Even after the U.S. Supreme Court and several other courts had weighed in on the issue, it was still apparent that, while an individual had a right to bear arms, the right was not without limitations. In fact, in *Heller,* the same case interpreting the Second Amendment right to bear arms to extend to individuals, the U.S. Supreme Court specifically noted the continued need for limitations and gun control by stating:

> Like most rights, the Second Amendment right is not unlimited. It is not a right to keep and carry any weapon whatsoever in any manner whatsoever and for whatever purpose: For example, concealed weapons prohibitions have been upheld under the Amendment or state analogues. The Court's opinion should not be taken to cast doubt on longstanding prohibitions on the possession of firearms by felons and the mentally ill, or laws forbidding the carrying of firearms in sensitive

places such as schools and government buildings, or laws imposing conditions and qualifications on the commercial sale of arms.

Based on these express limitations of the rights set out in *Heller*, lower courts have upheld many state and federal gun regulations. Federal circuit courts are struggling to interpret the reach of the Second Amendment protections outside of an individual in their home; this is especially true in the context of concealed carry permits and the rights of individuals to carry guns in public, which the *Heller* decision does not address. At this point, the U.S. Supreme Court has declined to hear any Second Amendment cases since *McDonald* in 2010. However, attorneys and activists on both sides expect it is only a matter of time.

Bringing the Debate to Campus

As activists, courts, legislators, and scholars try to make sense of the Second Amendment rights extended to individuals in *Heller* and the continued need for limitations on those rights in order to protect the public, a growing focus has been placed on legislations allowing the carrying of handguns on college and university campuses. As a nation, we continue to experience tragedies involving school shootings like the events at Stoneman Douglas, High School, Sandy Hook Elementary School, Columbine High School, Virginia Tech, Stoneman Douglas High School, and others across the nation in the past two decades. The expansive media coverage of these events brings in-depth stories of these horrors into our living rooms repeatedly and, combined with the knowledge of countless lives that have been ended too soon, has resulted in public outcry over the issue of the presence of guns in our school communities.

In addition to these devastating school shootings, mass shootings, in general, are occurring on a regular basis, keeping guns and gun control issues in the spotlight and gun legislation on the rise. In fact, one recent study found that a mass shooting leads to a 15% increase in the number of firearm-related bills introduced into the legislature that year (Luca, 2016). However, the legislation being introduced might be surprising to some. When Republicans hold power in the state legislature after a mass shooting, the number of laws enacted to loosen gun restrictions goes up 75% (Luca, 2016). This is consistent with the current legislation being passed over the last decade to allow concealed carry on college and university campuses, despite the fact that we continue to experience mass casualties due to shootings on school properties and in public places.

From the varying types of legislation being proposed across the states, it is clear that the public and state legislatures have very mixed opinions on whether, and to what extent, guns have a place on college and university campuses. For some, the increased number of mass public shootings and school shootings point to a need to relax existing gun control regulations and allow concealed guns on campuses (National Conference of State Legislatures, 2017). These individuals argue that persons with lawful, concealed firearms on campus could intervene in violent crimes and prevent more casualties (Carter & Turner, 2017). Some even argue that having concealed carry could have a deterrent effect on violent crime on campuses because potential offenders would have to factor in the uncertainty of whether or not the victim or someone else nearby is armed (Lott, 2010).

For others, the necessary solution is a heightening of firearm regulations to keep guns off campuses (National Conference of State Legislatures, 2017). These individuals are concerned that guns on campus would lead to an escalation in violent crime, suicides, accidental discharges, gun-backed alterations that otherwise would not have existed, and intimidation and fear in the classrooms. They feel that only by reducing the number of guns on campus will we reduce the amount of gun violence (Carter & Turner, 2017).

Present Landscape

Most of the 4,400 college and university campuses do not allow individuals to carry guns on their campuses (Armed Campuses, 2016). But as discussed previously, an increase in pro-gun support, litigation, and fear of killing sprees has compelled some colleges and universities to allow concealed guns on their campuses. According to the National Center for State Legislators, all 50 states permit citizens to carry concealed weapons under certain conditions or requirements (National Conference of State Legislatures, 2017).

As of 2017, 11 states allow concealed weapons on public college and university campuses (Arkansas, Colorado, Georgia, Idaho, Kansas, Mississippi, Oregon, Texas, Tennessee, Utah, and Wisconsin) (Winn, 2017a). Mississippi requires those who conceal carry to complete a gun safety course by a certified instructor. Kansas permits banning concealed carry guns on campuses with adequate security; Wisconsin can prevent concealed carry guns in campus buildings by posting signs prohibiting weapons (Winn, 2017a). As of this writing, Utah is the only state to have a statute that restricts public postsecondary institutions from banning concealed carry; therefore, all public colleges and universities in Utah must allow concealed guns on their campuses (National Conference of State Legislatures, 2017).

In 23 states, each postsecondary campus is allowed to make the decision to ban or permit concealed carry weapons (Alabama, Alaska, Arizona, Con-

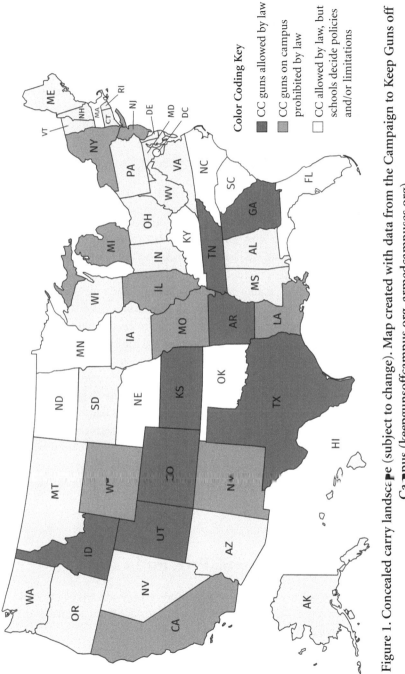

Figure 1. Concealed carry landscape (subject to change). Map created with data from the Campaign to Keep Guns off Campus (keepgunsoffcampus.org, armedcampuses.org).

Color Coding Key

■ CC guns allowed by law

■ CC guns on campus prohibited by law

□ CC allowed by law, but schools decide policies and/or limitations necticut, Delaware, Hawaii, Indiana, Iowa, Kentucky, Maine, Maryland, Minnesota, Montana, New Hampshire, Ohio, Oklahoma, Pennsylvania, Rhode Island, South Dakota, Vermont, Virginia, Washington, and West Virginia) (National Conference of State Legislatures, 2017; Winn, 2017a). Sixteen states currently ban concealed carry firearms on postsecondary campuses (California, Florida, Illinois, Louisiana, Massachusetts, Michigan, Missouri, Nebraska, Nevada, New Jersey, New Mexico, New York, North Carolina, North Dakota, South Carolina, and Wyoming) (National Conference of State Legislatures, 2017).

The Cost of Opting Out

Each state's concealed carry statute is somewhat unique with respect to college and university campuses, with some statutes banning concealed carry, some permitting concealed carry, and others mandating the allowance of concealed carry. Some states have left the decision up to the individual institution. Some statutes contain a provision allowing private colleges and universities to opt out of the requirement altogether. Other state statutes contain a provision allowing public colleges and universities only to designate certain gun-free zones on campus, such as sports stadiums and hospitals. However, there is usually an included requirement that in order to designate an area as a gun-free zone, the university has to pay for and provide certain security features, such as metal detectors and barricades (National Conference of State Legislatures, 2017). Kansas's law goes even further and requires universities that want to designate an area as a gun-free zone to provide adequate security measures, including both metal sensors and the personnel to staff them to ensure that no weapons are permitted to be carried into such an area (Oblinger, 2013). The costs of making that decision can be quite steep and may not be possible for some colleges and universities.

Arguments: Pros and Cons

As states continue to debate and develop new legislation regarding concealed carry on campuses, similar arguments begin to surface from advocates on both sides of the issue across the various states.

Arguments for Concealed Carry on College Campuses

The Deterrent Effect

Advocates for concealed carry on campuses consistently argue that having guns on campus has a deterrent effect. The 1989 book *More Guns, Less Crime* helped popularize this hypothesis by arguing that crime could be reduced by "shall issue" concealed carry laws because criminals would be deterred by the risk involved with attacking someone armed with a gun (Lott, 2010). John Lott and David Mustard extended research on this topic in 1997, creating an enormous dataset of crimes occurring in counties across the nation from 1977 through 1992 and arguing that state laws allowing concealed carry had reduced crime (Lott & Mustard, 1997). There was a huge response to this study. First, it started a debate among scholars on both sides of the issue and continues to be cited both for support and criticism by scholars examining the issue of concealed carry. Second, politicians, lobbyists, and groups like the National Rifle Association (NRA) called great attention to the results from this study and thrust it into the spotlight as evidence to advance the cause of expanding individual freedoms concerning gun rights (Ayres & Donohue, 2003).

The stated theory behind the argument that concealed carry has a deterrent effect on violent crime is the following:

> [C]riminals will be willing to arm themselves whether or not this is lawful, so that laws designed to restrain gun ownership and carrying will only serve to protect criminals, who will have a lessened fear of encountering armed resistance to their criminal designs. Allow law-abiding individuals to carry guns, so the theory goes, and the costs of engaging in criminal activity will rise, thereby dampening the amount of crime (Ayres & Donohue, 2003).

The idea is that if potential criminals cannot know in advance who is armed, the risk of entering into a violent encounter with any potential victim increases. One problem with this theory is that repeated college campus shootings have shown that the shooters often do not expect to survive their attack. Instead, they seem resigned to the idea that they will likely end up taking their own lives at some point during the attack or are committed to taking out as many victims as they can until they are eventually killed by law enforcement.

Another concern with the logic behind this theory is that the increased risk could also result in an increase in the number of criminals who decide to carry guns themselves and could potentially increase the necessity for criminals to fire their weapons quickly to disable victims from using a concealed weapon during an attack. Because of the risk that victims could be armed, criminals can no longer afford to hesitate before shooting once a criminal attack has begun (Ayres & Donohue, 2003).

Lott and advocates also argue that gun-free zones invite mass shootings and become a target for perpetrators to maximize causalities and reduce risk of harm to themselves (Webster, et al., 2016). Gun-free zones are typically considered areas that prohibit private citizens from carrying guns (depending on state or federal laws). Because the definition of *gun-free* continues to be revised, it is difficult to analyze research on this issue. However, it appears that some initial research may be inconsistent with Lott's claim. As one example, researcher and authors Webster et al. found that of the 111 U.S. rampage shootings (6 fatalities or more) over the past 40 years, 18 occurred in what could be defined partially or wholly as gun-free zones, with 13 of the 18 occurring in true gun-free zones (Webster et al., 2016; Defilippis & Hughes, 2015). Nearly 90% of these rampage shootings occurred in locations where civilian guns were allowed or where there were armed security or law enforcement (excluding the mass shooting of Dallas police officers on July 7, 2017) (Webster et al., 2016; Defilippis & Hughes, 2015).

Some studies also indicate that mass shooters target locations where they had a personal connection of some kind rather than a ban on guns at that location (Defilippis & Hughes, 2015). A Federal Bureau of Investigation (FBI) report shows that out of 160 active shootings occurring between 2000–2013, only 1 shooting involved successful intervention by an armed citizen (a former Marine) with a concealed carry permit (Webster et al., 2016; Defilippis & Hughes, 2015). Instead, 21 active shooters were reportedly stopped by unarmed citizens (Defilippis & Hughes, 2015).

Proponents of concealed carry on campuses would hope that the presence of guns would also deter other types of crimes. However, an examination of the Clery Act data suggests that for both Utah and Colorado, certain campus crime rates may have increased after conceal carry laws were passed: one report found Colorado's forcible rape rates increased by 25% (2012) and 36% (2013), while Utah's rates increased almost 50% for the 2012–2013 timeframe (Defilippis & Hughes, 2015). This preliminary data may point to the possibility that conceal carry laws do not deter campus crimes that do not involve mass shootings, such as sex-based crimes. However, much more research will need to be done on this issue before this argument can be validated.

The Intervention Argument

Another common argument for concealed carry on campuses is the intervention argument. Proponents of concealed carry argue that in the event of an active shooter on campus, concealed carriers would be able to intervene to prevent or shorten the attack. One study early on indicated that when someone draws a concealed gun in self-defense, the criminal retreats 55.5% of the time (Kleck & Gertz, 1995). According to the Bureau of Justice Statistics, in 2008, individuals who used self-protective measures against violent criminal offenders avoided injury or greater injury 46.5% of the time, and they scared the offender off 18.6% of the time (Bureau of Justice Statistics, 2008).

One problem with this argument is that, at this time, carriers of concealed weapons are not required to receive training on responding to active shooter situations, even in those states that still require an individual to have a permit to conceal carry. Usually, any training required by states can be completed in a single day and is comprised of information regarding basic gun use and safety and the law surrounding their concealed carry permit (Kreuter, 2016). Further, it is possible that law enforcement responding to the situation could have difficulty in quickly distinguishing the attacker from the concealed carrier who is attempting to defend when they approach and see more than one individual holding a gun. And having a mixture of citizens and law enforcement attempting to stop an active shooter may not be the best method for intervention. The FBI's active shooting data indicates that in 13% of their documented shooting incidents, the perpetrator was stopped and disarmed by unarmed citizens. In 3% of the situations, the perpetrator was challenged by armed citizens; four of these citizens were security guards on duty. Only one person was the average citizen or "good guy" with a concealed handgun (Weisser, 2014).

Arguments against Concealed Carry on College Campuses

On the other side of the debate, opponents of concealed carry argue that the mere presence of more guns on campus inherently increases the probability of firearms being used on campus either in violent attacks, suicides, or accidental discharge.

Violent Attacks

Because guns typically intensify violence, some argue that conceal carry on campus could increase violent crime on campus. These opponents feel that as the number of guns on campus increases, so does the opportunity for injury and death (Oblinger, 2013). However, American college campuses are extremely safe locations to be when compared to the levels of violence found in other U.S. places or segments of the population (DoSomething, 2017). The number of crimes reported for college and university campuses decreased by 35% between 2001 and 2014, with 2014 reporting the lowest number of on-campus crimes for every category except forcible sex offenses (DoSomething, 2017). And while violent crimes continue to be a concern for educational institutions, the rate of such crimes in schools has decreased over the last 20 years (Winn, 2017b). In fact, a U.S. Department of Justice study found that over 90% of violent crimes involving college students occur off campus premises (DoSomething, 2017).

Still, according to the FBI's data for active shooter incidents in the United States, there were 20 incidents in 2014 and 2015 (and across 26 states)—an increase from 17 to the annual total recorded for 2013 and the last year of the FBI's 14-year study (Schweit, 2016). Of these 20 incidents, 6 occurred in educational environments, 3 of which were institutions of higher education. The three incidents occurring in postsecondary settings resulted in 10 deaths (a total of 13 wounded). The FBI active shooter data notes that one shooter was a student, one was a former student, and one had no identifiable connection to the school. Further, one of the shooters was killed by a campus police officer, one shooter was restrained by students while trying to reload and until law enforcement arrived, and one shooter committed suicide after an exchange of gunfire with law enforcement wounded the student (Schweit, 2016).

So even if the statistics demonstrate that campuses are relatively safe places to be, the possibility of harm is still very real. Further, it is also evident that the statistical reality and the perception of harm are two very different things. The possibility of a violent attack may be low, but the perception of fear by those who fear harm from possible incidents remains high, despite the statistics. And at this point, there is no empirical research to demonstrate that a campus is more or less safe with concealed carry.

Escalation of Confrontations

There is also the belief that concealed carry will increase the likelihood of escalating everyday disagreements into shootings because of the availability and ease of access to guns on campus. The research on concealed carry also indicates that the most common reason for gun violence on college campuses is interpersonal arguments or confrontations that escalate into gun violence. Out of 85 shootings or unwanted discharges of firearms on U.S. college campuses over a 3-year period (2013–2016), only two of these occurrences involved an active shooter (Webster et al., 2016). Between 2013 and 2015, at least 14 of the shootings occurring on college campuses happened as a result of a verbal confrontation that had escalated to using a gun (Winn, 2017b). Some of these incidents include the following:

- December 12, 2017—Front Range Community College: A 26-year-old woman "displayed" a gun when confronted about cheating on a test (Hefty, 2017).
- September 1, 2017—University of North Florida: An 18-year-old-track team member was arrested for discharging a firearm in a campus dorm room (Campaign to Keep Guns Off Campus, 2017).
- July 14, 2017—Wichita State University: A university employee found a handgun in the restroom of a campus building (Campaign to Keep Guns Off Campus, 2017).
- August 20, 2016—University of Northern Colorado: A male was found dead in a campus parking lot with a self-inflicted gunshot wound (Campaign to Keep Guns Off Campus, 2017).
- October 9, 2015—Northern Arizona University: Following a fight outside of a dormitory shortly after midnight, 18-year-old-freshman Steven Jones ran to his car, grabbed a handgun, shot and killed freshman Colin Brough, and shot and injured three other students (Defilippis & Hughes, 2015).
- August 16, 2015—Texas Southern University: a heated argument in a parking lot turned deadly when one of the individuals killed one person and wounded a bystander (Defilippis & Hughes, 2015).
- January 30, 2014—Eastern Florida State College: a fight erupted in a parking lot; one of the participants grabbed a gun and injured one person (Winn, 2017b).
- April 16, 2014—Stillman College: After two students began arguing over a bet they had made over a video game, one pulled out a small caliber handgun and shot the other student twice in the torso. The victim was rushed to a hospital but did not die, and the other student turned himself in and was charged with attempted murder (Winn, 2017b).
- January 22, 2013—Lone Star College: A confrontation that began when two young men bumped into each other in the doorway of an academic building ended when one fired at least 10 shots. Three people were

wounded, including two students and a 55-year-old maintenance worker who was shot in the leg (Winn, 2017b).

- January 16, 2013—Chicago State University: A fight broke out after a basketball game and spilled into the parking lot. Amidst the confusion, 17-year-old Tyrone Lawson was shot twice in the back, killing him. Two older men were later charged with the crime (Winn, 2017b).

Suicides

The easy access to guns that comes with concealed carry on campus, it is argued, could also increase the number and success of suicides on campus. College students routinely suffer from stress, anxiety, and depression, which increases their risk for suicide. Recent reports from the Centers for Disease Control and Prevention (CDC) show suicide as the leading cause of death among individuals aged 15 to 34 in the United States, with firearms being the primary method used by males and the third leading method used by females (Romero, Bauman, Ritter, & Anand, 2017; Webster et al., 2016). Another report indicated that if a gun is used in a suicide, "the success rate increases to 90% as compared to 3% for a suicide attempt by drug overdose" (Lewis, 2011). However, at the time of this writing, only half of U.S. colleges track campus suicides, with little information to allow for connecting guns on campuses and campus suicides (Rock, 2018).

Accidental Discharge

Additionally, opponents fear the risk of accidental discharges in the campus setting. When students and faculty are rushing to class, carrying several items, a firearm could easily fall, causing a discharge. It is also argued that the presence of guns at events with large crowds and alcohol being consumed could result in an increase of accidental discharges (Lewis, 2011). Even if concealed carriers make every effort to carry safely, accidents happen. In terms of accidental injuries, several incidents have been reported thus far, including an Idaho professor who shot himself in a leg during a chemistry lab (Follman, 2014), a Utah student who accidentally shot himself in the leg while walking on campus (Everytown, 2017a), a University of Denver dental school employee who accidentally fired her handgun when it jammed while showing it to coworkers (Defilippis & Hughes, 2015), and a student in Mississippi who mistakenly shot himself while sitting in a car on campus (Defilippis & Hughes, 2015).

Juvenile Development

Confrontations that have the potential to escalate to violence may be due, in part, to the maturity level of young individuals. This can be especially problematic when young people are given the opportunity to carry concealed firearms in public places.

The teen years (12 to 17) as well as the emerging adult years (18 to 25) are a time of considerable biological changes that impact emotions, behaviors, socializations, motivations, and decision-making processes (Webster et al., 2016). Nearly 15,000 teens aged between 12 and 19 die annually because of accidental injuries, homicides, and suicides, constituting the three leading causes for these deaths. Most of these homicides (83%) were gun related and half of the suicides involved firearms (45%) (Xuan & Hemenway, 2015).

The development that occurs between the ages of 18 and 25, during emerging adulthood years, is considerable. Individuals begin to experience autonomy from parents or guardians and experience changing social roles in the world. Some of the different characteristics associated with the emerging adult developmental stages are identity exploration, the feeling of being in between the youth and adult status, a time of many possibilities, being self-focused, and experiencing instability (Sussman & Arnett, 2014). Some researchers have viewed the last three dimensions of change as a time when youth are more likely to take health and security risks, feel less vulnerable to consequences for decisions, and want to experiment more with life events (Sussman & Arnett, 2014).

During emerging adulthood, individuals may feel impervious to consequences that result from risky behaviors. This is also a period when individuals are believed to be more susceptible to developing substance and behavioral addictions (Sussman & Arnett, 2014). Further, college-aged students can be at risk for a variety of mental health issues, with the majority of mental disorders occurring before the age of 24. The process of transitioning from home to college life, adapting to new peers and social roles, and juggling coursework with employment or extracurricular activities can contribute to different forms of anxiety or depression (Webster et al., 2016).

For these reasons, college-aged individuals may be particularly at risk for gun injuries to self and others. A 2002 study looking at students carrying guns at college found that students with guns were more likely to engage in binge drinking, drink while driving, and receive injuries requiring medical attention (Webster et al., 2016).

The behavioral science addressing young adult developmental changes does not explain all unwanted behaviors in emerging adults, but it can highlight the early developmental stages as a time when impulsivity, risk-taking, self-control, and shortsightedness are often present as a distinct period in brain and behavioral development (Steinberg, 2012). When firearms on campus are added to the mix of college alcohol drinking, suicidal ideation during early adulthood, the possible onset of mental health issues, and the changing physiology of young adult brains, the outcomes can turn violent or deadly (Webster et al., 2016).

First Amendment Freedoms

While all of these arguments continue to be debated on both sides, an arguably stronger argument against concealed carry on campus has emerged. The argument is that the presence of guns in higher education classrooms is at odds with the First Amendment right to free speech and academic freedom. A quality education requires students and faculty to freely exchange ideas (Miller, 2011). Professors make every effort to try to make their classroom a place where students can feel free to think critically, challenge ideas, and have the candid discourse that is necessary for a valuable, educational experience.

The presence of guns in the classroom could endanger free speech and academic freedom in several ways, including interactions between students in the classrooms, a professor's engagement with students, interactions between professors, and dealings between professors and administrators (Lewis, 2016). Even if a shot is never fired and a gun is never seen, the possibility of a gun's presence in the classroom could be enough to threaten freedom of expression and stifle necessary academic discourse. Just as criminals could be deterred from violent attacks, students and professors might be intimidated and deterred from engaging in healthy debate over hot topic issues based on fear of a gun potentially emerging. Additionally, professors could fear giving a student a bad grade or challenging a student's view for fear of recourse involving a gun (Lewis, 2016). In addition to not being conducive to a learning environment, opponents argue that the presence of guns could hinder interactions between professors and with administrators. For example, professors may be less likely to vote against tenure or promotion of another faculty member or disagree with a proposal before faculty senate if they know that a gun could be involved in any recourse (Lewis, 2016).

Proponents of concealed carry counter this argument by claiming students and professors cannot be threatened by an object they are unaware of. However, people are afraid of the unknown all the time. In fact, it is precisely the fact that the individual does not know who has a gun and when or how it could be used on campus that makes people uneasy and discourages the free exchange of ideas necessary for a quality education.

Perspectives

Faculty/Administrators

States are beginning to document some of the implications for the policies that allow faculty, staff, students, or visitors to conceal carry firearms on campuses. At the time of this writing, the American Association of State Colleges and Universities (AASCU), along with more than 428 colleges, universities, community colleges and technical schools, and 49 college presidents across 43 states have joined a national campaign aimed at keeping guns off U.S. college and university campuses (Campaign to Keep Guns off Campus, 2015).

For college and university faculty, having guns on a campus raises questions about the ability to carry on free-flowing classroom discussions on controversial topics, handle disputes about grades, or provide office advising sessions with particular students (Horan & Bryant, 2017). In Kansas, for example, four faculty members at a state university reportedly changed their job positions as a result of the state's conceal carry laws (Lysen, 2017). After a 2015 conceal carry bill was passed in Texas, professors at one of the universities there chose to sue the state. Several other faculty in Texas left their education positions to teach in other states, while others reportedly withdrew their consideration to teach in some Texas colleges (Everytown, 2017b). In general, college campuses are often viewed as an ill-suited and unwanted place for citizens to carry guns. Estimates indicate the majority of college and university presidents (95%) and faculty (94%) are against having concealed carry guns on campuses (DoSomething, 2017; Everytown, 2017a).

The cost of complying with mandated guns on campuses laws can also impact the campus employee's perception of conceal carry laws. A 2011 insurance estimate provided by a Texas community college board of trustees noted insurance costs of $900,000 per year to allow guns on campus (Everytown, 2017b). A 2012 board of regents debate in Arizona estimated one-time costs of over $13 million to allow guns on college and university campuses in that state (Everytown, 2017b). And in 2015, Florida estimated a cost of $74 million for its state colleges to plan for police and both armed and unarmed supplemental security (Campaign to Keep Guns Off Campus, 2015).

Law Enforcement

The International Association of Campus Law Enforcement Administrators (IACLEA) has publicly denounced allowing guns on college and university campuses because of fears that such policies will increase violence on campuses

(DoSomething, 2017). Reportedly, nearly 80% of college and university police chiefs want the campus and local police departments to play a leading role in providing campus protection from gun violence rather than delegating that responsibility to citizens (DoSomething, 2017).

One reason law enforcement is opposed to guns on college campuses is because of the risks involved with inadequately trained civilians attempting to respond to gun violence. Police officers undergo training throughout their career to address the use of deadly force. When such a decision is made in a matter of minutes during a chaotic setting, the results can be a matter of life or death for both the "good guy" and the "bad guy." A study sponsored by the National Gun Victims Action Council (NGVAC) looked at 77 participants at different skill levels as they underwent three different self-defense scenarios. The results found some of the participants shooting innocent people during the scenarios and/or themselves getting killed. The NGVAC noted how none of the participants reached a level of accuracy in their quick decision-making process to actually stop a criminal or active shooter (Defilippis & Hughes, 2015). While much of the attention for allowing guns on campuses has focused on active or mass shootings, there are other types of situations on campuses—ranging from conduct disorders to interpersonal violence—that may also be affected by concealed carry on campus laws (Webster et al., 2016).

Students

Various groups have formed coalitions both for and against concealed carrying of guns on college and university campuses. In a 2012 study, researchers found that a sample of college students were much more likely to report being against concealed carry on campuses than in the community at large, suggesting that college campuses are different enough to warrant a restriction on carrying handguns (Cavanaugh, Bouffard, Wells, & Noble, 2012). In a 2016 study involving the opinions of 419 college students from a midwestern university, the researchers found that 53% of the respondents believed that teachers should be allowed to carry a registered handgun on campus (Lewis et al., 2016).

Public Opinion

A 2010 nationwide poll of Americans indicated that the majority of U.S. citizens are against concealed carry of guns in public places. Even stronger agreement was indicated for particular public places, with 9 out of 10 respondents expressing opposition to conceal carry in bars, restaurants, hospitals, government buildings, and on college or university campuses (Gifford's Law Center, 2017).

Tracking

The discussion points for conceal carry handguns often include the idea that such policies will reduce violent crime or help prevent mass shootings occurring, particularly in gun-free zones, by allowing citizens to defensively prepare for such incidents (Defilippis & Hughes, 2015). Given the evolving landscape of concealed carry on campuses, it may be too soon to verify the usefulness of these policies.

Tracking Data

The Jeanne Clery Disclosure of Campus Security Policy and Campus Crime Statistics Act (or Clery Act), a consumer protection law originating in 1990, mandates that all colleges and universities participating in federal financial aid programs collect, track, and disclose data about crime on or near their campuses (Aronowitz & Vaughn, 2013). Crime data is also collected nationally and published annually by several key sources such as the U.S. Department of Justice (including the FBI and the Bureau of Justice Statistics) and the Department of Education. However, many of the traditional sources of crime data have not consistently tracked detailed information about shootings in postsecondary education institutions.

While the U.S. Department of Justice publishes annual statistics for the number of students killed on campuses each year, those numbers have typically reflected shootings at K–12 schools and not higher education institutions. Further, the numbers that are provided do not always include characteristics about the shooting incidents, such as the type of weapons used or where the shootings occurred on the school premises. The nonprofit group Everytown for Gun Safety began tracking more specific data about gunfire (based on public documents showing where a firearm had been discharged in a school building or on a school campus), including incidents at postsecondary institutions (Everytown for Gun Safety, 2017a). Everytown for Gun Safety found that 160 school shooting incidents occurred between 2013–2015 in 38 states, with 47% of those incidents occurring on postsecondary education campuses.

Conclusion

By all accounts, Americans continue to struggle with the right to bear arms and the ability to safely control guns in society. What began as Second Amendment protection for militia weapons eventually led to questions of public safety and individual rights. The desire to uphold individual rights for defending self and home with a firearm made its way to school settings, particularly American college and university campuses.

This chapter reviews how concealed carry of guns on campuses began, what the current legislation is indicating, and the common arguments for and against concealed carry on campuses. While it may be too soon to fully analyze or predict what the future will hold for concealed carry firearms on college campuses, the growing attention to violent attacks brought on by mass public shootings and school shootings have compelled Americans to consider the advantages and disadvantages of relaxed concealed carry gun laws on postsecondary campuses.

Concealed carry of guns on campuses continues to raise questions and can present many challenges that will need to be addressed. For one, as states scramble to adapt to the changing legislation for concealed carry on college campuses, gun owners and campus facilities wrestle with the proper storage of the firearms that do not require quick access and are being stored for inaccessibility and an extended period. This issue extends to the proper securing of firearms that are stored in vehicles on college campuses or in specially designed containers for storing guns in vehicles. Another important consideration in terms of accessibility to guns is ensuring that the stored guns do not fall into the wrong hands, regardless of whether the "wrong hands" is an individual wishing to cause harm or an individual who simply does not know gun safety.

As the debate continues, we can see some positive outcomes at this time. Some researchers and policy makers have framed the guns on campus issue as a public health dilemma and are looking more closely at what contributes to mass and school shootings with more in-depth discussions and research aimed at making campus settings safer learning environments (Aronowitz & Vaughn, 2013). Others are leading the way in policy development. For example, most American schools have now created planned responses to potential school shooting incidents, either in writing or through practice drills (Winn, 2017b). At the postsecondary level, campus public safety leaders and subject matter experts came together in a forum through the National Center for Campus Public Safety (funded by the Department of Justice's Bureau of Justice Assistance) to examine the critical factors necessary for sound public policy to guide college and university campuses in concealed carry issues (Carter & Turner, 2017).

In moving forward, many states are also requiring some level of training for concealed carry policies and procedures before an individual can carry a concealed handgun. The training can include state regulations, legal protocols, and practical issues such as safely drawing a weapon, being able to shoot a target, or returning a gun to its holster. Currently, the training requirements vary from state to state, and the question of how much and what type of training is needed for a concealed carry is still being debated in many jurisdictions (Government Accountability Office, 2012). Requiring basic firearm safety and competency can help bridge the gap between concealed carry rights and gun responsibility.

Communicating information to faculty, staff, parents, and, perhaps most importantly, students, is paramount in moving forward in the concealed carry of guns on college campuses. For one, faculty will need to ensure that course syllabi provide students with clear information that not only informs but also does not create a fearful classroom. At some higher education institutions, students may be inundated with information; in others, the information can be confusing, if not lacking, as to what the policies and procedures are for concealed carry on campuses. In many locations, it will be up to the students to know where, when, and how they are permitted to conceal carry handguns on campuses. What may be less clear is how the concealed carry of guns on college and university campuses will affect the next generation of American college students and the overall culture on their campuses.

References

Armed Campuses. (2016). *Guns on campus' laws for public colleges and universities: A guide for students, parents, policy makers and journalists.* Retrieved from http://www.armedcampuses.org/.

Aronowitz, T., & Vaughn, J. A. (2013). How safe are college campuses? *Journal of American College Health, 61*(2), 57–58.

Ayres, I., & Donohue, J. J. (2003). Shooting down the "more guns, less crime" hypothesis. *Stanford Law Review, 55*, 1197–1206.

Bureau of Justice Statistics. (2008). *Percent distribution of victimizations in which self protective measures taken by the victim were helpful.* Retrieved from https://www.bjs.gov/content/pub/pdf/cvus/current/cv0873.pdf

Campaign to Keep Guns Off Campus. (2015, November 11). *Fact sheet: Why our campuses are safer without concealed handguns.* Retrieved from http://keepgunsoffcampus.org/blog/2015/11/11/fact-sheet-why-our-campuses-are-safer-without-concealed-handguns/.

Campaign to Keep Guns Off Campus. (2017, October). *Incidents in states that allow campus carry.* Retrieved from http://keepgunsoffcampus.org/blog/category/resources/.

Carter, D. L., & Turner, J. (2017). *Policy development and implementation of legislation permitting the carrying of concealed handguns on college and university campuses: Promising practices.* Burlington, VT: National Center for Campus Public Safety.

Cavanaugh, M. R., Bouffard, J. A, Wells, W., & Nobles, M. R. (2012). Student attitudes toward concealed handguns on campus at two universities. *American Journal of Public Health, 102*(12), 2245–2247.

Cramer, C. E., & Kopel, D. B. (1995). Shall issue: The new wave of concealed handgun permit Laws. *Tennessee Law Review, 62,* 679–681.

Defilippis, E., & Hughes, D. (2015, November). The numbers on arming college students show risks outweigh benefits. *The Trace.* Retrieved from https://www.thetrace.org/2015/11/campus-carry-risk/.

DoSomething. (2017). *11 facts about guns and college campuses.* Retrieved from https://www.dosomething.org/us/facts/11-facts-about-guns-and-college-campuses.

Everytown for Gun Safety. (2017a). *Analysis of school shootings (January 1, 2013–December 31, 2015).* Retrieved from https://everytownresearch.org/reports/analysis-of-school-shootings/.

Everytown for Gun Safety. (2017b). *Guns on campus facts sheet.* Retrieved from https://everytownresearch.org/guns-on-campus/.

Follman, M. (2014, September 3). *Idaho professor accidentally shoots himself while teaching class.* Mother Jones. Retrieved from https://www.motherjones.com/politics/2014/09/idaho-professor-shoots-self-guns-campus/.

Gifford's Law Center. (2017). *Concealed carry.* Retrieved from http://lawcenter.giffords.org/gunlaws/policy-areas/guns-in-public/concealed-carry/.

Government Accountability Office. (2012, July). *Gun control: States' laws and requirements for concealed carry permits vary across the nation.* Retrieved from https://www.gao.gov/products/GAO-12-717.

Hefty, J. (2017, December). Police: Front range student arrested after threatening faculty member with gun. *The Coloradoan.* Retrieved from https://www.coloradoan.com/story/news/2017/12/12/police-student-arrested-after-displaying-gun-front-range/947229001/.

Horan, S. M., & Bryant, L. E. (2017). Guns on campus: Creating research to inform practice. *Communication Education, 66*(4), 488–490.

Kleck, G., & Gertz, M. (1995). Armed resistance to crime: The prevalence and nature of self-defense with a gun. *Journal of Criminal Law and Criminology, 86,* 150–187.

Kreuter, N. (2016). *The key arguments for concealed carry on campuses don't hold up*. Retrieved from http://www.insidehighered.com/views/2016/04/12/key-arguments-concealed-carry-campuses-dont-hold-essay.

Lewis, R. K., LoCurto, J., Brown, K., Stowell, D., J'Vonnah, M., Dean, A., McNair, T., Ojeda, D., & Siwierka, J. (2016). College students' opinions on gun violence. *Journal of Community Health, 41*(3), 482–487.

Lewis, S. K. (2016). Crossfire on compulsory campus carry laws: When the First and Second Amendments collide. *Iowa Law Review, 102*, 2109–2144.

Lewis, S. K. (2011). Bullets and books by legislative fiat: Why academic freedom and public policy permit higher education institutions to say no to guns. *Idaho Law Review, 48*, 1–28.

Lott, J. R. (2010). *More guns, less crime: Understanding crime and gun control laws* (3rd ed.). Chicago, Il.: University of Chicago Press.

Lott, J. R., & Mustard, D. B. (1997). Crime, deterrence, and right-to-carry concealed handguns. *Journal of Legal Studies, 26*, 1–68.

Luca, M., Malhotra, D. K., & Poliquin, C. (2016). *The impact of mass shootings on gun policy* (Unpublished working paper). Harvard Business School, Cambridge, MA.

Lysen, D. (2017). *K-state faculty members leaving because of campus carry*. Retrieved from http://themercury.com/news/k-state-faculty-members-leaving-because-of-campuscarry/article_a732234f-73e3-528c-8e7e-1195ab22df7a.html.

Miller, J. H. (2011). The Second Amendment goes to college. *Seattle University Law Review, 35*, 235–263.

National Conference of State Legislatures. (2017). *Guns on campus: Overview*. Retrieved from http://www.ncsl.org/research/education/guns-on-campus--overview.aspx.

Oblinger, L. H. (2013). The wild, wild west of higher education: Keeping the campus carry decision in the university's holster. *Washburn Law Journal, 53*, 87–117.

Rock, A. (2018*). Almost half of U.S. public colleges do not track suicide*. Retrieved from https://www.campussafetymagazine.com/university/public-colleges-track-suicide/.

Romero, A., Bauman, S., Ritter, M., & Anand, P. (2017). Examining adolescent suicidal behaviors in relation to gun carrying and bullying. *Journal of School Violence, 16*(4), 445–458.

Schweit, K. W. (2016). *A study of active shooter incidents in the united states, 2014–2015*. Retrieved from https://www.fbi.gov/file-repository/active shooterincidentsus_2014-2015.pdf/view.

Steinberg, L. (2012). Should the science of adolescent brain development inform public policy? *Issues in Science and Technology, 28*(3).

Sussman, S., & Arnett, J. J. (2014). Emerging adulthood: Developmental period facilitative of the addictions. *Evaluation & the Health Professions, 37*(2), 147–155.

Webster, D. W., Donohue III, J. J., Klarevas, L., Crifasi, C. K., Vernick, J. S., Jernigan, D.,

Weisser, M. (2014, September). New FBI report casts doubt on NRA's "good guy stops bad guy" nonsense. *Huffington Post.* Retrieved from https://www.huffingtonpost.com/mike-weisser/fbi-report-active-shooters_b_5900748.html.

Wilcox, H. C., Johnson, S. B., Greenberg, S., & McGinty, E. E. (2016). *Firearms on college campuses: Research evidence and policy implications.* Johns Hopkins Bloomberg School of Public Health. Retrieved from https://www.jhsph.edu/research/centers-and-institutes/johns-hopkins-center-for-gun-policy-and-research/_pdfs/GunsOnCampus.pdf.

Winkler, A. (2011). *Gunfight: The battle over the right to bear arms in America.* New York, NY: W.W. Norton & Company.

Winn, Z. (2017a, August). A list of states that allow concealed guns on campus. *Campus Safety Magazine.* Retrieved from https://www.campussafetymagazine.com/university/list-of-states-that-allow-concealed-carry-guns-on-campus/.

Winn, Z. (2017b, December). The U.S. school shooting statistics everyone should know. *Campus Safety Magazine.* Retrieved from https://www.campussafetymagazine.com/safety/u-s-school-shooting-statistics-us/.

Xuan, Z., & Hemenway, D. (2015). State gun law environment and youth gun carrying in the United States. *JAMA Pediatrics, 169*(11), 1024–1031.

Cases Cited

D.C. Code §§ 7-2501.01(12), 7-2502.01(a), 7-2507.02 (2001)

Gun-Free School Zones Act of 1990, 18 U.S.C. § 922(q)(1)(A)

Gun-Free School Zones Act of 1996, 18 U.S.C. § 922(q)(2)(A), (3)(A)

Gun-Free School Zones Act of 1996, 18 U.S.C. § 922(q)(2)(B)(ii–iv)

Gun-Free Schools Act of 1994, 20 U.S.C.A. § 7161. Repealed. Pub. L. 114-95, Title IV, § 4001(a)(5)(B), Dec. 10, 2015, 129 Stat. 1966

McDonald v. Chicago, 561 U.S. 742 (2010)

United States v. Lopez, 514 U.S. 549 (1995)

United States v. Miller, 307 U.S. 174 (1939)

U.S. Const. amend. II

Index